The Future of Innovation

To past and future: Our parents and our children

The Future of Innovation

Edited by
Dr Bettina von Stamm and
Dr Anna Trifilova

innovaro

GOWER

Reprinted 2011

Published by
Gower Publishing Limited
Wey Court East
Union Road
Farnham
Surrey
GU9 7PT
England

Gower Publishing Company
Suite 420
101 Cherry Street
Burlington
VT 05401-4405
USA

www.gowerpublishing.com

British Library Cataloguing in Publication Data
The future of innovation.
  1. Change--Miscellanea. 2. Evolution--Miscellanea. 3. Creative ability--Miscellanea.
  4. Technological innovations--Miscellanea. 5. Educational innovations--Miscellanea.
  I. Von Stamm, Bettina. II. Trifilova, Anna.
  116-dc22

  ISBN: 978-0-566-09213-8 (pbk)
      978-1-4094-2185-6 (ebk)

Library of Congress Cataloging-in-Publication Data
Von Stamm, Bettina.
  The future of innovation / by Bettina von Stamm and Anna Trifilova.
      p. cm.
  Includes bibliographical references and index.
  ISBN 978-0-566-09213-8 (pbk.) 1. Technological innovations--Forecasting. 2. Technological innovations--Economic aspects. I. Trifilova, Anna. II. Title.
  HC79.T4V667 2009
  338'.064--dc22

                                                                                    2009029710

Printed and bound in Great Britain by the
MPG Books Group, UK

Contents

---

[*]   The keywords for each contribution are given in the Contents.

Part III   Innovation: But Not as We Know it   59

Part IV   The Good, the Bad and the Ugly   79

Part XI   Innovation From Everyone, Everywhere   286

Part XII   This is All You Ever Wanted ...   312

Part XIII Innovation Through a Particular Set of Lenses 358

Part XIV   Famous Last Words   469

List of Figures

Acknowledgements

L ike all innovation, the realisation of this book would not have been possible without sponsors, those who believed in the idea and those who were actively engaged in driving it forward. Hence we would like to give our special thanks to:

- Innovaro, our sponsor and here in particular Mark McBride, Vice President of Innovaro, who heard of the concept of the Future of Innovation from Bettina von Stamm and immediately recognised the importance of the project. He worked to coordinate sponsorship of the project as well as the application of the technical back-end. He is based in York, United Kingdom.

- **Jonathan Norman** and his wonderful team at our publisher, Gower Publishing, who 'really got it' and were just so supportive and a pleasure to work with.

- **Iain Bitran**, Executive Director of the International Society for Professional Innovation Management (ISPIM), for indirectly inspiring this book by giving the 2009 ISPIM conference the title that can now be seen on this book.

- **Debra M. Amidon**, Founder and CEO of Entovation International Ltd in the USA, who encouraged a group of contributors from her network into ours.

The structure we have given the book has inevitably had an impact on which contributions were finally selected for the book and which ones we had to leave (much to our regret) for people to discover and enjoy on the website alone.

We would like to thank *all* who have contributed. We are extremely grateful and proud of each and every one of our contributors, for believing in themselves, for believing in our initiative, and in the future of innovation. Not only were you disciplined enough to fit your views into 500 words, but you were brave enough to open up and share your innermost thoughts with a global community.

Then there are also our wonderful families without whose amazing support this endeavour would not have been possible.

Bettina von Stamm: Innovation comes from combining things in new ways (building on what was) and imagining what is not (yet). This book is dedicated to the generations before and to come: to my father, and my boys, Robert (9) and Tobias (7). My father has been the best mentor any innovator could wish for: listening, asking probing questions and then supporting whatever scheme I might come up with, without interference. My two most wonderful boys represent our future and are a source of reflection, inspiration and learning; an essential part in shaping my understanding of innovation, and the world.

Anna Trifilova: This book, to a great extent, is the result of many years of reading, writing, research, all of which represent time taken away from my daughter, Alexandra, and my husband, Andrey. No words can express my gratitude, appreciation and sense of indebtedness to them for their understanding, care, patience and belief in me and my academic research. I could not achieve much of what I do without them.

A Note About Copyright and Contributions

While some submissions have been officially endorsed by the author's company, such as in the case of Siemens and Nokia, the majority of contributions reflect personal positions, hopes and aspirations.

Copyright is retained by each individual author. Any replication of the material from the website should be cleared with him or her. Any material that you seek to reproduce, using the book as source, should be cleared with Gower Publishing.

We would also like to acknowledge that a number of our contributors were uncomfortable with our request for 'single author contributions'. We understand. However, it was important to us that each of the contributions to this project had a single voice and offered a very personal perspective. Of course, we recognize that in the world of innovation, most ideas and developments will be part of collaborative or team efforts.

We appreciate that the contributors have responded to our original vision and the constraints we placed upon them, and we are delighted that those of you who felt very strongly about acknowledging someone else's contribution and influence have found ways and means to express this.

Foreword
Our Debt to Innovation: Past, Present and Future

Gary Hamel

Inspired souls from around the world mapping the future of innovation – that's the idea behind this book, and I love it. It's hard to imagine a topic that could be more important for human beings, after all ...

We Owe Our Existence to Innovation

Our species exists thanks to four billion years of genetic innovation. Since time immemorial life has been experimenting with new genetic combinations, through sexual recombination and random mutations. As human beings, we are the genetic elite, the sentient, contemplating and innovating sum of countless genetic accidents and transcription errors. Thank God for screw-ups, for if life had adhered strictly to six sigma rules, we'd all still be slime. Whatever the future holds for bipeds like us, we can be sure that happy accidents will always be essential to breakthrough innovation.

We Owe Our Prosperity to Innovation

Most of us do more than subsist. From the vantage point of our ancestors, we live lives of all most unimaginable ease. Here again we have innovation to thank. A thousand years of *social innovation* has given much of humanity the right to self-determination. We are no longer vassals and conscripts. We live in democratic societies where we are free to think and do as we wish – essential prerequisites for innovation. Repeated bouts of *institutional innovation* – including the invention of central banks, stock markets, company law and patent protection – also paved the way for economic progress, by facilitating trade, capital formation and entrepreneurship. Humanity's giant leap into the modern age was powered by a hundred years of unprecedented *technological innovation.* The steam engine, the electric motor, the automobile, the airplane, the telephone, fertiliser, antibiotics, plastics, the integrated circuit – each breakthrough extended human capabilities and spawned millions of subsidiary inventions. And finally, it was *management innovation* – the invention of new ways of mobilising human beings to productive ends – that turned all this potentiality into widespread prosperity. If you have a car or two in the garage, a digital device in every pocket or a refrigerator full of food grown by someone else, you owe an enormous debt of gratitude to those early management pioneers who mastered the challenges of efficiency and scale.

We Owe Our Happiness to Innovation

As human beings, we are the only organisms that create for the sheer stupid pleasure of doing so. Whether it's laying out a garden, composing a new tune on the piano, writing a bit of poetry, manipulating a digital photo, redecorating a room or inventing a new chilli recipe – we are happiest when we are creating. Yes, we innovate to solve problems, to make money and to get ahead. But for most of us, innovation is not a means, it is an end. To innovate, we don't need a commercial or practical justification. We innovate because we were born to – we have no choice. From Mihalyi Csikszentmihalyi to Tal Ben-Shahar, the experts agree: human beings are happiest when they're exercising their ingenuity. Sadly, throughout history millions of human beings have had little opportunity to exercise their creative gifts – because they lived in an age when the tools of creativity were prohibitively expensive, because they were geographically isolated and lacked contact with other innovators, or because they worked in organisations where they were viewed as semi-programmable robots. Our generation, by contrast, is blessed. We have access to dirt cheap tools (a $100 video editing program, for example); we can connect with our creative fellows around the world and are able to share our innovations with any and all (thanks to the Web). Moreover, millions of us now work in organisations that are truly hungry for new ideas. Forget the Renaissance, the Enlightenment and the Industrial Revolution – ours is the golden age of innovation, and we should take delight in that fact.

We Owe Our Future to Innovation

It's lucky for us that the fires of innovation are burning more brightly than ever. Today, human beings confront a daunting array of problems that demand radical new solutions. Climate change, global pandemics, failed states, narco crime, terrorism, nuclear proliferation, environmental degradation – meeting these challenges will require us to invent entirely new innovation *systems*. We need to learn how to solve problems that are multi-dimensional and multi-jurisdictional. In the early years of the 20th century, Thomas Edison and General Electric invented the modern R&D lab, and with it a set of much-imitated protocols that would help to generate a century's worth of technological progress. Today, humanity's most pressing problems aren't merely technological; they're social, cultural, political – and transnational. That's why, like Edison, we must reinvent innovation. What's needed are new meta-innovations (like idea markets, crowdsourcing and folksonomies) that will facilitate innovation across disciplines, borders, institutions and ideologies. This is the only way we'll solve the make-or-break challenges now facing our species. Our future, no less than our past, depends on innovation.

Hence this book. Each one of us has a critical stake in 'the future of innovation' – and each one of us can help to invent it.

Editor's Foreword
The Story Behind the Story of the Future of Innovation

Dear Reader

We are inviting you to join us on a most amazing journey – a journey to discover 'the Future of Innovation'. For this journey we offer you a compass – the book; a map – the website (www.thefutureofinnovation.org); and some companions – the community.

The idea for this expedition came quite unexpectedly and serendipitiously – as much innovation does – and has been most captivating and engaging from the start. To pre-empt any questions you may want to ask about the beginnings of our journey, we decided to tell our story now. We would like to share some of the stages we went through, and outline some of the insights we gained during this experience – the experience of taking a peek into the future of innovation.

1st Stage: The Beginning

Let us hear Anna's story of the beginning: 'On an eve of the summer holiday, rather in a rush, I was writing a conference report on International Society for Professional Innovation Management or ISPIM (www.ispim.org) 2008 for the Russian journal *Innovations*. As part of it, I decided to interview two of that year's keynote speakers, John Bessant and Bettina von Stamm. Without any hidden agenda and inspired by the title for ISPIM 2009, "The Future of Innovation", I addressed one question to both of them: "What are your thoughts on the future of innovation?"

'To my great surprise, John and Bettina each described innovation rather differently. I wondered, how others would see it? It seemed intriguing, curious, fascinating and delightful to explore what leading thinkers from business, government, consulting and academia might consider the future of innovation to be. What would they consider the role of innovation to be? What would they define as its essence, chief constituent, primary element, vital part? I was intrigued as to what would come straight from their hearts when asked about the future of innovation. What would they put on just *one* page? In other words, I wanted to explore the global thinking on the future of innovation!'

This is where Bettina picks up the story. 'I was delighted to be contacted by Anna whom I had met at the ISPIM conference, and who had asked me to share my thoughts on the future of innovation. We had a great meeting and when I thought we had discussed all we had set out to talk about Anna introduced the idea of a book on the future of innovation. (Will you be surprised to hear that it was in a café? Best place for cooking up great ideas.) Having unknowingly been one of the triggers of the amazing venture, I was immediately taken by the idea of inviting people from around the world to share their thoughts on the subject. Hence it took little convincing, and a decision to pursue this joint project was made on the spot.'

So the seed was planted at the ISPIM conference in June 2008, showing its first shoots at our meeting in September, and began vigorous growth when we starting inviting contributions mid November. Now you see before you the beautifully grown, richly flowering results.

Little did we think at the time that the book would be an innovation in itself! Think about the following:

- For the first time in the development of innovation management large parts of its global community were asked one and the same question; a deceptively simple question that nevertheless involved a significant challenge for each contributor because their answer was limited to only 500 words.

- The invitation went out to a community of leading thinkers of diverse backgrounds: business, government, consulting and academia.

- As far as we are aware, this book creates a unique opportunity for readers to communicate directly with the authors: for each and every contributor a photo and contact details are provided in addition to their statement on the future of innovation.

- The book is not the destination in itself but rather a catalyst for further discussion, exchange, analysis and research – as well as offering insights and understanding on the future of innovation, gathered from people from around the globe.

- The project represents a real opportunity to create a road map for the future of innovation; a map platform for networking and collaborating on the global scale.

So, the book is an innovation in itself, and its journey shares many aspects with other innovations that, we are quite sure, many of you are only too familiar with: innovation starts with an idea; it needs diverse skills; it has to draw on a large network to make it happen; and it needs the critical help of a generous sponsor.

When we started uncertainty was rather high as we did not know what response we would get: we did not know whether we could attract contributions, we did not know whether a publisher would be interested – and we still do not know whether it will be a success in terms of units sold.

Soon after we started our initiative **Chin Hoon Lau**, State Assemblyman for Pemanis in Malaysia, emailed us with the following, 'Thank you very much for your kindness and invitation to contribute. This wonderful effort is like a giant fire cracker in the presently cloudy global financial sky. Yes I would like to send you my thought after finish re-visiting and reading my heart.' **Mariana Ferrari**, CEO of PROCESOi in Spain, wished us a 'great success with such an interesting initiative. Really, it's one of the best innovation initiatives I've heard so far … Congratulations!' **Dr Mohamed Mamdouh Awny**, Head of the Technology Management Department at Arabian Gulf University in the Kingdom of Bahrain, thanked us for our 'invitation to contribute to brainstorm on the future of innovation. Your initiative is an innovation in itself.'

We were amazed, touched and completely encouraged in our adventure, there was no holding us back now!

Speaking of selling, in some ways (and to some audiences) selling it was easy, with other audiences we struggled a little more. Well, thinking about it, that's to be expected with something like this which has never been done before! And, like all good innovations, it inspired many of those who came in touch with it, engaged them and made them part of the journey.

The first insight for you, dear reader, from our experience into the future of innovation is to keep an 'open heart'. The concept of 'open innovation', based on the understanding that innovation can come from anyone, anywhere, is not new, but it is nice that we received so much supporting evidence for it. We can confidently state: 'You never know when and where innovation might come from.' So, do not keep your ideas hidden inside you; no one will ever know about them unless you talk about them, as you will never know the value of your thoughts unless you share them. The innovation community cannot but open up to the concept of open innovation, an open spirit and an open heart, if it is to survive. Declare your ideas, and find your peers. Open up your heart and mind, and take delight, even if it is not you but someone else who takes your insights forward.

2nd Stage: Early Progress

We were aware of the tight schedule we had imposed on what was a global project. We were in doubt, a bit scared, but only initially; the speed and enthusiasm of the early responders justified our original assumptions.

Our journey into the future of innovation has attracted more than 350 contributions from over 50 countries. Who are they, and where exactly do they come from? Here we can name but a few – in the alphabetic order – to give you a flavour:

Companies: Aerospace, Fujifilm, IBM, InnoCentive, Jaguar and Land Rover, Kodak, Kraft Foods, Nokia, Nortel, Pfizer, Philips, Siemens, Smith and Nephew, Virgin Atlantic Airways, Unilever.

Consultancies: Atos, I-Nova, IDEO, Innovaro, McKinsey, PricewaterhouseCoopers, WhatIf.

Well-known authors: B. Joseph Pine II, Joe Tidd, John Bessant, JT Lawrence, Rob Atkinson, Praveen Gupta.

Journal editors from: Creativity and Innovation Management, Manufacturing Technology Management, Product Innovation Management, R&D Management.

Representatives of foundations: Information Technology and Innovation Foundation; Grundfos Foundation, Technology Partners Foundation, The Arab Science and Technology Foundation, South African Creativity Foundation.

Public sector representatives: Danish Technological Institute, Government of India, Max Planck Institute of Economics, NHS Institute for Innovation and Improvement, The R&D Society of Iranian Industries and Mines.

Technical universities: Delft University of Technology, Karlsruhe Institute of Technology, Lappeenranta University of Technology, Tshwane University of Technology.

From around the world: Australia, Austria, Belgium, Barbados, Bahrein, Brazil, Canada, Chile, China, Croatia, Cyprus, Denmark, Egypt, Estonia, Finland, France, Germany, Hong Kong, Hungary, Italy, India, Iran, Israel, Ireland, Japan, Jordan, Kazakhstan, Korea, Latvia, Lithuania, Luxembourg, Malaysia, Mauritius, Mexico, Netherlands, New Zealand, Nigeria, Norway, Occupied Palestinian Territories, Pakistan, Poland, Portugal, Philippines, Romania, Russia, Singapore, Slovakia, Slovenia, South Africa, Spain, Sweden, Switzerland, Taiwan, Turkey, UK, USA, Ukraine, Venezuela.

And this truly is just a small fraction of the background information we could give you. If you'd like to know more there is always the website!

Within the extraordinarily short time span of only two months we not only managed to invite a large yet select community to contribute, we also managed to convert most promises into deliveries! But, as pointed out before, in so many cases it was a rather easy sell: **Mónica Moso**, responsible for the programme of Networks and Alliances in the Basque Innovation Agency in Spain, shared with us: 'Well, I really wish to read this book as it is a great idea. I think that we need to dream collectively about the future, and this is a fantastic way to do it.' **Dianka Zuiderwijk**, Oil and Gas Business Assurance Manager at Lloyd's Register in the Netherlands, sent to us this comment 'Thank you for the opportunity to share my passion on this subject. I look forward to challenging my views with colleagues around the globe.' **Francisco Pinheiro**, Global Innovation Director at Atos Origin International in Spain, commented on:

> this wonderful 'journey' to give so many people the opportunity to be on board and contribute to the transformation of the present and the future. I would like to share the following statement which I like very much (and which can be applied to innovation and collaboration, and of course to the Future of Innovation journey): 'If you go alone, you go faster. If you go together, you go further'.

Venky Rao, Senior Vice President and Head of Innovation and Leadership Enablement at Satyam in India, concluded, 'Certainly this book will be influential in shaping the future through thought leadership from so many contributors. It is indeed a pleasure to contribute to such an exciting and important book. I wish to congratulate you on taking up such initiative and thank you for giving me an opportunity to share my thoughts.'

Dear reader, what you might want to take away as a lesson from this second stage is, don't shy away from ambitious targets, unless you reach for the moon you will never catch the stars. And don't let other people tell you 'it can't be done'. Use such comments to fuel your passion and fire, and show them that, indeed, it *can* be done.

3rd Stage: Gathering Momentum

The book in itself is only a start; it is rather static, while the future is always dynamic. We consider this book to be a root, giving life to a growing tree.

As a little encouragement and persuasion to continue and invite others to the journey, here some voices of those who have commented on their experience: **Ray Buschmann**, Principal and Owner of Solving the Impossible Pty Ltd, Australia, comments: 'You certainly had to be very disciplined to fit into the 500 words quota but I believe that is one of the brilliant concepts you have come up with: contributors are forced to be crisp and controversial.' **Miloš Ebner**, Director of R&D at Trimo d.d. in Slovenia, echoes him: 'Usually, because of the lack of time, I do not participate in such initiatives, but your approach was so different and innovative that you somehow easily convinced me.' **Jennifer Ann Gordon**, CEO of Cool Breeze Marketing, LLC in the USA, remarks 'I've been pondering, tilling my thought soil, planting little seeds. What a wonderful project!' **Debra M. Amidon**, Founder and CEO of Entovation International Ltd. in the USA, adds 'Your instructions to write something straight from the heart created something quite novel and relevant. You two have started something ... wonderful!' **Mark McBride**, Vice President of UTEK Corporation in the UK, concludes, 'Very frustrating that it was only 500 words as there is much background (justification maybe) that I would have liked to have added, but I guess that it will be one of the strengths of the book as it will deal in conclusions rather than waffle!'

Our choice of organising the contributions has invariably had an impact on which ones were finally selected for the book and which ones we had to leave for people to discover and enjoy on the website, much to our regret. Of course, *all* of the contributions can be found on the website.

The third insight into the future of innovation from our experience, for you, dear reader, is the belief that any good idea will find its recipient. We have already managed to persuade you to open up and cooperate globally; now we would like to inspire you to have the trust and confidence to continue that journey.

4th Stage: Full Steam Ahead

When we started reading through the contributions we were awed. Awed by the thoughtfulness and honesty, and the level and depth of insights people shared, at their passion and desire to contribute, to this book, towards the future, towards change. Not just any change but change for the better, change towards a better future. It was also the belief that creating that better future is in our hands that warmed our hearts and gave us hope. Particularly in times where every news bulletin brings announcements of more redundancies, a default reaction to economic crisis, and, in our view, not a particularly effective one as it demotivates even those left behind, and fundamentally disables the ability to innovate.

There would have been many ways to structure the book and to organise a flow. When we received the over 350 contributions, we were delighted and ... overwhelmed. Having had a first glance through them, the challenge was to make sense of the complicated and intriguing jigsaw puzzle that they represented.

We realised that the contributions were effectively three-dimensional scenes, rather those pictures full of apparently random dots, 'autostereograms'. Autostereograms are 3D images that are initially invisible to the eye before the hidden picture starts to emerge.

Once we had decoded the overall shape of the contributions, we decided to use them to tell a story, to take you on a journey, one destined to illustrate the overwhelming benefits, power and indeed beauty of the future of innovation.

We will share a story of the need for innovation, and about what drives such need. We will give voice to those who argue that the future of innovation will have to be different from the past, and those who warn of its dark side – not least because we, as humanity, seem to have reached our eleventh hour, and the way we have innovated has played its part in getting us there. This means that governments and education have important roles to play. Whichever way we look at it, in the end it is all about people, and it is about mindsets. If we can create the right conditions for people to get together, inviting innovation from everyone everywhere, and develop the ability to communicate our ideas in ways that others can understand, ideas that are based on real needs, creating real value, then we can truly come up with solutions that are all that we ever wanted. We will share stories from particular industries, and perspectives from particular countries or geographies.

Our contributors share our understanding of the value of this book:

- *'The result will be an important summary about the world's thoughts about the future of innovation and become a must-have book for everyone in the field of innovation.'* **Michael Dell**, CEO of RATIO Strategy and Innovation Consulting gmbh, Austria.

- *'The book is a really nice idea. Bringing together a snapshot of different viewpoints will be great to invigorate the debate on innovation.'* **Claudia Eckert**, Senior Lecturer of Design Group at The Open University, UK.

- *'The book will be useful for innovations in the future, including thinking, changes and activities needed.'* **Kari Sipilä**, Managing Director of Future Innovations (Management Consulting), Finland.

- *'I can't wait to see the result. With so much talent condensed, the outcome is going to be really something amazingly rich and diverse.'* **Ignacio Villoch**, Marketing and Communication Manager at BBVA Innovation Centre, Spain.

So our fourth takeaway for you is: cast your net wide, and trust that something will emerge. Don't try to force things, put your wish out to the universe – or to a group of wonderful people – and have the patience to watch a pattern emerge. Read up on complexity theory, it is a great guide to innovation!

The 5th Stage: Reaching Audiences

Dear reader, this book has something for each of you: for academics the book will provide insights into where to concentrate future research agendas; for people from industry it provides starting points for their innovations and models of innovation; for consultancies it describes the fields in which to develop expertise; for the public sector it raises awareness of cutting-edge advancements and thinking that might be important for the development of policies, infrastructure and support.

Read this book to find consolation, read this book to find inspiration and read this book to find out how you can embrace innovation to help shape a wonderful, exciting and worthwhile future.

This book is the result of our passion for innovation and has reassured us that there is a future for innovation. This book has also made us aware of how much there is to be done to create a desirable future. The contributions have helped us understand that in order to make the future of innovation bright and shiny, green and gold, human and social, proactive and supreme, we have to ensure that we draw on thinking from around the globe, and seek to achieve results that reach across the globe. This book is a manifestation of hope as well as a warning. You do not need any further evidence; this book is all you need to realise that the time for innovation is now, and that we need innovation in innovation. We need a new understanding of innovation management that draws on the concerns, insights, dreams, visions and hopes of the global innovation community.

Having thus set the scene, without further ado, let us now commence to convince even the last doubting Thomas that innovation is no longer a nicety, but a necessity.

Let us pick up the thread, and let the play begin ...

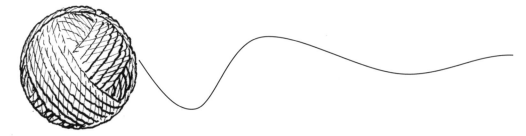

PART I
The Need for Innovation: Painting the Canvas

Innovation has increasingly moved out of the obscurity of R&D (research and development) departments into boardrooms, politics and social sciences, and the mainstream press. Here are a few quotations from:

- **Business:** *'We want to be Number One or Two in our chosen market segments but we need more innovation.'* – Beresford-Wylie, Executive Vice President, Nokia Networks.

- **Politics:** *'We need even more innovation.'* – German Minister for Education and Research BMBF Frieder Meyer-Krahmer on the role of research and technology transfer in the modern economy.

- **Trade associations:** *'We need more innovation, research and education. Because innovation is about ideas we must ensure that intellectual property is protected efficiently.'* – Jürgen R. Thumann, President of the Federation of German Industries.

- **The regional level:** *'We need more innovation, more investment, and growth-oriented politics. ... The future of Baden-Württemberg depends on its ability to innovate.'* – A regional politician at a press conference in 2005 in Stuttgart.

- **The European level:** The EU has declared 2009 the Year of Creativity and Innovation[1] with the aim *'to raise awareness of the importance of creativity and innovation for personal, social and economic development; to disseminate good practices; to stimulate education and research, and to promote policy debate on related issues.'*

- **The US:** *'If America recommits itself to science and innovation, then we can lead the world to a new future of productivity and prosperity,'* said Barack Obama in a speech in November 2008.

- **China:** *'If you wish to remain or become New Champions, you must be innovative and take the lead in doing so. Otherwise, you won't be successful.'* – Chinese Premier Wen Jiabao in his opening remarks at the World Economic Forum's Annual Meeting of the New Champions, 2008.

- **Korea:** *'Korea must encourage entrepreneurial innovation through the creation of more competitive private investment funds and industrial incentives, including both venture capital and private equity investment funds,'* – Derek Lidow, President and CEO, iSuppli Corp.

- **The chemical industry:** *'It's innovation that will drive that production curve to try and keep up with demand.'* – Monsanto's Chairman, President and Chief Executive Officer Hugh Grant in his letter to shareholders of 23 October 2008.

- **Telecoms:** France Telecom CEO declared in January 2009 that France Telecom will focus on investment and innovation to help it survive the economic downturn.

---

1 *The Future of Innovation* – the book and the website – were included into the national events of the EYCI 2009.

- **Insurance:** *'We will continue to deliver even more innovation performances grounded upon infrastructures developed during the first-stage management innovation process.'* – Kim Soon-Hwan, President and CEO, Dongbu Insurance, Korea, in the 2008 annual report.

On 27 February 2009 a search on google.com revealed 113,000,000 hits for innovation – in 0.13 seconds. There is no denying it, innovation is on the agenda. So, what is the outlook for innovation? ... Why do we need it? ... Do we need more innovation? ... Less? ... What is the purpose of innovation? ... Where is it needed most? The following voices paint the canvas of innovation in very bright colours.

We would like to start the contributions with Stefan Kohn as we very much like his title: 'The future of innovation is in our hands.' That's our firm belief too. The future is not something that just happens to us; it is not inevitable or imposed on us, and we are not simply puppets in someone else's play.

We all make decisions, grasp or ignore opportunities, reject options. We can participate or avert our eyes. The future is our decision. If we choose to experiment and it fails, we can brush that failure under the carpet or we can seek to learn from it.

The future is in our hands. We need to take responsibility for it – and accept that our decisions come with risks.

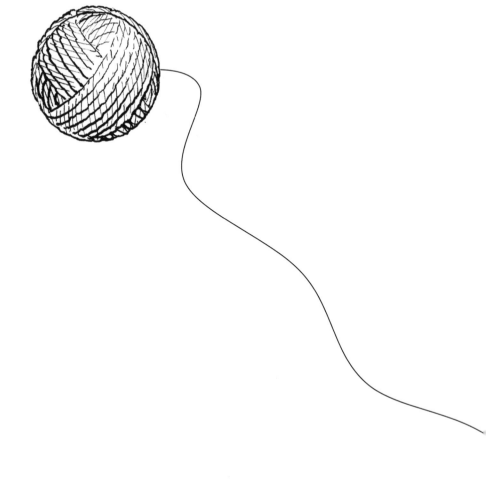

The Future of Innovation is in Our Hands

Name	Stefan Kohn
Affiliation	Fujifilm Europe GmbH
Position	Head of Innovation Management
Country	Germany
Area	Innovation management, fuzzy front end, culture
Email	kohn@fuzzyfrontend.eu

culture   responsibility   risk   globalization   mistakes

Before looking at the future of innovation it seems worth looking at its past. The term 'innovation' was created and introduced to economic science by Schumpeter in 1939. For a long time innovation just happened. It actually was a while before researchers started to analyse the innovation phenomenon and investigate how to improve it – how to *manage innovation*. This research stream started in the 1970s with studies like the famous SAPPHO study.

In the past 40 years innovation research has focused on trying to explain how innovations can be more successful. In the 1970s and 1980s we learned a lot about innovation processes and portfolio management. In the 1990s we learned about interdisciplinary collaboration and involving the customer and in the past 10 years we have been talking about – besides many other interesting and important issues – the importance of culture and its influence on innovation.

As a result of this research we see that the flop rates of new products and services dropped significantly till the middle of the 1990s, but since then they have remained on a quite high level. At the same time product lifecycles become shorter and shorter and thus innovation becomes more costly.

What can we learn from that? In my opinion the crucial learning is that innovation means, has always meant and will always mean *taking risks*. Neither the corporate planning staff nor the research community will ever – despite some interesting attempts in the 'computer-aided innovation' community – be able to find tools and methodologies to correctly predict which products will be successful and which not. In the end innovation becomes a matter of attitude and by that a matter of corporate culture and leadership. This is where we stand today. Companies need to accept that innovation has the risk of failure and the chance of success.

For the future of innovation this raises several challenging questions:

- In a world where we are more and more trying to avoid mistakes and errors – how will we be able to muster the courage to take the risk of innovation?

- In a world where culture is a local phenomenon but corporations are becoming more and more global – how will we be able to manage a diverse set of individual cultures of employees in different countries and markets and maintain an innovation-friendly culture that allows for mistakes and taking risks?

- In a world where responsibility is more and more placed in the hands of committees and consultants – how will we be able to identify and motivate the individuals who can be the innovation heroes with the spirit and the courage to fight for their ideas?

To answer these questions is the task of everyone working in the innovation field. And answering these questions will show the future of innovation.

Stefan raises several important and interesting challenges and you may want to ponder how you are dealing with them. Are you aware of them? Have you embraced them and are you working to start addressing them, taking others along with you? You may think, 'What can I do, as an individual? I cannot change the course of the world.' We do not agree. We may not be able to change the world immediately, but the choices we make may influence others. If enough of us embrace the change it gains acceptance, and at a certain level of acceptance it becomes the new norm. Think of Mahatma Gandhi. Think about something more abstract such as environmental awareness. Twenty years ago when Bettina started recycling, her parents' generation looked on in amusement and wonder, arguing that it was ridiculous to have a number of different rubbish bins. Now recycling has become the norm, and her parents are certainly doing it too.

Any change requires an awareness of the status quo. What is good about the change? What is less good about it and how can you evaluate these aspects from different viewpoints and through different lenses? Once you have done that you can decide what to do and how to approach the change. Unless we are aware of the challenges, and unless we are willing to start addressing them, the future – let alone the future of innovation – may be a little tricky. But then, as Eduardo Sicilia Cavanillas suggests in the opening to his contribution, unless there is innovation there is no future!

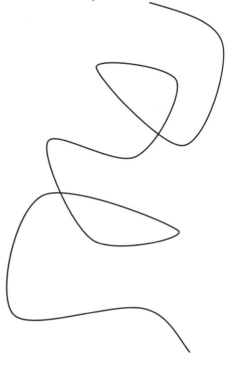

The Future of Innovation is the Only Possible Future

Name	**Eduardo Sicilia Cavanillas**
Affiliation	Consultancy
Position	Owner
Country	Spain
Area	Innovation and strategy
Email	sicilia.eduardo@gmail.com

innovation future change different management

It is rather bold to talk about *The Future of Innovation*. I would change the book's title to *Innovation is the Future*, the only possible future.

I do not think we can picture a future without innovation. We can see saturated markets, where supply is higher than demand, where it is difficult to stand out, where globalisation makes us equal and, finally, where technology and its breakthroughs surprise us at a speed we cannot imagine.

Who can survive under these rules? Those who innovate, those who are ahead of change. We are living absolutely exponential times, where everything happens rapidly, where change happens today and is here to stay. If economic prosperity doesn't force change, the present international economic crisis must do it.

Let me give some examples:

- The top 10 in-demand jobs in 2010 did not exist in 2004 – new specialisms, new skills, new performances, new position, new qualification, new kind of companies demanded today did not exist six years ago.

- Below is the number of years it took to reach a market audience of 50 million for the following products:

radio	38 years
TV	13 years
internet	4 years
iPod	3 years
Facebook	2 years.

- For students starting a four-year technical degree this means that half of what they learn in their first-year study will be outdated by their third year of study.

On their tenth anniversary, Google rebuilt their 2001 search index. It is hard to believe that in that index, searching on words such as 'iPhone', 'YouTube', 'gmail' gave us a search result of 'does not exist'.

However, there are two major challenges in innovation as the future: reach management, people and organisations. Not everybody is ready to follow a new lifestyle and way of producing.

There are people and organisations willing to accept 'the unexpected', but only a few.

Big organisations are reluctant to innovate and are full of barriers; people do not want to change. Big companies can accept new ideas, but they find it hard to let go of old ones.

Let organisations try to recruit employees with new, different profiles (why are most people in a company similar?), of different races, from different countries, cultures, education and backgrounds. This wealth will be critical for organisations. In addition, let us bring in entrepreneurial people who are not afraid of the risks of change. We should learn from their ability to fight, their devotion and their imagination.

I remember a recent domestic flight in the USA, there was an hour's delay. The five members of the crew at the desk of the airline American Virgin started singing and improvised a karaoke. First they sang, terribly badly, and then other passengers took over, one after the other. All the passengers looked pleased and people put up with that delay without realising it was because they were all so well entertained. 'Innovation is the future.'

A second challenge and a final wish: we have all the means, probably we have fantastic individual examples, but as an international community the willingness to compromise – so as to make the most of this intelligence and use it to make the differences between the two worlds, the rich and the poor, smaller – is missing. So my wish is, 'Innovate for a better future for the planet'.

While Eduardo cannot conceive of a future without innovation he also gives it a very meaningful purpose – the creation of a better, more equal future. Hear, hear! At the same time he brings to our attention a challenge that may prevent us from realising that future: the inherent human reluctance to change. He offers two potential tools for addressing the challenges of innovation, and for creating our future: diversity and entrepreneurship. Are these things you are trying to encourage in your life, in your company; at least in the context of innovation?

Eduardo is not the only of our contributors to believe in diversity. You will find that diversity is one of the warps, the long strands of a woven tapestry, in the future of innovation. We will explore diversity in much more detail a little later.[1]

Let us continue with the theme that innovation is our future. Arash Golnam who shares this view, goes a step further and declares that "the future of innovation will no doubt transform the future of mankind." He further predicts the emergence of technologies no one would be able imagine today, and for which the developing countries will play a major role in creating.[2]

---

1   See Part XX, 'Let's Get Together'.

2   For more thoughts on the role of emerging countries and indeed a number of different geographical and national perspectives please have a look at Part XIII, 'Innovation Through a Particular Set of Lenses'.

The Future of Innovation is Transforming the Future of Mankind

Name	**Arash Golnam**
Affiliation	The R&D Society of Iranian Industries and Mines
Position	Executive Advisor to the President
Country	Iran
Area	Innovation Management
Email	a.golnam@gmail.com

enhancing quality of life   developing countries   geographically dispersed   innovation science   intellectual property

The future of innovation will no doubt transform the future of mankind in a way that 'innovation' will be globally associated with enhancing the quality of life and improving standards of living.

The term 'innovation' will not be limited to the promotional tag lines of companies. Bridging distance, time and culture, innovation, incorporating a significant part of hourly news bulletins, will be heard and followed by people all over the world with as much or even more interest and attention as sporting events!

After witnessing an exponential growth in science and technology in the 20th century, which led to a tremendous transformation of people's lives, we will see technological changes and paradigm shifts considerably accelerating, leading to shorter lifecycles and the diffusion of breakthrough and radical innovation around the world at an enormous speed.

Needless to say, the existing theories of innovation will inevitably be rendered inapplicable for identifying patterns and indicating the likely course and impacts of innovation. As a result, in order to capture the extremely dynamic nature of innovation and its important social, technical and economic consequences, the academic disciplines – from engineering, medical and behavioural sciences to economics and business studies – will shape an interdisciplinary 'innovation management' body of knowledge which will be taught academically and practically at universities in form of graduate and postgraduate programmes or even at schools, providing powerful bodies of theories and predictive tools for analysis of innovation phenomena, patterns and context.

Had we been asked at the beginning of the 20th century to write down some predictions about the technologies which would be coming to market in 100 years' time we would never even have got close to imagining the scope and extent of product or process innovations that would turn up. Hence it can be confidently stated that a to us unimaginable range of unperceivable high tech innovations will be diffused over the next century. Such innovations will focus on and pay a special attention to renewable energy sources, green technologies, health improvement and other issues that will be crucial to human quality of life, while targeting a lower total cost of ownership in order to be affordable and therefore available to a wider range of users around the world.

With the emergence of new paradigms in the management of innovation such as virtual research and development (R&D) and new product development (NPD) teams, open innovation, R&D internationalisation and globalisation, the innovation process has become and will definitely become more geographically dispersed and technologically specialised, driven by advancements in information technology and turning the protection of intellectual property into one of the most critical and complex concerns in the innovation process.

Lastly, developing countries will play a major role in the future of innovation. As an example, in Iran the current Iranian year, 20 March 2008 to 20 March 2009, has been called 'the year of innovation and flourishing', reflecting the fact that the correlation between innovation from one side and economic growth, development and citizens' well-being on the other has been plotted to great extent by the governments of countries with economies in transition.

Arash re-emphasises the concept of innovation as enabler for reducing inequalities; innovation for a better, more exciting life. Who would not subscribe to this? How do we make this a reality? How do we make it happen?

*Arash hints at the changes we can expect in the future; the speed and the degree of them; suggesting that technologies we cannot even imagine will emerge over the coming century. Sometimes we wonder what else there can be, what else could be invented. Yet we know that there will be new inventions. Invention is something that is deeply rooted in the nature of humanity. Making this more explicit and accepted through educating on innovation at all levels is what Arash envisages. That's the first step to making it happen. He also points out that the future of innovation will expand the concept in terms of meaning and reach; going beyond what is has been in the past. What is the current understanding of innovation in your organisation and how do you educate your people? What can **you** do to move it forward?*

Arash alerts us to technologies that are unimaginable today; Eduardo makes the case for diversity, and Stefan started us off with the conviction that the future lays in our hands. Michael Dell believes in all of the above, and adds to them, introducing nature as an analogy for innovation – and declaring that in innovating for the future we ought not to forget to have fun. What an important point, not least because humour is known to be a great connector between the different parts of our brain, facilitating new awareness. Humour also dispels fear, encourages understanding, makes it easier to deal with failure and lightens the heart. Michael is not alone in this view: Juha Kaario offers a very similar perspective. But let's read Michael's words first.

The Future of Innovation is Without Psychological Inertia

Name	**Michael Dell**
Affiliation	Ratio Strategy and Innovation Consulting gmbh
Position	CEO
Country	Austria
Area	New product development
Email	dell@ratio.at

interdisciplinarity   product convergence   biomimetics   biomimicry   bionics

The future of innovation is ... disruptive, interdisciplinary, colourful, fundamental change, new paradigms, a curved road, challenging, sustainable and ecological, without psychological inertia. It is full of creative people from different fields, who create higher customer value sharing the vision of contributing to a better world. They work in trans-disciplinary groups and – have fun! Any more dreams? Any more positivism? We should not forget – *we* are those creative people, only *we* can contribute to this positive view.

'Who knows what tomorrow brings?' I know that some of you reading those few words actually heard the voices of Jennifer Warnes and Joe Cocker, few of you even sang along, inaudibly – a kind of 'mental karaoke'. So can I read your thoughts? No, I can't. Is this foresight? No, it's not. It's empathy, metacognition and self-observation, which allow people to understand how others might act.

Let's focus on the future of new product development. There is a need for products that are sustainable and environmentally friendly, more authentic and less 'more of the same', they have to simplify our daily lives and businesses.

The year 2009 is the 150th anniversary of Darwin's theory of evolution. So what and how can *we* learn from nature's IQ? Nature creates outstanding 'products' with definite uniqueness and no waste. Humankind still produces 3-ton cars moving 80 kilos of human 'luggage'. But evolution, in its innovation processes over some 100,000 years, decided not to invent products for carrying luggage, but instead produced highly efficient flyers, swimmers, walkers or wigglers.

One future scenario for new product development lies in the use of biomimetics, biomimicry or *bionics* (the amalgamation of *bio*logy and mecha*nics*) as a creativity technique. Biomimetics is a highly inter- and trans-disciplinary science which helps engineers to understand structures and processes in nature and apply those findings to technology and new products.

In the future ecology will become a 'sellable value' (even if, in the next few years, people will not be willing to pay more for ecologically friendly products). Product convergence will increase – products will co-evolve and merge together, based on evolutionary algorithms. In the end nobody will remember that the new product had 'parents from different worlds'. We will see smart materials, biomaterials, re-growing product parts, self-adapting materials, things that think and communicate, all of them with a strong tendency towards mass customization.

To cope with this *we* have to create new networks and teams; engineers working together with biologists, botanists and medical doctors. We need to learn each other's languages and become much more flexible than today. We also need new forms of cross-company cooperation and crossover organisations (particularly between economy and science), with ad hoc teams and the conscious integration of 'visionary jesters'. This requires lifelong eclectic learning, the combination of different fields of knowledge, open-mindedness and – positivism. *Have fun innovating the future!*

Doesn't a future that is fun, and that is in our hands, sound so much more appealing and worth being part of than a future that is being imposed on us?

Perhaps because our contributors believe in our own ability to help shape our destiny, and that this can be fun too, some of them, like Arcot Desai Narasimhalu, explicitly open their statements that the future of innovation is 'as bright and shiny as never before'. Why might that be? Read on and find out!

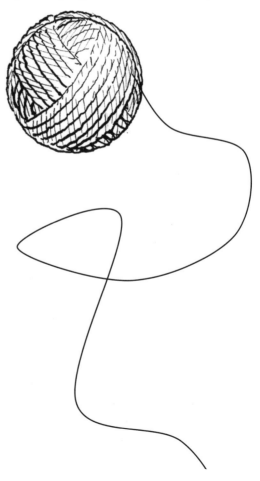

The Future of Innovation is Bright and Shiny as Never Before

Name	**Arcot Desai Narasimhalu**
Affiliation	Singapore Management University
Position	Director, Institute of Innovation and Entrepreneurship
Country	Singapore
Area	Innovation methodologies, innovation management
Email	Desai@smu.edu.sg

innovation management   opportunity identification   open innovation technical innovations

This bright shiny future is due to several reasons including better understanding of opportunity identification and innovation management, significant advances in technologies, new economic realities and the shifting focus to service innovation.

Innovation was perceived as an art practised by an exclusive few sitting in an ivory tower of a corporate headquarters of a company. The availability of methods such as Disruptive Innovation, Blue Ocean Strategy and Innovation Rules has empowered ordinary individuals to identify innovation opportunities as never before. This is a sea change in the sheer number of minds searching for the innovation needles in other otherwise chaotic haystack we call this world.

Calls for open innovation combined with the realisation that the best minds do not always reside within a firm have awakened companies such as Proctor and Gamble to devise new innovation management strategies such as 'Connect and Develop'. Increasingly complex problems and a wealth of talent distributed across different organisations and geographies can only heighten this awakening and create a series of innovation tsunamis due to the tectonic movements created by the open innovation community.

The speed and acceleration of new technology innovations are astounding. This community often creates new technologies without concern for monetisation. Researchers and practitioners ought to focus on effective methodologies for turning these technologies into wealth for individuals, organisations and nations. This is an area still yearning for clear and useful methodologies. How often do we see stacks of technologies sitting on the shelves of university departments and research institutes around the globe inviting exploitation? The innovation community is challenged to take the first steps in formulating an understanding that will help spin this 'intellectual hay' into gold.

New economic realities deserve close attention. Irrational exuberance, poor governance and unabated greed have resulted in the unprecedented economic crisis that stares us in the face. Hard times lead to questioning the status quo which in turn kindles our minds towards the creation of new innovations. So, expect new innovations to come from the unemployed, intelligent minds seeking a new lease of life based on their past experiences and new technologies. Now is a good time, if there ever was one, to expect a deluge of innovations to hit the market. Labour is cheap, rentals will fall and costs of setting up new businesses will be lower. With some help from an enlightened investment community, be it public or private, we can expect to see new entrants in several fronts.

New economic realities also encompass the emergence of BRIC Plus – Brazil, Russia, India and China not forgetting the Central Europe and Asia. Keen minds brimming with confidence that their time and turn have come will throw themselves intensely at creating new opportunities that will raise their standards to on par with or better than the those of current economic leaders.

As nations grow their economies, the cost of doing business in developed nations will only drive low value-added manufacturing to lesser developed countries. This in turn will reshape their economics such that more than 70 per cent of their GDPs and GNPs will look to the service component of their economies as the generator. Increasing dependence on the service component will draw the brighter minds to focus on innovations in the service industry.

Given the above development can there ever be any doubt that the future of innovation could only be bright and shiny.

The economic crisis we face today is an opportunity to for renewal and reconsideration, leading to a future of innovation that may be brighter than before. Part of this sparkle comes as more people engage in innovation and are less wary of innovation and change. It makes sense; when we understand something – in this case, innovation– we fear it less. We mention this as research shows that fear is a significant obstacle to innovation. If we start to understand, if we are less fearful, we can see light at the end of the tunnel, we can see into a brighter future.

A better understanding of how innovation comes about encourages us to seek diversity, and it is leading us towards new approaches, such as open innovation. Some of you may think that seeking for insights and ideas outside one's own organisation makes so much sense why make such a fuss about it? One reason to make a fuss about it is that engaging with open innovation requires a quite different perspective and mindset from the past mental models (most dominant in the heads of senior management) which were built on the belief that all great ideas are available in-house. If it is a mindset thing (and mindset is yet another warp in the fabric of innovation that we will explore in more detail later on) then it is worth celebrating that such a mindset change was possible for many people in a relatively short space of time.

Have you noticed that both Arash and Arcot see an increasingly important role for the developing and emerging economies? Do you? What consequences does this have?

Jan Buijs starts his contribution with a belief in a bright future for innovation, and agrees with Eduardo that there is no future without innovation. He throws three further considerations into the ring: the importance of timeliness, the ephemeral nature of innovation and the need for sustainability.

The Future of Innovation is Innovate or Die!

Name	**Jan Buijs**
Affiliation	Delft University of Technology, Faculty of Industrial Design Engineering
Position	Professor and Chair in Management of Innovation
Country	The Netherlands
Area	Product design
Email	j.a.buijs@tudelft.nl

invention   paradox   Al Gore   consumer   automotive industry

The future of innovation is bright: there is no future without innovation! Most known inventions, methods and products will ultimately be overtaken by new inventions, new methods and new products. Some people and some organisations will always be triggered to rethink the way we do things in the present. They will always come up with new ideas.

One of the core characteristics of innovation is that it is always temporarily. Take for instance the electrical car. It was, together with the steam engine and the combustion engine, one of the early attempts to make a self-propelled vehicle in the early days of automotive design. But the combustion engine became the dominant design, and now introducing an electrical vehicle is a big problem for the automotive industry. In absolute terms an electrical vehicle is not an innovation, it was here 100 years ago, but for most automotive companies it will be an innovation to introduce an all-electrical vehicle by 2015. All their engineering knowledge, design knowledge, marketing knowledge and manufacturing and maintenance knowledge are based on combustion engine technology. They have to re-invent nearly everything. And that is what I call innovation.

And not only the automotive industry has to re-invent itself – the same is true for the oil and gas industry, the infrastructure of petrol stations and the way governments get their money. In Europe the major determining factor for petrol prices are taxes, not the cost price of oil. We as consumers and users of cars will have to change our buying, driving and commuting behaviour as well.

If we look at the way we live our lives, and are aware that the majority of the world's population is waiting to get their fair share, we know that we need a couple of more planets Earth. Al Gore's *An Inconvenient Truth* is really at our front doors. So there is a very big need for innovation.

If we only want to have clean water for every person on earth, if we want health care on an acceptable level for everybody, if we want everybody to have a decent meal per day, if we want to reduce CO_2 emissions, if we want to get rid of poverty and if we want to live in peace, there is a lot to be done. And all these problems will ask for radical solutions. And radical solutions are per definition innovations.

So we need more innovations and more innovators than ever before. In that respect I see a bright future for innovation. But on the same moment I know that most people, and especially those who have power, will resist change. Most people will say in public 'We need innovation', but at the same moment they think privately 'I hope that nothing is going to change'.

That is the innovation paradox. Without innovation we will probably die, but keeping to the past we will surely die! That is the big challenge for all of us: innovate or die!

Jan doesn't mince his words and rightly so. The fact that a large proportion of humanity is still catching up, not only with the niceties we in most of the Western world take for granted, but even the basic necessities of life such as clean water and enough to eat, opens up an endless field for innovations. We cannot continue as we have before, there are just not enough resources if we continue our established trajectories.[1] It reminds us of The Sorcerer's Apprentice: *like him we have conjured up magic to do certain jobs for us, and it now feels as if we are not quite sure how to control the beast we have unleashed. We promote consumption and hold it up as a Holy Grail to which those 'not quite there yet' should aspire; we celebrate rising sales figures in the car industry or our ability to fly around the world for extraordinarily little charge, ignoring the hidden costs this generates and the blows we deliver to the delicate ecosystem we are part of. So we need better mastery of magic to set things right again; magic that is tempered by morality and by a better understanding of the impact of individual actions on the whole system.[2] Let us stress that again: we do need to start looking at and understanding our choices and their implications at the systems level. We can no longer ignore the implications of these choices for the wider context. We need to use the 'pain' we are experiencing now as a catalyst to drive us to innovate more responsibly and more sustainably.*

It is this pain and its potential role as a catalytic force that Joe Doering has made a central part of his contribution, along with some elaborations on the issue of timeliness.

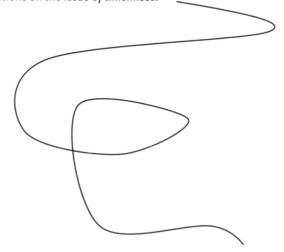

---

1   Many more of our contributors were concerned with the widening gap between anticipated consumption versus resources available and more space will be given to this in Part V, 'The 11th Hour'.

2   Here we refer to a lovely poem by Johann Wolfgang von Goethe, beautifully set to music by Paul Dukas, and visualised with Mickey Mouse as apprentice by Walt Disney. In the poem the great magician leaves and asks his apprentice to fill a bath with water. Unwilling to do the work himself the apprentice uses magic to get a broom to do the work for him. Unfortunately he does not know how to stop the magic, and nearly drowns, only just saved in time by the great master himself.

The Future of Innovation is a Function of Catharsis and Kairos

Name	**Joe Doering**
Affiliation	Nokia Siemens Networks
Position	Head of Asia South
Country	Malaysia
Area	Innovation management
Email	joe.doering@nsn.com

catharsis   pain   chronos   kairos   timing

New ideas have many ways of being created. One strong driver for humans to think about new ways of thinking, new ways of doing things, new products or new services is pain. Or better, a strong need or desire not to experience the same pain, the same drama, the same difficulty, the same embarrassment or the same bloody, sweaty or tearful (daily) burden or incident.

Most people reflect on their painful experience and learn from it. People develop new ideas out of pain and misery by thinking about new ways right after the pain was felt. As per Ancient Greek philosophy, the process of learning out of a drama is called *catharsis* (in fact, this is brutally simplified, but the right direction and makes the point). To understand more about new ideas or inventions as basic pillars of innovations, it is worth to study and to understand what a good catharsis is. This finally leads to new behaviour and finally to new management practices to drive innovation. Using dramatic occurrences – a crisis or a corporate drama to seed innovation – is the passive way to deal with catharsis as driver of innovation. To create painful changes, to create a crisis, to facilitate a drama or dramatic experiences (instead of ongoing corporate flat lining) are more radical paths to creating inventions.

An invention or idea may be brought up years or weeks too early or (in rare cases) too late to solve a need or fulfil a desire and for that reason such an idea will not become an innovation. Only an idea that comes up in the right moment, an invention that gets created in the right moment, has the potential to become an innovation. The Ancient Greeks called the right moment *kairos*. Kairos is distinct from chronos (running time) and is the point in time (the right moment, the right hour, the right year) when action leads into impact. When different flows of events interfere, connect and lead to a stage for something to be said (like 'I love you'), something to be done (like saving a life) or something to be invented, then this is kairos. Timing matters a lot to create an innovation (that is well known), thus the study and understanding of kairology (the science of the right moment) may lead to new ways to read signs that indicate that an idea is not ready to be brought to market and that the impact of an invention will increase when applied later, at kairos. Or that kairos has been missed. Inventions arising from a catharsis have a good chance of hitting kairos if the catharsis is experienced by a larger group, a society or the world economy.

We believe that the issue of timeliness is an important one, and we agree that if enough people are dissatisfied with a certain condition the likelihood that change will occur is high. Somehow we feel that a vision that paints an exciting future can be a motivator that is equal – if not superior – to pain. How about the vision of 'putting men on the moon'? Has that not motivated and inspired an entire generation? Is the energy we put into easing pain the same as the energy we put into a project that truly inspires us?

When are you at your most imaginative – when you are fearful, or when you are enthused and excited by a prospect? How about the notion that we 'stop innovating' as soon as the pain has ceased but continue innovation if we believe in our vision and the possibility of creating a better future? It seems akin to the idea of problem solving versus opportunity creation; the former starts with the present, the latter works back from a desired, preferable state in the future. Did not Antoine de Saint-Exupéry say in his book The Little Prince, *'If you want to build a ship, don't drum up people together to collect wood and don't assign them tasks and work, but rather teach them to long for the endless immensity of the sea'? Just a thought.*

Building on where Jan had left off, Janis Stabulnieks develops the theme of responsible innovation and of using innovation to address the world's problems. But, as he highlights, in order for this to happen we need an understanding of innovation that is widely shared; one that is much broader than the view of innovation that was predominant until the recent past; one that was limited to technology and products – a few people in white coats who invented things.

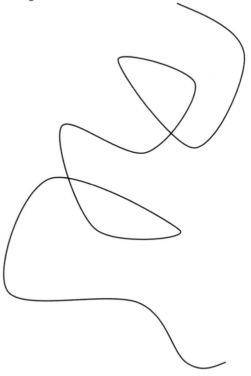

The Future of Innovation is a Common Understanding of the Global Economic Process

Name	**Janis Stabulnieks**
Affiliation	Latvian Technological Centre
Position	Managing Director
Country	Latvia
Area	Innovation management, acceleration of high-tech business
Email	LTC@LATNET.LV

**knowledge   creativity   economic development   common understanding
driving force**

The future of innovation is to find the shortest and most secure way to global peace and optimum welfare for every human being. But to reach it, first of all, we have to understand the meaning of the term 'innovation' in the correct way. In my opinion the simplest explanation of innovation may be the following: the endless process which guides us to a non-stop development of new technologies, new relations between people, new culture and even to a new way of thinking about how to make our lives better. We should understand the term 'innovation' in very broad sense – like education, science, culture, etc.

The history of humankind shows that innovation has taken place since very beginning of the era of civilization when, of course, nobody knew and used this term. Now, everybody likes to use this word to express his/her competence in economic development of society and/or certain business. However, many of them are using the word innovation in the most narrow meaning – new product on the market. In the worst case the word 'innovation' (in this case, meaning making money out of knowledge) is mixed up with the word 'invention' or 'science' (meaning making knowledge out of money). Hence, such very strange and to my mind senseless combinations of words as 'patenting innovation' (you can patent an idea, research results, etc.; innovation comes later), 'implementation of innovation' (implementation is a part of the innovation process) or even 'innovative science' (science is the creation of new knowledge and nothing more) have appeared and been widely used.

Therefore, last year I asked myself a simple question: is innovation a fashion word or a real term which describes the development of a highly organised and progress-oriented society?

The answer is in the question. Innovation should become a reality! We should all understand the term innovation identically, regardless of whether we are a politician or decision maker, professor or teacher, business advisor or company owner, banker, venture capitalist or business angel, schoolboy/girl or student. As a consequence, we will be able to manage innovation in the most effective way. This becomes more and more important if we take into account global changes in economies, systems of finances, technological development and, last but not least, climate.

We are on the eve of new technological revolution, when innovation will be the number one topic. Innovation is a driving force with unlimited power for the evolution. Only a combination of all components related to innovation – knowledge, creativity, intuition, communication, non-traditional ways of thinking and the ability to find new solutions for old problems – will bring us to an existence based on welfare for all and harmony with nature on planet Earth.

We could not agree more with Janis: innovation is not a fad it is here to stay and the challenge for all of us is to start making it a reality, in all walks of life. So let's hope that the vision of Arash and Arcot about a better understanding of innovation is realised. No, let's rephrase the last sentence: what can we, each of us individually, contribute to a deeper understanding of and purpose for innovation?

We would like to finish this section with Richard Philpott's contribution. Richard highlights some important challenges that we must face if we want to realise the potential of innovation, provides us with some thoughts on what trends are likely to affect us and offers insight into the future of innovation.

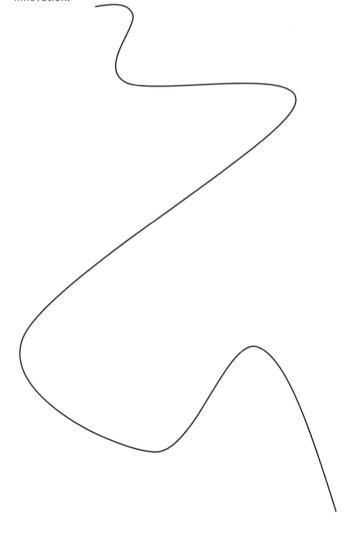

The Future of Innovation is Making Innovation Stick

Name	**Richard Philpott**
Affiliation	MyGreatIdea.com
Position	Director, Knowledge Transfer and Innovation Leadership
Country	UK
Area	Leadership; sustainability
Email	Richard@mygreatidea.com

sustainability   talent   systems   fatigue   performance

The future of innovation is fuelled by our ingenuity and commerce, our social and environmental needs and our insatiable appetite for the curious and new. However, some existing and future challenges and transformations will have a profound impact:

- 'Trend' fatigue, the next 'lean'?

- Demonstrable conversion of innovation 'rhetoric' to output.

- Building sustainability into every innovation thought process.

- Growing the pool of multi-dimensional innovation leaders.

- Rapid developments in digital communication.

- The increasing unpredictability of regional and global events.

Innovation has certainly been in the air for a while but its very definition may be its undoing.

Encompassing all aspects of the end-to-end process together with the less tangible cultural and environmental aspects means that it is hard to convey a concise picture or accurately measure progress. Its fashionable use in almost every aspect of business and increasingly in the social world is also potentially damaging. It's a great word and everyone seems to like the sound of it but the problem is that few understand how to really get a grip and use it to make a difference. Unless the output is convincing, there is a serious danger of it becoming as a fad.

Growing a pool of talented and dedicated innovation leaders is a key challenge. We need to better understand the attributes of our innovation leaders who have truly shown the ability to transform performance through their personal attributes and tools used. People respond to great leadership, we need better insight of successful profiles and implementation mechanisms to be able to select and train our future performers.

Environmental sustainability and innovation should go hand in hand. The sustainable agenda was very much on the fringes until people became impacted by global warming and diminishing resources (from a marketing perspective innovation is in need of the same hard-hitting messages to transform it from a nice-to-have to an essential). Current chaos in global financial systems is a timely reminder that our world is vulnerable to unforeseen events. Against the background of a recession it is easy for organisations to focus upon the short term but we have to get the message across that there is good long-term business to be made from sustainable processes and products. Innovation is a vital tool to help solve the mounting challenges and 'sustainnovation' will by necessity take a high place in tomorrow's agenda.

The rules for communications have been re-written with the advent of the digital age. Information, feedback, unsolicited comments and a whole variety of unexpected novelties have transformed and are probably bypassing historic ways of engaging and marketing. Innovation needs to move with this rapidly evolving area; such digital communities will probably be highly influential in the steering, building and destruction of future organisations. As we enter an era of more rapid change and unpredictability innovation systems need to be flexible and poised to respond to the next usurping technologies, events or culture changes in this increasingly helter-skelter world.

So, the future of innovation is bright, and is to be fun. Innovation is the means by which we can set right the wrongs of past developments, and by which we can create a better future for humanity. But in order to do that we need to create a shared understanding of innovation; grow a pool of dedicated innovation leaders; embrace collaboration; and draw on the immense diversity that is available to us. The future of innovation's driving force will be human ingenuity and the future is in our hands.

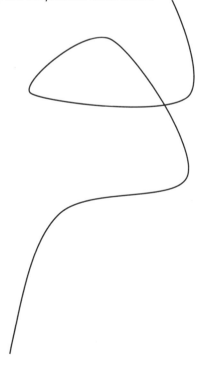

PART II
The Winds of Change: What Drives Innovation

With the broader canvas of innovation in mind then, what are the things that influence innovation, what are the drivers and enables of the change that is to come? What is it that creates an urgency and momentum around innovation? In what way are conditions different from the way they were even 50 years ago? Why is it that we are talking about so much more about innovation than ever before?

The contributions in this section will suggest why this might be and you will hear about the ever-increasing pace of change, of increasing connectivity and globalisation as well as instant communication and accessibility of information. This is about 'what has changed', 'what are the implications of those changes', and perhaps also where you might like to look to concentrate your innovation efforts in future, i.e. where potential innovation hot spots are. When composing this part of the story we found it often quite difficult to separate out causes and effects; they seem to be intertwined with no immediately obvious beginning or end. So it is not surprising that some identify causes that other describe as effects. What contributors made of the 'winds of change' in the context of innovation, what they see as force-fields in the innovation space will be explored in this section.

We would like to start with three contributions that outline what potential drivers as well as enablers of innovation are. Csaba Deák will start us off with three juxtapositions, arguing that the future of innovation lays in mastering the balance between the seemingly opposing aspects. Centralisation versus decentralisation is one of them. Let's hear what else he is picking up on.

The Future of Innovation is in the Mirror of Concentration, Dependency and Humanisation

Name	**Csaba Deák PhD**
Affiliation	University of Miskolc
Position	Associate Professor
Country	Hungary
Area	Innovation management
Email	deak.csaba@uni-miskolc.hu

concentration   dependency   humanization   dichotomy   factors

We can explore the future of innovation through three factors: concentration, dependency and humanisation. Concentration is evident in the divide between centralisation and decentralisation, as witnessed by the size of the innovation and research organisations. The dichotomy between separation and collaboration illustrates the dependencies of disciplines, geographical locations and business and academic sectors. Meanwhile, when humanisation is explored through the dichotomy of automation and human labour, it can be demonstrated that some human factors become less important while others need to be valued more highly.

Centralisation–Decentralisation

It can be argued that centralisation continues to gather pace. This is partly due to the targeting of financial sources towards innovation that has a visible impact. Company mergers and acquisitions also serve to reinforce the centralisation of research. Furthermore, smaller companies based on radical innovation are growing rapidly and dominating on them market.

Decentralisation will exist in the future, because small and medium-sized enterprises and other organisations will continue to participate in innovation as the moon-like satellites of bigger research centres. Many R&D organisations undertake research by dividing it into smaller units and the increasing popularity of open innovation is testament to the rise of this approach. Paradoxically, this openness serves to maintain the confidentiality and relative secrecy of research by restricting the number of members of the innovation team who are privy to the marketable results of the whole R&D project.

Separation–Collaboration

Specialisation will continue to increase within most disciplines and in some cases this will lead to the formation of new professions and branches of science. From another perspective, we will almost certainly witness further growth in geographical specialisation as cities and entire regions leverage their known strengths in specific fields of innovation.

The borders between disciplines will continue to fade and in some cases will simply disappear. Disciplines belonging to the fields of energy and the environment are a good example of this dynamic in practice. These days it is a standard requirement that one seeks the input of others for innovations in their respective fields.

The collaboration between academic institutions and industry through joint research is increasing. Universities appear to be transforming into 'knowledge factories': once solely devoted to developing human capital they are now amongst the most important R&D laboratories.

Automation–Human Labour

Innovation will become increasingly unimaginable without a strong technical background. The automation of innovation processes will lead to the ever-quicker realisation of results and this will be a major determinant in competition between researchers. As innovation becomes more complex so the need for more sophisticated tools will be heightened and the presence of effective innovation and project management methodology will be a key to successful projects.

Effective team performance will be critical to successful innovation in the future. We can expect to see research that originates in the fields of social science and psychology feature more prominently in product and process innovation, in technology and in natural science research. At the same time, the growing impact of organisational and marketing innovations will be felt in the research world.

Addressing the three dichotomies will require new ways of thinking around innovation. How well does your organisation do in, first, recognising these dichotomies and, secondly, addressing them?

We now turn to Han van der Zee who has identified four main drivers behind the need for new thinking, practices and structures.

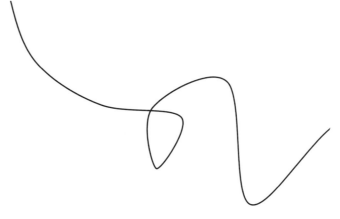

The Future of Innovation is A Quest for a (R)evolution in Innovation

Name	**Professor Dr Han T.M. van der Zee**
Affiliation	Atos Consulting Trends Institute
Position	Executive partner
Country	The Netherlands
Area	Business transformation and information technology
Email	han.vanderzee@atosorigin.com

**consumer needs   industrial convergence   value migration   globalization
eco-system**

Many companies experience the increasing impact of several changes in their business environments, which influence the way they plan and organise their business innovations. The current economic climate particularly tends to hamper bright ideas, preventing them from being conceptualised, designed and executed as they were envisaged during better and more certain economic times. However, innovation, that is generating knowledge and transforming it into new products, processes and services that meet (potential) market and customer needs, should continue to be the realm of future thinking, entrepreneurial managers. The alternative is just to slowly die and fade away. Unfortunately, future-thinking, entrepreneurial managers are not often greeted with much enthusiasm and eagerness by their peer (financial, operational) managers, to say the least. This implies that future-oriented entrepreneurial managers must become the coordinators and orchestrators of virtual and flexible networks of knowledge-generating entities beyond the traditional organisational borders, which will enable them to develop highly customised solutions and experiences for and with their customers.

During recent years, many companies' business environments have witnessed a number of structural developments. Together these have led, and increasingly will continue to lead, to an increasing demand for new thinking and practice. Four of these developments stand out in that they have and will have the largest impact on innovation concepts. These are industrial convergence, globalisation, value migration and the increased focus on individual consumer needs.

- **An increased focus on individual consumer needs** – To bind consumers' attention and satisfy their 'individual' needs, companies must increasingly offer 'experiences' or 'solutions' rather than just products or services. In order to identify such desires accurately, companies need to directly involve end consumers and customers in their innovation processes. Furthermore, providing suitable innovations and offering 'solutions' requires exponentially increased competences, which are preferably not all sourced internally.

- **Industrial convergence** – Industrial convergence, too, requires an increasing understanding of other industries. Technological developments force companies in the electronics, media, software, broadcasting, telecommunications, games, entertainment and education industries, for example, to rethink their markets radically. They are challenged to forge new alliances in order to generate new, converged products and solutions. Consequently, the scope of their innovation activities must span an increasingly widening array of industries and competences.

- **Value migration** – Whereas the traditional economy concentrated on manufacturing and assembling as the source of value, the information economy that is now dominant is rather more knowledge based. Today's productivity improvements are made possible by applying knowledge. Therefore real added value increasingly comes from R&D as well as marketing and sales activities. This development towards knowledge-intensive activities means that innovating organisations must take another step in the field of knowledge management, in order to sustain the knowledge already generated, expand their sources of innovation and establish learning organisations with respect to the wide variety of knowledge items companies must have access to.

- **Globalisation** – Increased globalisation forces and enables companies to get closer to their customers, suppliers, knowledge networks and manufacturers. The results are enhanced efficiency, increased access to resources and competences, cost reduction and true round-the-clock R&D operations, managed as global networks.

When business environments change significantly, as in today's economic downturn, innovative organisations are forced to change accordingly if their companies are to remain competitive. This implies that a new spectrum of business drivers and value-adding activities enters the innovation scope. It seems inevitable that the structural developments discussed above will have a significant impact on the way innovation is organised and structured in ecosystem-like networks of contributors of many forms, types and makes. The question for forward-thinking, entrepreneurial managers is, then, how companies' current innovation processes and functions can best be structured to meet these new requirements. It's obvious that 'open' will prove to be the keyword in this challenging, cut-throat innovation arena.

Han's reflections on Globalisation made us think. While there are certainly benefits in terms of efficiencies and pooling of resources, we believe that we are starting to see a reaction so this, a reaction that argues for a deeper concern for the local level. Think for food, for example. Sure, it is nice to have strawberries in winter in the UK – but at what cost? 'Locally grown' is definitely gaining in popularity, and we would bet that this will increase significantly in the future, with increased transportation costs and awareness of environmental implication of such offerings. However, we would not argue against the positive consequences of globalisation, nor that understanding implications of globalisations, and making conscious choices of whether and where to engage on a global level, is important. We would argue that one of the challenges of the future of innovation is to understand and deal with such complexities, and find solutions that allow to embrace both aspects of what could be seen as juxtaposition.

To help us navigate through the winds of change Csaba alerts us to three dichotomies we need to understand and balance, while Han emphasises the need to revisit existing structures, and the need for openness.

For us one of the biggest issues we need to understand and acknowledge is the systemic nature of the world we are living in, and the complexities arising from it. It is impossible to adhere to the clockwork analogy of Descartes any longer. We cannot believe that we can fiddle with one part of a system and not affect the others. The development of chaos and complexity theory, driven by a diverse group of people in the Santa Fe Institute in America, has helped much to increase our understanding of such matters.

Understanding the world in systems also implies that we cannot possible assume that we can solve the problems we are facing today with local solutions. As Einstein said, 'You cannot solve a problem with the mindset that created it'. Who remembers their maths lessons? Did you enjoy the bit on solving equations with unknowns? Do you remember that you need at least as many equations as you have unknowns? It's almost a forerunner of complexity theory, except that in complex systems there are so many variables that it becomes impossible to see for an equal number of equations. The trick in complex systems is to watch carefully, and almost with lateral vision, what is merging. Why lateral vision? Have you tried to look straight at a faint star? Have you lost it, and only found it again when you stop looking at it directly? Spotting emerging developments in complex system is a little like that. No doubt, our world is a highly complex, global system. This is not to say that solutions cannot emerge at a local level; in fact, they are quite likely to do so. However, we also believe that it is increasingly likely that similar approaches and solutions will start emerging locally – in several places at the same time!

Even around a century ago when the 'televisor' was invented it emerged in several places at the same time. As the wondrous product of mass collaboration, Wikipedia, states, progress in the art of televising came to a head in many places in 1925: Scottish inventor John Logie Baird gave a demonstration of televised silhouette images in motion at Selfridge's Department Store in London; in the United States of America AT&T's Bell Telephone Laboratories transmitted halftone still images of transparencies; also in the USA Charles Francis Jenkins was able to demonstrate the transmission of the silhouette image of a toy windmill in motion from a naval radio station to his laboratory in Washington.

The aspects our first two contributors have identified will only multiply the phenomenon of multiple, simultaneous invention and innovation. Are you aware of that, have you set up antennae to alert you to these things that are happening at mind-boggling speed? Just reading what Jongbae Kim writes makes us dizzy – yet that's what we have to prepare for!

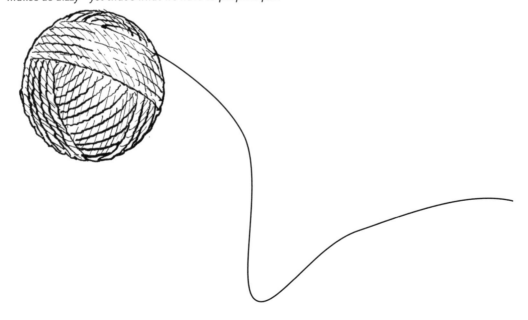

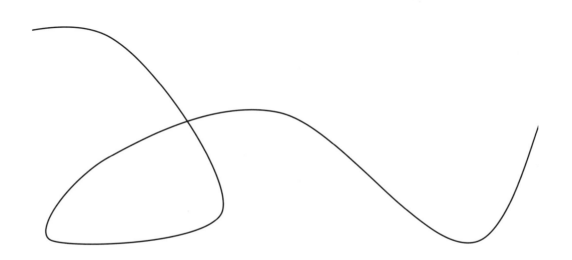

The Future of Innovation is Changing Across Three or Four Lanes all at Once

Name | Jongbae Kim
Affiliation | Sungshin Women's University
Position | Professor of Marketing
Country | South Korea
Area | Innovation management, NPD management
Email | jbkim@sungshin.ac.kr

innovation cycle   system   unlearning   business portfolio management
reversible lanes

The future of innovation is like changing across three or four lanes all at once on a road with the lanes vanishing or forming on occasion (i.e., the reversible lanes). The meaning of innovation doesn't change over time; that is, innovation in the future will also mean the ability to identify and implement new, better, more effective, more efficient solutions. However, in the future innovation is expected to occur *more frequently* and, at the same time, our understanding and knowledge of what is considered to be new, better, more effective, more efficient would be *broader*. Future innovation is analogous to the situation mentioned above, while innovation in the past is analogous to changing from one lane to the next on a straight road. The properties of future innovation can be delved deeper into as follows.

Changing Across Multiple Lanes

When we change across a number of lanes on a motorway, we cover a great distance in a short time; we will similarly cross a great distance in a short time to travel from past to future innovation. In the past, we only moved into the next lane when it was safe; in the future, organisations will have to manage the innovative side of their business at the same time as their existing business. In this context, the paradigm of business portfolio management may be changed. Of course, any innovation and the driving force behind it will apparently originate in the organisation's capabilities and the resources that have been accumulated over time. There are many cases, however, in which the method, the knowledge, the strategy, the organisation and the people that were useful to the existing business will be an obstacle to the successful implementation of innovation. Therefore, in order to operate in a way suited to the innovation, the organisation would have to 'unlearn' a sizeable portion of knowledge regarding the technology, the product and the market with which it has been familiar, and would have to change its corporate governance and culture, and its strategic alliances with external, heterogeneous organisations. While we stay at the first base, we cannot steal the second base.

The Road with Reversible Lanes

In the future, the lifecycle of a technology, a product or a market will be shortened since innovation will occur more frequently than in the past. Such a shortening of the innovation cycle suggests that, repeatedly, an organisation's existing business, technology or products will cease to have any meaning, just as the lane in the road suddenly disappears. In this environment of future innovation which is like reversible lanes, only an organisation equipped with a system that can effectively detect and cope with a changing situation will survive and prosper. When change has to be frequent, the winner will be an organisation with the sustainable capability to innovate.

A high-performing car, a car navigation system telling the driver of any changing road situation in a timely manner, a skilful driver, these are all needed when driving fast and safely on a road whose lanes suddenly form or disappear. Likewise, for operating successfully in the environment of future innovation, an organisation should have the necessary elements in place.

Jongbae is right, there is no one system or approach that will help us navigate the future, it will be a number of different things that will need to be in place simultaneously. It is about insight and understanding skills and tools, awareness and mindset. This also means that the creation of knowledge is less important than the ability to integrate that new knowledge, and combine it with existing knowledge sets. An ability to understand the implication of that new knowledge, and draw some fruitful conclusions from it, will set the winners apart.

The telecommunications industry is one area where the convergence of technologies has been particularly stunning and fast. Camera, phone, computer all morph into one – at least in principle. Henri Tirri observes acceleration and convergence, sharing a case study from the mobile computing sector as an example.

The Future of Innovation is a Corporate Activity

Name	**Henry Tirri**
Affiliation	Nokia
Position	Head of Nokia Research Centre, Senior Vice President
Country	Finland
Area	Innovation as a corporate activity, future innovation in mobile computing
Email	CDO.communications@nokia.com

ecosystem   corporate innovation   innovation flow   open innovation
Nokia Research Center

Innovation in mobile computing is changing. A collision between research styles is challenging the way companies innovate today and in the future. Through the advancement of technology, three distinct approaches have been thrown together and the outcome is the emergence of a new and exciting innovation culture. Companies that understand this and adapt, will gain a significant advantage.

Collision of Innovation Systems

Traditionally telecoms industry players innovated within silos, protecting their advances with intellectual property rights (IPR). This creates solutions that define specific standards, but mandate the rest of the industry adopt those standards to see them proliferate. The result is a power play to assert dominant ideas which through decisions over licensing fees and legal entanglements can lead to the demise of the best solutions.

But computer science and internet innovators traditionally operate with an altogether different style. The open and collaborative approach fostered by the Linux community and internet companies is based on speed and competence: a true meritocracy. With this type of innovation, being fastest is key. The approach is also self-balancing, as wide access to shared information demands that companies become more flexible in their approach to innovation; it creates real incentives based on commercial success.

There is no single right way to nurture innovation so businesses today must identify the style which will be most successful for them in the converging world.

Innovation Flow

Innovation cycles are accelerating dramatically. The speed at which new solutions reach the market can be a matter of months, if not weeks, and this timeframe is continually shrinking as online service organisations embrace a 'beta' culture. The internet has enabled innovators to share results and garner feedback faster. Feedback from peers, public betas and pilot studies is essential to fuel the accelerated innovation cycle.

Future innovation must also support scale; companies that can scale innovations quickly will succeed by gaining mass market acceptance almost instantaneously. A willingness to take risks and test ideas fast is vital; we call it a 'fail fast, scale fast' mentality, rooted in a culture of conducting pilots and trials. Often it isn't until you test a product or service that you really understand how customers respond. It is not unusual to see customers using products in unforeseen ways; embracing this can lead to runaway successes.

Nokia Sports Tracker (http://sportstracker.nokia.com/) is one example. Initially designed for runners and walkers, it has been used by everyone from kayakers to motorcyclists. Such unexpected adaptations have prompted Nokia to expand the mandate and functionality of Sports Tracker, conforming to the customers' needs rather than our preconception of what the service should be.

Collaboration also drives innovation forward at a pace that monetary investment alone can never match. Collaborating with leading research organisations globally, Nokia is building an Open Innovation network to co-create intellectual property and leverage each organisation's insight, expertise and resources. Through research partnerships we maintain a continual inflow of fresh thinking, which ensures we are always challenging established views. This is an integral element of our open innovation philosophy.

Innovate or Exit

As history shows, in the midst of change, one truth remains constant: companies that cannot identify and exploit the best approaches to innovation for their business will fail. From a personal perspective, I am proud to be leading research for a company whose strength is founded on a century and a half of innovation. From its roots in a riverside paper mill in south-western Finland to a global telecommunications leader, Nokia has learnt this lesson well.

The convergence of technologies, the combination not only of technologies but of industries – this heralds exciting times ahead. Information technology clearly plays an important role in the acceleration of the innovation cycle, and it also fertilises the innovation field. The accessibility of knowledge and the speed with which it can be accessed, as well as its independence from location, driven by the 'digital world', have cranked up the handle of communication, developments, decision making. Rob Atkinson elaborates on the role of ICT, and the digitalisation which is part of it, in driving, enabling and accelerating innovation.

The Future of Innovation is as Future Prosperity

Name	**Rob Atkinson**
Affiliation	Information Technology and Innovation Foundation
Position	President
Country	USA
Area	IT-enabled innovation
Email	ratkinson@innovationpolicy.org

past and future   America's economy

The future of innovation will continue to be based on information and communications technologies (ICT), in large part because ICT is our era's 'general purpose technology'.

Over the last 200 years, innovation has been driven in periodic waves by 'general purpose technologies'. These GPTs have three characteristics. First, they are pervasive in that they end up being used by most sectors. Second, their performance and price improve over time, sometimes quite dramatically. And third, they are at the core of a whole series of innovations in new products, processes, business models and markets.

In the past, different technologies, like the steam engine, railroads, electricity and the internal combustion engine, served as GPTs. Most recently, before today's ICT revolution, materials technologies served as the dominant GPT and underpin innovation in a wide variety of sectors. Plastics gave us more durable and easy-to-use materials. Cars and appliances depended on low-cost steel. Aluminium enabled jet aviation. Breakthroughs in chemistry provided us with better drugs, household products and clothing.

Today, however, the materials revolution has largely achieved its promise, particularly in developed nations, and relatively few innovations rely on materials technologies. Certainly many advances in the IT revolution depend on hardware innovations made possible by continued advancement in materials technology, but these improvements are not manifest in the physical nature of these devices but rather in their functional performance. Thus the value found in microprocessors has less to do with physical properties like size and weight, and more to do with functional properties, such as the number of instructions processed per second.

As a result, it is now the 'digital information revolution' that is driving innovation and enabling billions of people to live better lives. The materials revolution produced life-saving vaccines, but the digital information revolution is enabling the creation of a rapid learning network to enable our global health care system to quickly find out what treatments work best and which don't. The materials revolution produced the automobile and the highway system, but the digital information revolution is creating intelligent transportation systems and is letting us 'digitally travel' through telecommuting and teleconferencing. The materials revolution produced the telephone, but the digital information revolution is allowing ubiquitous communication from a wide range of devices and places. The materials revolution produced the electricity grid, but it is the IT revolution that is producing the intelligent 'green' grid.

In other words, the digital information revolution is not likely to produce a world that *looks* significantly different than the world of the recent past. But it is producing a world that *functions* in radically different and better ways, with individuals and organisations able to access and use a vast array of information to improve their lives and society. Indeed, after 5,000 years of civilization, we are only now moving from a relative inert and obtuse world to a one that will be intelligent and 'alive with information'. And in this world a vast array of opportunities for new products, services and business models will be enabled by the ICT revolution and the drive to create an intelligent world.

An interesting notion: it's not about how it looks but what's happening inside. However, we believe that if the 'what happens inside' changes this may bring up tremendous opportunities to also reconsider the 'how it looks'! How often do we find that the looks of something today have been shaped by something that is no longer part of it. Perhaps a short story illustrates what we mean. A young man, sitting with his friends at a declivous Thanksgiving dinner, shares a secret of his family's turkey cooking. He says, 'And before the turkey goes into the oven we break off one leg which then goes on top of it, that's why it tastes so delicious.' One of the guests asks why that might be and the young man replies, 'Well, I am not sure, but let me ask my grandmother.' Sure enough, during his next visit he brings up the issue of turkey cooking. His grandmother laughs and explains, 'Well, dear boy, the thing was, the oven we had at my parent's house was so narrow that the whole turkey would not fit in unless we broke off one leg!' It is not that you should challenge all the things you do all the time, but occasionally questioning why things are done a certain way and thinking about how they might be done differently could be a good idea.

Let us hear another proponent of the role of ICT in innovation, Eunika Mercier-Laurent, who especially views artificial intelligence as a great opportunity in the context of innovation.

The Future of Innovation is Eco-creating a Prosperous and Happy Future

Name	**Eunika Mercier-Laurent**
Affiliation	KIM
Position	President
Country	France
Area	Knowledge and innovation management, intelligent and creative technologies
Email	eunika@innovation3D.fr

e-co-innovation   eco-systems   education   technology   intelligence

To talk about the future of innovation we should imagine the future and be also inspired by the best from the past. In the context of today's economics, innovation is considered as the magic wand, able to miraculously change the world. It has to create jobs and growth, increase companies' productivity, help in the better use of natural resources, produce better and more affordable public services, including health and safety, and workable solutions for ageing populations, contribute to a high-quality education system, and help solve global warming and climate change. Maybe we ask too much? Could it really happen? What are the conditions to make it happen? What kind of investment is necessary?

First of all we need to innovate in the *way of thinking*. We live in a global world, dealing with ecosystems, talking about the Knowledge Society, yet we are still classifying things and working separately in narrowly defined domains, and are mainly considering technological innovation. The 'info-nano-bio' initiatives are fashionable around the world, but usually disconnected from what Zhouying Jin calls 'soft technology'. Some initiatives emerge around organisational, social or ecologic innovation but main actors are specialised in their domains and talk their specific languages. In EC programmes innovation is mainly research related and about technology. However, slowly a few multidisciplinary initiatives are starting to emerge. Europe is still watching, observing competitors in the US and in Japan.

According to my definition innovation is a process *from idea to sustainable success*.

Innovation capacity is mainly measured in number of PhDs, patents and publications and not in term of benefits it can bring to humanity without impacting ecosystems.

The future of innovation depends on our *capacity to innovate* in the way we think, use resources, move, manage, work and learn. That's why *education* systems have a great role to play in switching from 'in the box thinking' to system, global and holistic ones, in freeing imagination, in creating a common innovation language.

The *ecology* movement can be one of enablers for expanding the eco-industry and eco-technology into a cross-disciplinary eco-innovation.

Information and communication technology (ICT) can be a considerable help to the future of innovation. A new generation of artificial intelligence, including convergence of natural intelligences, will allow us to be more intelligent together. Another meaning of ICT could be intelligent and creative technology.

Innovation may *address needs*, make dreams come true or create new needs.

What could be the future needs and dreams of humanity? Good health, comfortable life, friends, be respected, peace, elixir of youth, more intelligence, travel to Mars, or simply having something to eat?

Briefly my vision of the future of innovation is the following: connected human knowledge cultivators work in perfect synergy with the artificial knowledge processors. They learn from each other. Computers help people by performing the tasks difficult or impossible for human to do in the world where the biological, social and machine components are well balanced, are sustainable indefinitely without destroying the environment, and enhance the human condition.

Point well made. We are expecting much of innovation yet it can only happen if we are willing to take the necessary steps to enable and support it. We need to look over our fences, and we need to move beyond our current understanding of innovation. We need to see technology as an enabler of innovation, as a means, not as the end result in and on itself.

While some of the above might sound as if the author believes the main driver for innovation in the future is technology. Eunika hints at innovation as a servant to human needs and aspiration. Technology is undeniably a major driver in the play of innovation, but we'd like to follow on with Kenneth Preiss who points out that human welfare – which is by no means the same as progress, but should be the ultimate aim of innovation – will depend more on social organisation than technological development. Let's see why.

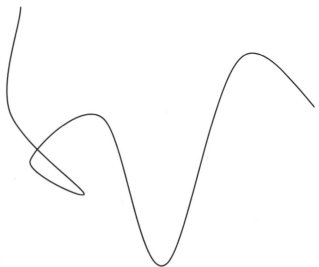

The Future of Innovation is Reinventing

Name	**Kenneth Preiss**
Affiliation	Ben Gurion University of the Negev
Position	Emeritus Professor
Country	Israel
Area	Political science, philosophy
Email	preiss@bgu.ac.il

sovereignty   prosperity   wealth   political science

The late Mancur Olson investigated data from wealthy and poor countries in order to understand why some are rich and some poor. The conclusion, given in his book *Power and Prosperity*, is that necessary conditions for prosperity are individual and property rights under law, and absence of predation by corruption or by special-interest groups abusing the legal process. Berman, in his book *Created Equal*, showed that in an ancient Middle East where people believed that natural phenomena resulted from manipulations by gods, kings being the sole intermediaries to those gods both universal and parochial, and where ordinary people were to heed every whim of the king, the Hebrew bible coalesced emerging beliefs into a revolutionary idea, that there was one God external to nature, who created nature, and that every individual was equal, with the status of a king, under that one and universal God. This is the basis of modern society and enabled the development of modern science.

Message Number 1: Human Welfare Depends on Societal Organisation More Than on Technological Development

When the modern concept of national sovereignty was developed, the impact of any process within a single country on its neighbours was minimal. A few examples from among many are: the world population was around 1.2 billion people, and the pollution per capita was less than today so the effects of pollution were not felt; the distance that military force could be projected from within a country was the range of an artillery piece; ideas travelled slowly since they were transmitted on paper that had to be transported to a population of whom many were illiterate. We introduce the concept of a country having many borders, one for each mode of influence on its neighbours; in those days all the borders of influence of a country coincided with its physical borders.

Today every country influences another. A few examples from among many are: pollution from every country has influence beyond its borders. Military destruction can be projected without reference to the border of the projecting country; Iranian rockets can reach Europe and India, and American rockets can reach anywhere; soon many countries will have that capability. A scene photographed on a cell phone can be rapidly shown anywhere to the illiterate as well as the literate, generating riots and upheaval. There are hence many borders of influence for each country, and these do not any more coincide with its physical borders. Sovereignty is becoming distributed.

It is not surprising therefore that nations are committing aspects of their sovereignty to international treaties and bi- and multilateral agreements, but this is still seen as a perturbation or add-on to the fundamental concept of absolute sovereignty. The new and developing concept of 21st-century distributed sovereignty is replacing 20th-century absolute sovereignty.

Message Number 2: Fundamental Concepts and Methods of Political Organisation Will Inevitably Change in the 21st Century

These paradigmic issues will be important innovation challenges for the 21st century.

Kenneth again raises the important issue to which we will come back in Part III: that innovation will go far beyond what many of us currently associate with it. It will go well beyond technology and R&D, it will even go beyond business model innovation. We are likely to see fundamental innovation in the way we as Human Race Limited will operate and function. What exciting prospect!

What then do we need to understand in order to not only be aware and ready for change, but perhaps also help drive it? It reminds us of something David Bernstein says in his book Company Image and Reality: *'Companies communicate whether they want or not. Deliberate reticence is itself a message.' A little further on he continues, 'Communication is the responsibility of the communicator. Misconceptions are the fault of the transmitter, not the receiver.' For us it translates into the fact that if we would like the future to be of a particular kind we need to get involved and let our voices be heard. The future is not something that just happens to us. There will be some people who will shape the future, and some to whom the future seems to 'just happen'. In our view, we may as well belong to those who do the shaping – rather than complaining later that the future is not what we wanted it to be!*

What then do we need to understand and know in order to get involved in shaping the future? Bengt-Åke Lundvall gives us some starting points.

The Future of Innovation is in the Learning Economy

Name	**Bengt-Åke Lundvall**
Affiliation	Aalborg University
Position	Professor
Country	Denmark
Area	Innovation in the learning economy
Email	bal@business.aau.dk

learning economy   collective entrepreneurship   diversity   social cohesion
new new deal

Innovations are New Combinations and They Come Out of Diversity

Innovation involves the creation of new knowledge. At the same time most innovations are new combinations of old insights. They come out of an interaction where people with different talents, interests, insights and experience get together in open communication willing to share their knowledge with others. Innovation processes that neglect the needs of users are inefficient. Science-based innovations that are not supported by experience-based learning are not successful. Therefore innovations are best seen as outcomes of 'collective entrepreneurship'. It means that generalised trust among people meeting at the marketplace and participatory democracy in working life contribute to innovation.

Innovation Thrives When Science Meet Practical Experience

Science plays a growing role for innovation also in more traditional sectors such as food, textiles and furniture. But without experience based knowledge about production, markets and organisation investment in science has little impact on economic performance. Innovation strategies and innovation policies need to be broad. Firms need to combine R&D with building a learning organisation that includes networking with external organisations. Public policy that aims at harnessing innovation for growth needs to combine Science and technology policy with institutional change in education and labour market systems.

The Learning Economy Poses New Challenges

We are in a learning economy where the success of people, organisations and countries reflects the capacity to learn. Old knowledge becomes less relevant as technologies change and global competition transforms working life making some types of jobs disappear and others grow.

Whatever knowledge you have, it does not constitute a lifelong guarantee for success neither for firms nor for individuals. This has major importance for the design of education and labour markets, and for strategies of management and trade unions. All institutions and strategies need to focus on how to facilitate learning at the level of individuals and organisations.

The Learning Economy and Social Cohesion

Some of the most successful economies in the world benefit from being advanced learning economies; they do not host radical innovations new to the world but they are outstanding in taking up technologies elsewhere. The Nordic countries are small and this should be actually be seen as a handicap in a knowledge-based economy. But they do very well because they have built generalised trust and this is reflected in how they learn. Firms engaged in innovation interact more with other firms and employees take more active part in processes of technical and organisational change. This reflects social cohesion. But the learning economy tends if left to itself increase the gap between those with higher education and the rest. Those with little education have less ability to learn and in the business sectors they are offered less opportunities to learn.

A New New Deal

This constitutes a major challenge for public policy in the learning economy. In order to keep the learning economy strong and vibrant there is a need to redistribute learning opportunities to the advantage of those with little education and few opportunities to learn. Here the current crisis may be seen as offering new opportunities. There will be many people out of job and some industries such as automobiles will be sacking hundreds of thousands of workers. In this situation upgrading the skills of workers is the best public policy for the long term. Giving them unemployment support for not working implies that their skills will be gradually eroded. Supporting ailing industries to keep them employed in their existing job is to postpone structural change that will have to take place in the near future.

As suggested earlier, diversity is one of innovation's strong points. Bringing together different bodies of knowledge, combining and re-combining insights and knowledge, leads to innovation and to solving problems and issues we might face. The combination of knowledge also points to another important change and enables of innovation: learning. It is no longer sufficient to apply knowledge, constantly we need to draw on different pockets of our knowledge to understand or respond to situations. However, this throws a gauntlet to current systems of education where the dominate mode is still one of 'right or wrong', of multiple choice question exams and individual-based assessments. This then throws a discussion and review of education into the mix. And only confirms that we cannot understand and change things unless we look at all relevant aspects of a system.

Following on from Bengt-Åke, John Bessant continues the theme of weaving different strands of knowledge together, and talks about some tools and capabilities that we need to develop in order to better navigate the future of innovation.

The Future of Innovation is Challenging the Frontier of Innovation

Name	**John Bessant**
Affiliation	University of Exeter Business School
Position	Director of Research and Professor of Entrepreneurship and Innovation
Country	UK
Area	Dynamic capability
Email	j.bessant@exeter.ac.uk

dynamic capability   sustainability   knowledge spaghetti   co-creation

Managing innovation involves 'dynamic capability' – it's an old problem which constantly needs new ways of dealing with it in the light of changing context. In that connection I think three trends will challenge us in the future:

1. **Sustainability** – a fashionable word but a huge challenge both for incremental innovation (really doing what we do but better, taking the waste out of our processes, redesigning existing products and services, rethinking business models to take account of sustainability issues) and for radical, discontinuous innovation. This means finding completely new ways of achieving many of the things we have taken for granted in fields like energy, resources, transportation – and rethinking not just our product and process innovations but the underlying business models which we use.

2. **Managing knowledge spaghetti** – innovation has always been about weaving different strands of knowledge together to create new things. 'Open innovation' isn't a new idea, but the challenge of making it happen in a knowledge-rich environment is huge. Whilst more technical knowledge is being created than at any other time in our history – estimates suggest close to $1 trillion/year is spent on public and private sector R&D – it is no longer concentrated in a few companies or countries but globally distributed. How do we make connections to that effectively when – in many cases – firms don't even have full knowledge of what they already know? And how do we work in markets which are also globally distributed, fragmented into smaller and smaller segments and increasingly virtual in nature? Our innovation challenge is about making connections – thorough structures, networks, technological infrastructures and, above all, through people. Knowledge broking will increasingly be a key skill within organisations and the basis of a growing service sector. Perhaps the biggest implication is that we will move from a situation dominated by economies of scale or capital intensity where large organisations are the main innovators to one where 'economies of knowledge scope' shape the landscape. Firms don't have to be big, but they do have to be connected. They don't need to know everything as long as they know someone else who has the knowledge they need.

3. **Co-creation with users** – users are not passive players in innovation and finding ways of engaging them in the front end, co-creating the solutions which they need and value will be a critical driver of change in the way we manage the process. We are already seeing acceleration in 'mass customisation' and this is going to be particularly important in services where developing partnerships with users represents the frontier of sustainable competitive advantage. Public sector service innovation involves multiple stakeholders in a 'contested' process – and

co-evolution amongst these players will be of growing significance. And extreme users become critical – their needs at the fringe today may well represent the new mainstream tomorrow. Innovators are increasingly going to need to look to the edge – for example, at the 'bottom of the pyramid' – for insights into what the next big waves will be.

While John picks up the thread of increased knowledge – or 'knowledge spaghetti', as he calls it – he also offers one approach that might help us deal with it. What should we do with the masses of knowledge and information that surround us? Well, to draw on John's first point, the first thing is, more with less. Sustainability has actually emerged as important themes and will be investigated in more detail in Part V, 'The 11th hour', and Part X, 'Let's get together'. The second is his last point: work together with users; they no longer want to stand at the sidelines but want to be involved in the development of what they are to buy and consume.

If John has offered sustainability, knowledge spaghetti and user involvement for consideration in our journey to shed some light on the future of innovation, Ray Buschmann suggests a further three areas: women, music and corporate climate. We can't help agreeing about the role of women! The influence of women in society is changing rapidly: women are in management, government, army, politics. Their role extends far beyond making decisions on sourcing children's care, medicine, food, clothes, shoes, household devices, holidays. No denying that shopping remains one of women's delights, but their contribution and role in influencing success or demise of innovation go well beyond that. Just consider what the car manufacturer Volvo set up some years ago: an all-women team designing a car for women. The rationale behind it? If we can satisfy women we can certainly satisfy men, easily! While women were seen to be more critical, they were also more engaged in trying to find solutions for things they felt were not right. Traits often associated with women, such as being emotional, intuitive and caring, were previously considered to be barrier to women's progress in business. In the age of innovation they are turning to their advantage: it is just these qualities that are required in innovation. Thank you, Ray, for bringing this up, now, the floor is all yours!

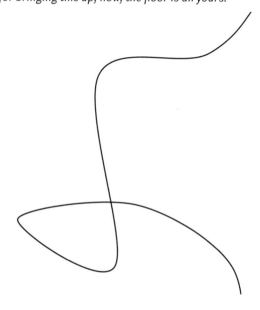

The Future of Innovation is Glimpsed by a Futurist Creativity Practitioner

Name	**Ray Buschmann**
Affiliation	Solving the Impossible Pty Ltd
Position	Principal and Owner
Country	Australia
Area	Practitioner and futurist
Email	rkbuschmann@solvingtheimpossible.com

new knowledge   women   jealousy   music   sustainable

Back to the Future

We are on a precipice of needing to rapidly change our thinking proactively forward, rather than using traditional solutions gathered from past experience, combinations and remembered scenarios, for innovation to rapidly succeed. I believe we will falter if we continue to innovate using an epitome of past knowledge that has no relevance, or equivalence, for the future. We need to quickly learn to generate new knowledge that currently doesn't exist.

Let the Women Lead – Innovation Reawakens

There is an ever increasing awareness that innovation is the best tool to help the less fortunate, neither relying on traditional handouts nor on bureaucratic processes where the original concept gets lost in wasteful and disgraceful inefficient use of resources. I believe that the socialisation of innovation is the giant horizon that will become the spark to revitalise people's interest, and help regain respect for innovation, as a valued craft.

Further, the catalyst for change needs to be led by women in these disadvantaged areas. Education is key: the most caring individuals to get that started are the future-generation mothers. Let's invest our innovation resources through ideas and helping others think creatively in a very different way. Already examples exist: an African merry-go-round brings enjoyment to children in remote villages, but more importantly, innovation in its design allows the device's turning motion to be connected to a water pump which produces clean drinking water for the first time from previously inaccessible underground aquifers, plus women no longer have to carry water for miles.

Music Finally Hits the Right Chord

There is something wondrous about music that none of us yet fully understands or utilises. Sure, hearing music of any sort – reggae, rock, classical, rap, blues – there is a distinctive change in our thinking processes and we, generally, derive great pleasure from the experience. But, my prediction is that one day we will really discover the core reason we have music, rather than just enjoyment – it will drive 'revolutionary new innovation' concepts characterised by mechanisms that can heal the sick, and move people into new, unchartered intellectual zones.

Valley of Death

The Valley of Death is a location that is frequently visited by ideas, often called the 'innovation implementation phase', into which ideas go, and then, unfortunately, quickly wither and die; incapable of being resuscitated, lost for ever. It's a harsh corporate climate: lack of funds at the optimum time for idea deployment because of the yearly budgeting cycle, too many competing opportunities, too long a time horizon for results, no efficient implementation process in place, and perhaps the grand-daddy of them all: pet jealousy/sabotage by many executives who didn't think of the idea in the first place. The terrain is alive with venomous creatures hiding under every rock, ready to strike and kill your project in seconds. Antidotes are available: take a full dose of 'innovation strategic alignment', and add a liberal spreading of 'sustainable growth'. These two mechanisms will substantially increase the probability of future business success.

We find Ray's mention of music particularly interesting. Of course, there has been research that plants grow better when being played Mozart, and that cows give more milk, but we are not aware that someone has explored how we can use music to improve the process of innovating! And why not? The use of other arts, such as drawing and acting, has shown positive effects on innovation, by connecting us to our emotions, by making use of a different part of our brain, and thereby stimulating a more balanced use of what our brain has to offer, and by stimulating a different way of approaching and representing a problem. Next time you are presenting a new idea or a new concept try singing it out – rather than using endless numbers of PowerPoint slides...

Patrick Poitevin is another contributor who offers a number of tools and thoughts that might help the innovation process, and relates back to Bengt-Åke's notion that innovation happens through combining and re-combining existing knowledge.

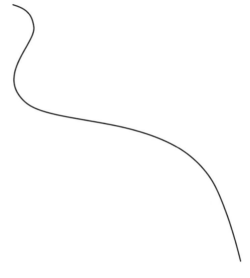

The Future of Innovation is Timeless and Broad

Name   **Patrick Poitevin**
Affiliation   Patrick Poitevin Packaging
Position   Technical Manager Cadbury
Country   UK
Area   Packaging innovation
Email   patrick.poitevin@csplc.com

definition   creativity   patents   change   needs

Why try to define or categorise innovation? Why try to understand and put it in a glossary? Innovation is timeless; at the same time, there is no such thing as innovation! Somewhere, sometime, the innovation is or has been available, maybe not in your own field, maybe not in your own environment or industry. So look broader, across industry, combine. It might even have been done in nature, that's what the field of biomimetics is about.

Innovation is broader than we think. It is not only about creativity, newness or patents. Applying innovation is creativity in design, concept, material science, environmental, improvements, changes, value engineering and cost savings. It is betting – not knowing – the topic or issue. It is about not getting absorbed into the system with opinions, constraints, culture, obligations. It is about know where to look, where to find the science. Collaboration, relations and networking are the future of innovation.

Focus on the solution, not the problem. Believe in finding, improving, creating, innovating. Don't give up. Re-consider and keep challenging.

Engage and commit yourself. It is not a job, it is a 24/7 marriage. Never switch off. Neither in exploring, nor in networking, nor in finding solutions. It is a passion, a hunger for newness, an open-mindedness about changes, and about being bold.

Understand the needs. Look for trends in any area and map the future. What is not available today or needed tomorrow might be available in the future. The future is near.

Consider economical, political, social or environmental changes. Challenge technologies and explore any kind or type of road map. Visit and re-visit and use or abuse different ideas, approaches and technologies in the area you would like to implement.

Observe behaviours of all kind, any gender, any age. Tune in on the gaps and the needs. Look and compare with nature. Innovation is not just on packaging or a product, it can be on a process, a behaviour.

Face and absorb negative reactions. It is part of the process. Treat them as food for thought and never give up. Park them if necessary and re-visit at a later stage. What might not be relevant at the moment, can be of use at any time in the future.

What an interesting list of dos and don'ts! This should give you some guidance when engaging in the process of creating the future, through innovation. You may also have noted that Patrick, like Michael Dell, sees great potential in looking to nature for guidance ...

A couple of thoughts on a focus on 'solutions not problems'. Somehow this is what we seem to do rather a lot: focusing on finding a solution without truly understanding whether the solution we come up with actually addresses the underlying problem. Often we confuse symptoms and causes, and are dealing with the symptoms without ever getting down to understanding the underlying causes. Think of how medicine is practised widely in the Western world: we deal with headaches by giving people tablets that cover up the symptoms; we do not set out to understand what has caused the headache in the first place. For ulcers we give medicine that placates our stomachs – instead of trying to understand and change what has led our stomach to be sore in the first place. Focusing on the underlying problems and finding ways to address these is one of the big challenges of the future of innovation.

If the previous three contributions were more about the tools of the trade, Tobias Rooney moves us on to start thinking of places where innovation activities might be hotting up.

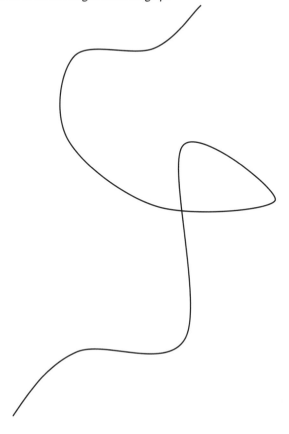

The Future of Innovation is Innovation Catalysts

Name	**Tobias Rooney**
Affiliation	Innovaro
Position	Principal
Country	UK
Area	Innovation strategy
Email	tobias.rooney@innovaro.com

catalyst   water   authenticity   healthcare

Innovation catalysts are external trends or events that destabilise a company's steady state. In destabilising they open up opportunities to innovate, and those companies that see and act first are those that benefit. Many companies are comfortable with their immediate environment outside their walls, more challenging is to look beyond this and watch broad, cross-industry, cross-society, cross-cultural trends.

Mainstream trends today are for example carbon, social networking or wellness. 'Mainstream' does not mean that their innovation potential is behind them, for in each of these there is still much to be done in terms of identifying technology coupling, viable business models and so on. But 'mainstream' does mean you can assume people get it and are investing to do something about it, the competition has started.

What is interesting is to explore the next wave of catalysts whose faint signals we can detect today if we know where to look, but remain below most people's radars. Three of the trends that we see emerging today are water, authenticity and health care insurance.

Water is the most apparent, and will go mainstream probably in the next year or so, already appearing in some of the national press and in industries. This is about water in a sustainable agenda. Water is becoming our scarcest resource and has no real substitute. Company water use and how this is presented to the consumer will become questions of business priority, just as we have experienced with the green agenda. Consumers will look for embedded water measures and choose products and even services on this basis. As shortages and awareness grow so changing consumer patterns and beliefs will be with us soon.

Authenticity is a more ambiguous concept with a more subtle impact. Authenticity is about who we believe. Historically this has been the press, the government, structures of authority. The growth of the web and changes in our lives have undermined this. Wikipedia is a growing 'authority' on the web, people turn to blogs and make lifestyle choices at odds with the dominant scientific understanding. All these factors are undermining the ability of structures of authority and companies to control what people believe. For businesses the challenges will be finding new ways to convey their message and tap into these clusters of interest.

Health care has been with us for some time so what is special about it now? The world of health care insurance is experimenting with many innovative ways of managing costs through the adoption of new technologies and the coupling of these with preventive medicine. This has put them at the forefront of understanding and valuing health management in a way that has escaped public health care systems. Through this we are seeing a quiet revolution in how health is managed at an individual level, how people can engage in their own health choices, and opportunities for technology that draw on this.

These are three catalysts among many that are on the horizon, and set to change the landscape and innovation opportunities for many companies.

Indeed, water and health care are clearly essential, but somehow we feel that authenticity might become an equally important consideration. How many of us trust what we hear from politicians or read in the press? How many believe marketing claims and company statements? We believe that those companies that communicate openly, honestly and show a sincere concern for their customers will benefit hugely from the trust such conduct creates; they will be perceived as the authentic ones. The shock of contaminated milk products that has led to the death of many infants in China is a reminder of the need for a new morality, new responsibility, new authenticity. Currently we worry about how to protect our intellectual property rights when bringing new products or services to the market; in the future we will also have to think about the rights of those who trust us; how can we as innovators protect customers and users from dangerous fakes? Don't you agree? Nanotechnology might reduce the threat of imitation and forgery, especially when it comes to medicine, water, food, and toys. Authenticity, reliability, genuineness – here you have some first indicator of places where you might want to look for innovation.[1] Are they relevant to your industry? Have you been considering them, perhaps looked for some partners with whom to explore these fields?

One way to explore possible futures, jointly or with partners, is what Andy Hines is contributing to the mix. While many of you are familiar with scenario building *he offers a particular slant on this approach.*

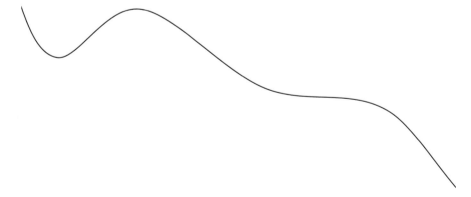

---

1   By the way, when looking at innovation through a particular set of lenses we will revisit the issue of healthcare again, certainly of great concern and interest to all of us.

The Future of Innovation is Provoking Innovation via the Future

Name	**Andy Hines**
Affiliation	UTEK – Social Technologies
Position	Director of Custom Projects
Country	USA
Area	Foresight, future, forecast, breakthrough, provocative
Email	andy.hines@socialtechnologies.com

future   futurist   product concepts

In exploring an innovation opportunity, a futurist will typically probe further into the future and consider a wide range of influential external factors. This approach expands the field of vision and opens up the opportunity space, enabling us to cast a wider net for ideas, which are then brought back to the present in order to be useful.

The value of foresight in stimulating innovative thinking was never more clearly brought home to us than during a recent focus group exercise involving innovative product concepts. The session began by introducing the concepts and asking consumers to rate them. Then, we did a 15-minute introduction of a future context we crafted using scenario storyboards. The same concepts were re-introduced and re-ranked. It was truly amazing to see the 'lights go on' as participants who had ranked the concepts poorly when trying to imagine them in the present, ranked them much higher after seeing the future context. Organisations searching for truly breakthrough ideas have a similar opportunity – to target their innovative concepts against the potential future contexts that their truly innovative concepts are likely to actually exist in.

Provocative forecasts are one of our many tools for stimulating innovative ideas. We map the system of the future of the topic, and then create an inventory of the key trends and values influencing that system. We stretch our thinking here by tapping the 'edges' of research and 'outliers' among experts. We then use various clustering techniques to identify the interesting themes that we build into provocative forecasts. We will stretch as far as the client feels comfortable with, keeping in mind that if we stretch too far, we risk losing credibility. We agree on the final candidates typically in a workshop (these are great fun!), and afterwards do any needed follow-up research.

Our goal here is to deliberately exclude the most likely forecasts. We are looking for higher impact candidates that will lead to really significant change. We are trying to challenge the thinking of the team to go beyond what they are already thinking. An example of a provocative forecast we created that proved too provocative involved products and services for the home. We called it 'Fur People'. It suggested that pets were becoming so important that they would increasingly thought of as people, and their presence would be increasingly important factors in home building and design – pet bedrooms, anyone?

The provocative forecast builds a picture of what a really different future might look like, and with this mental model in mind, innovators can have it and generate ideas that fit this possible future. Thinking about different future possibilities stimulates ideas that would not otherwise emerge. The innovator can take the creative insight and 'back it off' to fit with more likely market conditions. Maybe we don't need pet bedrooms per se, but maybe indoor cats need a more effective way to exercise? The value of the provocative forecast is in getting the innovators to these creative insights that they might not otherwise have come up with.

One of the key phrases for us from Andy's contribution was about concepts that had been received poorly when considered in the present, were appreciated much more when considering them in a future context. When concept are evaluated and selected in your organisation, do you project them into the future? Do you consider them in view of today's world or of the world of tomorrow?

Like Richard and Kenneth who have both argued for 'innovation, but not as we know it' Steve May-Russel starts his contribution with that belief; we need to rethink what we are doing, and he suggests that this requires to ignoring existing rules and accepted wisdom. He continues to elaborate why this is the case, and offers some thoughts on where you may want to start looking for the future of innovation. Just don't follow his recommendations in one aspect: do not throw away this book!

Perhaps one more thing. Many of us are no longer willing to accept suffering in this life for a promise of better conditions in the next one. While this may be so, this kind of thinking has left an 'invisible' legacy which means that we need to rethink not only what we are doing but also why we are doing it, and for whom. It is in our hands to create a better life now, right now, right here, or the reverse. Rethinking starts with the understanding that first and foremost you are the one who has to do the 'doing it'; there is no one to do it for us. So, as Steve invites us to do, don't fear to break the rule, what if we don't have a second chance?

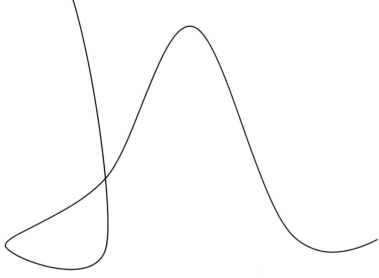

The Future of Innovation is Innovation

Name   **Steve May-Russell**
Affiliation Smallfry Product Design and Innovation
Position   CEO
Country   UK
Area   Product and enterprise innovation
Email   steve@smallfry.com

**sustained growth   future planning   innovation roadmap   innovation mindset
creative thinking**

The future of innovation will be to throw away the book, break the rules, change the process and challenge everything. Have a go, be surprised and do it again (differently).

In this age of fast and continual change, we are at the point where the corporate world is slowly realising that innovation is the only way to survive and sustain growth. As there is a global rush to write innovation into the corporate systems and make sure there is a sound 'innovation strategy' in place, it will become increasing necessary to do all of those 'different' things that are the mainstay of innovation in increasingly different ways; to innovate the way that you currently do your innovation.

Structure, process and formula, the keystones of a well-oiled corporate machine, are the enemy of innovation. To stay ahead of the game you will need to break down the barriers of hierarchy, risk, fear and blame, take a voyage into the unknown without a defined destination and harness the power of teams from diverse backgrounds, cultures and disciplines. It is essential to ask stupid questions, be curious, probe unusual avenues and reject the accepted facts. Most of all you must be prepared to take risks and tolerate unexpected result (there is no such thing as failure).

One thing is guaranteed and that is innovation will not come from where you are carefully watching. It will almost certainly come from the left field, somewhere that never seemed relevant, something overheard, an idea misunderstood or an article in a magazine you were just flicking through. It will not come from formal routines. We talk to our clients about taking an 'innovation holiday' a deliberate break from the usual daily structures, people and environment. This is key to breaking out of your regular mindset and common discourse. For most people the problem is not learning new things but forgetting what they already know in order to see things in new ways.

Children have the most creative and fertile minds because they have not yet learned what is and is not possible. In the commercial world designers and other 'creatives' have the benefit of a mindset that thrives on challenging and questioning everything on a daily basis. This is not an exclusive skill, no one of us is as good as all of us. So take advantage of cross-fertilisation. Put the right minds together and feed their imagination.

Finally, in order to understand what the future of innovation will be for you and your company, it is important to establish what innovation means to you. At Smallfry we define innovation as 'the strategic implementation of good ideas for commercial gain'. This helps us to focus on bringing ideas to market in a form that is profitable for our customers. Strategy, implementation, ideas and gain are the critical words in our definition. Innovation may well have other meanings and goals for you.

If you learn one thing from this it should be 'if it ain't broke, see where you might break it, for the better'.

How does your organisation do on 'breaking things that ain't broke'? Is your organisation happy to break all rules – or even a few – to go to the future and face the winds of change? And how about the appetite for 'stupid questions'? As Steve points out, children never cease asking the 'why' question that can drive us adults around the bend ... yet these are just the questions we need to ask if we are to innovate – and perhaps bringing children in to ask 'stupid questions' is not a bad starting point!

Coming slowly to the end of this section we would like to bring to your attention two more voices. The first one is that of Paul Matthyssens who lays out a future that is characterised by what seem to be difficult–to–reconcile opposites.

The Future of Innovation is a New Combination Logic

Name	**Paul Matthyssens**
Affiliation	University of Antwerp
Position	Professor
Country	Belgium
Area	Innovation management
Email	paul.matthyssens@ua.ac.be

**absorptive capacity   open innovation   dominant design   dominant logic
market driving**

Future innovation will require the bridging of seemingly inevitable dilemmas embedded in our innovation frames. An innovative perspective on innovation is required urgently.

Firstly, the innovation of the future combines the *creation of a new dominant design with a new dominant logic*. The strict division of technological innovation and value (strategic) innovation cannot be sustained any more. Disruptive innovators combine *both* types of research simultaneously. For instance, the iPod combined a new product concept (vis-à-vis the Walkman) with a new concept of acquiring and delivering songs via the web (iTunes). Real breakthrough innovations break industry rules. The dilemma of 'technology push versus market pull' will not count any more.

Innovation leadership will build on a *market-driving* logic where innovations shape market behaviour and restructure markets. Disruptive innovations combining new category creation with technological revolution will be sought. Functional foods are a good example of such a market-driving innovation.

Secondly, future innovation will increasingly combine *companies' own competence building and consequent IP protection with open innovation models*. Also here, it is not 'either … or'! Both types of innovation are needed simultaneously to build disruptive innovations. The core technological competences need to be protected while at the same time the innovation process must be opened up to suppliers and customers. Such *vertical* open innovation ties will have to be combined with *horizontal* partnerships (i.e., partners from adjacent supply chains) in order to make substantial progress. An example of such collaborations is a partnership of gas supplier ATO with food processing machines supplier Stork and food producer Unilever in order to produce and conserve a new type of avocado mousse.

This leads into a third combination challenge. The case of the development of new food categories such as probiotics requires the collaboration of different industries such as biotechnology, pharmaceutical, food and packaging. Innovators are forced to *combine different technologies* rather than excel in one technology only. The innovations of the future will further integrate intelligence with hardware originating in multiple technologies (e.g., mechatronics) and integrate different types of sciences into new materials such as the combination of life sciences and performance materials resulting in 'smart materials' at DSM. In the past the technology specialists showed the way. In the future, smart combiners will lead the pack.

Finally, innovation becomes all the more an activity requiring ambidexterity. This implies a *combination of routines leading to efficiency, speed and control with dynamic capabilities for stimulating their 'absorptive capacity'*. The latter leads to early recognition of trends, sharing and experimentation. An ambidextrous organisation does not accept the traditional time-cost-quality trade-offs. Individual value optimisation will not preclude corporate social responsibility. Local relevance will be combined with global efficiency and relevance. Due to their ambidextrous structure and culture, companies such as 3M or Google will further stretch their 'pipeline'.

To conclude, we believe the dominant innovation logic has to be revised. Top innovators must question their one-dimensional views on so-called innovation dilemmas. Rather, they will bridge these extremes exploiting their 'combination skills'.

We quite agree, the future will no longer be about 'either … or'. It will be about 'and'. Figuring out how to achieve the 'and' will be one of the most important and at the same time difficult challenges of the future. One of the examples Paul highlights is the need to protect one's intellectual property, while at the same time engaging in and embracing open innovation. This needs careful consideration: what is our essence, what should we not give away under any circumstances, and what can we share? Achieving the 'and' means having to juggle ever more balls in the air, having to deal with ever higher levels of complexity. Without having mentioned it explicitly Paul highlights these increasing levels of complexity that need to be understood and to be taken into account in the future, and it is these increased complexities and paradoxes that require us to rethink innovation itself.

In our final contribution in this section Bill Fischer talks about increased complexities too, and suggests what the implication of this might be.

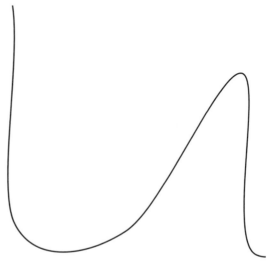

The Future of Innovation is Going to be Different

Name	**Bill Fischer**
Affiliation	IMD
Position	Professor, Technology Management
Country	Switzerland
Area	Innovation culture
Email	fischer@imd.ch

demographics   complexity   mindset   culture   leadership

The future of innovation will be more important than ever, but most likely quite different from what we have thought of as 'normal' innovation in the past. More important because as global population grows, available resources shrink, the environment worsens and the business environment becomes more complex, we'll need more innovation than ever to move human prospects forward.

We start with the sobering realisation that the global economy is much more complex than any competitive terrain that we've innovated in before. In addition, the pace of change appears to be accelerating. All in all, innovation will be more essential in the future than it has ever been in the past and, at the same time, more challenging to do well!

The very nature of how we innovate will change. The old (and often misleading) stereotype of the single individual, or even small team, will fade as multi-site, multi-organisational and multicultural collaboration becomes the norm. This will result in truly global approaches to idea sharing, shaping and ownership that go well beyond what we have mastered in the past.

We must recognise that few firms are prepared for this. They often lack the appropriate mindset, sufficient competencies and even access to the necessary ideas that this new innovation approach requires. Yet, if they limit their innovation activities to the confines of their own organisation, they are condemned to underachieve. Increasingly, we will be seeing that the potentials and weaknesses of our value chains are as important as our own competencies, and building innovation partnerships up and down the value chain will become an imperative. This, then, will require coordinating other people's innovative assets, in a way that is more challenging than merely managing one's own commercialisation funnel.

We must build organisational 'cultures' that treat ideas as the raw materials for building an organisation's future. That means idea-work must be recognised as a legitimate, and vital, part of what we're all doing. It also means that the right attitudes are necessary, if we're going to take knowledge and innovation seriously, and that processes need to be in place to assure that we are getting enough good ideas into the firm and moving them to the right people in order to add value and bring about commercialisation. We need to measure how much smarter we are as an organisation, from year to year, and think about what investments need to be made to raise our return on brains.

Leadership must also change. The ideal is 'smart people leading smarter people', and the role models for this are those virtuoso performers who have inspired others to work beyond their normal aspirations. This is leadership as a contact sport, but the goal is for the knowledge workers to believe that they are working in absolute freedom, while leadership believes that it retains complete control.

Bill reiterates some changes that we have already encountered in this section before, such as increased complexity and the need as well as benefits of collaboration. He drives this line of thought further by highlighting areas where change will have to occur as a consequence of the previously mentioned changes. The plot thickens, and the systemic nature of change is becoming ever clearer. He emphasises that with increased complexities we need to review our values and behaviours, i.e., culture, and we need a different kind of leadership. In the future that is upon us 'command and control' are no longer working, it is a negotiation process, a process of achieving buy-in, of inviting people to join in by offering a persuasive and worthwhile vision.

We are particularly intrigued by his concept of 'ideas as raw materials'. Building an organisation's success on what human minds rather than mother earth have to offer has significant implications. Or would you argue that human resources should be managed in the same way as natural resources? If we want people to contribute and share their ideas we cannot use the Taylorist man = machine analogy. We cannot treat people as numbers who execute tasks and just take orders from those who have risen to the ranks of management. Invariably this means that different skill sets are required in the leaders of the future. This too has implications for leadership, and only increases the need for social and interpersonal skills at all leadership levels.

But before we delve into the people issues too much let's have a closer look at why we will have to pursue 'Innovation – but not as we know it.'

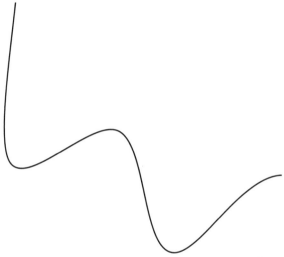

PART III
Innovation: But Not as We Know it

Several of our contributors have already hinted at the idea that innovation in the future will be different from innovation in the past. In terms of a simplified answer to the question why this should be we are entirely with Albert Einstein who said that we keep doing the same things and expect to get different results. If general validity of this statement is assumed than even innovation itself cannot remain the same, if we are to achieve different results.

This section has some overlap with Part I, 'The Need for Innovation', with Part II, 'The Winds of Change', as well as with Part V, 'The 11th Hour'. Part I has dealt with the need for innovation more generally, Part II has drawn on contributions that have focused on what is changing/will change and the implications of that, and Part V will look particularly at issues around sustainability. This section brings together contributions that argue for innovation around innovation itself. We felt that the need for a new look at innovating around innovation was such a big issue that we wanted to create a dedicated section to it.

So what's our contributors' take on this? Why do they argue for a 'different kind of innovation', and what do they consider to be the driving forces behind this changing take on innovation?

Let's find out by looking at what Al Saje and Trevor Davis have to say.

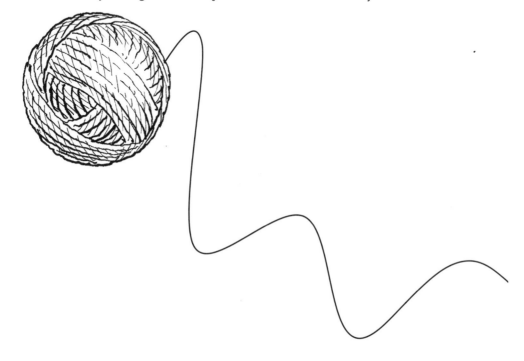

The Future of Innovation is After the Watershed

Name	**Al Saje**
Affiliation	Jaguar Land Rover
Position	Manager Future Business and Market and Competitor Intelligence
Country	UK
Area	Design of organisations, products and process for innovation, management of complexity and variety
Email	asaje@jaguarlandrover.com

Innovation   discontinuity   supply chain   environment   complexity

The next five years will set the tone for future innovation well into the rest of the century. While the future world is founded on what we know today, there are some fundamental discontinuities that shape the way it will develop. Oil and commodity peaking, global warming, population growth: the world is discovering that economies have nowhere to go without an engine for sustaining that growth. Cheap energy, limitless natural resources and unbounded credit are (nearly) at an end, and the world has to mine other sources of value.

It doesn't sound easy, but there's plenty of need and appetite for innovation. The attraction for what big investment there is will be to bring down the energy intensity of economies, to prolong and enhance life – and to support whatever it takes for people to scrape out a living and provide an escape from daily cares. The developing technologies for the new world are already starting to build products and services: nanotechnology, biotechnology, information technology and cognitive technologies. That's an exciting set of new principles that will provide completely new value and new products on their own, interact and blend into existing products and services. New materials and sensors, body and mind enhancements, new ways of connecting, entertaining, working and travelling will all see huge growth. And there will be a major focus on re-using investments already made to give products and sectors a new lease of life.

But it's not only which technologies will change the marketplace, but also who will be doing it and how. Nurture, education, experience and networks will still provide motivation, creativity and knowledge. Nations will guard their competencies in difficult times. However, the process of creativity and innovation can, and will, see a revolution. Customers are increasingly the source of innovations, and processes and extended development networks will entice them increasingly into the creation of new products. Distributed research and development already happens today, but there is huge potential to exploit the last decade's worth of innovation knowledge. This learning will find its way into standard methodologies. The codification of innovation into innovation tool-sets will better allow the inclusion of remote experts, developers and entrepreneurs to work together as a virtual organism rather than a traditional organisation. Each member of the extended team will get what they need while playing a full role in contributing and learning, shaping and developing the project. Teams will not stop at internal boundaries, but will extend down into the supply chain, through manufacture and out into distribution and retail with both core and transient players. New measures of value and risk will come into play and will need the combined involvement of many players to handle the complexity 'right first time'.

As the low growth world develops, so too will the ethos of innovation. Economic and environmental development will converge around 'reduce, reuse, repair, recycle' principles to conserve resources. Innovation will thrive even in this climate to radically change the world we know today.

AI brings to us a vision of a future where the what as well as the who of innovation is very different from what we know today. New technologies allow to intervene at levels that were impossible before; people who were never before involved in the development of new products and services are entering the scene – at an individual as well as a national level. What is Trevor Davis' perspective on the new take on innovation?

The Future of Innovation is For Us to Decide

Name	**Dr Trevor Davis**
Affiliation	IBM
Position	Global Expert Innovation
Country	UK
Area	Business model innovation
Email	Trevor.davis@uk.ibm.com

innovation   collaboration   change   future   frontier

Clearly the balance of power is shifting in the world beyond the current economic distress. There are new technologies and emerging business models, powerful global players in China, India and Russia, aspiring nations in Eastern Europe, the Middle East and Latin America and the diffuse threats of terrorism and extreme ideologies. We have reached a further New Frontier and that requires a re-evaluation of the future of innovation.

In the past two centuries a technological revolution in agriculture led to a productivity explosion, followed by a similar expansion based on manufacturing goods. Many organisations have still not learned to fully exploit the value creation potential of those innovations and yet we are already in the middle of the next wave; that of service innovation and global integration, creating the largest labour force migration in human history and characterised by urbanisation, pervasive communications and global resourcing.

In my view, the world is changing and an old era is ending. The old innovation thinking and methods will not do. The trend to open innovation is a first and strong indication of what we can do, but we need more. We need innovation for this New Frontier, bringing together open and 'closed' models and more.

To be successful as innovators going forward we need the courage of our old convictions coupled with a collective and open willingness to challenge the status quo. To borrow from Senator John F. Kennedy at another time of paradigm shift, 'The motto of the American Old West was not "every man for himself" – but "all for the common cause."' Those innovators (in so many dimensions) were determined to collaborate to craft a strong new order, to overcome uncertainty and difficulty and we need to adopt the same spirit for our innovation efforts. After all, if the innovation experts and enthusiasts don't, who will?

Some will say that all of the innovation horizons have been explored and that more effective execution of existing approaches is all that is required. But few business leaders in my experience consider that their problems can be solved with contemporary approaches. So we stand today on the edge of this New Frontier – the frontier of goods into services, of changing demographics and political balance – and there are fresh opportunities for innovation and innovators.

Why should we rely on approaches developed for an older world, when there is clearly a chance to rewrite the textbooks in the way that Robert Cooper (phases and gates) and Henry Chesborough (open innovation) have in their contributions over the past 25 years? Perhaps the future for innovation will be written by all who read this essay, a 'Wikipedia' effort for the New Frontier.

We believe that Trevor is right, things will not just swing back to where they were before the current crisis; we are experiencing a seismic change; the economic and social landscape will not look the way it used to, we will see a different landscape emerging – and it is up to us to help shape it.

Both Al and Trevor look at the wider picture and share the conclusion that current views on innovation will have to change, that technological innovation alone is no longer enough. To go into the future a reshaping of innovation at a more fundamental level will have to take place. The level they are talking about is about the way we operate, interact, function as the human race. Nothing short of a social and organisational revolution.

Is it likely to happen? Is our collective awareness developed enough to understand and embrace the challenge? Karmen Jelcic feels that we have some way to go yet.

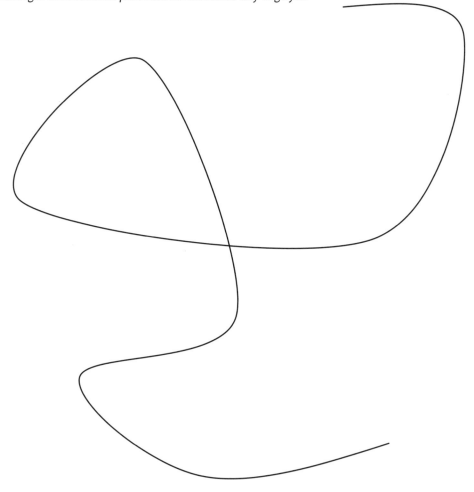

The Future of Innovation is Good Enough for the Future?

Name	**Karmen Jelcic**
Affiliation	Professor
Position	Director of Croatian IC Centre
Country	Croatia
Area	Intellectual capital management and measurement
Email	karmenj@cik-hr.com

ignorance of new economic reality   intellectual capital as key resource

The EU has a strategic goal for the 21st century: 'To become the most competitive and dynamic knowledge-based economy in the world.' Powerful words for those who understand what it is all about. Meaningless for the majority of the EU working population, who would be needed to make it happen. Many are not even familiar with the term 'knowledge economy', let alone its implications. Others think it has to do with educational and school issues, not business. Too few have realised that we are living and working in a transitional period, with the industrial economy giving way to the knowledge economy and that the change of paradigm, which is happening right now, is inevitably going to affect business in yet unknown ways. Because of that, I think it should become an imperative at national, regional and corporate level to inform and educate as many managers as possible on this matter (in other words, political management, which is responsible for shaping the business environment as well). Only if we learn about the features of knowledge-based economy and understand in what ways this global phenomenon affects our local business, can we prepare for the challenges of the 21st-century economy.

Governments and leading institutions should be among the first ones to receive such education in order to be able to guide other economic players. Only a critical mass of people, who understand the new economic conditions and know what to do in order to create value for themselves, their company and their country under such circumstances, can ensure the transition into knowledge-based economy.

The year-long fall in productivity worldwide and the severe financial crisis indicate that the old way of reasoning and doing business is not serving us well in the new economy. Dr Ante Pulic, an authority in intellectual capital (IC) measurement, says it is because businessmen and analysts have been ignoring for too long the key value creation factor of knowledge economy, IC. Having refined the skill of managing tangible assets throughout their career, many managers feel more comfortable in continuing to focus on money and physical assets, even though they sense the need for change of focus to intangibles. This is a perfect way to waste much of the intellectual capital that exists in companies and could ensure the wished-for goals: competitive advantage, an increase in value creation capability and secure working places.

Worldwide, many respected experts on managing and measuring IC are actively contributing to a better understanding of and development in this field. However, others still ignore the existence and impact of a new economic reality and provide outdated solutions for new problems. There are too many political leaders who make decisions regarding the economic development of their countries without consideration of new age needs. And there are too many managers who manage resources and measure business performance in the traditional way, unaware of the fact that this might be endangering the existence of their companies.

I am sure that they are giving their best. But the best of the past is not good enough for the future. A wise man once said: 'Our development is not endangered by that, what we do not know, but by that, what we think we know.'

Let us start to discover and understand what we think we know and how this gets in the way of moving forward! Let us not be like Goethe's Faust who said, 'And see there's nothing we can know! That all but burns my heart right out.' Let us rather see what Jinsheng He has to offer on the topic of knowledge.

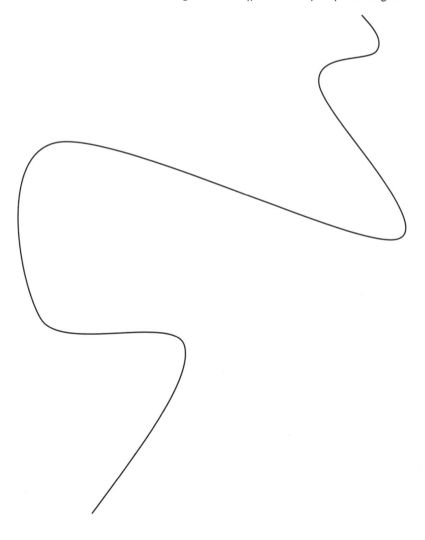

The Future of Innovation is Driven by Knowledge Cultivation

Name	**Jinsheng He**
Affiliation	Tianjin University
Position	Professor of Management
Country	China
Area	Theoretic thinking for innovation resources and mechanisms
Email	jshe@tju.edu.cn

**knowledge cell   new stimulus   thinking ability   innovation bar
catalysis mechanism**

Knowledge development[1] is the core activity of innovation. Innovation's future cannot be separated from the rules and trends of knowledge development. I believe that knowledge develops organically. This means that new knowledge is developed from existing knowledge, with the human brain making connections between new stimuli[2] and existing knowledge. Like plants, animals and living things, knowledge development is through growing.

Knowledge is the result of thinking.[3] Man can only think relating things to existing knowledge. Thinking is the ability to relate new information, new problems (called new stimuli), to existing knowledge, to devise new concepts or new cognitions through reaching some kinds of explanation[4] built on existing knowledge. New knowledge is the process of extending, penetrating, softening and diffusing existing knowledge. From a knowledge perspective innovation cannot occur in a void.

As the basis of thinking, existing knowledge not only provides materials of thinking, but also provides the start point for new knowledge, logistics and methodologies of thinking. Thinking, basically, is a system which includes both a person's specific bodies of knowledge and his or her ability to infer and reason with respect to a certain area. This knowledge system is a system of 'knowledge cells' more than anything else. It consists of interrelated knowledge and external information. The relationship may be cause and effects, essence and appearance, form and content, logistics or dialectical. A good knowledge cell is reliable and consistent in itself. Fragmented knowledge (e.g., partial understanding of things) can be referred to as 'segments of knowledge'. The knowledge cells form the foundation, indicate directions and constrain domains of new knowledge development.

---

1   For the purposes of this article, we define 'knowledge' as what we learn, what we feel and what we think.

2   Knowledge in broad sense includes information and knowledge.

3   Without doubt, knowledge is the miracle power of human brain.

4   'Explanations' means to get some kinds of view: reasonable or not reasonable, understanding or not understanding, agree or not agree, so as to get various kinds of thinking relationship.

While a new stimulus is the source for introducing new thinking, it also provides new sources of material to think about. New stimuli come from the environment around the thinker; people can only produce innovation relating to their own environment.

Knowledge cells exist in the minds of people who have knowledge. New information or new knowledge can be combined with a certain existing knowledge cell; such as to extend, delete or reform segments of the original cell. In this way, new knowledge cells come into being.

Knowledge cells, new stimuli and the ability to think are three great resources which decide the ability to innovate from a knowledge point of view. The quality of knowledge cells depends on people's learning capacity. The quality of new stimuli is decided by the social, economic and technology environment. The thinking ability is decided by intellectual power which in turn depends on human development itself.

The endowment of these three resources can decide a nation's ability to innovate. The mission of innovationists is to bring these resources into full play. There are three mechanisms to promote innovation:

1. 'Innovation Ba' mechanism: knowledge development through gathering and communicating 'knowledgeable mass' and the facilitating of interactions between knowledge cell/cell segments.

2. Activation mechanism: cultural and psychological adjustments so as to create an atmosphere of boundaryless cooperation within innovation bas.

3. Catalysis mechanism: teaching, coaching, consulting, coordinating are functions of catalysis which greatly accelerate the combination of knowledge cells and cell segments.

Accordingly, the developed countries will still be the main forces of innovation for the near future. China needs another 20–30 years to become the major innovator of the world.

Jinsheng has a point, new knowledge does not materialise out of nowhere. It builds and evolves from what we know, even though we might see the occasional 'quantum leap'.

Maybe finding out what we do not (yet) know, and finding ways of consciously 'clashing' different bodies of knowledge, can help us to accelerate the revolution Al and Trevor were talking about. Is such a revolution likely to happen? Debra Amidon, our next contributor, is quite hopeful. Drawing on the positive energy, collaboration and resolution to stand together to avoid future wars we saw towards the end of the Second World War she has faith in humanity's capacity to come up with similar approaches and frameworks to address today's burning issues.

The Future of Innovation is as an Instrument for World Peace

Name	**Debra M. Amidon**
Affiliation	Entovation International Ltd
Position	Founder and CEO
Country	USA
Area	Knowledge innovation strategy
Email	debra@entovation.com

knowledge   innovation   peace   economics   intellectual capital

'Creation of a dynamic world community in which the peoples of every nation will be able to realize their potentialities for peace.'

Henry Morgenthau, Opening Address at the Bretton Woods Conference (July, 1944)

Ours is a future to innovate. Knowledge societies – more a function of human beings than technological innovation – should unleash the capabilities of imagination, insight and interaction. We need to convert current fiscal and political threats to opportunities; but how?

In July 1944, towards the end of the Second World War, world leaders abandoned gold as a currency in the hopes it would create a less combative world stage. Today, a global knowledge commonwealth is replacing the world of nations. We are dependent upon the knowledge and success of others across organisational and cultural boundaries. The new currency of intellectual capital – properly leveraged through human relationship and structural capital – is an asset of abundance, not scarcity. Globalisation demands new rules. Old rules no longer apply; new ones are being innovated.

Leadership in the knowledge economy is different from the industrial or even information economies. It is an economy in which the innovation capacity of every human being, enterprise and nation is fully engaged. It is an economy in which culture and heritage are respected, commonalities are more important than differences, and aspirations can be shared. It requires a fundamental new mindset and common language to harness capabilities across a global, networked world.

The *concept* of knowledge innovation (KI) is action with understanding and purpose – the creation, evolution and application of knowledge for the success of an enterprise, the vitality of a nation's economy, and the advancement of society. The *concept-in-practice* is a knowledge innovation zone (KIZ) – a geographic, industry or virtual space in which knowledge flows from the point of origin to optimal need or use.

Until the past century, distance and communication made the movement of goods and knowledge arduous. Knowledge moved along trade routes – from the Appian Way to the Silk Road.

Today, trade routes morph into trade 'nodes' – or zones of innovation. Nurturing and managing the instantaneous flow of knowledge in these market spaces – digital cities, internet villages and knowledge corridors – requires innovation strategy to replace traditional business planning practices.

The *BusinessWeek* chief economist writes about 'innovation economics' and G7 discussions have expanded to G20. Economists and business leaders globally are coming to agreement: innovation is the best way to build a future within which we all thrive. After centuries of war punctuated by uneasy peace, Europeans formed the European Union – a mechanism to erase old differences which were leading to ever more efficient wars. They established a common currency; and ushered the dawn of collaborative advantage. The Middle East is doing the same.

The United Nations was created to maintain political stability around the world. The World Bank and IMF were created after World War II to ensure the movement of financial capital. Today we need similar infrastructure for the worldwide flow of intellectual capital. With the recent collapse of old structures, we should architect new rule-sets to guide our collaborative innovation. We need a Bretton Woods for the knowledge economy – purposed to create a global innovation platform for peace and the world trade of ideas. History will document our success ...

Let us hope that the current crisis has the same galvanising effect with some positive outcomes too, and let us hope there will be a point in the future where history looks back at the beginning of the 21st century and admires the resolution and determination, the foresight and the courage with which we have addressed the preservation of our future.

To get another handle on how we might try to understand ways in which innovation in itself has to change, we felt that the contribution from Milton Jorge Correia de Sousa might be quite helpful here. He suggests looking at innovation at three different 'units of analysis' – to find out what this means please read for yourselves!

The Future of Innovation is Innovating for a Meaningful Future

Name	**Milton Jorge Correia de Sousa**
Affiliation	Hay Group
Position	Consultant
Country	The Netherlands
Area	Innovation management
Email	milton_correia_de_sousa@haygroup.com

meaning   leadership   permeation   sustainability   empathy

My view of the future of innovation is from a management perspective at three levels: the individual, the organisation and society.

Innovation and the Individual = the Search for Meaning

Meaning in life is a basic human need. It is the vehicle through which great things are done. Innovation, as an instrument of renewal, provides the fuel for the search of meaning. This aspect of innovation will become essential in the future, as people and organisations recognise the need to be part of something greater than themselves. By making innovation part of the organisation's DNA, people will increasingly recognise opportunities to develop themselves and to find ways of contributing not only to the organisation but also to society in general. In the future, innovation will be recognised as a key element in the search for individual meaning, creating greater workforce engagement in organisations and helping to develop great leaders.

Innovation and the Organisation = the Key Management Instrument

In the future, innovation will drive every decision and permeate every single process in organisations. Innovation will become the key management instrument, through which strategy will be both conceived and executed.

For many years innovation has been seen as the unmanageable hidden process, given to serendipity and pure luck. It has also been confused with research or the development of new products and services. People are now realising that innovation, and most of all sustainable innovation, is the fundamental driver behind such diverse elements as total quality management, customer satisfaction, growth, process efficiency, profitability and a whole range of key management areas. It is through systematic and purposeful innovation, combined with collaborative leadership and courage that organisations can strive. Systematic innovation allows organisations to tap into people's hearts and minds for creative ideas, to reach and process knowledge in varied forms and to create new added value to all stakeholders. Innovation, in this sense, will no longer be left to serendipity or even just a process; it will be that and much more. It will be engrained in the thinking process of every person in the organisation, the fundamental question in every leader's decision, be it for recruitment, developing a new product or selecting the organisation layout.

Innovation and Society = Building Bridges Through Open Innovation

As organisations open up their innovation models to incorporate external people and entities from around the globe, barriers are torn down and room for understanding and empathy is created. This is not about exploiting resources anymore but about truly valuing and integrating ideas and contributions from people in every corner of the world, regardless of their race, creed or culture. In the future, open innovation will be an important instrument for a better, sustainable and peaceful world. It is already happening. This future is very close.

The purpose and focus seems to change in what Milton describes. From a technology focus we shift to a human-centred focus; engaging in innovation becomes a question of engaging people's hearts as well as minds; in his vision innovation becomes part of a mindset, a part of the fundamental fabric of individuals, organisations, societies. It is quite interesting to have observed over the past decade that the understanding of innovation, and what its essence is, has started, slowly, to gravitate towards a perspective that has 'mindset' at its centre. So, not surprisingly, you will find a section dedicated to it later on (Part VIII). For now let's stay with why we will see innovation, but not as we know it.

With a change in understanding followed by a change in purpose and meaning comes the need to take a fresh look at how we then measure and assess innovation performance. That is exactly what Davide Parrilli has made the central argument of his contribution.

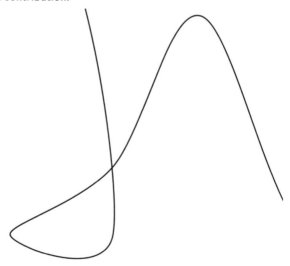

The Future of Innovation is Driven by Hardware and Software

Name	**M. Davide Parrilli**
Affiliation	University of Deusto
Position	Associate Professor and Director of IM2 Master
Country	Spain
Area	Innovation and clusters
Email	m.d.parrilli@dbs.deusto.es

Innovation system   learning   interaction   efficiency   effectiveness

In the current state of political, economic and social turmoil that affects the world, innovation is badly needed. Rigid cultural frameworks and standardised production practices may only lead to old solutions to old and new problems. The global community is facing new needs (e.g., services for children, disabled and elderly people, control of pollution) and stronger pressures (e.g., increasing population density, limited resource endowment). All this may lead to ethnic, religious, racial and social clashes or wars that, due to the scale reached by globalisation, jeopardise the future of mankind. Innovation is required to propose new solutions that respond to those demands and reduce those pressures.

Many mainstream economists and their organisations believe that innovation inputs are measured by investment in R&D and human capital (e.g., number of doctors) whereas innovation outputs are measured in terms of patents and sales. These aspects are certainly important, yet they do not disclose the whole nature of innovation, which implies a number of tacit knowledge flows that rely on informal exchanges and interactions among participants interested in finding optimal solutions to existing problems. These knowledge flows are often 'hidden' and do not automatically produce visible effects on explicit innovation processes.

Many world regions exhibit low standards in the above-mentioned indicators of innovation inputs and output; yet they also present wealth and welfare, good social interactions that may (or may not, in the short term) be translated into visible economic output. This seems to imply that new indicators have to be identified to explain why regions and countries with low standard innovation indicators present high levels of wealth and welfare. These countries and regions may well exhibit high propensity to social interaction and to the socialisation of economic activities that represent a conveyor of knowledge, insights and experiences along local to global networks, thus a driver of innovation. As the European Innovation Scoreboards (2007) show, in these territories innovation may be less radical and more incremental, less based on R&D and more focused on day-to-day observations, interactions and attempts to improve existing goods, services, processes, organisation and market channels.

This means that innovation can still be based on standard input and output measures that contribute state-of-the-art knowledge, new inputs and hypotheses, experiments and test; yet this mainstream view needs to be complemented with a view to adopt and utilise social/experiential knowledge pools that may enrich the former as catalysts of more ideas, insights, participation and networks. Both are necessary and may help to build up different systems of innovation that respond to the needs of countries, regions and localities.

Theorists in Aalborg, Cardiff, Lund, Sofia-Antipolis, Utrecht, Manchester, San Sebastian, Boston and Berkeley are currently working on this issue trying to identify intra-firm, inter-firm and systemic organisational mechanisms and practices that promote innovation in a less patent form and that can be measured through more flexible, qualitative indicators. Others are working to specify these forms and mechanisms even further by adding cognitive and/or psychological drivers (e.g. motivation, self-realisation through entrepreneurship, reputation, trust) that help to understand the realm of innovation in depth. They are a vanguard that may really help elucidating the deeper and often hidden innovation dynamics.

Public policies need to respond to this complex nature of innovation. They have to take into account that investing in the 'hardware of innovation' – infrastructures (e.g., science and technology parks, business incubators, universities) and human capital (e.g., doctors, S&T graduates) – does not guarantee an effective innovation system; public and private efforts need to target also the 'software of innovation' that is the social relations and the interactions leading to learning and to efficiently and effectively exploit the afore-mentioned 'innovation hardware'.

All the re-evaluation and particularly finding new measures requires that we can make sense of what is happening, and of what we want to happen. Milton started his contribution with the importance of meaning. Making sense of change, and understanding the deeper meaning behind it, are elemental to engaging people's hearts as well as their minds. We believe that people will not change, not truly, deeply and fundamentally, unless they understand in their hearts why this change is necessary or desirable. Accepting something with our minds is an important but not sufficient step. We all know what is good and what is bad for us. But how often do we follow our hearts, in spite of what our minds might be telling us? Just think about New Years' resolutions which many of us have probably made over the years. How many of your resolutions were still in place a few months into the year, despite your good intentions? Think about your biggest purchasing decision, which for most of us is probably buying a home. How did you arrive at the decision? Be honest. In our experience most of us will know that 'this is the place for me/us' when they walk through the door. That's when we make up our mind – and spend a significant amount of energy on justifying that decision with rational aspects afterwards – post-rationalisation. This kind of behaviour is exactly the reason why estate agents might show you all sorts of places that do not seem to fit your instructions; they know that we will know what we like when we see it, but are often not aware of what we want until we do so!

Understanding sense-making, ever more so in today's complex world, is important in the creation as well as the implementation of innovations. This is at the core of G.K. VanPatter's work. So let's see what he has to say about it.

The Future of Innovation is SenseMaking for ChangeMaking

Name	**G.K. VanPatter**
Affiliation	Humantific
Position	Co-founder
Country	USA and Spain
Area	Organisational and social transformation
Email	gvanpatter@humantific.com

SenseMaking   ChangeMaking   complexity navigation   understanding   thinking

Before change happens

New seeing happens

New understanding happens

New thinking happens

The 21st century is already presenting all of us on Planet Earth with many challenges and opportunities that have never been seen before. To many of us it has been clear for some time that the days are gone when all of the challenges facing Planet Earth could be solved by creating more products and services however human-centred and sustainable they might be. Gone are the days when the complexity facing organisational leaders could be understood by simply studying 'users'.

Today organisational leaders recognise that they face a continuous stream of giant complexity arrays. Inside and outside their organisations complexity is rising and timeframes are being compressed. Old notions of brainstorming ideas are impotent when the challenges and opportunities remain fuzzy and undefined. The simplistic days of brainstorming as innovation are long gone.

For 21st-century organisations creating paths through continuously changing complexity a different set of capabilities and tools is required to those from previous eras. Organisational leaders working with Humantific recognise that before change happens, new seeing has to happen, new understanding has to happen, new thinking has to happen. In this context of complexity there is rising awareness that SenseMaking is the 21st century fuel for organisational innovation.

SenseMaking is making the strange familiar. In an organisational context SenseMaking is the strategic activity of making sense of ambiguous complex situations. At Humantific, we do this using visual methods and tools, including words, images, drawings, diagrams and charts. This involves not only visual thinking, but creating visual ordering systems.

ChangeMaking is making the familiar change. In an organisational context ChangeMaking is the strategic activity of moving from an existing state to a co-created future state. At Humantific, we

Figure 1   SenseMaking for ChangeMaking

do this using hybrid methods from the emerging/converging fields of design thinking, innovation acceleration and transformation science.

While every innovation cycle requires both SenseMaking and ChangeMaking the big news is that the proportions of one to the other are radically changing as challenges become more complex. In large-scale innovation challenges a significant degree of SenseMaking often must be undertaken before ChangeMaking can begin. This paradigm shift is radically transforming how organisations are gearing up to overcome the complexity navigation crisis and get ready for change.

At Humantific we understand that in the 21st century, SenseMaking and ChangeMaking have become equally important partners in the quest to create a more human-centred world. There is a lot of work to be done. Let's get to it!

'Understand before you act' might sound quite common-sensical, but then, how often is common sense found? Many things are obvious with hindsight, but rather difficult to anticipate without it. We like the analogy that Edward de Bono uses when explaining the phenomenon of 'hindsight'. Think about a tree, and an ant sitting on one of its leaves. To find the way down to the trunk is rather easy – but what about the other way around? How about navigating the way from the trunk to a particular leaf? The options are endless and finding the desired leaf seems almost impossible.

As the world is becoming more complex, understanding the interactions and interrelatedness of individual parts and the systems of which they are part is becoming ever more important. Before we implement innovations we need to understand their impact on the wider system. A lack of consideration for the wider context has led to many of the problem we are facing today. So we quite agree with Manuel Mira Godinho who opens with the statement that future innovation will be, to a large extent, about reversing the negative effects some of our previous innovations have had.

The Future of Innovation is About Reversing its Past

Name	**Manuel Mira Godinho**
Affiliation	Technical University of Lisbon (UECE-ISEG-UTL)
Position	Associate Professor
Country	Portugal
Area	Systems of innovation; intellectual property
Email	mgodinho@iseg.utl.pt

innovation   spillovers   climate change   urbanisation   megacities
Malthusianism

The future of innovation will to a large extent be about the development of solutions to reverse the negative effects from many of the most important innovations humankind has introduced over the last 250 years.

The Industrial Revolution opened the door to unprecedented economic growth. This was only possible through a massive exploitation of natural resources, including the atmosphere, in which CO_2 and other pollutants have been released without control, until recently. As a result of such trajectory mass consumption started to disseminate around the globe, initially to consumers in Western Europe and North America, but now to many other parts of the globe.

Over the last 20 years alone the raising of the emerging economies and the concurrent growth in the developed world has doubled the consumption load on Planet Earth. A linear projection suggests that if this growth path extends into the future, world consumption will double again by 2028 and triple by 2040.

Most of this mass consumption is concentrated in or around urban areas. A specific aspect of urbanisation has been the emergence of megacities of more than 10 million inhabitants. In 1950 New York was the only one of such cities. By 2005 the number of megacities had grown to 25. The development of large cities undoubtedly offers huge opportunities for those living in them, but it also poses new problems such as the ones revealed by the recent terrorist attacks. In economic terms, the growth of large cities has pushed natural resources exploitation into new frontiers.

As natural resources become scarcer market prices will raise, holding back economic prospects. But it will be very hard to reverse the legitimate expectations of the peoples living in China and in the remaining emerging economies. The inertia of the current trends will certainly continue to exert an enormous pressure on resources and drive global warming to a new height.

The challenges are so formidable that no one can anticipate whether proper answers will be found. Metaphorically, one may say that Thomas Malthus's ghost is back haunting the enormous tasks we are facing.

What the past has taught us, however, is that every time humans have been confronted with similar challenges, such as the Black Death which struck Europe in the Middle Ages, they have been able to bring back their societies to the departure point and moved further ahead afterwards.

In short, more often than not, gloomy Malthusian views tend to be overcome by practical solutions. This indicates that human inventiveness will probably now again generate technological innovations to counter many of the current problems. New innovations are already being developed to offer cleaner energies and products based on alternative materials. But one thing seems certain: there is no simple technological fix for the problems we are dealing with. Innovation will need to go much beyond the mere advancement of science and technology. Given the complexity and size of the challenges we are facing, radical institutional innovation will be needed to overcome them.

We cannot emphasise this enough, we need to understand the effect our innovations have on the wider system in the longer term. If only we had listened to the wisdom to what we considered to be 'primitive' peoples as captured in the following piece of Iroquois wisdom:[1] 'In our every deliberation, we must consider the impact of our decisions on the next seven generations.' Would we have encouraged depletion of our natural resources if this had been the major guiding principle? Would we have set economic growth as our major – it sometimes seems only – maxim and justification for decisions?

How would decisions in your organisation, in your life stack up if measured against their impact 'seven generations hence'? Like decisions in many organisations more generally, the decisions around innovation have generally been made without long-term considerations, driven by the excitement of what is possible. It could possibly be argued that many innovations have caused more long-term harm than long-term good – that at least is the view of quite a few of our contributors.

So, in our Part IV, which is quite large, let's take a look at the dark side of innovation!

---

1   The Iroquois Confederacy, or Haudenosaunee as they prefer to refer to themselves, is a group of first five, later six Native Americans nations that existed long before Europeans started arriving in America. Their constitution, also called Longhouse Construction, dates back to at least 1100 AD.

PART IV
The Good, the Bad and the Ugly

Now then, the dark side of innovation. In our passion for innovation we may sometimes forget that where there's sunshine there is also some shade. We call for innovation, for more innovation, for radical innovation. Yet in this call, do we caution to consider whether it might be Pandora's Box that we are opening? Do we remember that there are not many things that are either all good or all bad? Can you think of something that is only good or only bad, regardless from whose perspective, in which context and in which time and combination? Insulin helps to keep diabetes under control – too much of it can kill. Nuclear power can produce energy in an environmentally friendly way (considering the very short term), yet it can cause mayhem and destruction. Even sunshine, the source of all life, can be life threatening; if you are in the desert then it can become life's worst enemy.

In our first contribution of this section Nigel Roome reminds us that an awareness of the destructive powers of innovation was introduced into our consciousness three quarters of a century ago. However, from the perspective then it was introduced as 'creative destruction' with the understanding that the new that was introduced was superior to what existed before. Well, we guess, that's considered to be progress.

Let's hear Nigel makes of 'creative destruction' today.

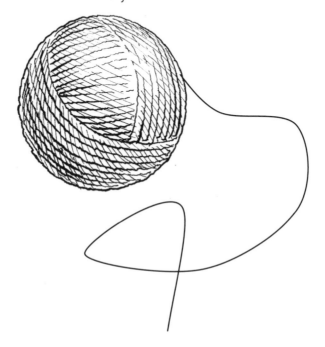

The Future of Innovation is Innovative Innovation

Name	**Nigel Roome**
Affiliation	TiasNimbas Business School
Position	Associate Dean and Professor
Country	The Netherlands
Area	Future of innovation
Email	n.roome@tiasnimbas.edu

creative destruction   governance   social environmental   economic value

Schumpeter recognised that entrepreneurs foster technical and financial innovations to create new value while simultaneously destroying the value in the products and services made obsolete by those innovations. Schumpeter's view of innovation, as creative destruction, was historically developed by looking back to the case of the railroads. A present-day, future-oriented view of innovation provides a different perspective on creative-destruction, and offers new insights into the 'future of innovation'. These demands will require 'innovation in innovation'.

Recent technological and financial innovations are leading to a more closely connected world, a world founded on silica and digital technologies and advanced materials for engines and machines for communication and transport. Combined with knowledge about the organisation of transport hubs and networks these innovations provide for safe, reliable and rapid connections that span our world. These innovations are the essence of globalisation – a process by which the world is connected through human agency.

These connections create the impression that the world is smaller and faster, when in fact it is simply that the transport of resources, goods, people and ideas is more rapid and intense. Just as railroads distorted our understanding of time and space, so the innovations driving globalisation distort our notion of time and space. The implications are simple to state but incredibly complex to resolve.

First, distant production facilities and markets can be opened up and managed, new ideas can be disseminated and new offerings distributed in our era of globalisation. Yet no business innovation, technological or managerial, is problem-free. Each ingenious, human-generated construct (technology, product, service or business model) has the potential to produce bad as well as good outcomes. Often those undesired effects are distributed through complex natural and human systems to appear in the form of changed climate, accumulated toxic chemicals or the destruction or depletion of natural and stock resources. A tyranny of small decisions means the sheer weight of human demands can place pressure on otherwise resilient natural systems. Globalisation enables this to happen on a scale previously not witnessed.

Second, innovation remains a process of creative destruction but, in this era of globalisation, the pace of innovation and the rate of change through complex pathways do not match. Economic value is created more rapidly as the lead time for innovation reduces, whereas the destruction of value following from those innovations is mostly focused on environmental and social capital which is diminished through pathways that are complex and difficult to measure and predict.

The paradox is that entrepreneurs push for innovations which rapidly succeed one another, even before their effects are fully understood or agreed, and institutional responses developed to remediate their implications for the fabric of our planet and society. This is the innovation equivalent of a financial pyramid scheme, a present reality with no integrity and no future.

The solution is found in the deliberative governance of innovation – combining wisdom and responsibility found in precaution and anticipation with the zeal and excitement of new knowledge and enterprise in innovation. This would be an innovation in innovation.

First of all, we marvel at our contributors' ability to make connections between each other's contributions that they surely could not have intended when their pieces were written (as no one knew what everyone else was writing)! Nigel provides yet another great link between the sections, picking up on the need for innovation in innovation, and reminding us of the destructive force of innovation. In fact, he argues that the potentially destructive force of innovation is what causes the need for innovation in innovation. Human ingenuity has the potential to create good as well as bad and we need to find ways to maximise the good while minimising the bad.

This is exactly the point Arvind Srivastava is making, illustrating his point with examples.

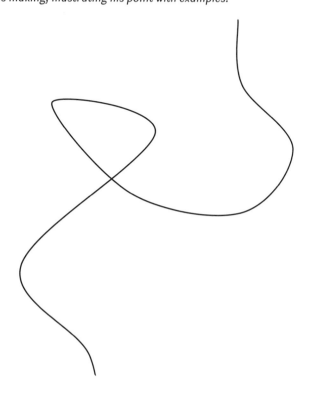

The Future of Innovation is a Warning

Name	**Arvind K. Srivastava**
Affiliation	Accelper Consulting
Position	Vice President
Country	USA
Area	Innovation management
Email	Arvin@accelper.com

virus   terrorist   society   value

Human thinking has evolved over past centuries in an accelerated manner. We see a practically infinite number of new products and services around us. Since innovation is an applied creativity and creativity is a unique combination of two or more ideas or products, we expect to see more and more innovation in the future. The rate of innovation is already exponential as there are more opportunities to innovate.

There are however a few words of caution – we should be concerned about the areas where innovation is applied. Let me elaborate. There is good innovation and bad innovation. Good innovation means producing something that creates or enhances value to the society and bad innovation destroys the society.

While a number of people are engaged in good innovation, perhaps equal number appears to be engaged in bad innovation – examples include virus creators and terrorists. Virus creators are very innovative in creating new problems for computers causing data loss, wasteful duplication efforts and a net loss to the society.

Today practically every nation feels threatened by terrorists who are also very innovative in their ways. Recent events have indicated that they have outsmarted the best brains of the societies which are trying to protect themselves from terror attacks.

The problems posed by viruses may be handled by another stream of business that sells products to counter them but terrorism is the true threat to society. Our perpetual desire to become good – better – best, a key driver to the future of innovation, shall just remain a dream if we are not able to handle the issue of terrorism effectively. We need to put in resources and prioritise our efforts to counter the threat of terrorism innovatively.

When you are innovating, do you consider the possible negative consequences or just get excited by the potential? Do morality and conscience play a role in your organisation's innovation considerations? Have you a 'code of conduct' for innovators?

The biggest challenge here is probably how to prevent 'bad innovation'. Is bad always bad and good always good? Does not even this depend on context? What kind of yardstick or measure can we use to decide this difficult question? Is nuclear energy good or bad? Are there truly things that do not have 'the other side of the coin'? When we innovate, can we always see or at least anticipate the downsides of our invention? How do we account for the fact that the downsides of innovation may only emerge over time? Side effects and long-term effects are generally not obvious at the outset. Think of asbestos: when first introduced it was most welcome as a fire-retardant building material.

Patrick McLaughlin is one of our contributors who takes a closer look at the monsters that innovation has created. Remember when we spoke about The Sorcerer's Apprentice *in Part I, 'The need for innovation'? He sees retrenchment into the status quo as a consequence of scrupulous – or badly communicated – innovation. But read his own words.*

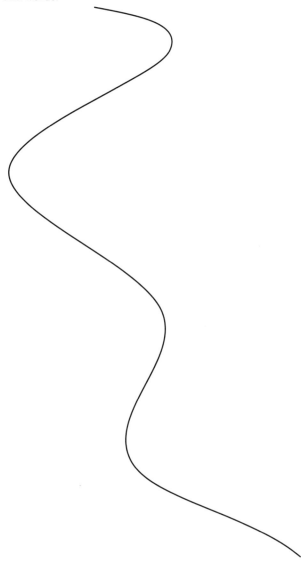

The Future of Innovation is a Shaw Perspective

Name	**Dr Patrick McLaughlin**
Affiliation	Cerulean
Position	Managing Director
Country	UK
Area	Discontinuous innovation/radical innovation
Email	patrick.mclaughlin@cerulean.com

discontinuous innovation   radical innovation   non-conformist   innovators   risk

'The power of accurate observation is commonly called cynicism by those who have not got it.'

George Bernard Shaw (1856–1950), Irish literary critic, playwright and essayist; winner of the 1925 Nobel Prize for Literature

Discontinuous innovation in the 21st century created monsters in the form of bio-engineering, nano-technology, social engineering, financial services and intelligent weaponry. As a result society came to see this type of innovation as politically incorrect, and advocated preservation of the status quo as environmentally friendly, acceptable and without risk. This future is a neo-medieval dark age where discontinuous innovators are treated as rebels and non-conformists, and where such thinking – questioning the extant system – is considered to be heresy. There is a requirement to conform to the strict orthodoxy demanded by the machine bureaucracy of governance. Yet within this restrictive environment, as in medieval times, a renaissance is beginning; and as it does, it draws together the innovators, the people who do not fear new or radical technologies, applications, methods. Like points of light coalescing in the darkness, these groups of innovators apply their craft to bring step-improvements to products, processes and the human condition. Although adopted in time, when the benefits are visible to those in control, the early stages of these innovations are fraught with danger. Not the fear of failure or fear of rebuke for making mistakes that was a feature of such innovation in the 20th century, but a fear of being ostracised, exiled or even 're-educated' for not following the 'rules', as laid down in the governance manuals.

For in this future, the risk aversion, political correctness and torrent of rules and regulations that characterised the late 20th and early 21st centuries has grown into a fully formed and fearsome bureaucratic fundamentalism. Here people are rigidly controlled and dissent is ruthlessly suppressed in order to 'protect the majority' – a majority whose 'needs' are defined by the state. Your safety is our highest priority, they cry, and use this mantra to suppress anything that could be conceived as radical or potentially dangerous to the status quo. Unlike others in this dystopia, these Big Brother administrators have access to the rebellious underclass of discontinuous innovators. These non-conformist radicals are hounded from mainstream society, yet also farmed to ensure that any new innovations are appropriated by the state to ensure the maintenance of the established order.

The innovators scavenge for resources from each other or from the edge of mainstream society. They hunt out new ideas and reflect collectively on their failures and successes. They share knowledge. Dissent is encouraged, experimentation abounds. Through their collaborative network, they develop a high level of consciousness about the enablers for discontinuous innovation. In this future discontinuous innovation is not a 'desirable feature' but a lifestyle for these rebels. And yet the innovations they produce are consumed by the society that abhors their non-conformity – a symbiotic relationship with the innovators being tolerated as long as they remain invisible and provide a flow of innovations to the host.

Does a microcosm of this future already exist in some organisations?

Might your organisation be one of those Patrick talks about? Where innovation suffers as a consequence of 'bad innovation'? Are you one of those rebels he talks about, and are you experiencing the dark ages of innovation? Do you and like-minded people in your organisation have to go into hiding to escape the witch hunt of the 'preservers of the status quo'?

We think that there might be two issues with the monsters of innovation. The first comes back to the afore-mentioned systemic level: have the true consequences of the monsters' behaviour at the systemic level been taken into consideration? The second is that we might perceive an innovation to be a monster because its benefits might not have been communicated clearly enough. We tend to be afraid of what we do not know or do not understand. Hence, if innovations are sprung on people, or if people find out that innovations are 'used on them' without their knowledge, rejection might only be a logical consequence. Remember us mentioning David Bernstein? Another of his arguments is that people, in the absence of information willingly given, believe that there is something to hide, and nothing works as fast as the bush drums of scaremongers and misinformers.

Let's listen to another voice, that of Robert Veryzer. He too is concerned about the downsides of innovation, cautioning about its detrimental effects.

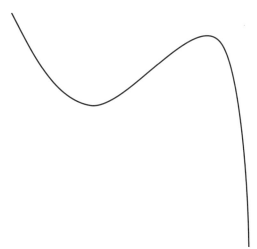

The Future of Innovation is Presenting a Paradox

Name	**Robert W. Veryzer, PhD**
Affiliation	R. Veryzer Research
Position	Professor
Country	USA
Area	Discontinuous innovation and product design
Email	rveryzer@gmail.com

innovation   technology   latent dangers   estrangement   innovation ethics

The future of innovation will present a paradox. Advances and 'progress' will be mixed with developments that actually diminish the quality of life (or health) enjoyed, although the detrimental effects will often not be immediately or readily apparent or even universally acknowledged. This is not to suggest that the future of innovation does not hold great wonder and tremendous potential for significant benefit. Certainly innovation can and likely will (and at this point must if it is to happen at all) provide the means for enhancing the quality of life – in part by reversing the extensive damage done to the world in which we live.

The paradox is evident in the tension between the drive for innovations offering increased utility or convenience, and innovations that ultimately prove deleterious. Detrimental effects are too often not 'discovered' (either uncovered or admitted) until well after a damaging 'innovation' has worked its way into the consumption stream – what can be termed 'latent dangers.' Along with this is also a tension between innovating for innovation's – or profit's – sake, and innovation that truly benefits humankind. Such innovations may give rise to another aspect of the innovation paradox – 'estrangement.' This refers to a subtle loss of connection to basic human nature. Mixed (positive and negative) potentials seem inherent in innovation, there is a gain, and what is lost may go unrecognised – yet not entirely unfelt (at least on some non-conscious level).

All of this places an even greater onus on the developers of innovations and innovative products, particularly discontinuous innovations where responsibility and accountability must be embraced and also enforced (through rigorous, objective, truth-seeking testing and approval processes). However, for innovation to be kept from going awry requires the development of a long overdue sense of 'innovation ethics' with an evaluative emphasis encompassing innovation foresight and vision regarding potentially detrimental as well as more subtle negative effects on people and life patterns. Regulatory mechanisms both within and external to firms should extend from this sensibility. Even though prediction is notoriously difficult – and often widely misses the import and reverberations innovations may have – nonetheless, it is crucial that the full impact (both benefits and true and complete costs) of innovations be determined before they are introduced into manufacturing processes and the markets of the world in order to avert diffusing, accumulating catastrophic effects.

It is easy to get caught up in the enthusiasm for innovation, easy to consider only the gain and not the more subtle loss – or even danger. However, a perspective simply lauding the future with its most assuredly robust stream of exciting innovations is not only incomplete but naively short-sighted if not irresponsible. The 'gain' is readily seen (even though it may be grossly underestimated or does not ultimately materialise in a commercially viable way), and in many cases proves more significant or far-reaching than expected. Yet, it is for the darker, more worrisome side of the bargain inherent in innovation (and innovative new products) that attention, diligence, and action are required.

There clearly seems to be consensus about the damage we have done to our environment, and that we need more, not less, innovation to get us out of the hole we have dug for ourselves. We should listen to Robert's words of caution and bring them to the forefront of our attention every time we get too excited about possibilities, without moderating our excitement by a consideration of the downsides. We should also acknowledge that we are dealing with a paradox here, with situations where there is no clear-cut answer and no 'black or white' scenario.

This, too, is the view of Jan Grundling who advises us to evaluate the value and implications of an innovation before implementing it.

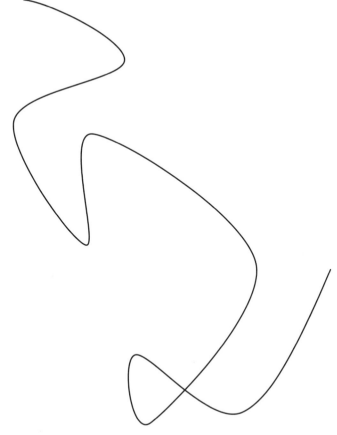

The Future of Innovation is a Re-directional Perspective

Name	**Jan P. Grundling**
Affiliation	Tshwane University of Technology
Position	Head, Centre for Entrepreneurship
Country	South Africa
Area	Management of innovation
Email	grundlingjp@tut.ac.za

redirecting   eonic   **public good**   anticipation   life order

Any individual innovation act and all innovations should always be evaluated in terms of its potential and real contribution to the public good. This evaluation process entails a mental application in which the individual evaluates the value of the innovation idea to the current and the anticipated future situation. Based upon the outcome of the evaluation the individual decides whether to implement the innovative idea or not.

Hence, a critical factor often ignored in the innovation evaluation process, is that we are all infected by a condition known as the 'Higher Order Syndrome'. Affected by this syndrome we unconditionally assume amongst others that complex life forms are preferential to simpler life forms, and that complex life forms are more intelligent than simpler life forms. The net effect accumulates in a human-centric, biased innovation process – as *Homo sapiens* represents the most complex life form on earth – in which the final beneficiary is humanity and the final evaluation is made by humans. Innovations are therefore not only made by humans, but also serve the purposes of humans. This bias is so strongly built-in that the whole innovation development process has become de-historicised and it is preferably discussed as an 'offspring' of the genetic evolutionary development process of *Homo sapiens*.

Whilst this approach may be necessary and even useful for the next few decades, the question arises whether this single innovation directional approach is sufficient for the next millennia and aeons when conditions on Earth to sustain life continue to deteriorate? Will progress then still be defined in terms of greater complexity or will it be more appropriate to define progress in terms of intelligence moving to more simplistic systems that can survive with less – ultimately when Earth dies – as in the case of modern technology where the trend is to make things smaller and simpler? Will it then not be possible to export special kinds of Earth life forms even to other places in the universe where conditions demand less consumption of raw and survival materials?

Beginning to redirect innovations also in the opposite direction of understanding and creating intelligent simpler life forms and technologies could just affect the sustainable reproduction and growth of intelligent life on earth and the universe. Further, it will install an innovation approach which serves the interests of all life entities on earth and not only the self-interests of man.

Accompanying the re-directional approach, the adoption of a very long-term approach is considered crucial as change in any system normally tends to flow through predictable close change and statistical predictable contained change, to unknowable open-ended change which does not necessarily follow a contingency sequence. In this regard it is assumed that the short-term future will be primarily dominated by close and contained change from which consequences can be deducted. On the other hand, we can only foresee the real long-term future (millennia and aeons) as being open-ended change which will necessitates the establishment of speculative expert teams. These teams should be responsible to create and develop 'Life Analysis Protocols', scenarios and plans for the future, and produce abstract innovative ideas on how to deal with the challenges of the far distant future.

Do you know the remarkable film Mindwalk, *based on the book* Turning Point *by Fritjof Capra? While quite a 'slow' film it is well worth watching, particularly if one aims to understand complexity and the systemic nature of things. In the story one of the three main characters, a physicist, has withdrawn from the world of science as she has realised that the inventions she got so excited about and helped to advance have the potential of destroying the world. The issue with inventing things is, once something is invented, you cannot 'un-invent' it. You cannot take back knowledge that has been created nor can you prevent it being used and abused, and developed and taken further than you ever dreamed off. Patents and regulations might hold things off for a while, but ultimately it cannot be stopped. We also believe that in these times of instant communication and almost effortless sharing of knowledge people will invent what can be invented. What is more, the chance that several people in different places around the globe will draw the same conclusions from a number of different knowledge sets is only increasing. Remember the example of the 'televisor' we mentioned earlier?*

So what do we do about the 'ethics of innovation'? Not much, given the evidence of the recent past, as presented by Karl-Erik Sveiby.

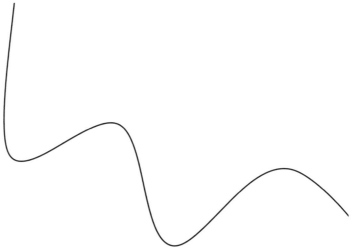

The Future of Innovation is Always 'Good'?

Name	**Karl-Erik Sveiby**
Affiliation	Hanken School of Economics
Position	Professor
Country	Finland
Area	Knowledge management
Email	karl-erik.sveiby@hanken.fi

pro-innovation bias   collateralized debt obligations   negative consequences
indirect consequences   risk

Is innovation always good? Let's look at one example. A financial innovation, collateralized debt obligations (CDO), was developed in the late 1990s by the US financial industry. CDOs bundled loans with bad risk in packages together with loans of better risk, which could be resold at high premiums. The CDO innovation opened up a new lucrative market segment: 'sub-prime' loans to American home owners with poor collateral. The global banking industry boomed and huge profits were pocketed; bank executives preened in the media.

The CDO bubble burst in late 2007 and the indirect consequences were dire. True, a US recession was long overdue, but it was the poorly understood indirect consequences of the CDO innovation that triggered it. It turns out that very few, if any, bank executives had understood the true risks involved. The experts did not warn people either; true, there were a few who did, but they were silenced or even ridiculed. And the regulating bodies sat on their hands for eight years happy with the surging markets.

Was CDO a good innovation? Yes, in the short term for the chosen few, in terms of financial remuneration for bank executives, brokers and shareholders. But the Americans have only begun to count the long-term indirect consequences: social disaster and ruin for hundreds of thousands of home owners, while the bill to the American taxpayers stood at 2.2 trillion dollars and counting according to FED at the time of writing.

The CDO case displays the intrinsic dilemma: an innovation is by definition new and unknown outside the company that invents it. Innovative technology is deliberately designed to be unique – a prerequisite for profitability and competitive advantage.

Is an innovation beneficial for people in the long run? What is the total value of an innovation including the indirect and intangible consequences? What does a responsible innovation process look like? These fundamental questions are difficult to answer, but it appears few are even trying to do so.

Indirect consequences tend to be predominantly unexpected, negative and long-term, as Everett Rogers noted as long ago as 1971 in his classic work *Diffusion of Innovations*. The trouble with the current pro-innovation bias and the lack of serious critical study of innovation is that fundamental questions are never asked. Not by industry, not by governments, not even by innovation researchers.

In a content study of 1,084 publications on innovation in 1968, Rogers found 0.2 per cent discussed the indirect consequences of innovations. The proportion had not changed in 1981 and emerging research at my university, Hanken School of Economics, suggests that the proportion is roughly the same today. Why?

We don't have to evoke disaster scenarios like the UK astrophysicist Marin Rees did in his book *Our Final Century* (2003) in order to be concerned about a future with continued irresponsible innovation. Innovations in fields like nanotechnology and gene-manipulated organisms share some uncanny features of the CDOs: indirect consequences for society outside the target group of paying customers are unknown; experts in the field are few and generally on the payroll of industry; environmental consequences are taken into account only to the degree they are regulated by law, and the issue of long-term indirect social effects is not even on the agenda.

We talked a little about timing and the time horizon before. Karl-Erik's contribution brings it home even more. He is not only emphasising possible long-term implications of innovation that we often neglect to consider, he also points towards indirect effects, making it ever more important that we truly need to understand the implications of our decisions at a systemic level. We can no longer afford to argue with the gains – in the short term. We need to develop systems and approaches that are anchored in the implications of our actions in the long term!

To guide our decisions we need a 'cradle to grave' approach, a concept that has been introduced in design and manufacture some time ago (though there still is a long way to go yet). Interestingly at a recent conference we heard reference being made to a concept of 'cradle to cradle', driven by the argument that we need to recycle and reuse things rather than disposing of them. When you innovate, do you keep recycle, reuse and material reduction in mind?

Another contributor having an issue with our current thinking around innovation is Yvonne Buma. Let's see what she has to say.

The Future of Innovation is in a Stakeholder-driven Economy

Name	**Yvonne Buma**
Affiliation	Gideya
Position	CEO
Country	The Netherlands
Area	Shareholder economy
Email	Yvonne@gideya.com

stakeholder   shareholder   employee   communication   sustainability

The challenge we have at the moment is to move from innovation being a key issue in some organisations and for some governments to an overall innovative economy. Will the current economic crisis be the catalytic factor that will take us there? Will we be able to draw the necessary conclusions and change some of the basic assumptions of our economic system?

At this moment we witness the results of the fundamental flaw in the shareholder orientation in our economy. The focus on short-term results for shareholders has led to many of the problems we see at this moment. Greed, short-term thinking and lack of nerve are the key words, and one thing we know is that these are not the *qualities* needed for innovation.

The focus should shift to stakeholders, not shareholders alone; the most important stakeholders being people that work for the organisation, society as a whole and those who provide the capital. In this vision managing the satisfaction of all stakeholders (not just one) should be the main goal of organisations. Bering focused on stakeholders will nurture human capital, and assumes long-term strategies and taking risks that are necessary for the sustainability of the organisation and its environment and therefore is supportive of innovation.

For innovative organisations (whether profit, non-profit or governmental) the most important stakeholders are the people working there, the talent that will help to be competitive and innovative. The networks we use for innovation and Web 2.0 are after all manned by the people that work for our organisations. Without them they don't exist. In his *Harvard Business Review* article of November 08 Michael Yaziji even states that they are so important they should get the bulk of the revenues instead of shareholders. Even if we don't adhere to this specific point of view, what is happening at the moment is the opposite. A recent Dutch survey showed that 17 per cent of employees are thinking about leaving their job within a year because of the organisational culture, not being recognised for the work they do and feeling that their employer doesn't value them. So focusing on the employees as important stakeholders, and taking care of their needs, is essential if we want to keep our main innovative force. This at least requires trust, recognition of their contribution and open communication.

That society as a whole also needs long-term investment and vision is obvious. Sustainability is the key word here. And yes, we do need capital, and capital should be rewarded, but the reward of capital should not be the sole concern of organisations. Sustainability, long-term results and the nurture of human capital are at least as important and need to be re-evaluated.

So let's change. Governments can help by giving companies back the right to protect themselves against unwanted attacks, by developing rules and regulations that are supportive of stakeholder-oriented companies with a long-term strategy, by restructuring the banking system and by creating measures that support R&D, the valuation of human capital. I am sure many great suggestions can be found in this book.

Yvonne is picking up the issue of long-term thinking, proposing that putting people at the centre is critical, as well as indicating an important; she also points out the role of government can play to help this along. Both issues, people and the role of government, will be discussed in more depth in subsequent chapters.

What has gone wrong with our approach to innovation? Let's take a look at what Serafin Talisayon has to say about this.

The Future of Innovation is Dependent on Non-technological Spheres

Name	**Serafin D. Talisayon**
Affiliation	CCLFI.Philippines
Position	Director for R&D
Country	Philippines
Area	Knowledge management, organisational learning
Email	serafin.talisayon@cclfi.org

social innovation   peace   value creation   intangibles   conflict resolution

The future of innovation will be influenced by the fact that the pace of technological innovations has outstripped that of political, social and ethical innovations needed to solve the problems made worse by the technological innovations themselves. Mankind has demonstrated that its ability to technologically innovate is far greater than its ability to anticipate, learn and solve the negative social consequences of those innovations.

Innovation in the future will be driven by common threats confronting humankind. Ironically, most of those threats are manmade. Innovation will proceed in the general direction of preventing and resolving conflicts, governance at all levels, advancing human rights and human security, making cross-border agreements in preventing and fighting crime and terrorism, eliminating social exclusions and other social ills that lead to poverty, generating consensus on environmental problems and solutions, and value creation.

Innovations in value creation, either for the commercial sector or for the social or development sector, will be important in redefining and advancing wealth creation for all. Wealth creation in the new global economy has been less and less through extraction and processing of natural resources and more and more through the application of human knowledge and creativity. Both pursuit of corporate profits as well as nurturing community or social development have been found to be dependent more on knowledge and other intangibles such as social and cultural capital, and less on tangible assets and infrastructures. Now and in the future, we can expect that creating and managing knowledge and other intangible assets, personal and organisational learning, and facilitating innovation itself, are playing greater roles. Innovations will move from the physical hardware and software types to also embrace the biological-ecological, behavioural, organisational, network-social, legal-legislative and symbolic-representational types.

Development itself is being redefined. The pursuit of peace, including the use of new international sanctions to support local application of violent modes to secure long-term planetary peace, is also being redefined. As humankind's only home planet gets more crowded and problematic, we are forced into a common journey of learning how to live together and how to creatively convert our ethnic, religious and political diversity from a disadvantage to an advantage.

Humankind's capacity to innovate will need to be focused on questions of 'what for' and 'for whom'. It will have to revolve more around finding new and better questions, than on finding correct answers to old questions. I anticipate more innovations in how people recognise and manage their own mental boxes and judgements, and how people can perform this reflective process through open dialogue within a diverse group. I sense a future where innovations will give humankind a better capacity to reflect and learn together as a group, and therefore co-create a consensus on how they can more effectively address problems they face as a group.

What really struck us with the above contribution was Serafin's phrase of 'humankind's only home planet'. While innovation is much about experimentation, our home planet is perhaps one of the few things we should avoid taking terminal risks with! The good news is that the inevitable openness, driven by instant communication and easily sharable knowledge, resulting it greater transparency, will make it increasingly difficult to keep experiments hidden, be they good or bad. Hopefully that will allow us to react to any 'bad' innovation – or bad application of an innovation – in a swift and decisive manner.

Fundamentally, our contributors are raising the questions: what is it that we are innovating for? Whom is it that we are innovating for? These are just the questions Josephine Green is raising in her contribution.

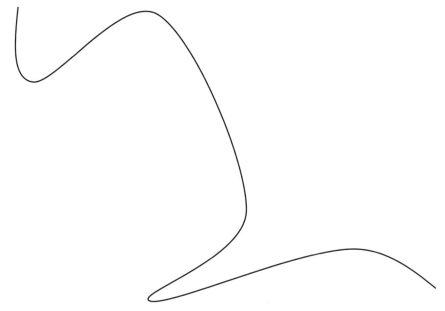

The Future of Innovation is For What and By Whom?

Name	**Josephine Green**
Affiliation	Philips Design
Position	Senior Director of Trends and Strategy
Country	The Netherlands
Area	Strategic futures, social foresight for strategy and innovation, sustainable solutions, design, innovation
Email	josephine.green@philips.com

sense making   new consciousness   crossroads   social innovation   systems

We hear so much about creativity and innovation, releasing it in ourselves, in our society, in our institutions, but wait a minute, innovation for what and by whom?

The world is changing. The forces that shaped the 19th and 20th centuries have gone, leaving the institutions, the companies, the ways of thinking and the ways of working less relevant if not redundant. This is inevitable. The socio-techno-economic forces underpinning the industrial era have changed, making many of the solutions of the last century not only less sense making but increasingly non-sense making. With a new paradigm comes a new consciousness, a new set of values, new behaviours and new solutions. If all this is happening, and more, then it seems somewhat facile to push the creativity and innovation button without a more in-depth process of imagination and learning around the kind of society we want, the kind of future we long for and the values that we need to underpin such a society.

We stand at the crossroads of a unique opportunity. Given the state we are in, we have to re-invent just about everything, including new ways of living, new ways of producing, new ways of delivering our social industries, such as health, education, mobility, and even new ways of measuring progress and growth, beyond productivity and consumption. At the same time the new socio-techno forces shaping our next future come to the rescue by enabling a more systems approach to living, one in which people are connected in an ecology of places, information, activities and experiences. Health offers an example. The future of health is about putting people at the centre of the system and connecting them to their circles of care, loved ones, health practitioners, medical centres etc. Such systemic and structural re-invention is based on new values, new needs and new technologies.

This emerging possibility, however, is less about the market and market innovation, based on consumer needs and driven by experts, and more about social needs and social innovation, based on stakeholder needs and driven by the collective and collaborative participation of those stakeholders. Less about products and consumption and more about ecosystems and value. Such necessity and such visions change everything, including *why* we innovate, *what* we innovate, *how* we innovate and *who* innovates.

We are living through the death of one paradigm and the emergence of another. If in this process we simply continue to innovate for innovation's sake, based on old thinking and past/best practice, then we increase the nonsense. If on the other hand we take the opportunity we enhance future relevancy and sense making. Hence the need a priori to ask the big question: creativity and innovation for what and by whom?

Like G.K. VanPatter in Part III, Josephine is talking about sense making, and a need to take a close look at things that made sense in the past, but have lost their meaning in our quest to move forwards. We have reached a turning point – a situation that can viewed as a threat as well as an opportunity! A shift, a change, the emergence of something new is always full of opportunity. Just think, we, all of us, where ever we are, have the opportunity to shape and influence the future! As was said at a recent innovation conference, 'Imagine the opportunity, any one of you out there might come up with an idea, with a suggestion, with a thought, that will influence the future of all of us.' As a new canvas opens out before us it is our privilege as well as our responsibility to do our hardest to start painting a picture that our children's children can be proud of.

We are entirely with Josephine and believe that the question we should never start asking ourselves is, who we are innovating for, and why. Innovation is not an end in itself, it is a means to an end. And that end is the creation of value; value not at the individual level – though of course there is no harm in that – but at the systems, at the society level.

While also posing more questions another of our contributors, Leila Hurmerinta, has some suggestion as to the 'what'.

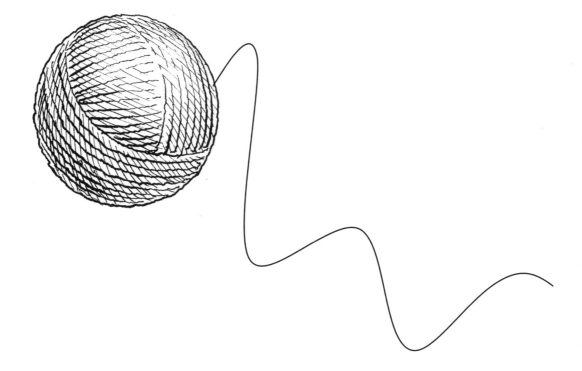

The Future of Innovation is Make it Smart!

Name	**Leila Hurmerinta**
Affiliation	Turku School of Economics, Department of Marketing
Position	Professor
Country	Finland
Area	Innovation management, smart technology
Email	leila.hurmerinta-peltomaki@tse.fi

innovation   smart technology   smart product   challenges   risk

The development and application of smart technology is an ongoing phenomenon in the 2000s. It has aroused enthusiasm among product developers and researchers, whose interest lies in the technological details – how things work. Smart products are based on smart technology that aims at balancing a situation or activating a function. Smart products absorb information from their environment, process it autonomously and then act in some logical and repetitive way, or suggest action. The core function is information exchange between a customer/user and its environment.

There are, however, many known risks or challenges. How can smart products be made to communicate and respond to each other? How can they be made reliable enough to enable users to trust the outcomes? How will users retain control of or a feel for the product? Sometimes we stop doing things we think might cause some problems in the future. Sometimes our enthusiasm for new technological inventions makes us blind to these visions. Do we have our eyes open now?

Smart technology communicates with us, and with other smart products. We still have control – but for how long? The danger is that we are developing something that is too smart for us, something that will soon no longer need us – a Jurassic Park. In time the smart network surrounding us will have no humans, only beings communicating with other beings, producing and accumulating knowledge. We will be kicked out of the network. Is this possible?

People using smart products give the responsibility of thinking, deciding, communicating and acting to others: they outsource certain human activities to technology, which thinks and acts in our best interests – as long as it serves us. For people with restricted capabilities this is an ideal situation, and it is what companies are doing as well. The world is networking, and companies are outsourcing many activities and resources in the interests of effectiveness and efficiency – but they stop at core competence: there are skills that no company is ready to share with other network partners. Where does smart technology leave the ones who can choose?

Learning by doing assumes a whole new meaning: what are we learning in this new situation, and what will we forget? Smart technology is making us passive by taking from us the one thing that made us human – our creative intelligence, our core competence. We are no longer processing, analysing and interpreting, and storing information, we are learning to manage and utilise others' knowledge as one operator in the network. And here is the risk: we are losing control over the technology and ourselves; we are regenerating.

Older people try to prevent dementia by exercising their brains on complex exercises. And what are we doing? We are promoting dementia by outsourcing human thinking activities, and what's more, we are even doing it to young people. Schools are already calling for mathematical skills. What should we say? You can find them in chips?

Again this contribution urges us to understand implications, in the wider context as well as from a human perspective. Advancement of technology not in order to replace fundamental human processes and activities but to support and encourage them. If we do not understand that now, will the dystopia of the film The Matrix, *where humans live in a dream world generating electricity to support the governing robots, become reality?*

What an appropriate place to share the story of Lutz Kucher who encourages us, like Josephine before, to rethink our motivation for innovation, and to reflect on what really matters.

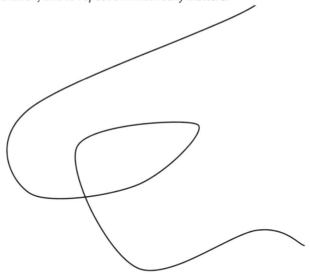

The Future of Innovation is in the Rich Soil of a Potato Field

Name	**Lutz Kucher**
Affiliation	Kucher+Thusbass Design Brand Soul
Position	Founding partner
Country	Germany
Area	Brand design, design innovation
Email	kucher@lutzkucher.eu

potato field   quality of life   sustainable   innovation turning commodity
story telling

Paul, an independent consultant in the area of innovation, was strolling aimlessly through the streets of a wintry Munich. It had been his last working day before Christmas. He had had a great year and you would have had expected that he would be quite satisfied. But his look was telling a different story.

While strolling around, he had passed probably hundreds of shopping windows, most of them lavishly decorated for Christmas. Yet he started to feel considerably irritated, because in way too many of them *innovative* or *innovation* seemed to be the main and ultimate selling arguments.

Innovation seemed to have degenerated into a selling commodity. Into something, whose sole purpose seemed to be to boost consumption. Progress, fired by its *innovation engine*, had developed its very own momentum, not caring much whether this progress really served the people or increased their quality of life.

Paul had stopped in front of an electronics store. He saw mobile phones, telecom services, mp3 players, internet games, blue ray players etc. All kinds of high-tech gadgets. Sure, all of them were significant technological innovations, he thought. But then again, did those innovations really help to make our lives better?

Considering his own last projects, he was wondering whether he himself hadn't lost touch with what really mattered. Too much innovation for its own sake. And definitely not enough reflection about the effects of it on our life.

All of a sudden a guy with headphones in the ears came around the corner and run almost into him. The guy mumbled a muted *sorry* and rushed on. 'People seem to have no time any more. Not much desire to talk if it can be avoided. I guess we are all haunted by our *to-do lists* ...' thought Paul.

Thinking about time and to-do lists, a memory of his grandpa came to his mind: Paul must have been around eight years old, and he was visiting his grandpa who was planting potatoes on a field. When he arrived, his grandpa stood aside the field, leaning casually on the spade and chatting lively with a neighbour. They were laughing and seem to have a good time. After the neighbour had finally left, his grandpa had shown him all kinds of things he needed to know in order to plant a good potato.

'My grandpa always had time and he was at one with the world,' thought Paul, 'and my guess is, that back then nobody talked much about *innovation*. He was wondering whether the hypothesis could be stated, that having a content life and *innovation* were not necessarily connected? Or maybe even not at all? And if so, the question was, what needed to be changed so that *innovation* could contribute again to a content life?

Paul's face now showed a quiet smile, for he had a clear idea what needed to be done. He wanted to find an answer to these essential questions! And he even knew where to start searching:

Next spring on the rich soil of his grandpa's potato field.

We need to take stock of where we have got to, and we need to consider carefully where we want to go next. We do not have to follow the trajectory we are currently on – because if we do, there might not be a future for which to innovate, as Elko Kleinschmidt rightly points out.

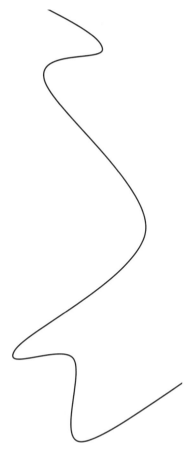

The Future of Innovation is Dependent on Having a Future

Name	**Elko J. Kleinschmidt**
Affiliation	McMaster University
Position	Prof Emeritus
Country	Canada
Area	Process of new product development
Email	kleinsc@mcmaster.ca

climate change   consumption   habit changes   breakthrough   marketing

After 26 years of academic and practical work with the processes of new product development (NPD), portfolio management for new products and global NPD I have observed how time consuming and difficult it is to really get new developments accepted and fully used. At the same time I have always had great interests in and concerns about the long-term impact of our innovations (and our related style of living) on the global ecology which is today the global warming situation. The future of innovation in my opinion is based on a marketing innovation (a marketing programme or approach) that will succeed in convincing the developed world to be willing to accept major changes in their present consuming behaviour and the willingness of the rest of the world not to attempt to aim for the consuming behaviour of the developed world. According to the specialists on global warming, only a few decades are left to make the needed changes.

The present consumer behaviour of the developed world as represented by car ownership, housing requirements, even travel and many other heavily material consumption-based material things and services is the major source of the global warming . At the same time, the rest of the world (the great majority of the world population) is trying to emulate the developed world and who can tell them they cannot do this considering their often wretched living conditions?

What is needed for a future in innovation is an innovative marketing programme that is simple and convincing so that the developed world consumer is willing to change from a high materially based consumption to a significantly less material and energy-consuming consumption and is willing to pay the price for such a change. At the same time, the developed world will have to transfer considerable funds to the developing world to improve their living conditions and convince the rest of the world that a high standard of living is not necessarily based on high material consumption.

The present marketing approach to reduce for example 'dirty' energy use, using less energy in general, reuse material things, etc. is changing habits very slowly or marginally in the developed world, even if supported more or less by local governments, NGOs and international organisations. New technological innovations will help but again only rather slowly (no incentive to develop them if not fast economic return is promised). Changing habits will require all kind of major marketing innovations to get real change. Presently we talk a lot about needed changes but many other urgent developments, e.g., pressing economic conditions, changing governments, local strives, seem to have our immediate attentions, replacing so-called more 'distant problems' from our concern for important long-term and worldwide innovations.

So, where are these important innovations and who will do them and how will they be introduced and launched in time to make a real difference? To have a long-term future of innovation we need such innovations.

The plot thickens; we need innovation, the wheel of innovation is spinning faster and faster, which means that increasingly we need a different kind of innovation, and we need to understand implications and consequences of our innovations – in the long run, and at a systemic level.

It seems that up to now we have explored whatever was possible, regardless of whether it – or the consequences of its introduction – were actually desirable and truly beneficial. What about giving innovation the purpose to changing things for the better, and for innovating for the long run rather than the short term? While we can already hear the voices of those who argue with the stock market's demands and the necessity to deliver satisfactory performance on a quarterly basis we would like to counter with the question, 'Can we really afford to keep using this as excuses not to act for the benefit of a future?' Let's keep Elko's opening words as a constant reminder: 'The future of innovation depends on having a future'!

Perhaps it is time we called for responsible innovation, for balanced innovation, for considerate and thoughtful innovation; for innovation that supports and sustains life on this planet. The concern for our future – that there will actually be one – was felt by many contributors, that's why we have decided to dedicate the next section to those who have made that the central theme of their contribution.

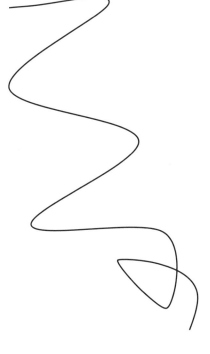

PART V
The 11th Hour

If the focus of the last section was to explore the dark side of innovation and concerns resulting from that more generally, the special focus of Part V is to give voice to those who made our current preoccupation with consumption and growth and an urgent need to move sustainability higher up the agenda their main focus. We would argue that the current economic crisis is a final wake-up call, a last opportunity to reconsider our economic maxim and attitude towards the planet that is our only home, before we reach a tipping point from which there is no turning back. We truly believe that we really are at a watershed, and that action needs to be taken urgently. As Kate North, our first contributor in this section, impresses on us, it *is* the 11th hour.

We felt that it might be quite useful to share the words which have led Kate, and us, to choose to reference the prophecy of the Indian Hopi tribe in this context.

We are the Ones We've been Waiting For

You have been telling the people that this is the Eleventh Hour.

Now you must go back and tell the people that this is The Hour.

And there are things to be considered:

Where are you living?

What are you doing?

What are your relationships? Are you in right relation?

Where is your water? Know your garden.

It is time to speak your Truth.

Create your community. Be good to each other.

And do not look outside yourself for the leader.

We are the ones we've been waiting for.

– The Elders Oraibi, Arizona Hopi Nation

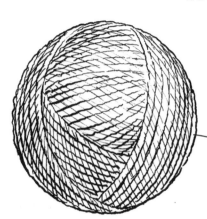

The Future of Innovation is Within Us

Name	**Kate North**
Affiliation	Encompass International
Position	President
Country	United States
Area	Workplace strategy
Email	kate@jknorth.net

creative talent   collaboration   networks   Me Inc   transformation

Hopi Indian stories reveal we've entered the 'Eleventh Hour'. Given the daily reports regarding our global economy, environment and political unrest, it's difficult to deny this as one plausible reality. Whilst this haunting concept heightens my personal sense of urgency, I'm also filled with tremendous hope. As the Hopis' story unfolds, the message reveals: 'the time of the lone wolf is over ... we are the ones we have been waiting for'.

As I reflect upon the 'future of innovation', my foundational premise is based upon my deep belief that we have embarked upon a global transformation and its rapid emergence is calling forth a new ways of working and 'being'. Demanding higher levels of courage, collaboration and creativity to solve the complex challenges we now face.

No longer can we suppress our growing desire for an authentic and meaningful relationship to our work.

No longer can we deny the opportunity to come together to solve critically emerging issues facing our planet.

No longer will we allow the challenges of organisational innovation to suppress our efforts.

For decades, the mechanistic era has created barriers for the evolution of ideas to be explored in traditional business environments. Whilst many organisations have declared their desire for a more trusting, open, empowered culture, the reality is this type of organisational change is difficult and it will take time ... perhaps more time than we have.

My own experience has taught me the desired shift I seek is not something outside of me, nor is it up to someone else to manifest, but it is inside me, I own it. This desire for a cultural shift to support innovation, beckons an individual commitment to personal development. This includes a deep understanding of our 'full self' and congruency with our values. New skills, such as meditation and dialogue can offer the stillness, clarity and purpose we seek. The art of strengthen our individual 'presence' will become a necessary trait as we more vehemently engage virtually and cross-culturally.

As we know, this type of personal/spiritual development is not for the faint of heart and requires tremendous desire, perseverance and time, all of which can be easily sabotaged in a corporate world built on speed and quarterly results.

Through my work, I've observed many large organisations struggling to find an integrated value proposition that truly attracts and retains creative talent. As the benefit of being 'inside' an organisation lessens and the frustrations increase, the concept of 'Me Inc.' may become a more probable reality for those driven to expand, innovate and create. 'Opting out' of traditional organisations to seek a bolder canvas with like-minded colleagues and networks may indeed be a welcomed alternative.

If the future of innovation expands in these unexpected networks and on the fringes, what new collaborative models might emerge? How can they best be supported and harnessed? What would a successful relationship look like between private and public enterprise?

We are the ones we have been waiting for.

We could not agree more with Kate's observation of a current surge for authenticity, for meaning and for belonging to something that is worth belonging to. Just consider a few facts. Surveys indicate that over 50 per cent of the people, particularly in large organisation, are not engaged – an additional 15–20 per cent are even negatively engaged, which means they are acting destructively. To explain quickly, engagement has two components: an emotional one, which is about taking pride in working for a company (or team, or leader), and a rational one, which is about understanding how your job fits into the bigger picture. If you have engaged people in the organisation you will find that they are willing to go the 'extra mile', that they feel they can contribute and that attrition rates are likely to be low. At the same time a survey from 2005 indicated that a large majority – generally over 70 per cent, varying slightly across European countries – would gladly give their time for free, if it involved something that is worthwhile and that they believed in. In our view this not only indicates a desire for meaning and belonging, but also to contribute. Don't you think that the desire to be engaged and contribute together and the need to innovation would make rather complementary companions?

By the way, did you note that Kate emphasised that we cannot look to others to achieve the change we need, that we have to look to ourselves, each and every one of us?

Something worthwhile, something to be proud of, a feeling to contribute to a better future. Surely, innovating with sustainability in mind meets all these requirements, as Daniel Weule believes too!

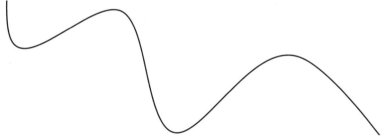

The Future of Innovation is Ecological Innovation

Name	**Daniel Weule**
Affiliation	5 D Consulting
Position	Managing Director
Country	Australia
Area	Strategy and organisational development
Email	Daniel@5dconsulting.com.au

sustainability   ecosystem   ecology   creation   transformation

When we mention the word 'innovation', revolutionary inventions and the stories that accompany them come to the fore for many. Walkmans, Post-it notes, Liquid Paper, iPods, and more recently eBay, YouTube and Google are all products that some way or another became worldwide hits and generated huge amounts of revenue for those behind them. These products fulfil the prevailing definition for innovation: the commercialisation of ideas where the interplay between a market and an idea gives us a 'score' in currency as to its success. Is the future of innovation a continuation of this lineage? Of course those in the business of innovation know there is much more to 'it' than the creation of revolutionary products but have we really taken the time to think about what this might be?

Innovation is fundamentally a vehicle for value creation. The relentless pursuit of value creation through innovation has produced a relentless wave of technological advancements, but at what cost? The future of innovation cannot be solely about creation of wealth as a dominant objective but must also factor in sustainability.

This reference to sustainability is an ecological one, but not in an environmental sense alone. The ecology referred to here concerns business inputs and outputs and the level to which these feed a system rather than depleting one. Traditional business approaches, and innovation for that matter, could be viewed as a closed pipeline. Large volumes or inputs are drawn in one end and smaller outputs emerge at the other to be commercialised. This formula is finite and on a planet that is naturally ecological potentially disastrous.

The industry that is innovation, be it incremental or radical, can play a leading role in the creation of new ways of doing business that consider the impact of any enterprise on the system with which it interacts. Innovation is the engine that can create ecological systems for our enterprises so any waste becomes a resource or an input to another value creation system, where the vast resources of the global corporate world can be leveraged to enrich rather than deplete resources.

Why is this the future of innovation? There is a certain desire and momentum that accompanies the idea of innovation. This momentum is a perfect delivery mechanism for building a more sustainable way of doing business. Transformation of any kind requires the following:

- **Motivation** – Innovation is sexy – people naturally like to be associated with new and interesting ideas and trends.

- **Capability** – Innovation is the science of creating something new – the discipline of innovation brings with it a suite of tools and approaches that support the creation of 'new'.

- **Patience** – Innovation tolerates false and slow starts – Piloting new approaches kills new approaches as go/no go decisions are based on sales performances alone. The prototyping or user co-design approaches used in innovation allows more time to meet the more complex needs of an ecosystem.

- **Learning** – Innovation feeds innovation – Innovation can be in its own sense a learning ecosystem where learning is recycles to apply a needed where needed.

Innovation has so much to offer. Why don't we apply it to the most important issue facing us – our future?

Of course we very much liked the statement 'Innovation has so much to offer' – in fact we could not agree more – but again it is the call for a systemic understanding, for a perspective on sustainability that goes beyond the environmental sense alone, and the concept of a far-reaching transformation that truly resonates with us. It is a relief to see that the awareness that things have to change and that sustainability has to be one of the evaluation criteria is spreading. What can you do to help it spread faster?

Let's now hear from Rosa Maria Dangelico who is telling us why her view of the future of innovation is 'green', and who shares some examples of the 'greening of product development'.

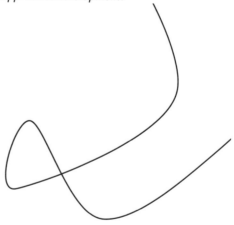

The Future of Innovation is Green

Name	**Rosa Maria Dangelico**
Affiliation	Polytechnic University of Bari
Position	PhD student
Country	Italy
Area	Product innovation, environmental sustainability
Email	r.dangelico@poliba.it

green products   environmental sustainability   Italian cases of excellence

In a world where climate change, resource consumption, pollution and waste are becoming more and more critical issues, both society and companies are required to take action. Within this context, green product innovation can play a fundamental role in helping society to reach the target of environmental sustainability. In fact, green products can be defined as products that strive to protect the natural environment by conserving energy and/or resources, and reducing pollution and waste in one or more phases of their lifecycle, such as production, use and disposal.

The relevance of green product innovation is becoming more and more widely recognised. For example, the Commission of European Communities highlights that green products can lead to a new growth paradigm and a higher quality of life through wealth creation and competitiveness. Moreover, among the first 50 innovations of 2008 listed by *Time*, there are some green product innovations, such as the Italcementi photocatalytic cement. This Italian green product innovation can contribute to reducing the air pollution due to traffic in cities and galleries.

Other Italian cases of excellence related to green product innovations could be mentioned. Think about the Phylla Concept, the experimental urban vehicle, recently developed by CRF (Centro Ricerche Fiat) together with Environment Park, and Politecnico di Torino. This car reduces pollution and waste by integrating many environmentally friendly aspects such as electric propulsion and photovoltaic panels, is made of environmentally friendly materials and uses renewable energy sources. Another Italian case of excellence is Novamont, named European Inventor of the Year 2007, a leader in bioplastics, biodegradable and compostable plastics.

Developing green product innovations is not only beneficial for the natural environment but also for companies. In fact, integrating the environmental dimension into product development may be a significant source of competitive advantage, since it provides product differentiation, enhancement of firm reputation and low-cost manufacturing (by means of increased efficiency in the use of resources, reduction of pollution and waste from production processes).

However, several challenges are associated with the development and diffusion of green product innovations. First of all, the development process requires a high level of integration of competencies and knowledge about the environmental impacts of products and processes between different functional areas within the company, investments in eco-design competencies and the adoption of lifecycle thinking.

Secondly, one of the greatest barriers to the diffusion of such innovations is the lack of customers' awareness of the need for and benefits of such innovations.

However, in my opinion, over the next years green product innovation is destined to become more and more widespread, representing the only way for society to effectively face the challenges of resource limitations and increases in waste and pollution.

Then, if you asked me how I see the future of innovation in one word, I would answer: I see it 'green'!

We have taken the liberty to checking out the Italian cement company's product and this is what we found:

What does Italcementi's TX Active® product line consist of? TX Aria® – *Linea Ambiente (Environment Line), with its de-polluting effect, is the specific binder for paints, mortars and "rasanti" (leveling compounds), plasters & coatings, and concrete for photoactive building elements. TX Aria® can effectively abate the airborne harmful pollutants that are produced by human activities (industry, transport and residential heating units). TX Aria® can be used for both horizontal and vertical structures as well as tunnels, where air quality and safety conditions are eventually improved. TX Aria® is the first active way in battle against store of substances coming from smog.*

Isn't that amazing? Walls, paints and cement that absorb pollution! Of course, it would be better not to produce pollutants in the first place but, realistically, before we reach that stage it's quite a way to go. If in the meantime we can limit the damage we do we have already made important progress.

And yet again we hear about the need to understand the system well beyond the individual product. Rosa also acknowledges that taking environmental considerations into account increases levels of complexity – more aspects to consider, more possible interaction between the different aspects. But can we really afford to ignore this?

One aspect is made clear by Part IV as well as both Kate and Rosa's contributions: we need to re-evaluate, reconnect, re-assess how we go about doing things. Dorothea Seebode acknowledges that this is quite difficult but does not stop there. Conversations are great to facilitate such a process; having a framework to help structure such conversations is even better. We are delighted that Dorothea is sharing the framework she has developed here with all of us here. Her framework helps understand what is needed, and that it is actually us, as individuals, who have to change in order to affect the bigger picture. And by the way, keep a look out for a book and a website on The Future of Sustainability!

The Future of Innovation is Reconnecting to Life

Name	**Dorothea Seebode**
Affiliation	Royal Philips Electronics; Philips Research
Position	Senior Director Sustainability
Country	Germany
Area	Innovation facilitating sustainable development
Email	dorothea.seebode@philips.com

**sustainability   disruptive innovation   eco-system change   co-creation
transition**

'Re-connecting to the fundamentals of life' is in my view the essence of the innovation we need to realize *now* to secure our future.

The world's vital innovation challenges can be directly derived from the WWF's powerful *Living Planet Report* 2006. From it we see a world populated by societies that are out of balance, as the developed nations over-consume while less developed nations are not able to provide their people with sufficient health care, education and employment. Already today on global average we consume beyond the biocapacity of the *one* planet we share.

In our current globalised industrial socioeconomic system, regional and global problems are highly interlinked. They can only be solved once we really understand the causes for the current crises, manage to coherently align on environmental, social and economic priorities, and agree on consistent action aiming to re-establish healthy symbiotic, closed-loop ecosystems. Such an ambition is not a minor one. Yet realising how immense this challenge is, and then making it explicit as *the* globally shared innovation priority would not be a bad start.

How could that happen? Conversations facilitated by the *innovation framework for sustainable development* help to uncover how to facilitate a transition from the current economic paradigm to one more balanced.

In Figure 2 the horizontal dimension represents the nature of 'ecosystem change', providing a space for 'incremental' innovations within

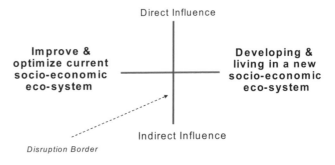

Innovation Framework for Sustainable Development

Figure 2   Direct and indirect personal influence

the existing industrial paradigm. These help to 'flatten' the currently observable unsustainability on the left side. Here notions like 'energy efficiency' play an important role. On the right side, radical or breakthrough innovation will facilitate the build-up of a new socioeconomic system. Renewable energy plays an important role and a closed-loop economy will require new financial mechanisms, business models and impact metrics.

The vertical dimension captures people's influence on the required change, recognising that everyone can change her or his behaviour. The upper half represents the spaces in which people have direct influence on their lives (e.g., at home or in their professional lives), while the bottom part captures those spaces that can only be influenced indirectly (e.g., by a political vote or by joining an NGO).

For a multinational corporation optimised to deliver to the mass in the current industrial paradigm, one of the biggest challenges is to understand the 'disruption border' between the existing and the emerging system and adjust its governance, management styles, business and innovation processes and product offers accordingly. It will be essential to uncover 'industrial paradigm myths' and sense 'emerging paradigm values'. We are currently locked in a prison of existing infrastructures and regulations that hinder new technologies to unfold their potential; emerging needs of 'Cultural Creatives' often stay unserved. Investment decisions should be made under new criteria and should be financial flows redirected. The future of innovation is about finding transition paths leading us from the mass-oriented industrial paradigm to the networked knowledge society, co-creating context relevant, closed-loop solutions respecting the limits of our planet.

Reconnecting to the fundamentals of life and learning from nature could inspire the disruptive innovation required to find a new path towards 'symbiotic prosperity'.

Wow, an invitation to challenge our most fundamental assumptions around our 'operating principles' at the organisational as well as the societal level. Within her last sentence Dorothea draws together a number of key threads found in many contributions: knowledge society, networking, co-creation, closed-loop, or cradle to cradle, solutions. The wonderful thing is that Philips is taking this framework forward, and you can follow its development at www.bamboostones.net.

Kate quoted the Hopi Indians saying, "We are the ones we have been waiting for"; Dorothea says. "Everyone has to change his or her behaviour". We have to face the mirror, and start with ourselves if we want to affect others. Not a comfortable thought for most of us. It's easy to say "things have to change". It is rather more difficult to say, "I have to change" – and not only say it but also act on it.

However, preaching without practicing is no longer acceptable. Sincerity and authenticity are key. If you do not really mean this people will sense your doubts in your tone of voice and spot it in your actions. For example, if you say radical innovation is important, and than shut down the long term, speculative project in favour of rescuing next quarter's results, the message will be heard loud and clear. If you say you want innovation, and follow up by saying, but it should fit in with existing operations processes and structures, the message is loud and clear: innovation is nice, but not really that important. And each individual will set their own priorities accordingly. You need to live what you believe and believe what you live. The future of innovation is about people, from people, for people. The future of innovation will be to improve the course of humanity. Or, as Lotte Darsø puts is, "The future of innovation will serve humanity first".

The Future of Innovation is Humanity Before Economy

Name	**Lotte Darsø**
Affiliation	University of Aarhus
Position	Associate Professor in Innovation
Country	Denmark
Area	Social innovation, innovation pedagogies
Email	LDA@dpu.dk

artful   co-creation   humanity   leadership   learning

The future of innovation will serve humanity first. Instead of business models we will have partnership models for innovation based on diversity, participation and co-creation. Economy will be considered a means to generate innovation and the economical profit that is produced will be fed back into new cycles of innovation *for* a sustainable world. The future of innovation depends, however, on the quality of our thinking and on the level of our moral development. It depends on the audacity of our visions and hopes for the world. It depends on learning from our mistakes and on using the wisdom gained.

Innovation is powerful. Through innovation we can solve the most important problems and challenges of the world, but through innovation we could also destroy and thus create even bigger problems. Inherent in innovation are the powers to create goods, services, communities, infrastructures and technologies. The future of innovation must be dedicated at serving humanity in creating sustainable food and health, in creating jobs, in creating community, in short it must focus on sustaining life. In the future nobody will waste energy, time or money on creating and producing yet another product only to compete with masses of similar products. On the contrary, people will serve the needs of the world by following their wildest dreams of creating products that make a difference. Products that help others survive and thrive, products that are well thought out as not endangering any species or planet earth.

There is much to be done. Every conscientious human being must mobilise his or her talent in order for our wanted future of innovation to materialise. I'm currently working with education and learning: Leadership and Innovation in Complex Systems (www.laics.net). I strongly believe in learning as the way forward – not teaching, training or educating – but rather understood as providing fertile grounds for creating local and global learning communities, for connecting people, for hosting dialogues and for developing leadership. We need new ideals and role models for leadership. We must support leaders who *care* about people and planet – and profit, of course, but as a means, not an end – and who make wise decisions and know how to nurture and support people in creating genuine value. Innovation must have direction and must be meaningful to the people involved. We need leaders, who can lead corporations and multinationals through powerful and meaningful visions for creating beneficial global growth. We need courageous leaders, who value humans more than profit and who dare to open new doors and walk new routes for innovation. We need artful leaders, who are conscious of the multiplicity of forms, expressions and 'languages' that can help surface human talents and resources, and help connect people across the planet around important challenges.

The future of innovation involves compassionate partnerships where people generate values and qualities, which will build a far more vital and durable economy than we experience today. The key to the future is, in fact, social innovation.

Now how is that for a challenge: placing sustainability instead of economic profit at the core of our paradigm! While the essence has been lurking in many contributions Lotte is the first one to mention it explicitly: 'The future of innovation depends ... on the level of our moral development.' A tall order, and a great challenge, particularly when large parts of the world's population are still struggling to satisfy most basic needs such as access to clean water and food. A tall order it might be but we do have to aspire to achieve it. Lotte also identifies what is needed to help us move towards a new kind of morality: learning and leadership.

The sense of urgency and call for a comprehensive review of our most fundamental assumptions and paradigms is not only felt in the developed countries such as the USA, Italy, Germany and Denmark from where our contributions in this section have come from so far. The need is shared and felt with the same urgency in emerging countries, as you can read in the contribution by Chin Hoon Lau from Malaysia.

The Future of Innovation is Enabling Hope at the Frontiers of Systems, Values and Politics

Name	**Chin Hoon Lau**
Affiliation	Johor Legislative Assembly
Position	State Assemblyman for Pemanis
Country	Malaysia
Area	Innovation in culture and politics
Email	lauchinhoon@gmail.com

humanity   systemic   value   political   innovation divide

The future of innovation is tightly coupled to its ability to enable the future in the way humanity aspires to. Humanity is very often felt through innovation. Humanity shines brighter as innovation finds its way to more and bigger purposes. Humanity is where innovation triumphs and its future is assured.

This very uncertain time, which can be hard and cause suffering, blesses us with a historic window for rebuilding. Seeking collective security and strength, a nation may choose to resurrect the past (be it in a guise romantically real or imaginarily idolised), or charge forward to innovate the future. The world will become more and more divided along the line of innovation positives and innovative negatives with widening conflicts and confrontations.

To fill up this innovation gap, every nation and responsible leader needs to know where they stand in the scheme of global innovativeness, which will be an indication of the state of their future. Present competitive and productivity reports, which are a picture of our immediate past, are definitely insufficient to diagnose and identify weaknesses in human capital development strategy and investment. A global comparative study of innovation capability of nations is called for to enable positive intervention, support and international collaboration at an earliest possible stage. Such global innovation commons will definitely be more productive than the 'new world order'. Furthermore, shared boundary innovation made feasible through the intensified cross-cultural interactions shall alleviate the 'clash of civilisations'.

Political leaders tend to get addicted if not tied up to vested interests in the status quo. As a result, they rarely learn and innovate. Change takes place normally only as a response to external pressure. As the innovation projections of a nation become available, political parties and stakeholders will have to be more accountable to and be evaluated by what they have done to secure a better future for their people, rather than hiding under historical report cards or present tangibles.

There is a need for intervention at the most sensitive roots of problems or needs of most nations: their value systems. The mismatch of value over time, space and contextual framework, or its mismatch with the desired outcome, is the main cause of loss in economic sustainability, social cohesion and, most sadly, the opportunity to advance. Innovation frameworks and tools must be utilised to translate intangible values into a quantitative value scoreboard; for instance, to project how by degrading the public education system into a tool for political agenda or religious utopia, the children will be deprived of being educated as liberated beings with the knowledge and strength needed to guard their traditions.

Innovation must not be perceived as another disappointing piece of cancer research. Innovation does not just work on laboratory mice. Innovation works on humans too. Advances in innovation in corporate management and technology can be drawn to help leaders solve complex problems. Systemic innovation is the path where the building blocks of experience cross and come to a synthesis and identify further challenges, and this is where decision-makers place their hope.

Chin Hoon too has picked up the topic of humanity, of the need to rebuild and the important role of leadership. He too emphasises the need to look into the mirror to identify our weaknesses, to discover what we need to change and to collaborate across the globe to realise the innovation that is needed.

We also like his reference to 'guarding their traditions'. Innovation does not mean discarding what has been before, but it does mean re-evaluating what has been before with the ambition of preserving what is worth preserving, and changing what needs to be changed.

In our penultimate contribution of the 11th hour we hear how Lynne Schneider knits together the strands of complexity, sustainability, government and local communities.

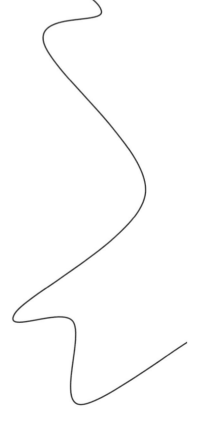

The Future of Innovation is Peace Driven by Local Communities

Name	**Lynne Schneider**
Affiliation	Enterprise Strategies and Solutions Inc.
Position	President
Country	USA
Area	Economic and wealth creation/stability operations
Email	lynne.schneider@att.net

community   entrepreneur   peace   innovation   local

Our world in this 21st century is more complex than most of us had imagined, with an interdependence of people everywhere more profound than we had realised and with challenges, risks and reverberations that most of us cannot claim to be able either accurately to predict or adequately to understand. More than ever, rigid doctrines and dogmas are inadequate and counterproductive. Accurate observation, careful analysis and a basic, common commitment to good governance, at all levels, in all spheres, are required if we are to avoid upheavals, political, social and economic. Social, cultural and economic, rule of law and governance factors are so intertwined in what we call 'development' or stabilisation that it is at our own peril that we will emphasise one at the expense of the others. Indeed, globalisation itself now makes it mandatory, more than ever, for us to seek innovative approaches and solutions that are holistic to the challenges and the opportunities of development. It is crucial that these innovative and sometimes simple solutions are developed in partnership with the local indigenous population, who in the end must live with the results.

If there are faulty infrastructures and inadequate public systems, weak markets and limited opportunity, it becomes exceedingly difficult to build healthy cities and villages where people can have a realistic chance to move out of poverty – specifically when there is war raging in the streets. Sustainability is central to stability whether it be in microfinance institutions or in medical and educational institutions or in restored historical sites, monuments and urban parks. The ability to develop and manage both financial and operational efforts with cost-effective budget and the necessary control systems, appropriate planning and strategic positioning, transparency and good governance are all essential.

Experience shows that the development of an active, organised and effective civil society is the strongest assurance not only of continued economic development at the grass-roots level, but also of social stability. Civil society can advance the public good through the creation of private institutions, including not-for-profit but self-sustaining institutions, which counterbalance the habit of looking primarily to government to address the full range of local social needs and therefore undermining the very goals which we seek.

Examples of innovative and creative solutions to alleviate poverty and to improve the quality of life of the local population abound. Innovative solutions need not be complicated and the efforts to collaborate with the local indigenous population must seek to leave behind institutions and civil societies that are, or have become stable, competent and self-reliant. Only then will peace endure.

Innovation to alleviate poverty, innovation to achieve sustainability, innovation for peace and, most importantly, innovation with those affected by it, rather than for them. We like to think that people do not resist change so much as they resist being changed. People, local communities, need to be involved in innovation, and in creating a sustainable future.

We would like to close this section with another story – or rather the vision that Osman Ahmed has created of a sustainable future.

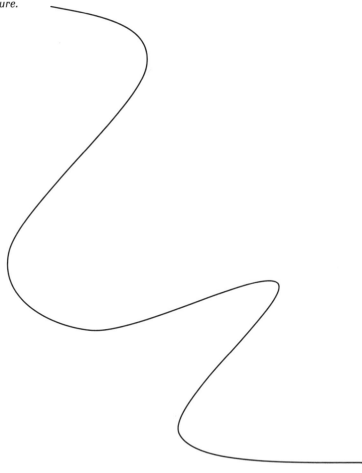

The Future of Innovation is Sustainable Building and Environment

Name	**Osman Ahmed**
Affiliation	Siemens Building Technologies, Inc.
Position	Head, Global Research and Innovation
Country	USA
Area	Building, energy, environment, and sustainability
Email	osman.ahmed@siemens.com

building   energy   environment   sustainability

It was a dark winter morning in a suburban Chicago town, the year 2030. Thomas Jones, a proud director of operations for this sprawling community, is about to start a new day. Tom's township just won an award for being the first to become completely carbon neutral, for recycling 100 per cent and reclaiming all its utilities, meaning that no landfill is required. His town operates a solar thermal station and a Photovoltaic plant, a wind farm and a natural gas based co-generation where it can burn trash and bio-fuels.

But what makes this town so innovative is how it shares its carbon neutral programme with several cities around the world. Interestingly, it is the town's plants and the infrastructure systems that share information with other plants of the sister cities; they learn from one another's experience autonomously for better overall carbon performance. In another example, a nano-wall supplies solar power for both cooking and lighting for homes in suburban Harare. However, that same technology, with some tuning, can also convert an office interior wall into a display for computing or personal conferencing. The office is located where Tom lives.

Behind the prairie settings of Tom's town, breakthrough innovations are at work to make the township and its lifestyle sustainable. A high-capacity nG wireless network serves as the main communication artery. In addition to providing infotainment, the network picks up the readings of about a million of intelligent wireless sensors along with the location of each occupant and creates innovative solutions. For example, Tom knows precisely how much water is needed for each section of the landscaping, thus eliminating the need to water the entire landscape. Tom shares same technology with Qingdao's eco-block in China that advises residents when to wash clothes and at what temperature settings. The same network provides Tom with a real-time train schedule, offering free rides and a few free carbon brownies. The train company operates a variable-schedule and variable-capacity train operation in order to minimise the municipality's overall operating carbon footprint by synchronising each passenger's morning schedule. The actual train schedule then is used to optimise the entire local transportation systems including buses, trams and electric cars, even organising the charging of batteries.

Tom was born in 1990 and as a young adult he saw how global financial meltdown and economic downturn impacted the life of millions around the globe. But economic challenges also brought the world together and people found innovative solutions for global problems such as climate change and carbon footprint. Technology innovations were made in the areas of material science, ubiquitous and pervasive intelligent sensing, hyperconnectivity, bio-mimicry, knowledge creation and sharing, and above all helped to create a new, shared mindset focused on sharing and applying technology innovations for a peaceful and sustainable global living. The examples from nature influenced and taught humans to look for sustainable solutions in a big way such as nano-material for building found to behave like stone, exhibiting superior thermal performance but using low-embedded energy or honeycomb structures found to be superior in retaining heat within a home.

Unlike his parents, Tom enjoys richer life experience because an intelligently connected and networked physical world often works autonomously or semi-autonomously. The sharing of technology across the borders without any boundaries has put global innovation on a new pedestal.

We feel that with each piece of this book a richer picture is emerging, one that is becoming increasingly difficult to refute, and one that is increasingly urgent. Not one of us can afford to stand on the sidelines, we all share the responsibility, we all share the responsibility to act.

Having said this, a responsibility to act at the personal level alone is not enough. We have already heard learning and education being mentioned, and the odd reference to political leaders and governments being made. While the responsibility for finding solutions can certainly not be left to politicians and governments, as Lynne has pointed out, they certainly have an important role to play. In the following section we share more contributions that particularly emphasised the role of education and government – let's see what people have to say!

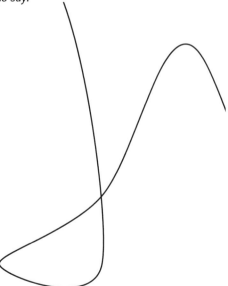

PART VI
The Roles of 'Big Brother' and Education

Particularly in Part V we have emphasised the importance of all of us taking responsibility, and of all of us embracing and engaging with the necessary change. However, while this remains utterly and undeniably true there is of course also a role for governments to play! One aspect that is emphasised in this section is the role of education. The way we learn, the way we think, what skills and viewpoints are imbued in us shapes our attitude towards creativity, experimentation and investigating alternatives as well as taking initiative and feeling responsible.

So what did our contributors have to say about that? What is it that they believe government can and should do? And why is it so important to keep a close eye on education?

Atta-ur-Rahman, our first contributor, provides a nice agenda of how and where governments might want to focus.

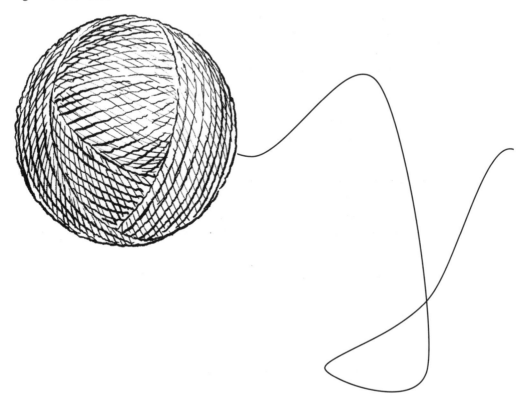

The Future of Innovation is in Unleashing the Creative Potential of Your HR

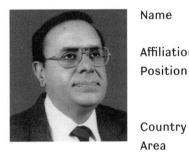

Name	**Prof. Dr Atta-ur-Rahman,** FRS, UNESCO Science Laureate
Affiliation	COMSTECH/Pakistani Government
Position	Coordinator General/Federal Minister/Chairman, Higher Education Commission Advisor for Science and Technology to the Prime Minister
Country	Pakistan
Area	Medicinal chemistry, spectroscopy, higher education, cricket
Email	ibne_sina@hotmail.com

**creativity   socio economic development   technology
foresight   entrepreneurship   knowledge economy**

We live in a world in which natural resources have diminishing importance. It is the ability of nations to innovate through unleashing the creative potential of their human resources, thereby allowing them to develop new products and processes, which determine the process of socioeconomic development. Nations which have realised this paradigm shift that has taken place over the last few decades and have invested massively in strengthening science, technology and innovation, and prepared the necessary high-quality human resources have progressed rapidly, leaving others behind.

The future of innovation will be dependent on the following key factors:

1. **Appropriate educational systems:** An educational system which unleashes the creative talent of the young is essential for innovation. The educational process should make the students understand the basic underlying principles, and apply them to solve real-life problems.

    This requires a substantially different type of education to be imparted, focused not only on the mastery over the subject but also on the development of various other skills such as the ability to think critically, innovate, communicate effectively, work efficiently in teams, develop entrepreneurship and risk-taking skills, and face and manage changes in a flexible and enterprising manner.

2. **Attracting creative workers:** It is important to develop and introduce a system of facilities and incentives that attracts the brightest youth towards scientific careers and a system which supports and rewards innovation. This would require investment in building a solid infrastructure for research and internationally competitive salaries.

3. **Fostering innovation/technology foresight exercises:** Dynamic innovation systems involve an interplay between a number of different parts of the society which include the government, private sector, universities and research institutions. Countries need to formulate their

respective science, technology and innovation (STI) policies, after carrying out comprehensive technology foresight exercises.

4. **Science and technology parks and business incubators:** Science and technology parks and business incubators will play an increasingly important role for promotion of innovation in the future. These should provide (i) office/lab space for new start-up companies in cutting edge and emerging fields for development of innovative products and processes; (ii) legal and business services to facilitate patent filing, company formation, business plan development etc. (iii) access to highly qualified workers in closely located universities and laboratory facilities in the universities.

5. **Incentivisation of private sector R&D:** In order to promote innovation, governments will need to encourage the private sector to invest in establishing R&D facilities by (i) offering tax relief on R&D investments; (ii) providing grants from the government to the private sector for establishing and operating laboratories; and (iii) offering long-term tax holidays on new high-tech products developed on the basis of indigenous R&D.

6. **Knowledge networking:** Increasing globalisation is creating huge opportunities for reaching across continents and benefiting from investors in distant lands. The future of innovation will be linked to the ability of the inventors to be able to disseminate the information about their discoveries as widely as possible in order to derive maximum benefit from global opportunities. For this to take place effectively, knowledge networks must be created through the collaboration of government research laboratories and industry at the regional, national and international levels.

The explosive growth of knowledge is resulting in rapid technological changes. The future of nations will therefore depend on their ability to compete globally through innovation and effective change management.

Atta's advice places a very strong emphasis on education – and a different kind of education than the sort we are likely to find today. If the emphasis is on creativity, experimentation and lifelong learning than we cannot preach about 'one right way' nor should we use multiple choice exams to test successful 'knowledge transfer'.

What we would also like to emphasise from his contribution is Atta's urgent advocacy for a systemic approach. Doing one particular thing is not enough, it is the systemic approach that makes a difference, combining an creativity-encouraging education system with the development of a networked infrastructure in which players from different parts of society can interact and innovate. The future will belong to those countries who are able to provide such context.

Our next contributor, Hyam Nashash, provides another interesting argument why focusing on education – focusing on our children – is so important.

The Future of Innovation is Innovation for All

Name	**Dr Hyam Nashash**
Affiliation	Al Balqa' Applied University
Position	Faculty Member
Country	Jordan
Area	Innovation in education
Email	hyam_nashash@yahoo.com

simplicity   educators   educational systems   creativity   network of innovators

The future of innovation is perceived as the right path that will advance a sense of overcoming the real challenge of making governments effective and responsive to the needs of citizens by bringing together the common features and aspects among people to share and replicate.

Further, the future of innovation is best viewed as the process involving learning and knowledge management that will serve citizens and strengthen democracy. It heavily relies on guidelines for good practice, in which empowerment and accountability are considered the base criteria to nourish innovations.

But the financial crisis, escalating wars, unemployment, diseases and, above all, poverty are all issues that affect the world, stunting its ability to stimulate the environment in order to reach the best possibilities in achieving a better life for citizens.

Searching for common ground to serve those who need to be served, you need to think of everyone; in this case we have to draw a clear pathway to build a global network of innovators that can share and disseminate the knowledge and provoke the world to decrease the differences among people.

Simplicity is the key to things that should be accessible by everyone. Achieving that is what we call innovation. Dreams are our path, and activating those dreams is the process of turning hopes into plans. So, to attain that, I believe that children are our target; they should get involved in connecting their dreams and turning them into reality, through our providing the adequate environment. And to do so, getting into the educational system is the perfect way to smooth the boundaries between adults and children, to make those boundaries much more porous.

Moreover, let the educators keep an open eye on the kids while trying to provoke them to always keep an open mind, because it is the silly questions and imagination triggered by nature, the sort that children ask and dream up, that eventually lead to creative thinking. While testing the extreme questions and ideas that come up, educators can explain any misunderstandings and help the children keep improving the idea to what they consider an innovation.

True creativity and innovation are thinking what no one else has thought about and doing things in a different, simple manner. And when doing that, the right tool has to be grasped. Serendipity may be useful to generate ideas and turn on the imagination that helps the process of creation our new world, where different ideas from different resources are the solution.

Champions have to be found and maps and guidelines have to be drawn in order to establish a network of innovators. They ought to be linked by innovative links, have different specialisations, and trust the knowledge we have developed.

Accordingly, pioneering is hindered by the difficulty of knowing what to do next, and we know that every innovation is restricted by invisible forces. But, we have to continue searching and trying, and that's what we call the future of innovation: innovation for all.

Finally, innovation is not limited to the creation of new ideas but it also promotes social responsibility and inspirational capacity that can benefit all, and novelty must be there to tackle challenges as well.

We just love Hyam's statement that 'Dreams are our path, and activating those dreams is the process of turning hopes into plans.' We love the idea of innovation for all, of innovations for which dreams lead the way, a new generation that is being praised for asking silly questions. Does that not sound rather different from what we are experiencing today? What is the reaction to 'silly' questions in your organisation, in your department, in your family?

Hazim El-Naser continues the story by emphasising the link between technological innovation and a country's competitiveness, offering his thoughts on government's role in enabling this, and asking what particular challenges for Arab countries might be.

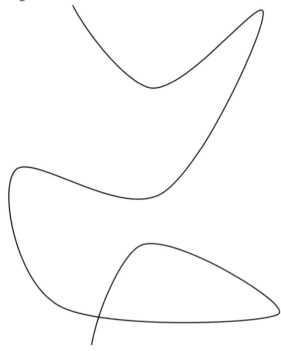

The Future of Innovation is Infrastructure and Competitiveness

Name	**Hazim K. El-Naser**
Affiliation	Chairman, Orient for Engineering Consultancy and Design
Position	Member of the Jordan's House of Representatives; Former Minister of Water and Irrigation and Minister of Agriculture
Country	Jordan
Area	Infrastructure and competitiveness
Email	hazim_elnaser@yahoo.com

infrastructure   research   development   competitiveness   innovation

The future of innovation is driven by technology's ability to create new forms of value, and where competitiveness is a major performance engine towards achieving socioeconomic success within the social, economic, policy and political schemes. In fact, technological innovation and competitiveness go hand in hand in the creation of internationally tradeable products that are competitive in terms of cost and quality with those of other nations.

In a national context, competitiveness is related to the innovative capacity that a country has. The process of innovation is now considered to be the driving force for competitiveness in order to maintain national sustainability, reduce poverty and increase the standards of living.

Technological innovation is driven by how much countries or firms spend on research and development (R&D), which involves constant improvements to the cost, process, efficiency, quality and quantity of products.

The responsibility of innovation does not only lie with the private sector: governments have a very important role to play in building, improving and shaping the market economy, and in finding new means and environments for healthy governed competition. Governments should provide the following main functions: (i) provide macroeconomic stability; (ii) set up the necessary legal system and regulatory framework including competition and entry and exit laws; and (iii) address market failures i.e. having the right policies.

Improving all those aspects requires true and effective partnership between governments and their private sector in sharing this responsibility specifically through areas such as (i) education, (ii) technology and innovation, and (iii) physical infrastructure.

A simple question – yet complicated and critical – that everybody in our region enquires about is why Arab countries are still lacking in technological innovation and are less competitive in the world's global market. The answer is not easy; however, some thoughts can be shared in order to identify major proposals and approaches that are of great importance to our future economies and for the sustainability of the generations to come.

As mentioned earlier the key to innovation and competitiveness is R&D. Unfortunately, despite the strong economies in some of the Arab countries, R&D expenditure is the lowest of all similar economies. That spending on R&D is only modest is clear in the academia arena, and even then, what spending there is is mostly for promotional purposes. Most of such research is theoretical and not linked to industrial and societal needs. Such R&D is mainly supported by international agencies and local governments. When it comes to R&D for the benefit of the private sector, it is usually minimal and lacks any sorts of financial allocation. Some private sector entities and industries allocate some financing for R&D but it is mostly for the sake of promotion, compliance with national laws or to get some benefits of tax exemption as stipulated in certain tax laws in some countries.

Mobilisation of private sector resources within the Arab world to boost innovation and infrastructure development is essential to achieve long-term goals of competitiveness. However, in order to motivate the private sector, the establishment of a re-ordered regulatory framework and the introduction of competitive markets and commercial practices into the related sectors are essential steps to enhance the innovative role of the private sector.

The ultimate objective for Arab countries is to enhance their living standards and to catch up with the developed world in terms of income and technology through innovation and entrepreneurship. Increases in labour productivity, a well-functioning market economy, institutional development and necessary government actions are the key to achieving sustained long-run growth in living standards.

A clear call for action from policy makers and governments; and a clear mandate for innovation to play its role in the improvement of people's lives.

Mario Coccia picks up the story suggesting that it is the conditions of democracy that provide the most fertile ground for innovation due to the fact that it is human processes that underlie both democracy and technological innovation.

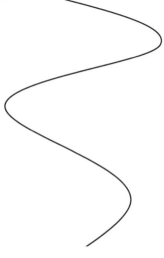

The Future of Innovation is Through Democratisation

Name	**Dr Mario Coccia**
Affiliation	National Research Council of Italy and Max Planck Institute of Economics
Position	Economist
Country	Italy
Area	Economics of innovation and political economy of science
Email	m.coccia@ceris.cnr.it

**technological innovation   democratization richness   economic growth
human resource investments   better living**

Nowadays the best opportunities to improve living standards and reduce poverty come from technological innovation, which is a leading factor underlying economic growth. According to my point of view, based on our scientific findings, *there is higher technological innovation when the countries have more democratisation.* Democracy is the best environment and political regime under which technology can originate, develop and diffuse, generating benefits for firms, institutions and people. Democracy and technological innovation richness can transform today's luxury goods into tomorrow's cheaper and widespread goods and provide services that lead to longer, better and healthier living.

In other words, 'democracy-intensive countries' generate a higher rate of technological innovation, since democratisation is an antecedent process (*cause*) to technological innovation (*effect*), which is also a major well-known determinant of economic growth. This insight is important, very important in the modern era to support future economic growth in view of the accelerating globalisation.

Why does democratization have positive effects on technological innovation? The determinants of these fertilising effects of democratisation on technological innovation and in general technical change are due to higher levels of literacy, schooling, education and media access, broadening the middle classes and reducing the extremes of poverty. In short, the underlying causes of this positive relationship between democratisation and technological innovation are due to the vital role of human capital in both processes.

However, democracy has also some drawbacks. Pareto points out that democracy can turn into plutocratic demagogy: the governing class is made up of people who try to govern in their own interest, arousing support through cunning and deceit. Moreover, the recent terrorism wave is a form of warfare that is a continuous threat against freedom and democracies. Although these drawbacks as well as threats to democracies, which are friction forces to the diffusion of technological innovation, scholars, policy makers, and politicians, in the future they will have to focus much more on policies based on sustainable democratisation processes that, as proven, support science, technology, and innovation and therefore economic growth and global wealth and well-being of countries and worldwide community.

If Hazim's argument was one of innovation for economic growth and competitiveness, Mario shares the interesting observation that you are most likely to see innovation thrive under democratic circumstances. In other words, if you would like your country to be competitive, you need innovation, and if you want to see innovation, you need to encourage democracy! Democracy drives competitiveness, now there's an interesting thought ...

Drawing on three contributions we feel that a new wave of democratisation of and innovating in politics is already happening! The first witness we would like to call upon is Carol Patrick who draws our attention to local government innovating, not least out of necessity. Our second witness, Rodica Doina Dănăiată, shares two specific examples of e-government with us while our third witness, William Lightfoot, reminds us of recent consequence of social networking on politics, not least the 2008 election outcomes in the United States.

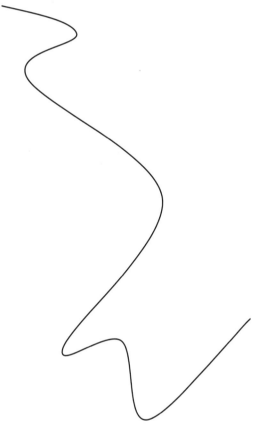

The Future of Innovation is Innovation with a Public Face

Name	**Carol Patrick**
Affiliation	Kent County Council
Position	Head of Innovation
Country	UK
Area	Innovation management
Email	carol.patrick@kent.gov.uk

public   transformational   culture   risk   local

Since starting my job, nearly 18 months ago, many people have said to me 'There is nothing new about innovation', which is strange when you think about it as that is precisely what innovation is.

Despite rumours to the contrary, the public sector and, more specifically, local government have always been innovative. To be fair it has to be – money and resources are always in short supply, daily demands from central government and the public and its political focus has ensured that innovative practices, services and processes are the life blood of any local authority.

Compared to central government we are far more agile. We are not remote from our customers but present in every locality. We have to meet the needs of a large, dispirit group of individuals and communities and therefore we cannot afford to remain static.

Local government is a transforming and transformative place. We have to be inclusive, diverse, accessible and simple. Our services must be understandable, be underpinned by great design, flexibility and focus. We need to be all things to all people whilst retaining a personal look and feel.

This is in essence an overview of what all innovative organisations should be.

We have to retain core products but deliver them in new and exciting ways. We need to remain efficient and cost effective without losing that personal touch. At a time when it would be easier to retain the status quo, the majority of local authorities continue to strive for innovative ways to make the lives of its customers better and easier.

Maintaining an innovative culture can be and often is difficult to maintain. The huge pressures on most staff to deliver day-to-day services can push out innovative ideas. This is particularly true in these difficult financial times when meeting targets can become the key driver – something that needs to be guarded against. I would argue that it is now that real and sustainable innovation can be most beneficial – if you can keep the faith. We need to keep risk in proportion and look at the endgame. Staff should continue to be encouraged to develop and share ideas and use new communication platforms to manage knowledge across a wider arena.

We need to ensure that we better enable individuals, communities and businesses to share in an 'innovation world'. This is I believe is the most exciting part of being involved in innovation at a local level. There is a palatable sea change in this area and increasingly residents are now actively engaged in developing innovative ideas, on their terms.

I look forward to seeing even greater ideas emerging from local government and believe that this sector will continue to lead the way when innovation is discussed.

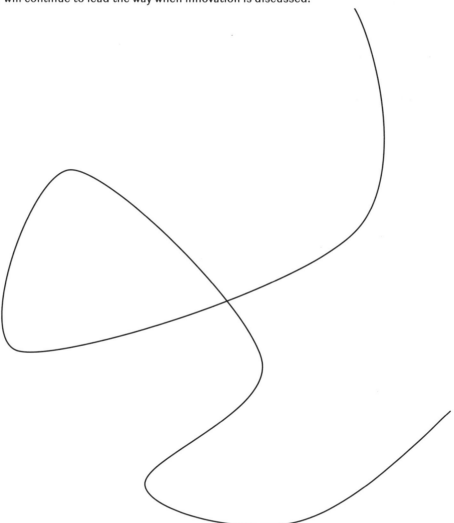

The Future of Innovation is in e-Government

Name	**Rodica Doina Dănăiată**
Affiliation	Universitatea de Vest Timisoara
Position	Professor
Country	Romania
Area	E-government
Email	doina.danaiata@feaa.uvt.ro

electronic government (e-government)   transformational government
(t-government)   e-government as a system   information ecology   co-evolution

Technological and institutional innovation in public administration usually goes by the name of electronic government. I have selected some innovative approaches that in my opinion can play an important role in the future.

The Transformational Government Approach

Twenty-first-century government is enabled by technology: policy is inspired by it, business change is delivered by it, customer and corporate services depend on it, democratic engagement is exploring it. Technology alone does not transform government, but governments cannot transform to meet the 21st-century citizen's expectations without it.

Known as an initiative of the UK government, *transformational government* (t-government) is an ambitious vision for the delivery of public services in the 21st century, using the power of new technologies to change the way government works. Achieving this vision will require key transformations: citizen- and business-centred services enabled by IT, a shared services culture, governmental professionalism, a systematic focus on innovation.

But, is IT really transforming government? The answer clearly depends on what is meant by IT: an ever-expanding set of practices as well as tools. It depends still more on what is meant by transformation. Modern governments with serious transformational intent should see technology as a strategic asset and not just a tactical tool.

The Information Ecology Approach

Inspired by Davenport's work on *information ecology*, a new approach of e-government is proposed in the e-government literature. Some upholders of this approach (V. Bekkers and V. Homburg) consider that e-government can be seen as a system which is marked by strong interrelationships and dependencies between different parts. E-government is not only about the use of information communication technology (ICT), it is also concerned with other aspects of the organisational environment in which ICT is used, such as the strategy of the organisation, the qualities of staff, the dominant culture and the structure of organisation and the distribution of power and power resources within the organisation.

In an information-ecology of e-government, there are different kinds of actors and different kind of tools. Hence, actors see different kinds of opportunities for e-government. This is why it is the local context that determines what kinds of technologies and opportunities will be envisioned. This is the main reason that e-government has different features is different places, and even within the same municipality we can see a striking variety of e-government applications. Not only technological considerations play an important role in the selection process. We should also consider the interaction between the technological environment of e-government and other environments, like developments in the political, socio-organisational, cultural and economic environment. The relationship between these different environments can be understood in terms of co-evolution.

In conclusion, I believe in the innovative power of these two approaches in tandem: while the first puts emphasis on the strategic role of ICT, the second calls attention to the interaction of technological environment with other environments. If my short reflection upon the future of innovation in public administration could stimulate further thinking, experimenting and debate, maybe it is possible to innovate.

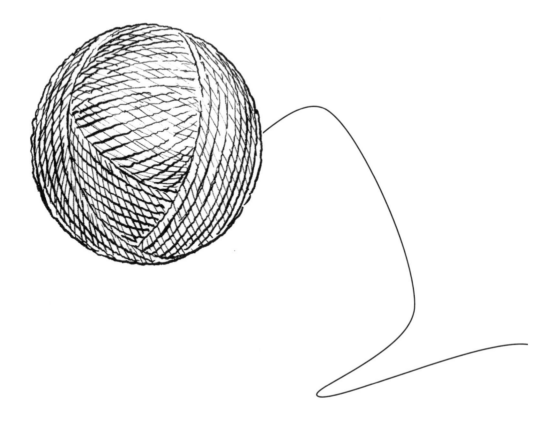

The Future of Innovation is in Social Networks and Sustainability

Name	**William S. Lightfoot, PhD**
Affiliation	Brenau University
Position	Dean, School of Business and Mass Communication
Country	USA
Area	Change management; new product development
Email	wslightfoot@gmail.com

social   networking   sustainability   green   environment

The future of innovation surely includes the effects of a couple of phenomena that are forcing upon us many new ideas, new challenges and, consequently, new and as yet unidentified innovations that will have far-reaching and longstanding impact. This essay focuses on social networking and developing a sustainable environment as the basis for future innovation.

The last few presidential elections in the United States have begun to show the power of the many ... many people linked electronically, contributing relatively small sums of money to the candidate of choice, on a repeated basis. Leveraging social networking technology, tools and techniques, candidates have begun to master the skills necessary to accelerate change. Imagine if this concept was morphed into real-time voting through the US congress, on issues and laws. Instead of politicians being 'elected' to represent us, and then free to vote according to their own interests, they instead become 'elected' to vote the way the 'instant' majority tells them to – in real time, while they are in their seat in Congress. The populace – at least those engaged actively – could both read important papers, and view (and possibly even participate in) the debate on the floor of the house or the senate regardless of location and time, and then vote. The nature of politics would change as our politicians would no longer be in control of how they vote ... the innovation is the process by which we vote – adapting social networking protocols, combining them with reality television, *et voila* – we would have a political system that would become much more compelling and influential. The technology is there ... it is our collective will that must come together to give us a greater voice in our system ... not just an occasional, third- or fourth-party one. Consider how many other ways our lives are being and will continue to be altered as a result of social networking.

The second area of interest comes from an exploration of issues related to sustainability and our environment which must come together in a way that encourages us – as stewards of the planet – to develop a healthier, more sustainable way of life. Anyone who travels to an underdeveloped or developing nation will find pollution – particularly in larger urban areas – a major issue. In Beijing, you count blue sky days, and when you have one, it defines your trip. Other cities have clans of people living off the refuse in landfills. At some point, communities will begin to develop the will to use renewable energy resources, and to learn to treat life as something to value – in all forms

– or to face imminent decay in the overall quality of life. Communities – including governments and corporations – will ultimately come together adopting policies, processes and practices in support of and continuously healthier and more sustainable lifestyles.

Are these ideas necessarily innovative? Certainly not! But within these phenomena lie the technologies, processes and societal innovations that will lead to real change, and new ways of doing things.

Wouldn't it be marvellous if the social networking tools now available to us could force some more transparency and honesty in politics? If that is already an exciting if perhaps a little exotic prospect, then how about civil servants as 'social innovations designers'? If you think this is just not credible let yourself be convinced by what Oliver Will has to say on this topic.

The Future of Innovation is Making Paradoxes Work

Name	**Oliver Christopher Will**
Affiliation	Strategy-Consultant (former civil servant)
Position	Managing Director
Country	Germany
Area	Strategy and innovation
Email	will@strategiemanufaktur.de

innovative government   living paradox(es)   social innovation designer
mastering passages   mental maps

Re-imagining the Role of Civil Service Leadership for an Innovative Society

The future of innovation – what does this mean with respect to government administrations and the civil service? Innovation in the public sector needs a different perspective, because of the long-term implications of its measures on the whole of the society and the economy.

It is a crucial task for any government administration to identify and implement new, better, more effective and more efficient solutions; in other words, to meet the challenge of being a permanent *social innovations designer*.

A globalised and flat world means to a certain extent the end of sovereignty and decision-making-processes as we have known it for the last 200 years. Governments still might be the most influential single players on the ground as we can observe in the current economic crisis, but even then they must act within governance structures rather than in a monodimensional and hierarchical way. This has been described in literature as a shift from government to governance. Probably *metagovernance* might be the more appropriate term – which means the sovereign use of all the three types of ruling: hierarchy, market and network.

What does this mean for leadership in the civil service? The crucial question is: how to innovate the mindset of the civil service? What should be the mental maps of an innovative civil service in government? Mental maps that guide beyond limitations in various perspectives.

The Balancing Map – balancing innovation and stability

Leadership in a government administration is more challenging than in any other organisation, because it cannot focus on one single interest only. A permanent rethinking capacity is necessary as well as the ability to design and implement new and innovative elements within a legal framework guaranteeing reliability and stability. Thus an innovative administration has the task to be 'a living paradox'. Examples for this are:

- stabilise the staff (-identity) to promote innovation and change;

- stabilise the organisation under uncertainty but prepare it to adopt innovations at the same time;

- stabilise government institutions whereas they are undergoing change itself and initiate social innovations in the society at the same time.

The Beyond Boundaries map – being bound but thinking beyond

An innovative government administration is a multi-perspective corpus. It is going beyond, but is bound to one strong purpose: the public good. An innovative civil service has the capacities to

- combine inside and outside perspectives;

- combine today and tomorrow perspectives;

- combine symmetric and asymmetric collaborative skills.

The Oscillodox map – choosing the appropriate side of a paradox

An innovative government administration creates and brings into practice new solutions by oscillating between contrasts. Such as:

- stability and innovation;

- commanding and cooperating;

- transforming and preserving.

An *innovative government is* and always will be accountable and responsible to their citizens, therefore it has to be a government which initiates as well as stabilises passages to the future in a world of uncertainty – *a government mastering passages.*

We quite like the idea of creating mental maps to guide innovation leadership. What is it that we need to navigate, what are the aspects to be taken into consideration? What Oliver has done is identify two key paradoxes that we need to learn how to embrace if successful innovation leadership is to become reality. In our enthusiasm for innovation we often forget that too much innovation leads us to the edge of chaos – or beyond! How much change can we cope with? How much change is helpful? How much change is necessary? To decide that is at the bottom of Oliver's balancing map. The second map, the beyond boundary map, is another interesting concept. What came to our mind is that innovation without boundaries is rather tricky! What if we asked you, 'Have you got a good idea?' What are you supposed to reply? A good idea for what, a good idea to achieve what? And if you came up with ideas, how would we know which ones would be the best, unless we had some criteria for evaluating them? Oliver refers to the criteria that should be used by civil servants for evaluating ideas the public good.

Of course, in order to have a future of innovation it is not only government that has to have an 'ability to identify and implement new, better and more effective solutions', as Oliver put it. As Susan Krup Grunin declares in her statement, 'The future of innovation lies in changing our organisations to foster creativity and innovation.' Let's read her argument.

The Future of Innovation is Dependent on Education of a Different Kind

Name	**Dr Susan Krup Grunin**
Affiliation	University of Virginia
Position	Faculty/author
Country	U.S.
Area	Organisational effectiveness/strategic human capital management
Email	skg9c@uva.edu

creativity   education   critical thinking

The future of innovation lies in changing our organisations to foster creativity and innovation in thoughts and ideas. We need to restructure our educational institutions so that students do more thinking and less memorising, develop their right brain more and are encouraged to question more. We need for our workplace cultures to allow our workers to have time to reflect and brainstorm. In order to create we have to have opportunities to collaborate and think rather than just produce. We have to break the business model and have outlets for encouraging and rewarding paradigm shift ideas.

We have to focus less on process and more on capturing the ideas that are out there. How do we capture people's passions or even dare to spark new passions? This is about involvement, motivation and educating our educators to teach from the heart and not just follow a curriculum. It is about getting us all to understand what it means to think critically; to make it okay to ask questions that need to be asked for which there may be no answers. We have to seek new perspectives and encourage an even greater exchange of ideas between our professions and occupations. New ideas often come from outside the mainstream paradigms. But unless and until we find a way to garner these ideas they may be lost forever. We have to find ways to start new conversations and to capture these ideas that are incubating.

We also have to recognise that software tools are wonderful in assisting us with collecting and sharing ideas but those tools do not replace the need for having a setting that fosters creative and innovative thinking. The internet is there as an amazing tool that could be used to inspire, reward and capture creativity and innovation. Maybe we change our patent and trademark process to allow for new ideas posted on the internet to be considered as initial patents until the legal process for awarding a patent can be completed. This might stimulate more idea sharing and less fear of losing intellectual capital for putting forth an idea that is starting to take shape. We should also find ways for individuals who do so to find some benefit and reward for generating the ideas.

We also have some critical world issues that need immediate attention and new solutions. Sustainability and the environment are two of those key issues that need innovative and creative strategies. We need to focus on how we harvest and produce regenerative energy and how we reuse, recycle and reformulate so called 'waste products.' We need to develop nanotechnology and use our software and hardware to foster ways for our scientists and engineers to solve many of our world problems.

But, unless and until we can dramatically change our educational institutions and workplace settings, we will continue to miss the next great ideas that will lead us into the new frontier … whatever that might be.

Susan argues that in order to achieve organisations that foster innovation and creativity we need to start people off on that trajectory early! Ah, how we love that! When you think about it, it also seems to make much more sense: stop educating creativity and questioning out of children in the first place and you will have less of a hard time drilling it back into them in adult life! We love even more that she uses words such as passion *and* heart *and encourages everyone to think and develop as well as collect and share ideas.*

That the current educational paradigm is clearly not set out to nurture and support creativity is illustrated by Alisdair Wiseman's story, which follows.

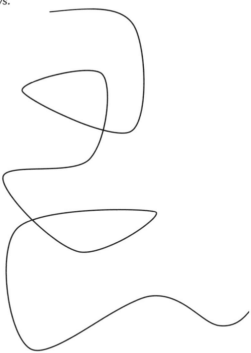

The Future of Innovation is About Aliens

Name	**Alisdair Wiseman**
Affiliation	The Innovation Zone
Position	Director
Country	United Kingdom
Area	Innovation culture, innovation behaviour
Email	alisdair@innovation-zone.com;
	www.innovation-zone.com

socialisation behaviour deviant ambiguity fuzziness

The future of innovation lies in our hands. We must all encourage innovative behaviours wherever we see them, especially in young people. Sadly, the many agents of socialisation that exist throughout society operate in completely the opposite direction. You see, society needs innovation and all the beneficial changes that flow from it. Yet, it craves the stability that comes from maintaining the status quo. This is where innovation gets into trouble because most of its principles run counter to our social programming. Society says establish order; innovation encourages chaos. Society says eliminate ambiguity; innovation revels in fuzziness. Society says conform; innovation dares to be different. In the end, society plays safe and opts for stability, keeping a watchful and often disapproving eye on what it sees as deviant innovative behaviour. Let me illustrate ...

I recently worked with an interesting chap called Simon. He admitted that he hadn't been creative since he was ten. When I asked how this could be, he told me he had arrived at school one day and the teacher asked his class to make models of aliens. So, the kids all went in alphabetic order to the 'makings' box – a chest full of old breakfast cereal packets, duct tape and the like. Simon's surname begins with 'S', so he had time to think about what he was going to do.

'My alien lives on Jupiter – a big planet with immense gravity,' he thought. 'So, my alien will be short and flat, not tall and skinny.'

I remember being incredibly impressed that a ten-year-old had such a good grasp of astrophysics. Anyway, Simon extracted an egg box and a short length of rubber tubing from the 'makings' box. They fitted his design exactly. He poked a hole in each egg well, cut the tube into six equal lengths, and inserted one into each hole in the orange-painted egg box. He was rather pleased with his alien. It could walk on its six feet, get nutrients from the surface through the bottom of the tubes and it could breathe through the tops of the tubes – very neat!

Soon, it was time to share their creations with the rest of the class. And so came a procession of humanoid aliens, each with a head, a body, two arms and two legs. When it was Simon's turn, he explained that his alien came from Jupiter and proudly presented it to the class. There was a long, tense silence. Then the teacher said,

'No, no, no, Simon! Aliens don't look like that!' (I have often wondered how she knew with such certainty that aliens didn't look like that.) Anyway, in that instant, the lights went out on Simon's creative abilities. He had dared to be different and was humiliated in front of the entire class – a lesson he wouldn't forget in a hurry.

As innovators, our mission is clear: we must encourage all forms of innovative behaviour, especially the young, if society is to reap innovation's rich reward. Go to it!

Have you ever had an experience such as Alisdair's Simon? Or are you one of the lucky ones who have escaped those who like to stamp out creativity at first sight and who can only see the world in terms of 'black and white'? Think about what kind of thinking is encouraged in schools – at least in the vast majority of schools that we are familiar with. Whatever the question is, there tends to be a clear 'right' or 'wrong'. It is one specific answer that is sought, and when you fail to deliver that particular answer you have 'failed'. Such excesses of education culminate in exams that exist of multiple-choice questions. No thinking required, just a good memory, a good short-term memory. Such kind of approach to learning and education will never lead to an ability to deal with the unexpected, it will not lead to the creation of new knowledge, it will not enable us to imagine the unimaginable. But has not Albert Einstein pointed out that, 'Unless an idea is utterly ridiculous at the outset there is not hope for it'?

Our future does not require the learning-by-heart of answers and solutions that already exist. Our future requires education that encourages the identification of new connection, of looking at what everyone has looked before but seeing what no one has seen before. Education of such kind is different, it is difficult and it is scary. How are teachers supposed to evaluate and grade? Do our teachers have the skills to provide such education?

We don't believe that we have the luxury of time to wait for the education of a new generation of teachers. Nor can we just continue on the same educational course. So, what might we be able to do? Might Tomás Garcia's idea of the innovation university be a solution?

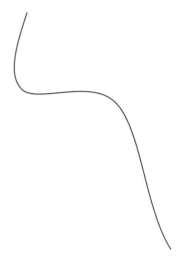

The Future of Innovation is the Innovation University

Name   **Tomás Garcia**
Affiliation Buenaidea
Position   Director
Country   Spain
Area   Innovation training and education
Email   tomas.garcia@buenaidea.es

education   design thinking   cross-fertilization   innovation management
university

This is the era of cross-fertilisation and diversity for creative thinkers. Radical innovation approaches are focusing more on hybridising different concepts to build up new and remarkable solutions. Challenges and business problems are not dealt with in only one dimension. Multidisciplinary teams providing different knowledge and skills are becoming the right melting pot to constructively generate resolutions that integrate many different and maybe not connected perspectives.

The business world is moving into a multidimensional context. Innovative companies face challenges from the technological perspective deriving their specific problem into a more generic domain (knowledge-based innovation or structured knowledge derived from the past human innovation experience) and start the search for solutions in other industries and even other worlds (i.e., nature). The generic solutions found will be used as food for thought and springboard to spark creativity to create their pursued specific solutions. At the same time, they try to understand, from a very ethnographic point of view, what are the hidden motivations and needs of their users by observing their behaviour and reaction when experiencing products and services in a given context or scenario. This user-centric innovation methodology along with design thinking skills becomes the critical capabilities of an innovative company. And what about the business perspective? Isn't it critical to find the right path for a business opportunity? Isn't it part of the innovation definition that beyond the idea and its value lies the reward of innovation?

Where do companies have to look to get these talented innovators bringing these skills and new approaches? At business schools? Design schools? Universities of technology? The answer is obviously at all three at the same time. Business, technology and design are key success factors to achieving value in innovation and if we want to officialise it as a discipline, why not reform radically the current unidimensional academic format? Why not create a University of Innovation?

Stop. The first one has been already been created. The Aalto University in Finland is a merging of the Helsinki School of Economics, the University of Art and Design and the Helsinki University of Technology aiming to build a science and art community providing new possibilities for multidisciplinary and strong education and research.

This is the first step. Then, the University of Innovation should programme all the competences, methodologies and disciplines that foster and leverage the most important enabling process in organisations: sustainable innovation. Academic innovation may also bring basic and applied research in new approaches, methodologies and models that would catalyse creativity into value in faster, easier, more efficient ways.

In a recent article, Alfons Cornella, CEO of the innovation network Infonomia, said that management is so real-time due to the speed of markets that all management becomes innovation management in the end, a management of the permanent change. That's quite an interesting subject to study at the University of Innovation.

Here it is again, one of the warps of the future of innovation's fabric: diversity. Nothing better than diversity to deal with complex situations and challenges. We don't want to throw our weight around but meeting complexity with complexity is the only way to find an adequate solution, according to the pioneer in the fields of cybernetics and systems theory, William Ross Ashby. His Law of Requisite Variety *states that: 'Any effective control system must be as complex as the system it controls.' Or in other words, a wide variety of available responses and actions is indispensable in order to ensure that a system which aims to maintain itself in a certain state can actually adapt itself satisfactorily if it is confronted with a wide variety of perturbations from the outside.*

We believe indeed that such universities of innovation are indeed emerging! They go under the word 'D-School' (at Stanford, USA, and set up with the involvement of innovation specialist IDEO), the Rotman School (part of the University of Toronto, Canada) and the Zollverein School of Management and Design (Essen, Germany, unfortunately struggling somewhat). We can also see first shoots where universities design joint courses for students of business, art and engineering, e.g., in London where the engineering and business schools of Imperial College collaborate with the Royal School of Arts, and a similar project at the afore-mentioned University of Helsinki in Finland.

For serious innovation to emerge around education Praveen Gupta sees the need to move innovation from an art to a science, and shares what a course syllabus on the science of innovation might look like.

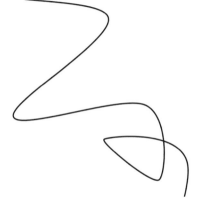

The Future of Innovation is the Science of Innovation

Name	**Praveen Gupta**
Affiliation	Accelper Consulting
Position	President, Accelper Consulting
Country	USA
Area	Innovation research and consulting
Email	Praveen@accelper.com

**business innovation   creativity   breakthrough innovation
science of innovation   innovation science**

Innovation has become a competitive advantage in the knowledge economy. The age of mass customisation has arrived when customers demand innovative solutions instead of R&D-developed products pushed through sales channels. In future, this will require innovation on demand and in real time. Such demand for innovative solutions will mean we need to transform the field of innovation from an art to a science. There needs to be more work done on engineering the innovation process for learning science behind the creativity and innovation, and develop a simple competency model to teach innovation in colleges to both faculty and students. Colleges employ tremendous intellectual resources for teaching stale material, and miss the opportunity to bring out their intellectual best.

To support the view of innovation science, we are publishing the *International Journal of Innovation Science* from the first half of 2009. We have developed a college-level curriculum to teach innovation to college students, and industry professionals. The course syllabus includes the following:

- evolution of innovation;

- the creativity, invention, and innovation;

- requirements for innovation on demand;

- innovation and cognitive science;

- the innovation framework;

- activities-based types of innovation;

- the portfolio of innovations;

- measures of innovation;

- innovation rooms or laboratories;

- idea management systems;

- 'go to market' and commercialisation;

- vision and strategy for innovation;

- innovation for growth opportunities.

Building a scientific model of the innovation process must become a necessity for academia as well as industry. In future, the innovation will become a standard business process similar to sales or purchasing process. Organisations will employ innovation leaders, innovation analysts, innovation engineers, and even innovation scientists or researchers. Universities will be teaching courses in innovation science, employees will seek certification in innovation and corporations will seek individuals with proficiency in innovation.

Moving on from the industrial age and information age, the coming years will be defined as the age of innovation. In the innovation age, people will increase the usage of their brain from the currently known average of about 5 per cent to a higher level. A slight increase in the use of the brain to generate significantly more intellectual property will be beautiful. Businesses will need to develop many innovative products every year, some businesses will let the customer design their own products and then assemble from the parts a business will offer. Businesses will need every employee's intellectual participation, not just that of R&D employees, for process, product, service or business-model innovations.

One of the most commonly asked questions is about future innovations. The auto industry may transform into a cottage industry where each car dealer will become an assembly plant for building and selling cars on demand. Personal transportation vehicles may even change from a car to a hybrid system that will fly as well as run on the road, or they might be personal flying jets with enough sensors to prevent collisions. The toy industry will be like the food industry where toys will be designed and assembled on demand in a toy cafeteria. Nanotechnology will mature such that new small shops or businesses will serve customers' specific 'nano' needs, probably creating new jobs.

Praveen seems to have read Einstein too, as the comment that we human beings only use a small portion of our brains' capacity is one often attributed to him. Creativity and lateral thinking are essential tools to make better use of our brains. Developing these skills, early on, and making these skills desirable is essential part of that journey. We need education, in the kindergarten, primary and secondary school as well as university and beyond, that encourages, nurtures, teaches and appreciates creative and innovation skills and that allows us to embrace uncertainty and thrive in emerging, ever changing conditions.

Or we need to remember to stop educating creativity out of children, and remember that ingenuity and creativity are a fundamental aspect of being human; let's remind ourselves of that, and celebrate it, as Marci Segal has started to do.

The Future of Innovation is Behaviours Change and a New World View

Name	**Marci Segal**
Affiliation	World Creativity and Innovation Week April 15–21
Position	Co-founder
Country	Canada
Area	Management consultant for creative thinking in organisations, creativity activist
Email	marci@creativityday.org

children   collaboration   creativity   Margaret Mead   fun

A child in kindergarten today will retire in 2073. What will our world be like then? We don't even know what 2011 will be like. Paraphrasing Dorothy as she told her dog Toto upon landing in Munchkinland in *The Wizard of Oz* film, 'We aren't in Kansas any more.' Conditions will have changed, so too our standards for brilliance. For example, current experimentation with three-dimensional printing may create a future where consumers download and print their own products – pens, auto parts, jewellery. Creative intelligences will be at the forefront as needed skills to embrace life and thrive in the era of innovation.

Innovation connotes society, collaboration. It occurs when others value and participate with the invention in meaningful ways. Ideas for invention are fuelled by personal creativity defined as new ideas and relevant new decisions. Everyone has the capacity for creativity and each expresses it uniquely. As Margaret Mead once said, 'In so much as a person has done something new for himself, he can be said to have committed a creative act.'

In the future for innovation, personal creativity as a desired skill base will be supported, not like it was 30 years ago. In 1980, a professor of cultural anthropology was asked by an undergraduate studying creativity[1] to define it from her perspective. 'Creativity,' the professor said, 'is bad manners. Imagine doing something creative at the dinner table. You get your hands slapped. That's what creativity is.'

What we were taught both overtly and covertly about creativity when we were small will evolve. The pre-innovation era 'hand slap' will be replaced by the innovation age 'hand shake'. We will invite curiosity, encourage the production of alternative solutions before settling in on a 'right' answer, and cultivate visualisation, the enjoyment of fantasy and fun. We will look at things from many perspectives and extend the boundaries of what is known or assumed. We will ask new questions from which we will create new solutions and we will be emotionally aware.

Our children will seek satisfaction and find the good life in ways different from our own. In schools they will learn skills and practise strengthening their social, technological, economic,

---

1   The author. It's a true story. The professor was anthropologist Dr Jill Nash at Buffalo State College, home of the International Center for Studies in Creativity.

environmental and political literacy. They will be inspired to think, question, imagine and synthesise. At home they will learn about ways to envision and manifest meaningful change from examples set by their parents.

The future of innovation will be defined as everyone having confidence in their capacity to use their creativity to make the world a better place and to make their place in the world better too. Further, people will know they can safely partner with others to allow meaningful innovations to succeed. Since 2002 people in over 48 countries have been celebrating World Creativity and Innovation Week, April 15–21, to celebrate and promote the emerging innovation era worldview. Won't you too? For information see www.creativityday.org.

Let's hope the stories told by Alisdair and Marci about attitudes towards creativity will become a shadow of the past. Let us look forward to an enlightened age where people are celebrated for the ingenuity and praised for their imagination. Did you also notice that Marci also connected to Praveen's vision of ultimate customisation and localised production?

But let's stay with the topic of children, and let's not fool ourselves that Marcia's notion that 'Our children will seek satisfaction and find the good life in ways different from our own' lies only in the future! Just hear what Sergio Alanis Rueda has to say.

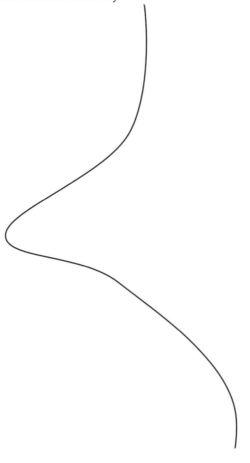

The Future of Innovation is in Linking Our Present and Our Future

Name	**Sergio Alanis Rueda**
Affiliation	Entrepreneur – technology-based business
Position	Innovation leader
Country	Mexico
Area	Product innovation
Email	checo_al@yahoo.com; salanisr@siosi.com.mx; salanisr@adetek.com.mx

Gen Y   killer-app   early-late majority   Geoffrey A. Moore   crossing the chasm

I am 35 years old, and chances are that you, like me, grew up reading the local newspaper. A printed version of course. Perhaps you still do, and maybe you are reading these lines in a printed format ... [editors' comment: *indeed you are!*]

For sure, once you used to have a 'killer-app' wired in to your living room: a 'telephone'. I am sure you won't remember your first date's phone number, but I am positive you still remember the butterflies in your stomach attached to the *ring-ring*? Remember when s/he went overseas for the summer, and you had to pay a massive phone bill to get in touch? Wait endless days to send or receive a letter in the mailbox? Insane, isn't it? Lots of time consuming activities, delays and lots of money spent. Right! But that extra effort helped us to build character, patience and discipline. Live by a natural principle: choose the right timing and location to plant a seed, water it, take care of it and wait for the harvest season. And at the same time, I bet that you grew up in a hostile environment for new ideas. Our systems were designed for standardisation, and odds are you were always a heretic.

We are innovating in the present, but our past is influencing the way we innovate today, for better or for worse. A lot of us, a lot of our companies, are still designing products for the early-late majority segment.

Still don't know what I am talking about? Don't know how much your local newspaper costs? For you a time-consuming activity is 35 seconds long? Do you use Twitter? If you do chances are you are Generation Y. Cool! You are the future of innovation. Fearless young people, that love to communicate their ideas. Bold people, who have no respect for the status quo. New citizens – not companies – who can make a contribution in order to leverage our standard of living. For them location is not an issue, and that's great, especially for developing countries like Mexico. If only we could figure out how to retain and profit from that talent.

But, is Gen Y going to have the character, patience and discipline to pull this off? They are not used to waiting until the harvest season; they want immediate satisfaction. Everything they need is at their fingertips, and most of the times for free. Effortless!

We need to learn how to link our present and our future, we are living in a unique threshold, right in the Geoffrey A. Moore chasm.[1] We need to trust Gen Y! Yes, it is a basic principle for the future of innovation. We must invite them to our new ventures; we must learn from them, we should spend more time and money with them ... so at the end of the day, we are all creating the future of innovation together.

We need both parties desperately. We cannot afford, as a society, not to cross the chasm!

Parts of what we might think is the future is here today already. Parts of the wider systems in which we operate have advanced and adapted faster than others. We need to keep pace with it, our education and political systems need to keep pace with it. If we cannot find a way to do so we will create another decisive divisor of humanity: those who know and those who don't; and such a new divisor could be as destructive and tension-ridden as the divisor of rich and poor. Education and government have a fundamental role in preventing this new rift from opening and widening.

We would like to close this section with the thoughts by Mariana Ferrari who sums up our thoughts on education in the context of innovation nicely.

1   The chasm refers to a gap between the early adopters (enthusiasts and visionaries) and the early majority (the pragmatists).

The Future of Innovation is Dependent on Innovative Behaviours

Name	**Mariana Ferrari**
Affiliation	PROCESOi
Position	CEO
Country	Spain
Area	Innovation management
Email	marianaferrari@procesoi.com

behaviour   talent   education   brain preferences

The future of innovation relies upon developing innovative behaviours in people of all ages, starting at the age of five, when kids begin their formal education and placing a special emphasis on developing innovative behaviours at work.

People who have an innovative behaviour are sensitive enough to perceive an existing problem, sufficiently creative to imagine a solution to the problem, ambitious to seek support for their idea and perseverant and goal-oriented to implement it.

The brain is a thinking organ, which learns and develops through its worldly interaction and through perceptions and actions. Brain preferences refer to how well an individual, depending on the social and cultural context and their experience and education, utilises their cerebral resources and how that makes them stand out from the crowd. Most people are bi-preferential, meaning that they will normally access two of the four brain areas with total comfort, while the other two will remain secondary areas.

The school system has to work on training the different areas of the brain that makes an individual creative, goal oriented, ambitious to seek support and organised to complete tasks. In other words, it needs to teach kids to 'think, discover and create' new things. Unfortunately, most school systems are still focused on developing the logical/analytical areas of the brain (left hemisphere), frequently forgetting to work with the right hemisphere, the one in charge of creativity and relationship building.

Beyond school, developing innovative behaviours at work must be the most important priority for human resources (HR) directives. To do this, HR departments should understand employees' brain preferences to train personnel in those areas of the brain that are not preferred. Training everybody on creativity and lateral thinking won't make an organisation more innovative; it will just make it more creative. However, training innovators in planning and planners in creativity will boost the overall innovation capacity of the firm. On the other hand, HR departments could focus their efforts in creating organisational learning systems, making teams more collaborative and creating ways of promoting, measuring and rewarding innovative employees. After all, if we all agree that innovation is a key corporate strategy, why is it that it's not measured and rewarded?

Innovation is about people. Innovation won't happen unless we educate people to be ambitious, creative, risk takers, passionate about what they do, goal oriented and open minded in order to keep learning throughout life. People are the cornerstone of innovation and unless we don't focus on both raising innovators and developing and managing innovators at work, we won't be able to boost innovation as the key corporate strategy of this decade.

When you think back to your education, do you remember it being open minded, passionate, stimulating? Interestingly, when we thought about it both of us could remember inspiring teachers – though generally singular (teacher) not plural (teachers). We also thought we share that when Bettina chose her elective courses which defined the second part of her MBA one of her selection criterion, perhaps the most influential one, was how exciting and interesting the lecturers were; her argument was, if someone is passionate and interesting in his teaching I will always learn; on the other hand I can be immensely interested in a topic but if the presentation is utterly boring I am bound to switch off. It's the same with music: the most exciting piece, presented in an unengaged, boring way will not be able to rouse you as much as a simple piece performed with utter passion and commitment. Innovation is about people. With that closing statement Mariana did not only provide us a nice wrap-up of the education topic, she also provides the perfect connection to our next section: innovation is about people!

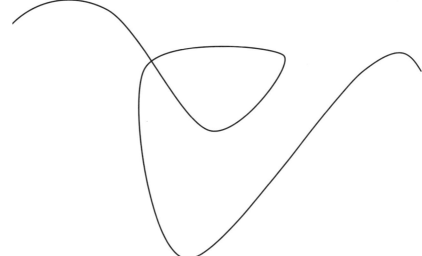

PART VII
It's About People, Stupid!

Innovation. If you look back even just 10 years most of the talking and thinking around innovation was about technologies, R&D, processes and structures. Whereas, fundamentally, it starts and ends with human beings. The good news is, companies have started to figure this out too. We'd like to share some insights on the journey of understanding innovation based on Bettina's research into *Innovation Best Practices and Future Challenges*. In the first round of interview-based research, conducted in 2001, most organisations were involved with introducing processes to manage innovation effectively such as stage gate and the understanding of innovation seemed primarily focused around technology and products. In the second round (2003) it seemed that the discussion had moved on to what kind of structures and roles were needed to support innovation. By the last round (2006) many organisation had broadened their understanding of innovation and were also seeking 'new ways of doing business'; many had also realised that processes and structures alone would not make a real difference, and that they would have to take a closer look at values and behaviours (e.g., culture), and leadership styles. Does that resonate with you? While they are helpful, it is not processes that make innovation happen, it is people.

We are delighted to have noted the emphasis by so many of our contributors on the need for a human-centric approach to and understanding of innovation. So, not surprising, we have decided to dedicate a section on the exploration of this topic.

We will start with the contribution of Abbie Griffin, who kindly, and without knowing, provided the title for this section.

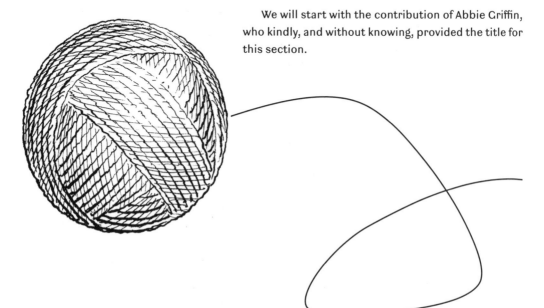

The Future of Innovation is About the People, Stupid!

Name	**Dr Abbie Griffin**
Affiliation	University of Utah, David Eccles School of Business
Position	Royal L. Garff Presidential Chair in Marketing
Country	USA
Area	Managing innovation, people
Email	abbie.griffin@business.utah.edu

innovators   development people   R&D personnel   champions   inventors

The future of innovation is about the people, stupid. Firms have spent an enormous amount of energy and money installing and improving their processes for innovating and creating new products. However, innovation doesn't happen because of some process that has been installed in the organisation. People make innovation happen. And the future of innovation – and by that I mean the more radical, creative and breakthrough innovation – is quite bleak unless and until firms invest more time and energy in supporting the people who deliver these types of innovation.

The majority of the individuals responsible for breakthrough innovation come out of the technology side of the firm. In general, these individuals, sometimes called 'hero scientists', are deeply trained and well versed in technologies new and old. However, technology developed just for technology's sake may not ultimately result in profits for the firm. Remember IBM's Josephson Junction (http://en.wikipedia.org/wiki/Pi_Josephson_junction)? Great technology, but not really converted into a successful product that made money for the firm.

Technology is only one side of the coin, however, in achieving breakthrough innovations. We find that 'serial innovators', individuals in large, mature firms who are associated with one after another new product development breakthrough innovation success, are more than just technologists. As with many technologists, they exhibit creative capabilities. However, they are differentiated from others because they have additional knowledge across multiple other domains. For example, they have a strong understanding of business and the firm's strategy, which allows them to pursue projects that will be acceptable to management. They believe that technology is only a means to an end – and that end is to make money for the firm. They have strong knowledge both of the market in aggregate and market trends as well as of individual customer needs. Additionally, they develop the political skills necessary to obtain firm acceptance of the projects they pursue. They are successful because, rather than starting from a technology, they start from an 'interesting problem', which they define as being important for some set of customers to have a solution to, has the potential to bring in significant revenue, fits with the firm's strategy and likely is a soluble problem.

Not all technologists have the potential to become serial innovators. However, squashing those that do have the potential may result in a firm not being able to come up with game-changing new products over the long run. Thus, the firm needs to put mechanisms in place that will allow them to identify potential serial innovators early in their career and provide them with additional training and knowledge about business, strategy, marketing, understanding customer needs and managing the politics of the organisation. Additionally, the firm will have to manage these individuals differently than the 'average' technologist, giving them more freedom and access to travel and investigation budgets.

There you have it. If you want to succeed with innovation you have to understand, nurture and invest in people. Abbie already hints at the fact that the people who drive, especially radical, innovation are of a particular kind. We will hear more about this a little later on.

First we would like to hear a few more contributors putting forward their arguments for putting forward a human-centric future of innovation.

We would like to call on Jean-Pol who proposes to rethink our understanding of innovation – read on for why that might be!

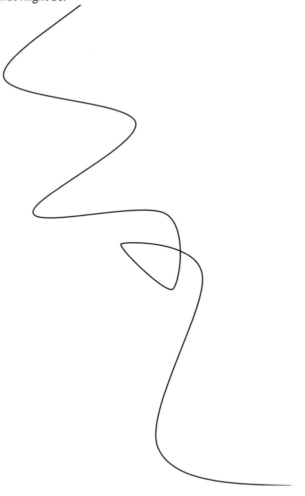

The Future of Innovation is Rethinking Innovation

Name	**Jean-Pol Michel**
Affiliation	Centre de Recherche Public Henri Tudor
Position	Director, Member of the Managing Board
Country	Luxembourg
Area	Innovation management, service innovation
Email	jean-pol.michel@tudor.lu

service innovation   organisation innovation   open innovation
knowledge management   RTO

My proposition refers to the book *Rethinking Science*, by Helga Nowotny, Peter Scott and Michael Gibbons. I wish it to be understood as a plea for science to be given a radically different place in society. The authors of the book don't consider science as an isolated pillar of society. By isolating science from the other activities, it looks like the world could be divided into full-scientific activities and science-free activities. Instead of this dichotomic view, science has to be seen as an embedded quality of all the human activities in the modern society. So, there is a certain intensity of scientific activity in each human action.

I think that the future of innovation is rethinking innovation in such a radical way. To the collapse of the academic ivory tower proposed by 'rethinking science', I would like to add the demolition of the scientific management theory (or Taylorism). Even if these two positions, scientific academism and scientific management, seem archaic for many of us, the mindset they contributed to develop is still deeply anchored in the today's practices. Just as scientific academism has created a certain science conception, so scientific management has created a certain innovation conception that all intellectual workers have to be withdrawn from the workshop to be gathered in the design or planning offices. It looks like the world must be divided into full-intellectual activities and non-intellectual activities.

Instead, my proposition is that there is a certain intensity of innovative activity in each economic, social, political or cultural action. As a consequence, the future of innovation is a new culture of management which is committed with the presence of a certain intensity of positive indetermination or innovation ability in all the human activities. This new paradigm has to get rid of the current belief that the human is always the problem to be managed. On the contrary, the new paradigm puts forward humans as offering the best capacities because they are 'not entirely predefined'. By humans, I mean workers, shareholders, clients, suppliers, competitors, external experts, scientists, regulators, members of professional associations, communities of interest, labour unions and others. Such a type of management is largely open to the outside of the organisation and is focused on human capacities, human interactions and knowledge management. The knowledge is seen as the result of a new mode of science-based production discussed in Gibbons' works.

Rethinking innovation in such a way is particularly important in service activities which have a high intensity of labour and human interactions. In financial centres like Luxembourg which must compete internationally with low-wage regions, science-based innovation towards excellence and exploration in business services is mandatory. Rethinking innovation in services is also a good opportunity in relation to fast-growing demand for new social and cultural services.

To progress toward a new paradigm, we need large-scale experiments. The institutionalisation of European research and technology organisations (RTOs) gives an opportunity for such experiments. RTOs are defined as autonomous organisations dedicated to science-based innovation services. While RTOs' core business is innovation, their emerging organisational and management models could be the drafts for tomorrow standard organisations. So, RTOs as living labs for new management experiments could be one of the valuable roadmaps for building the future of innovation.

Jean-Pol suggests a scientific view of innovation – which reminds us of Praveen's earlier statement in Part VI, but one which has the human being at its centre. In how many organisations you know are people considered to be a problem, numbers to be managed rather than an asset to be treasured? Even if organisations write in their official documents that 'people are our greatest assets', in how many organisations are people truly treated as such? Does not especially the current economic climate show again that people in organisations are mere numbers, to be reduced in bad times and to be acquired again when needed?

Second let's listen to what Miloš Ebner deduces from Blade Runner *and how he arrives at a people-focus future of innovation.*

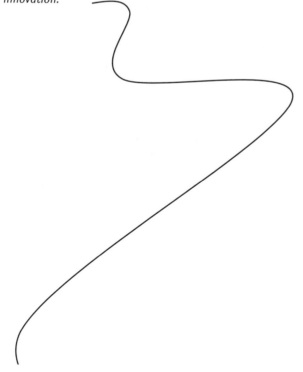

The Future of Innovation is Managing *Blade Runner*

Name	**Miloš Ebner**
Affiliation	Trimo d.d.
Position	Director of R&D
Country	Slovenia
Area	Innovation management
Email	milos.ebner@trimo.si

**complex innovative environment   managing innovation   managing change
open innovation   open business model**

The future of innovation is in managing change, surprise and volatility, and the complex environment of the future. The multi-ethnic, multilingual, multicultural, multifocal, climate-changing and chaotic future described 20 years ago by Ridley Scott in his legendary *Blade Runner*.

It has already been stated frequently that the world in 1914 was much more 'global' than it is today. At the same time, we can see a lot of evidence that the current financial situation is pretty similar to that in 1929 and even more to the one in 1873.

So, there is nothing new in the world! Basic rules are still valid and cyclical, 'cause and consequence' patterns are still working. So, we have to observe and find (old) patterns in new things. We have to put new tools, new technologies, new ways of communication into same cause and consequence model that has cyclically emerged from the ancient past up until today.

The majority of us will probably agree that bits, neurons and genes will be the building elements of the near future and that networks, biotechnology, nanotechnology, neurotechnology and clean-technology will shape our technological environment in times to come. Health care, longevity, security and clean and sustainable energy are themes that are already clearly emerging from any serious demographic, social or scientific analysis. Yet however well we understand these themes, we do not know which new gates will open in the future. On the other hand – do we need to know more than that?

For me the pattern is clear: we are (again) entering 'the Time of Revolution' and the only thing we can be certain about the future is uncertainty itself!

And yes, we already know enough – in such an unpredictable, radically changing environment we need to develop the ability to adapt fast, to manage change, to cope with surprise and to detect and use new possibilities as soon as possible.

To do that we need models for the fast exchange of resources (people, capital, ideas ...), global talent search networks, knowledge supply chains and knowledge engineering and sharing; additionally, we must establish collaborative virtual workspaces, collaborative learning and innovation networks, innovation alliances and pattern recognition models. For sustainable globalisation we should strive towards the diffusion of innovation and use of open innovation and business models. To cope with that kind of future, education systems have to be radically changed and the power of intellectual property rights must be reduced for the benefit of humankind. Other social and economical patterns have to be abolished or modified.

But above all: *a radical future needs the right people*! People who can cope with change: self-motivated, self-confident, self-initiative, flexible, energetic; individuals who know where and how to connect into networks but remain autonomous. Future researchers must have a 'dual mind': both technical and market-driven, realistic and creative, individuals who can take the initiative and good team players. They will need to be more like research managers than the typical researchers of the past. People who understand that knowledge and flexibility are the currency of the future. People who can observe, communicate, collaborate and innovate in a complex, fast-changing environment.

Then and only then new perspectives will open and we will be able to say the same thing as applicant Roy in one of the last scenes of *Blade Runner*: 'I have seen things, you people wouldn't believe ...!'

As we enter yet another time of revolution – rather than evolution – where one of the few certainties is change, the only thing that will help us get on and get through are people, the right kind of people. We could not agree more.

Let's turn to Tim Jones who is another contributor who talks about the 'right kind of people': the kind of people who ride the winds of change, who are the representatives of the knowledge economy. You may want to give this contribution to your human resource department and ask them what they are doing about the scenario Tim describes.

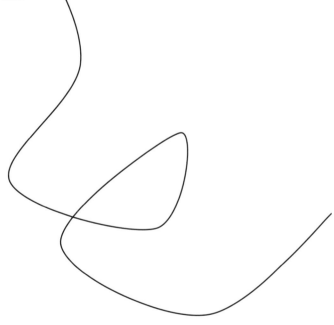

The Future of Innovation is Accessing Future Innovation Talent in a Flat World

Name	**Tim Jones**
Affiliation	Innovaro
Position	Director
Country	UK
Area	Innovation strategy/future growth
Email	tim.jones@innovaro.com

talent   flat world   complexity   open innovation   knowledge transfer

As globalisation finally starts to make the innovation world a flatter one, connectivity to the key sources of innovation – anytime, anywhere, anyhow and any-who – is driving new perspectives about accessing and recruiting the leading talent. This presents both opportunities and challenges.

With rising innovation spending, should companies build more internal innovation capabilities or should they look to better exploit others' investments? Equally should they be proactive in predicting new hotspots and act early to establish key relationships or sit back and be a fast follower?

While outside-in and inside-out open innovation have been challenging to some, as we move to open business model innovation, complexity increases significantly: in particular, the shift from technology transfer to know-how transfer will raise key questions, such as how will companies manage and value knowledge transfer as the limitations of intellectual property (IP) systems become apparent? As firms release their proprietary hold on knowledge, how will sharing it be monetised? So, how should companies balance the need for gaining prowess in conventional open innovation with shifting to the new world of knowledge transfer ahead of their peers?

Most companies see that, to be the exemplar innovation company that they aspire to be, they will need to manage globally dispersed networks of talent drawn from a plethora of individuals and companies, and manage these on a project-by-project basis. Attracting internal and external innovation talent is already being recognised as a top priority for many US organisations struggling to find the right resource. When you fold in the future role of India and China, the global marketplace for leading talent is becoming flatter. By 2012 outsourced R&D in India will account for US$20 billion and programmes involving research are forecast to rise from 10 per cent today to 30 per cent. In China, the future shift is even greater: by 2015 cost issues will be irrelevant and by 2020 as much research will be taking place in China as in the US.

These are catalysts for a shift towards truly 'flat world' innovation. The best future talent will be free to choose what projects they work on, for which companies they like. As free agents become the norm, the innovation expertise that companies need to bring into the fold will reside in a more fluid market.

If you are going to attract the leading talent are you going to access global talent locally or are you going to rely on the network effect bringing the talent to you? And, in such context, how will you engage with the best on a basis of reputation?

The authors of *Funky Business* identified a challenge: 'organisations worth working for' have to attract the 'people worth employing'. In the emerging world where innovation talent is global, fluid and attracted by the challenge and the reputation more than the pay cheque, this is needs a tweak. Innovation winners in the next decade will be the 'organisations worth working *with*' who will in turn need to attract the 'people worth *accessing*'.

If the future of innovation is about people, if it is about the right people, and if these ones are elusive, what might an environment attractive to them look like? While we will be exploring the conditions in which innovation thrives in more detail in Part IX, for now David Robertson gives us a glimpse in his contribution of the things we might need to consider in order to create such an environment.

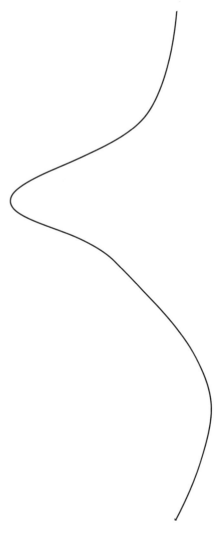

The Future of Innovation is in a Lesson from Napoleon

Name	**David Robertson**
Affiliation	IMD
Position	Professor of Innovation and Technology Management
Country	Switzerland
Area	Creating an environment for innovation
Email	David.Robertson@imd.ch

open innovation   crowdsourcing   implementation   Netflix

Managing innovation can be as frustrating as raising children. You have the responsibility. You do your best to establish the right environment. But in the end, you have to leave the creation of the innovation to the team, and the growing up to the child. Naturally, you want to offer both the best chance of success, so you focus on the environment, where there may be room for impact. But how much impact can you have on the future of innovation, and where should you direct your efforts?

Psychology or Economics?

I looked into the first question with co-authors Nicholas Dew and Philippe Margery. Based on a quantitative review of 31 existing articles looking at the antecedents of innovation performance, we were able to offer some insight into whether it is the psychology or the economics of the environment which impacts innovations more. More simply put, are rewards such as bonus, pay, equity and promotions (economics) more powerful levers for generating innovation outputs than setting up a situation where people feel safe experimenting and potentially failing (psychology)?

The Hard Impact of the Soft Side

We found that the correlation between psychological safety and innovation performance was twice as strong as the relationship between economic levers and innovation. We describe psychological safety as an environment where peers and supervisors empower individuals or teams that want to investigate a new opportunity or technology. And perhaps more important, psychological safety is also characteristic of organisations that effectively extract the learning accompanied by failure, as opposed to punishing the innovator.

The Future of Failure

Our takeaway from these findings is that managers who aspire to drive innovation need to carefully consider how to manage failure. Transferring that employee who was unsuccessful at entering a new market to the mailroom is not the answer. Conducting thoughtful after-action reviews of projects, both home runs *and* dismal failures, is more consistent with creating an environment of psychological safety. Adding that employee who was unsuccessful at entering a new market to the next innovation team is doubly consistent with the idea. It ensures that what was learned the last time will not be repeated this time. And it sends a message to the rest of the organisation that learning is more valued than failure is penalised.

Culture and Safety

This approach may be easier to adopt in different parts of the world. In Silicon Valley, it has been said that a failed entrepreneur is more likely to gain venture funding than one who has never tried. In Switzerland, entrepreneurs with good businesses regularly refuse venture funding as it would make any possible future failure too visible. And an entrepreneurship student from Japan told me he would love to start a company, but never would because if he failed, he would not be able to attract a wife. Within each of these diverse contexts, it is our challenge as managers of innovation to bring a culture of psychological safety to the organisation and free our people to be creative.

What kind of rewards does your organisation offer for innovation? Is emphasis placed on hard factors or soft issues in the context of creating an environment for innovation? In how far, do you think, is the current economic climate and organisation's response to it likely to create a climate of psychological safety? And how does our need for more ground-breaking innovation to get us out of this current crisis tally with our immediate response to it?

Of course the current situation creates fear, and in most of us only enhances the reluctance to try out and embrace something new. That, so Paul Graves argues, is the reason why we need to give space to the innovators amongst us.

The Future of Innovation is a Mindset

Name	**Paul Graves**
Affiliation	See Severn - Business Innovation
Position	Founder
Country	USA
Area	Brand strategy, communication, interatives and Experience Design
Email	paul@seeseven.com

mindset   connect   invest   ambition   selflessness

Thomas Kuczmarski put it well when he described innovation as 'a mindset, a pervasive attitude or way of thinking ... beyond the present to the future ... the penchant for seeing beyond what is and focusing on what might be.'

In this present world of economic chaos and social turmoil, 'what might be' seems like a hard place to go. It's too far away. For some it might not exist any more. Surviving the 'now' seems to be the common order for the day; or more accurately, downsizing now seems to be the status quo – indeed, 'flat' is the new 'up'.

What a shame. For in this place we can potentially ignore the power and real opportunity of this present moment – where we can sow and commit our all to our most precious and essential drivers of innovation; the human heart, soul, mind and strength. Tomorrow's ideas reside in the DNA of every future innovator. Accessing them requires unlocking, liberating and the chance to dream today – now, right at this very moment. Being given this chance translates in real terms into designer managers, creative directors *et al.* laying down their textbooks, theories, agendas, meetings and egos and becoming true innovation leaders; rolling up their sleeves, leading by example by 'doing it' not just 'reading about it', 'speaking about it' and 'talking about it'; but creating real, gritty, textural environments where tomorrow's innovators can experience a safe but dynamic place to start to learn, experiment and grow.

This means that today's innovation managers must stand alongside the next generation; enabling them on a daily basis to explore, embrace and own ambition, curiosity and courage, and understand the power to act, transact, relate and connect through the power of innovation. After all innovation is ultimately a bridging mechanism that allows humans to relate and it's this next generation of designers who represent the future of that connection through innovation – whether it be tangible, virtual, offline, online, deliberate, systematic, process, 3 D, 4D or something else.

For managers, this downtime represents the time to take time; to invest in people and resist the temptation to lay them off; to see beyond the short term; to be interruptible; to listen; to ensure the next generation of innovators are given time and place to enquire, explore, research, breathe in the world, get it wrong, get it right, ideate, translate, iterate, collaborate, give up, start again …

So in short, the future of innovation requires selflessness on the part of today's innovators. True innovation is to see a vision bigger than one's self; to embrace 'cathedral building vision' not 'rock hauling mentality'. Who knows if we will see true, radical innovation in this generation, given these times? Depends on one's perspective. Mine is inextricably linked to the notion that I will have only truly innovated if I am able to transfer something on to someone today that translates into something truly greater, bigger and more meaningful into the world our children will possess tomorrow.

We have heard already that those innovators we keep hearing about need to have special skills. In a rather subtle way Paul has introduced us to a group of people who might do well as such innovators: designers (that's his background). There are more of our contributors who pick up on the topic of design, designers and design thinking and so, you have guessed it, we will explore this in a little more detail later on in Part XII, 'This is all you ever wanted'. The thing we are taking away from this contribution is the emphasis on innovation for the future, innovation beyond our own horizon, and our responsibility for passing our passion on to the next generation.

Let's now hear from Jeremy Myerson who gives us a reason why the future of innovation has to be people centred, and expands on the topic as to why designers might have an important role to play.

The Future of Innovation is People Centered

Name	**Jeremy Myerson**
Affiliation	Royal College of Art
Position	Helen Hamlyn Professor of Design and Director, InnovationRCA
Country	UK
Area	Design, innovation
Email	Jeremy.myerson@rca.ac.uk

design culture co-creation ethnography prototyping

The future of innovation will be people centred. By that I mean that innovators within organisations of every type will make unprecedented efforts to get closer to their customers, to understand better the motivations and needs of the people who will use their products and services. Against the background of a global credit crunch, the future of innovation will demand a completely new relationship between producers and consumers that is less transactional and more interactive and creative.

In the recent past we've had technology-centred innovation which has given the world a lot of clever and often irrelevant things that people struggle to use. We've had marketing-centred innovation which has segmented consumers according to formulae and stereotypes, with predictably limited results. And we've had design-centred innovation which has vaulted over the messy realities of user behaviour with an elevated appeal of style and form.

People-centred innovation will harness aspects of all three previous waves. It will look to science and technology to solve functional problems related to need; it will set human desires in the context of market shifts; design will continue to play a critical role as interpreter and developer within the innovation process. But something fundamental will be different.

The starting point will not be a technological breakthrough, a striking piece of market research or an aesthetic brand heritage. The starting point will be a holistic co-creation exercise with key user groups. People-centred innovation will make consumers genuine co-designers in the process and not test subjects to be studied, analysed and marketed to.

To achieve this, designers will be required to redirect their skills from the back end of innovation (development, specification, production, branding and so on) to the front end of innovation, where discovery, user understanding and need definition will become important partnership activities with consumers. Designers will, in effect, become the main facilitators of the co-creation process, using their creative abilities in new ways.

What gives designers the right to assume a more prominent role in my version of the future of innovation? Three reasons in particular come to mind. Designers are increasingly adept at rapid ethnography, at studying consumer behaviour from an anthropological standpoint and translating that immediately into new design concepts.

Designers are also good at experimentation, at modelling the future through the ability to make multiple prototypes. James Dyson is a classic innovation experimenter who succeeded with his dual cyclonic vacuum cleaner after more than 5,000 prototypes.

The third reason why designers will be key to people-centred innovation is in their ability, in the words of IDEO general manager Tom Kelley, to 'cross-pollinate'. This cross-pollination enables the lessons of one market sector, culture or industry to be readily applied to another – for hospital emergency departments to learn from what happens in Formula One pits, for example, or for aerospace technology to be adapted to ergonomic office chairs.

For design to assume new responsibilities at the front end of innovation, a new type of designer will need to emerge – the T-shaped designer, in which deep discipline knowledge in design (the vertical of the T) will be complemented by the ability to reach out to other fields of expertise, most notable science and business (the horizontal of the T). That is why the ground for a more people-centred version of innovation is being laid now in education, as student designers, engineers, technologists and MBAs emerge from their departmental silos to work together in cross-disciplinary teams.

It is a future laced with pitfalls as well as potential. But, given the black economic forecasts, a people-centred future of innovation is the only one worth fighting for to bring back the customers, retain their interest and restore confidence.

We have heard about the 'right people' required to realise the future of innovation from several contributors earlier. It seems that Jeremy has identified a potential target group here: he points to the potential role of designers in the context of innovation, as well as highlighting that a different kind of innovation might be required to develop the right kind of designer to take up their role at the front end of innovation.

Designers are clearly one group of people to take note of in our ambition to understand the future of innovation. There clearly are others, and Piero Formica makes the argument for entrepreneurism as the other name of innovation.

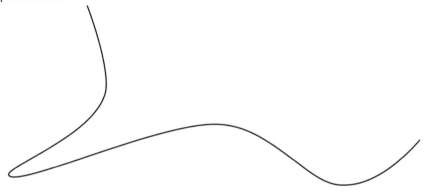

The Future of Innovation is to Think What No One has Thought of (Yet)

Name	**Piero Formica**
Affiliation	Jonkoping University – International Entrepreneurship
Position	Professor and Dean
Country	Sweden
Area	Innovation and entrepreneurship
Email	Piero.Formica@hj.se

**entrepreneurialism   knowledge   innovation   intellectual capitalists
brain circulation**

There is a direct link between the entrepreneur and the innovation process. Innovation is knowledge turned into action through creative endeavour that highly depends upon the willingness of individuals to start new firms. Thus, entrepreneurialism accelerates that process by increasing the opportunities for the successful commercialisation of innovation.

In the 19th century entrepreneurial scholars, such as Marie Curie – an enterprising woman who became personally involved in the industrial application of her scientific results – showed preference sets affected by the convergence of two character profiles: namely, that of *homo scientificus*, breaking away from convention to search for ground-breaking discoveries, and that of *homo economicus*, with a special acumen for marketing and sales. During the 20th century, self-made men like Henry Ford revolutionised the mobility industry by manufacturing groundbreaking vehicles. Ford did not listen to current customers who were trying to make the horse and buggy go 60 miles per hour. Inventors like Thomas Edison, the wizard of Menlo Park, fostered interactions and networking conducive to successful business models by 'selling customers the fewest number of light bulbs necessary to supply them with the light they wanted'.

The 21st century is the century of intellectual venture capitalists, those who make geo-economic changes and move to new places by acquiring a sense of discontinuity. Intellectual venture capitalists are in essence knowledge entrepreneurs who hold intellectual capital and are willing to undertake risks investing it towards the pursuit of larger pecuniary benefits – that is, they have the ability and the potential to transform knowledge and intangible assets into wealth-creating resources.

Over the century, an abundant supply of such intellectual capitalists would encourage intangible assets-intensive processes, whereby companies making decisions for outsourcing innovation 'learn' rather than 'control'. The focus is on what companies *do not know they do not know*. To be brave enough to sail in uncharted waters, they have to learn how to govern the impact of leverage on intangible assets. In doing this, they rely on the performance of the intellectual capitalists acting like the 'merchants of light' of Phoenician and Renaissance times who saw into distances most could not.

Intellectual venture capitalists encourage brain circulation, which is the best way to get an exchange of knowledge, and therefore they help entrepreneurial spirits to embark on innovation journeys. The resulting intellectual exchanges foreshadow processes of cultural integration, knowledge creation and result-oriented innovation actions that will be unfolding all through the century.

The international mobility of talented individuals helps countries, regions and territorial communities close their productivity gap vis-à-vis the most advanced economies, since it promotes entrepreneurship-led innovation. This reduces the risk of talent drains into the most advanced economies.

Open boundaries, education without borders, physical and virtual journeys into other places and disciplines: all these are ingredients that foster new ideas. The international mobility dimension we are experiencing at the dawn of the 21st century is the precursor of societal breakthroughs that, respectively, the Phoenicians and medieval communities of scholars made by intuition rather than through a laborious linear logical process, which was the style of innovation embraced by the Ancient Greeks.

Like Tim Jones before Piero talks about the mobility of people, and like others in this section before, Piero too talks about special skills that are required; in fact he introduces a new profession, the 'intellectual venture capitalist'. As he started his contribution with emphasising the role of entrepreneurial people in the context of innovation we feel that it is only appropriate to draw on Stefan Lindegaar next, who talks about intrapreneurs and shares some tips on how to identify them.

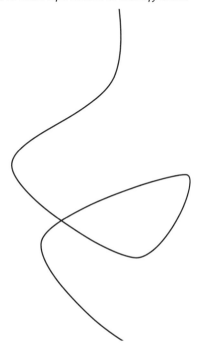

The Future of Innovation is Driven by People

Name	**Stefan Lindegaar**
Country	Denmark
Area	Open innovation, intrapreneurship
Email	stefan@stefanlindegaard.com

innovation leaders   intrapreneurs   T-shape

Companies need two kinds of people to make innovation initiatives successful. They need innovation leaders who focus on building the internal platform required to develop organisational innovation capabilities. This is work on the strategic and tactical level.

Innovation leaders are often also involved as coaches and facilitators for the second group required for innovation, the intrapreneurs who turn ideas and research into new products and services. Intrapreneurs are much more operational minded, and they are rare within most companies. Usually, about 10 per cent of white-collar employees have an intrapreneurial mindset and skills that enable them to contribute in one or more phases of a process in which the goal is higher than incremental innovation. With some efforts, you can train another 20–30 per cent of employees within your company.

How can You Identify the Intrapreneurs?

Here are some ideas:

- First, always remember that you're looking for people who can make things happen rather than people who have lots of ideas. Most organisations have tons of ideas, but lack people who can turn those ideas into reality.

- Ask candidates how they have created results as an individual. Most people will tend to hide behind a team effort. Ask for cases where they used passion and drive to make things happen. Enquire about how they overcame organisational, technical or market obstacles. Ask how they make decisions even when they feel they do not have enough information.

- Ask questions in a direct or even provocative way. Watch for behavioural responses in answers. If someone becomes defensive and combative, they may lack the optimistic attitude and openness required to drive innovation. Look for people who reply in a constructive way that persuades you they can successfully deal with obstacles.

- Watch for a strong customer focus. This is especially important for intrapreneurs as they need to have a business mind that thinks about jobs to get done for customers. Check if the potential intrapreneur gets into customer focus by himself or needs to be prompted. It is not enough for an intrapreneur to say he focuses on customers; he must convince you he has this mindset. Some people try to fake this. If you get this sense, keep asking questions until you can decide whether the person is bluffing.

● The design and innovation consultancy IDEO uses the term 'T-shaped people', which can be used to identify intrapreneurs as well as great people to work with. This implies you should look for people who have a principal skill that describes the vertical leg of the T – they may be mechanical engineers, industrial designers or have a deep knowledge on go-to-market strategies. But they should also have some depth in other skills that are needed to be successful. They should be able to explore insights from many different perspectives and recognise patterns of behaviour that point to jobs that need to get done. You can look out for this by having potential intrapreneurs describe their own T-shape.

Have you noticed that Stefan, like Jeremy Myerson, talks about T-shaped people? Just don't expect everyone to become T-shaped! As soon as we have discovered something interesting new many of us feel that we all have to become like that. That's not what it is about. It is about variety; it is about different strength and weaknesses; it is not about all of us aiming for the same mediocre average. We need people who excel at certain things, and we need those who can act as bridges, or translators, between those specialists. As with so much else in the brave new world, it is not about 'either or' but 'and'.

We have talked about designers, about entrepreneurs, intrepreneurs and T-shaped people. To thrive in the new world of innovation there is more to come, as described and supported by Rob Dew.

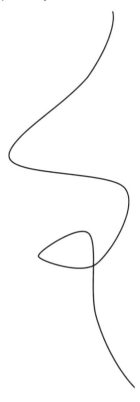

The Future of Innovation is Beyond Traditional Boundaries

Name	**Rob Dew**
Affiliation	Coriolis Pty Ltd
Position	Managing Director
Country	Australia
Area	Innovation management, entrepreneurship
Email	rad1@ecn.net.au

boundary spanning   education   economics   networks   new product development

In the future companies will not remain the main unit of innovation in our society. Increasingly nation states in the third world will innovate to resolve problems like poverty, infrastructure, famine and civil unrest. In the first-world nation states will innovate to reduce health care costs, improve public service sector effectiveness and reduce governance complexity. More supra-national groups like the EU may also emerge.

At the same time lower business transaction costs from new technologies and a trend towards contracted, temporary labour arrangements will accelerate individual level innovation. The nature of work will change – earning money from several different sources will replace a job with a single firm. New business models, a new employer–employee psychological contract (more like a client-supplier relationship) and increased boundary-spanning behaviour will result. This will make firms more transient and act as a virtuous cycle to further increase individual innovation. New careers like the following may emerge:

- professional innovators (counterparts to accountants, engineers and lawyers);

- cognitive coaches (mental fitness trainers offering therapy and technology);

- network entrepreneurs (profiteers who connect previously separate groups);

- consumer assistants (who guide consumers through market 'confusopolies').

The economic changes above will cause and be caused by education designed to develop innovation capability. First-world education systems will de-emphasise left brain development and linear thinking to enhance lateral thinking skills and creativity. Education will also fragment more, with many just-in-time type courses emerging to displace undergraduate and postgraduate degrees as the premier method of formal knowledge transfer.

The system changes listed above will both cause and be caused by key innovations:

- Innovations in pure maths will improve our understanding of networks, emergence, turbulence and dynamic evolving systems. This will result in innovations for traffic management, disease response, weather prediction and market failures.

- Cross disciplinary research will become the norm. Consider how fluid dynamics might help with economics, how neural networks could be applied to creative works of music and fiction for increased commercial appeal and how clinical trial protocols could support venture capital investment decisions.

- Products that combine hardware, software, chemistry and biology will enable us to augment our bodies, minds and children for improved health, sporting ability, mental capability and beauty. These products will also replace legal and illicit drugs and may be bundled with other devices. Imagine buying a video game console designed to release mild hallucinogens and stimulants for more intense game play. The business gives away the hardware and software, but charges for the pharma consumables (super Coke meets Xbox).

- Communication innovations will make internet access as ubiquitous, mobile, reliable, fast and inexpensive as wearing a watch to tell the time. Users will wear technology that unobtrusively enables them to be online constantly. Interface innovations will affect, in real time, conversations to change experiences like work, driving and dinner.

These innovations will mean that geographic diversity will be less relevant than cultural diversity and innovation managers will need better tools for diversity management. What a time – I wouldn't be dead for quids, and if I can just hang on long enough I should be able to buy a lot of longevity from Walmart, Google or Monsanto!

New roles, new professions and again the emphasis on different approaches to and emphasis in education. Does all this newness scare or excite you? Would you prefer to be one of those who are at the receiving end of the changes or be one of those shaping these changes?

It seems that many of this book's contributors feel that the future is for the latter: for the visionaries, for the dreamers, for those who dare. To speak in the words of Dean Bellefleur, '"innovator"'will be the coveted title to aspire to'.

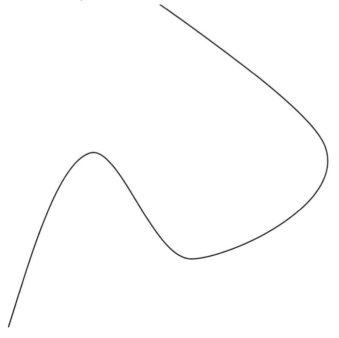

The Future of Innovation is the Purview of the Imaginative

Name	**Dean Bellefleur**
Affiliation	D-idea
Position	Founder and Creative Director
Country	Canada
Area	Radical innovation and commercialisation
Email	dean@d-idea.com

radical   **virtual innovation galleries**   design

The future of innovation belongs to the imaginative. Humanity has stargazed, seeking inspiration, since before recorded time. Be it accidental or systematically executed the results shape and sustain our way of life. Unlike days of old however, when passion motivated the soul of an innovator, agendas today synthesise the direction and pace of innovation.

As the nursery rhyme goes, butcher, baker, candlestick maker, all the way to lawyer, Indian chief. Notice the absence of the dreamer, visionary, risk taker or tinkerer. Imagine a prolongation of the Renaissance period, flower power and Carnaby Street, Kennedy's Camelot and Armstrong's walk on the moon. Creative periods in contemporary history when ideas captured on cocktail napkins spurred quantum leaps of innovation, surely an eclipse of the future. To this end a critical mass of creative spirits fused with teams of practitioners and entrepreneurs are today persistently networking global communities of innovation. These interconnected communities will function as catch basins were the slightest ripple of an idea is amplified as the idea resonates amongst a growing array of human competences. It is this network of visionaries that will redirect the thrust of development for the next millennium.

That intrinsic desire to create is the portal to future innovation. Imagine virtual innovation galleries tapping the infinite flow of ideas streaming from diverse expressions of intuition collated from the minds of the creative class. Comic book illustrations translated into reality and commercialised with a prerequisite to advance the well-being of humanity. Designs inspired from nature – for whom better to adopt as design mentor but Mother Nature herself? Infusions of the classics, contemporary and primordial recollections integrated in constructing environments that deflect the intrusion of bureaucracy from disturbing the creative process. Artists and patrons, visionaries and risk takers, the marriages of convenience dovetailing to yield contributions of merit.

Let's explore this virtual innovation gallery concept for a moment. Ideas visit us in the form of images or vignettes. Therefore, the gallery is predicated on the manipulation of images. Much like completing a jigsaw puzzle, through rapid successive selections governed by principles of trial and error the completed image emerges. Product modelling from projected three-dimensional images extracted from networked communities of innovative libraries would be the modus operandi. Selections triggered by associations gleamed from a pool of personal globe wandering experiences thus retaining the signature of humanity.

Where once actors and sport celebrities commanded prestigious salaries the innovator will have displaced these individuals. Acknowledged for advancing the well-being of both planet and humanity, innovator will be the coveted title to aspire to. Intellectual property will be the nightmare of the past and seen as the barrier to the rate of innovation that it truly is. The future of innovation is for those with a creative eye, a will to challenge the status quo and disseminate knowledge for the development of an idea.

The innovator as celebrity, how about that? Now think about what celebrities tend to have in common ... what is the fuel that propels them past others, be they actors, pop-stars, artists? Let us ask you one question, do you believe that any one can reach the top of whatever the chosen profession is without one essential ingredient? Do you know which ingredient we are talking about?

Right, passion. Without a passion for what you do, for what you are trying to achieve reaching the pinnacle would be quite impossible. This is why we could not agree more with Kobus Neethling who declares that the innovation journey has to begin 'as much in the heart as in the mind'.

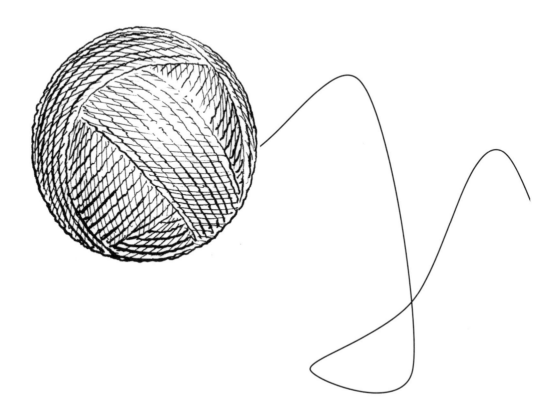

The Future of Innovation is with Heart and Mind (or Not at All)

Name	**Dr Kobus Neethling**
Affiliation	South African Creativity Foundation
Position	President
Country	South Africa
Area	Global
Email	kobusn@sacreativity.com

8-dimensional thinking   heart-innovation   courage   nbi

The future of innovation is in its essence a journey which needs to begin as much in the heart as in the mind. In my work in more than 30 countries and which spans two decades I have witnessed an overbearing, close-minded perspective on innovation – as if innovation is predominantly a discipline of 'things'. The shaping of a better planet for all of us is and will become even more complicated and unpredictable and therefore we will need a new kind of wisdom, courage and purpose-driven passion to innovate for the benefit of all.

Although we look back in awe and admiration to the groundbreaking innovations of the 20th century we also have to admit that most innovations served only the needs of a few. Naturally we have to continue our pursuit of cutting-edge technology, ideas and systems but the context in which these innovations take place, is and remains the fundamental issue. Of all the innovations that I have been involved in or researched the one that comes the closest to heart and mind innovation and the one that considered the context of the dramatic changes that the innovation would bring with immense sensitivity is the creation of a new South Africa. In a television series that I wrote called *Creating a Miracle*, I highlighted the critical factors which led to this unique societal innovation:

- a rare integration of spiritual, creative and pragmatic leadership;

- a bringing together of opposite visions into a single shared vision;

- the creation of new symbols, values, attitudes, principles, customs and practices (and the letting go of the traditions, norms and conventions which would obstruct or frustrate the creation of a free and democratic society);

- respect for and inclusion of ideas from every group affected by the innovation (the term I used was that every chair around the table was filled – failure in whatever form of innovation is often the result of 'empty chairs' – through ignorance or arrogance critical role players and idea creators are ignored);

- an extraordinary insight into the essence of the innovation that was required (there are times when adjustment or conversion innovation would achieve the desired goal – in the box innovation – but here only 'beyondness innovation' would had any possibility of success).

The future of innovation depends on a clarity of understanding regarding the *why, what, how* and *who* of substance and intent. The initiators and the managers of newness also need to be the producers of exceptional ideas (ordinary just won't do it any more) as well as courageous human beings who understand that authentic innovation and crucifixion are never far apart. As my mentor Paul Torrance said many times: 'Creative people can perform miracles but they are always in danger of crucifixion.'

There will always be many levels of innovation and many definers of this concept. And we can still choose to keep on improving the lives of a few privileged people and making the 'thing world' a better place. But I believe that we also need a radically different kind of innovation that will not hesitate to find breakthrough solutions to poverty, diseases, international conflicts and the present destruction of our planet – at the beginning of the 21st century our track record looks very average and mundane.

And maybe the time has arrived to elaborate on the words of Aristotle: 'Innovating the mind without innovating the heart is no innovation at all.' If innovation of the heart and mind could create a new society, why are we still lingering?

Now how about that for an innovation agenda? Clarifying the why, what, how and who and then setting about, heart and mind, to achieving it? (Do you remember Josephine Green also talking the important of understanding the 'innovation for what and by whom' in Part IV?) This innovation roadmap, with the ingredients Kobus names such as a special kind of leadership, bringing together opposites, and respect, can be applied to our individual journeys, to that of organisations, to societies and to humanity. The more people we can engage in joining us on the journey the more likely that we will be able to discover a new land, a new future – and potentially a better one.

In a way what he says resonates with what Paul Graves said about the need for innovators to display a degree of selflessness, and to be able to keep the bigger, longer-term picture in mind. In order to go beyond selfishness we need the passion and determination to achieve the vision, to make the 'thing world' a better place, as Kobus puts it.

Passion, determination. We believe it is time to bring up the 'e-word': emotion. Ask yourself the question, what drives me on to go beyond the expected, beyond what I thought possible? Would it be a rational argument? Would it be facts and figures? Perhaps. But what if strong feelings were involved? What if you were inspired, felt passion, felt love? Would that not spur you to much greater performance? Does not the saying go, 'Love gives you wings'? So what about if the future of innovation got emotional? That's just what Brigitta Sandberg believes will be happening.

The Future of Innovation Gets Emotional

Name	**Birgitta Sandberg**
Affiliation	Turku School of Economics
Position	Assistant Professor in International Business, Coordinator of the Global Innovation Management Master's Degree Programme
Country	Finland
Area	Innovation management
Email	birgitta.sandberg@tse.fi

innovation management   emotions   feelings   social behaviour

Innovations are often associated with projects, strategies and technologies, i.e., 'the hard stuff'. In the future, however, more and more companies will realise that if they are to get into the minds (and wallets) of customers they cannot ignore 'the soft stuff'. Emotions are bursting out and they come in many guises. Not only are they featuring increasingly in customer behaviour and employee management, they are also infiltrating technologies and getting into products.

In their search for new products and services that are meaningful in customers' lives, firms are already giving more and more thought to how users' emotional experiences affect their purchasing decisions and product use. The big question for the future will be how to manage these emotions. How can they trigger, monitor and influence customers' emotional experiences? Techniques such as emotional mapping and customer experience management will have a place in the basic tool-box of marketers, whereas product developers will devote more and more time and effort to emotion-based architecture and emotion-driven design.

Emotions are an inherent component of social behaviour, and thus we could claim that every organisation, whether traditional, network or virtual, is an emotional space. Their influence is likely to be particularly strong on behaviour when people faced with a complex task are in need of extensive information processing, which is often the case in innovation development. Those involved are often bombarded with information characterised by uncertainty and ambiguity, and from this they have to make decisions that chart the course of their development project. In the future, with tighter deadlines and increasing stress, individuals will be required to understand and to manage their emotions. Given the increasingly global availability of talent, expertise and knowledge, the burning question facing managers will be how to recruit, commit and manage increasingly diverse and mobile employees, individuals who are seeking goal fulfilment and want to have fun along the way. Consequently, emotional intelligence is emerging as a critical factor in innovation management.

Firms trying to develop something genuinely new are focusing more on intelligent products that can communicate with their environment, make decisions and autonomously adapt to changing circumstances. However, one might ask whether intelligence without emotion is possible. It has been acknowledged that emotions help humans to make decisions and to act in unfamiliar circumstances. Similarly, products endowed with emotions will be able to experiment and learn. Thus, if the idea is to create truly intelligent products that are capable of carrying through complex real-world tasks, they should be emotional: artificial intelligence requires artificial emotions. Emotional robots are already in the pipeline. Their path from the cradle to the community may be long, but it is inevitable. Their emergence will bring new challenges. How would one engage in social interaction with machines that have feelings, and ensure the effective control and ethical treatment of these sensitive creatures?

In sum, so far emotions have been an untapped resource in innovative organisations. In the future they will play an increasingly strong role in various areas of business life. Now is the time for firms to decide whether to treat them as a threat or an opportunity. Whatever they do – they cannot take the emotion out of their reactions!

Does emotional intelligence get airtime in your organisation? Is it felt to be important that you understand your own emotions and those of others, and to act appropriately using these emotions? Well, that's the definition of emotional intelligence. In all the things we learn, are we encouraged to understand our own emotions and how they affect others? Or are we encouraged to be entirely rational and ensure our emotions go not get in the way of 'sensible decisions'? How many of us are scared of emotions? How much is showing emotions publically socially acceptable? Of course, a lot of what is and is not acceptable will depends on the context of our national culture. The point here is, really, that our emotions will affect our behaviour, and depending on our behaviour innovation will happen, or not.

As we said in our introduction to this section, it is only recently that leaders of organisations have started to look at values and behaviours in order to understand innovation performance. For the penultimate contribution to this section we would like to give the floor to Dennis Stauffer who takes a closer look at behaviours and leadership in the context of innovation.

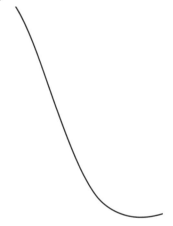

The Future of Innovation is the Innovacians

Name	**Dennis Stauffer**
Affiliation	Insight Fusion. Inc.
Position	Founder
Country	USA
Area	Innovation climate/culture, innovative leadership
Email	dstauffer@insightfusion.com

mindset   behaviour   culture   leadership   climate

Innovation today is widely seen as an organisational process. We're developing ever more sophisticated tools and techniques to drive that process. Yet we're still not as focused as we need to be on how people are actually behaving. We would not expect someone to suddenly become a musician, by simply being put into an orchestra. Yet many organisations act as though they expect to create 'innovacians' that way. (Or, assume they can't be created at all, only found.)

As we go forward, we will increasingly view innovation as a set of behaviours … learned behaviours of not only successful new product developers, and innovation teams, but of entrepreneurs, designers and even emergency responders. We're all facing relentless change. So our ability to adapt, improvise and solve novel problems will increasingly define how effective we all are in all aspects of our lives. A musician is a musician, with or without an ensemble. Each of us needs to develop our innovacianship.

The behaviours of such a virtuoso are no secret. The shortlist includes creativity, a willingness to take risks, thoughtful experimentation, acceptance of ambiguity and uncertainty, and the pursuit of multiple perspectives and interpretations. It's about skilfully and persistently challenging the status quo – including our own ideas and observations. And it's learning how to effectively apply these behaviours in combination. No savvy innovation practitioner would attribute an organisation's innovation successes to a single factor. Innovation requires an interrelated series of tasks. And so it is with individuals. It requires a collection of cognitive lenses or mental models, a certain mindset reflected by our values, beliefs and actions.

Anyone who wants to create an orchestra needs musicians. The most successful organisations, communities and nations will be those who learn how to instil these behaviours. We've long recognised that leaders are not just those with formal titles. Anyone can and should see themselves as an informal leader. Everyone should also see themselves as informal innovators. With that realisation, and the ability to monitor and measure those behaviours, we will recruit, train, promote and reward those who reflect the most innovation-friendly attitudes and beliefs. One of the most critical leadership skills will be the ability to recognise and develop innovacians.

We're certainly not there yet, and it won't be an easy transition. There's considerable resistance to these behaviours inside a great many businesses and institutions. Still, it will happen because those who figure it out will have a huge competitive advantage. While those who resist too strongly won't survive. We were all born with the ability to innovate. The challenge is to make that ability blossom, partly through skill-building and mostly by getting out of our own way ... and by creating a climate that welcomes skilled innovacians into the band.

Some points Dennis has made we would like to highlight are:

- *that we can learn the behaviours that lead to or support innovation – again the link to education;*

- *that 'innovative' behaviours are interlinked with a particular mindset;*

- *that mindset, behaviours and actions are also interlinked;*

- *that leadership plays a key role in identifying and promoting 'innovation' behaviours; and*

- *that we are born with an ability to innovate.*

If the ability to innovate is about values, behaviours, mindsets and emotions, than perhaps we need to shift our focus from trying to understand the processes and structures that support innovation to a better understanding of our emotions, and of how our mind works. That's just what Aino Kianto is proposing.

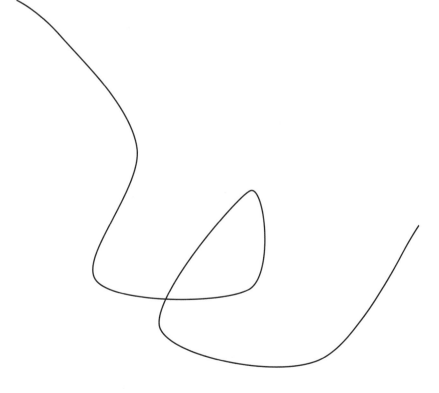

The Future of Innovation is What We Imagined it to Be!

Name	**Aino Kianto**
Affiliation	Lappeenranta University of Technology, School of Business
Position	Professor
Country	Finland
Area	Knowledge management, dynamic capabilities
Email	aino.kianto@lut.fi

creativity   imagination   improvisation   intuition   inspiration

Where do the new ideas that form the seed of any innovation arise from? Arguably, human creativity. However, while an abundance has been written on the technological, economical and organisational antecedents of innovation, human creativity has attracted much less attention by innovation scholars outside the field of psychology. I believe that if we are to understand and accelerate innovation, what we need is not a better administrative process or better-refined innovation funnel models, but a fuller understanding of the human bases of creativity and imagination.

During my years of working in the field of innovation, it has never ceased to puzzle me why even when the innovative individual is examined, our basic metaphor for the human mind seems to be that of a rational calculative human-machine. Why could it not be joyful human, playful human, dreaming human? Surely the underlying metaphor and presumption of ourselves and others guides and delimits our capacities for innovation.

Also more generally, the existing approaches to understanding the human mind seem to stem, more or less explicitly, from the presumption of individuals as – at least boundedly – rational, calculative creatures. But what about the imaginative capacities of the human mind? Imagination, intuition and inspiration have been left aside in the literature on innovation, even though everyone who's ever had a new idea will surely recognise these factors as related with the creative process.

We have a wonderful set of theories and models portraying the innovation process as a managed process proceeding through pre-ordained steps. However in a world characterised by continuous turbulence and discontinuous change, these planning-based approaches only can be useful to a limited extent. Rather than a directed, purposeful and linear process, could we see innovation as a deeply emotional operation characterised by serendipities and guided by intuition, taking place as improvisation-in-action?

In understanding how imagination and non-linear processes of creativity figure in innovation we have much to learn from two sources. First, imagination is perhaps at its purest and most observable form in children's play before they have been overly socialised into the limiting realities of the surrounding educational systems and societal demands. Is there something we could learn from children about how to keep alive and to support the ability in adults to step outside the box and to question existing paradigms? How could we avoid being bounded and blinded by our expertise to retain the skills and courage to improvise and take conscious side-steps outside of the normative template?

The second context to learn from is the creative industries. How are artists able to continuously generate new ideas and implement them? Where can they find the inspiration providing the needed energy for taking the leap towards the unknown – a leap necessary in imagining what doesn't yet exist? And what about musicians jamming together or actors putting up an improvisatory play unfolding in real time while taking the audience in? Could we use them for learning something about how to build those exhilarating moments when the space between people almost seems to materialise as new ideas are spontaneously created and executed and the whole truly becomes more than a sum of its individual parts. Surely understanding these issues would be just as useful for engineers struggling with NPD and managers striving to create business model innovations as for the professionals in creative industries.

To conclude, the future of innovation lies in better understanding the imaginative and improvisatory capacities of the human mind.

Understanding the human mind – sounds like quite a challenge! But it seems that understanding the human brain, influencing the way we think and shaping a particular mindset were on the minds (excuse the pun) of several people who have been thinking about the future of innovation, as Part VIII shows.

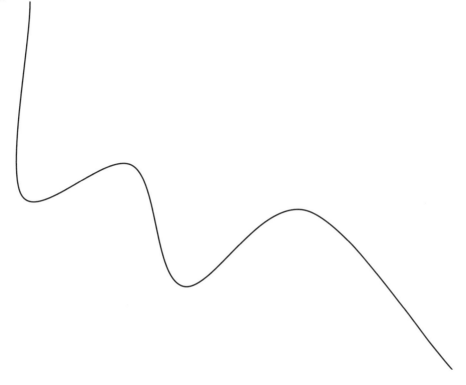

PART VIII
A Question of Mindset

'Mindset' as a topic in the innovation debate – in our view a most critical one! We believe that it is a question of mindset whether or not we will succeed in creating more innovative organisations, whether we will be able to release creativity, embrace failure and accept the 'silly' questions. Is it obvious that embracing innovation and mindset are connected? Is it quite obvious to everyone – or only once the connection has been made for you? We are not quite sure, but we know it is essential to get this piece right if we want to create our future, through innovation.

We would like to start this section with Martina Sheehan who pins her hope for the future of innovation on an increased understanding on the human brain, an understanding that will help to improve our individual as well as collective ability to innovate.

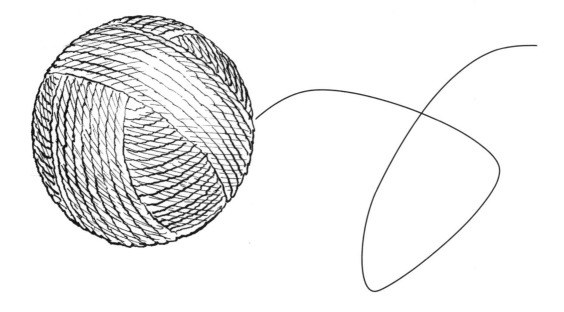

The Future of Innovation is All in the Mind

Name	**Martina Sheehan**
Affiliation	reinvention
Position	Director
Country	Australia
Area	Innovative thinking
Email	martina@reinvention.com.au

brain   neuroplasticity   mind   thinking   train the brain

I believe that the future of innovation rests in the individual human brain. We all have a complex and unique neuro-net that dictates our interpretation of the world around us. The combination of our experiences, our influences and our innate personality determines how we see the world, or at least how we interpret what we see.

I believe that the future holds a growing understanding of how the brain works and how this impacts on our response to our world. There are already mass market products that have opened people's eyes to what scientists came to realise in the 1990s: the brain is plastic and can be trained. While many of these products are just a bit of fun and focus on things such as avoiding the impact of ageing on the brain, I believe they are just the beginning of a paradigm shift. The area in which we see this principle applied most seriously is sport. Anyone related to sport recognises that excellent performance requires more than physical capability. Without the right mental approach, a talented person will simply slip in with the masses. With it, they can be the best in the world. But is this just the luck of the draw, or is it possible to harness this aspect?

I expect that it will only be a matter of time before it will be commonly accepted that we can train our brains for any focus that takes our fancy. We do it now, but without conscious intent. What we use gets stronger and what we ignore gets weaker. So every choice we make in how we direct our attention and feed our brains is training our brains. Imagine if we took control and said 'I want to be more innovative!'

What sort of brain training would make someone more innovative? I believe innovative thinkers need to be able to do two key things:

1. see a potential need;

2. generate potential solutions.

Innovative thinkers of the future will therefore have brains that are strongly trained to:

- observe the world around them with curiosity;

- recognise connections between seemingly unrelated things;

- believe that there is always a better way;

- care about the needs of others;

- build on others' ideas and enjoy it when others build on theirs;

- believe there are no limits to new ideas.

To have brains that are strong in these areas, they must train themselves to use these capabilities regularly and consistently.

If innovative thinkers are also to be good at applying and implementing solutions, they also need to do something that is exceptionally hard for any brain: move from open, creative, possibility thinking, to decisive, analytical, completion thinking. But even this is possible if we learn how to harness our brains and become masters of our own minds.

I believe the future of innovation is bright if we apply growing understanding of the human brain, and find ways to make it fun and rewarding for everyone to train their brain for innovation.

A brain that is elastic, a brain that can be trained – perhaps we can train our brains to be less afraid of change? Perhaps we can learn how to teach 'old dogs new tricks' after all? There is actually some research that indicates that even listening to a different radio station helps to get the grey cells going (again), as does learning a new language, as does exposing yourself to any new thing.

We cannot resist asking whether today's education provides any help in developing the skills outlined by Martina? Does training in your company? Is it part of what your HR people are looking for in the recruitment process? We feel an 'innovative brain' training programme coming along! Perhaps this could become part of Tomás Garcia's innovation university? Exciting prospects indeed, and not too far fetched, as Alex Bennet's deeper dive into our brains' functioning shows.

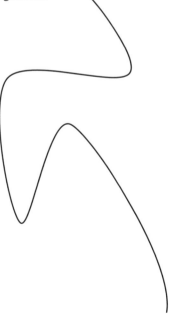

The Future of Innovation is Tapping into the Unconscious and the Collective Conscious

Name	**Dr Alex Bennet**
Affiliation	Mountain Quest Institute
Position	Co-Founder
Country	USA
Area	Tapping into the unconscious, inner tasking
Email	alex@mountainquestinstitute.com

**unconscious   conscious   strengthening of connections
we are learning from ourselves   nothing is static in life**

The future of innovation lies in the strengthening of connections and relations between the individual's external reality and the internal functioning of the mind/brain, and among our social networks. All that exists and the potential for all that will be is emerging from (1) the hierarchy of invariant forms in the human cortex, (2) associative patterning throughout the mind/brain, and (3) new forms of social networking that are making exponentially increasing information patterns readily available to growing numbers of people around the world.

We are learning from ourselves. For example, object-oriented programming emerged from a growing understanding of the invariant forms in the human cortex. As we continue to push the edge of this understanding, we find that there are six levels in the cortex, with each higher level storing invariant forms relating to but not additive of forms stored at the lower levels. Further, along with billions of connections throughout the mind/brain there are continuous connections upward and feedback loops downward through all six levels of the cortex. And everything that comes in through our senses is complexed with and valued by all that is within in a continuous learning process. Nothing is static in life. There is a continuous creation of new combinations of patterns emerging from the mind/brain and introducing new ideas into the physical world. Then, when these new ideas are visible to others – communication to a larger whole through words, actions and products – the same process that was inside the mind/brain now occurs outside as social networking and brings together invariant forms of colliding ideas in a virtual brainstorming process.

Knowledge is best considered as the capacity (potential or actual) to take effective action. Innovation is the presencing of ideas, whether by an individual or through a group of individuals. From the individual perspective, there is expanding knowledge on *ways to access* the patterns that are continuously recombining (complexing) in the human unconscious, which is arguably a million times more powerful than the conscious brain. For example, meditation practices that have the ability to quiet the conscious mind can allow greater access to the unconscious. A second example is inner tasking, a widespread and often-used approach to engaging the unconscious. This is when you tell your unconscious to work on a problem or question as you fall asleep at night, then lie in bed the next morning as you wake and listen to your own, quiet, passive thoughts. A third example is hemispheric synchronisation, the use of sound coupled with a binaural beat to bring both hemispheres of the brain into unison. What occurs is a physiologically reduced state of arousal while maintaining conscious awareness and a doorway into the subconscious. The idea is to tap into the creative power of the mind/brain. Couple this with the rise of social networking and collaborative entanglement and imagine the potential for creativity and innovation!

Just imagine indeed. Tapping into the power of the unconscious. A hugely powerful concept – not least because the conscious mind filters out so many things in order to be able to deal with the multitude of influences.

We would like to mention the work of Guy Claxton here who has written a book worth reading entitled Hare Brain, Tortoise Mind, *in which he explores different kinds of thinking. He associates the mode of 'hare brain' as being more interested in finding answers and solutions than in examining the question, valuing explanation over observation, seeking and preferring clarity, and neither liking nor valuing confusion, and treating perception as unproblematic. Now, anyone who would argue that such a mode of thinking is suitable for innovation?*

Just as well there is a second mode, which Claxton refers to as, the 'tortoise mind'. In 'tortoise mode' people are more concerned with understanding the questions than with providing an answer fast. The process of processing the information is less conscious and people often feel that the answer has come 'out of the blue'. Claxton argues that there is a significant advantage in allowing the process of 'slow thinking' when assessing a situation. We would argue that there is a significant advantage in applying the 'tortoise mode' in the context of innovation! However, today people are often not 'allowed' to let 'things sink in'. The emphasis, particularly in new product development, is on speed.

Though not exactly on the topic of 'mindsets' we would like to hand straight over to Mónica Moso as she picks up on the topic of networks and their potential as well as impact on innovation.

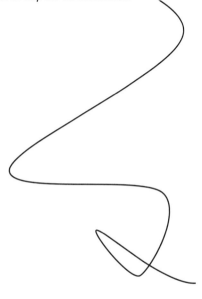

The Future of Innovation is Cognitive Spiders

Name	**Mónica Moso**
Affiliation	Innobasque – the Basque Innovation Agency
Position	Responsible for the Programme on Social Innovation
Country	Basque Country – Spain
Area	Innovation networks
Email	moso.monica@gmail.com

**relational innovation   networks and innovation   innovative interaction
social innovation   intellectual capital**

In my opinion, thinking about the future of innovation implies thinking about the fascinating and complex history of humanity. As if it were a good painting, it is important to look at the lines and details but, at the same time, one should go back two steps to see the whole picture. The future of innovation will probably depend on the human ability to deal with knowledge and innovation as a *whole*; taking into account all individuals, ideas, values and emotions, as well as groups, territories, environments, etc. The integration of all actors and components in the new scenarios will involve more heterogeneous nodes, multiple links and interactions that will enrich the nature of innovation. A key step in the evolution of humankind has been the creation of small networks of cooperation among individuals (such as families, tribes, cities, etc.) in order to survive within different ecosystems and to adapt to changing environments. The speed of the adaptation has increased in specific historical cycles, which has allowed a larger amount of intra- and inter-group interactions, favouring the creation of more extensive networks. These new larger networks facilitated the transference of knowledge and the socialisation of innovation. In fact, the human body, understood as a group of nodes (such as cells, neurons, etc.) connected by links, is a perfect example of a complex system enclosed within the context of a network. From a global point of view, *the concept of network* is a key concept for future scenarios of innovation, where the nodes, the links and the nature of the connections will facilitate or hamper the process of generating an innovative future.

Individuals are born, live and die within diverse networks: metabolic, neuronal, social, cultural, environmental, institutional, etc. Nowadays, there is a 'great collective brain' whose maximum exponent is the Big Science that has grown exponentially in the last decades. The great paradox is that as our knowledge increases, our sight becomes more trapped by the lines of the painting, being unable to distinguish the whole image. The creation, development and dissemination of knowledge has been, partially, a consequence of the hyper-specialisation into cognitive disciplines, which has produced multiple and varied advances. At the same time, this specialisation has also resulted into the fragmentation and polarisation of knowledge into many areas whose study and research are weakly interconnected. Thus, Sociology studies social groups, Biology studies the cells, Physics studies the atoms, etc. The challenge of the future will be to move *from thinking and acting through networks* towards *thinking and acting in networks*.

It would be desirable for 'network thinking' to result in the capacity to increase our specialisation, without losing the transversal knowledge. In this way, the strength of the thinking system would lie in the combination of certain strong nodes and the existence of multiple connections with other less developed nodes. The future of innovation will depend on the excellence of knowledge and on the capacity of associating ideas, which is one of the keys of creativity: the main basis of innovation. New learning and thinking models should be developed in order to study systematically and understand holistically the different spheres of innovation: scientific and technological, social, economical and cultural.

My dream is that in the future there will be millions of 'cognitive spiders', as many as individuals in the world, which will make social and innovation networks together.

Focus on understanding the brain, cognitive spiders, networking thinking, it seems that the future of innovation is all about the way we think – which is just Natalie Turner's argument.

The Future of Innovation is Dancing with Dilemma

Name	**Natalie Turner**
Affiliation	Entheo
Position	Founder, Creator
Country	UK
Area	Innovation management and leadership development
Email	Natalie.Turner@entheo.co.uk

leadership   thinking   organisations   dilemmas   networks

The future of innovation is in the future of how we think. Our thinking patterns to date have brought us to where we are now but are vastly inadequate and insufficient for the challenges that this century and beyond will pose.

As human beings we constantly face choices, dilemmas about how we choose to live and act. These dilemmas are going to become more intense as our simplistic good and bad, right and wrong view of the world continues to crumble around and within us. This will have a profound effect on individuals, on organisations and fundamentally on our concept and practice of leadership.

The future of innovation will require us, as individuals, to learn and think in the spaces between short-term commercial results and compassion for people, for robust internal processes and pioneering and change. This will require us to know deeply who we are, to become self-observers, skilful in the dance of holding often conflicting dilemmas, and to know how to act for the greater good.

The future of innovation is going to require different forms of organisation where information can flow freely, where new connections can form and change shape, and where trust is central to the success and utilisation of our networks. In these porous and increasingly self-organising systems, fuelled by new ways of working, the debate between 'open' and 'closed' innovation will become meaningless, as information and learning flows and groups of people form and disband depending on the dreams they collectively want to create.

The future of innovation will require completely different types of leadership; those who have a deep sense of who they are, those who learn to respond and adapt to an ever-changing business environment and those who use multiple levels of intelligence; an integration of the cognitive, the emotional, the psychological and the spiritual. Leaders must become meaning makers, connectors, skilful at a range of verbal and non-verbal communication patterns; these are the individuals who will have the courage both to create the future and to lead others through this increasingly ambiguous and uncertain world.

If this is the requirement for the future of innovation, what should we be doing now to prepare for it? What are the implications for how we educate our children, for how we prepare young people for work, for the design of our organisational structures and communities? What are the implications for how we develop the skills and competences of our current and future leaders?

As the drivers for global transformation continue unabated the complexities facing us are becoming ever more multifaceted. We have always innovated, we will continue to do so; it is not so much what is the future of innovation, but what is the future we want to create?

Interestingly Natalie starts with different ways of thinking and leads us on to organisational forms and leadership. Leadership is turning out to be another of the future of innovation's warps, the long strands that run through, that are essential and that cannot be ignored. We are quite surprised it has not come out even clearer than that. It seems to be subordinate to other aspects, yet we believe that leadership is and will be a main issue.

Allow us a brief discourse. When interviewing the owner-founder of a medium-sized architectural practice that was located near Kensington Gardens in London, the owner constantly emphasised how important their location was. He explained, 'It is hugely important to be able to go out and clear one's head, particularly in our line of business which relies heavily on creativity. I very much encourage my staff to make use of the fantastic park that is just outside our doorstep.' However, when asked whether he himself was gallivanting about in the park at lunchtimes, he replied, 'No, of course not! I'm far too busy for that.' Onto the next question as to whether his staff were actually making much use of the park he answered, 'Funny you should ask that, they actually do not.' This should not come as a surprise. We observe what people do rather listen to what they say. Professor Albert Mehrabian has undertaken research into how we as human beings construct meaning. He found that only 7 per cent are based on the spoken words: 38 per cent are based on the tone of voice and a mind-boggling 55 per cent are based on body language. Leaders need to lead through actions, not words.

Leading on from Natalie's question about what kind of future we want to create, Ignacio Villoch points out that the creation of our future is already in progress; we are the ones who are making it happen.

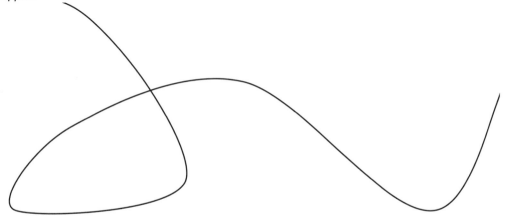

The Future of Innovation is Our Call

Name   **Ignacio Villoch**
Affiliation BBVA Innovation Centre
Position   Marketing and Communication Manager
Country   Spain
Area   Innovation marketing
Email   i.villoch@grupobbva.com

vision   people   emotion   global

The future of innovation will not happen to us. We, the people, will make it happen. Actually we are already creating it with our choices, hesitations, the actions we take – and the ones we do not dare to take. Our ideas and visions are shaping that future. We are already living it.

The future of innovation can only have one purpose: to make people's lives easier. It is useful, practical, focused on actual solutions, meaningful, user-centred, functional and ergonomic. It must add value, close gaps. It is simple, not superficially high tech. Regardless the technology we apply, it needs to be accessible to everybody, both to the digital natives of the gamer generation and to their grannies. Technology only works as a facilitator.

It is based on digitalisation and connectivity: if it can be digitalised, it will be. It is miscellaneous, enriched by user-generated contents, html tagged, geo-positioned and mobile. The solution you may need in any given moment is reachable whenever and wherever you are.

The future of innovation is P-2-P, collaborative, customised and self-expanded: individual wikipedic knowledge knows no barriers, no borders. It is open, intuitive, sees possibilities and generates opportunities. It finds serendipitous discoveries that reward endeavour and hours of code embedding, experience designing and linking.

Nonetheless, the future of innovation requires, establishes and promotes a new mindset. It is multitask, multimedia, multi-sensorial, multi-ethnic, multi-stakeholder, diverse and convergent; East meets West, North encounters South, feminine views generate *evenomics*, and new lifestyles merge leisure and business. It is bound to be free and open-source; the so called *emerging countries* will catch up quickly and take the lead. They are young, affluent and willing to live their exciting moments as other societies have already done so in the last half century. Millions of people are climbing the development ladder unstoppably and creating powerful trends. It is urban, young and is fun.

The future of innovation faces – and solves – serious challenges attached to *globalisation*. Leveraging on lessons learnt from the past, it promotes sustainable development harvesting natural resources matching scarcity and biodiversity with the needs of growing demographics. It is environmental friendly, carbon neutral, recyclable and long-term conscious. It is transparent, acts locally with a global mindset. Control returns to the hands of the people, self-organised in NGOs and counterbalancing the momentum of short-term driven corporations and governments. The future of innovation is tolerant of ambiguity, capable of combining multiple solutions to multifaceted challenges.

The future of innovation is about us, sharing, creating and uploading our contents, networking, connecting conversations and turning ideas into facts and those into attitudes. It means empowering people that turn communication into action with their fingertips. The human being again is in the spotlight, can be heard and seen, is confident and creative in a new Renaissance.

The future of innovation is kaleidoscopical, hybrid, mobile, connected, distributed, articulated, flexible and begins now. It is our call. Are we going to miss it?

If we are creating the future, and if 'The future of innovation is about us, sharing, creating and uploading our contents, networking, connecting conversations and turning ideas into facts and those into attitudes', then one thing becomes of critical importance: language. Whether we are sharing a vision of the future, whether we are able to communicate and sell our ideas, one thing is critical, that we communicate in a language that is clear, and one that does not have any hidden agendas.

Let's see what Jennifer Ann Gordon has to say on this topic.

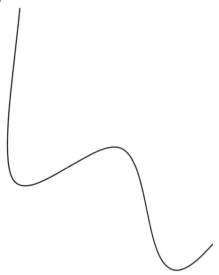

The Future of Innovation is Dependent on a More Open Language

Name	**Jennifer Ann Gordon**
Affiliation	Cool Breeze Marketing, LLC
Position	CEO
Country	USA
Area	Language for innovation
Email	jgordon@CoolBreezeMarketing.com

language   listening   creativity   safety   change

The future of innovation will require a more honest, sincere and open language, a language with more space around words. This spacious language of innovation will be free of hyperbole, superlatives and blame. It will be the language of being at cause, rather than at effect. And, most importantly, it will be the language of listening.

A new language is fragile, though. We will need to guard our linguistic environment, against the corrosive corporate speak, the speculative Wall Street jargon and the greed-driven media hype which all cripple innovation.

To invoke change, our language needs to be positively oriented, rooted in hope and judgement free. This is the space between the words. When despondency and anger are present in language, there is no room to breathe new thoughts. The innovator's language needs to create a place of safety, a big place where people can venture forth into new mental territory without judgement. The crux of this language is the listening between the words ... the wide open space of silence where creativity flourishes. People need to feel safe in their own skin before they are willing to take risks. And, in order to feel safe, they need to feel listened to. Meticulous listening is required to speak this new language. Impatience in this area slows progress dramatically.

Dr Barbara Cavalier is in the business of improving companies' voices on the frontlines of sales and service. When asked how she goes about this, she replied that she spends most of her time listening. Only then can she address the voice, or power, of the organisation. This listening is the space between the words, the silent vocabulary of the innovator.

The language of innovation is the language of being at cause, rather than effect. It is not *anti-* or deficiency language. For example, the *anti-violence* against women and girls campaigns. *Anti-violence* means what? What does a violence-free environment look like in positive terms? Paint me a picture that I can embrace, please. Or *Breast Cancer Awareness*. What about *Healthy Breast Awareness*? Can you paint me a word picture which inspires me to celebrate my wholeness and be proactive about my health care, rather than pushing me by creating dread, fear and paranoia?

Deficiency language, the antithesis of the innovator's language, finds no better lairs than the insurance industry and Wall Street, the vocabulary of which – such as *risk, chance, death, percentage, liability, fault, loss*, etc. – revolve around people's terror of death or loss.

Innovators are alert to their thoughts and words, well knowing that these define worlds. We can ask ourselves: What is my language magnifying? Does it blame or accuse? Does it label me or others? Does it inspire? Does it invite others into new territory? As we speak from our 'ears', curiosity and connection to others, we attract all the nutrients, light and people we need to grow better companies and a better world.

Open language, honest language, language that is positive, constructive and inspiring. How about the language in your organisation? Is the aim to inspire? Is its aim to be open and honest? Are people able to get their voice heard?

Someone else who is talking about language is Arne Stjernholm Madsen, though he talks about it in the context of needing to find a language around innovation in order to make innovation happen.

The Future of Innovation is in Our Minds

Name	**Arne Stjernholm Madsen**
Affiliation	Novo Nordisk A/S
Position	Innovation Management Partner
Country	Denmark
Area	Innovation management
Email	astm@novonordisk.com

**innovation management   dynamic capabilities   spheres of innovation
conscious leadership   meta-layer**

If we go 50 years back, companies didn't have strategies. Or, of course they had; they lived their strategies in their daily work. But there was no language to name what you were doing until the birth of *strategic management* in the 1960s. Igor Ansoff published *Corporate Strategy* about diversification in 1965, and Boston Consulting Group launched their popular portfolio matrix a couple of years earlier (the one with cash cows, stars etc.). But until there were such concepts and models to describe strategy making, it was no deliberate management discipline. In other words, you could see the practical results of your strategies, but there was no framework for reflecting and *learning* about strategy making. 'You can't tame, what you can't name.'

Innovation unfolds in real life, no doubt. But until the management vocabulary includes 'divergent thinking', 'architectural innovation', 'absorptive capacity' etc. etc., plus a number of models and tools to make the concepts operational, innovation is no deliberate management discipline. Today we face such transition from *innovation* to *innovation management* in the corporate world. It's about utilising what I call the four Cs of innovation:

1. Innovation takes place in a societal Context, e.g., the market with its turbulence of changes, new competitors, technological development, politics, laws and regulations etc. In this sphere you find many different 'schools of thought' both regarding business models and competing technologies, expressed within other companies, within universities, research labs and within the public in general.

2. Integrated in the societal Context, the organisational life unfolds as self-organizing patterns of behaviour, or Culture. In this sphere you find competing 'schools of thought' within the corporation. It's also the hotbed of emergent innovation.

3. A more formal structure is expressed in management systems, processes, competences etc., or the overall Capabilities of the corporation. In this sphere the official choices between the many ideas and thoughts are made and articulated into strategies and plans, based on the established mental models of the organisation. In other words, it's the home of planned innovation.

4. Finally, there is a possibility for the organisation to learn and reflect, to identify the mental models at stake in both the emergent and the planned innovation, and to experiment with alternative ways of seeing the business. I call such activity Conscious leadership of innovation. This sphere is a dynamic 'meta-layer' for adaptive innovation management.

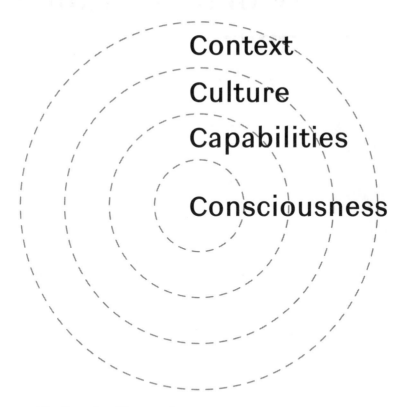

Figure 3   **The four Cs of innovation**

To initiate and guide an expedition through these spheres would be an act of conscious innovation management. By doing so, top management not only takes the step from innovation to innovation management, but also makes innovation management a *dynamic capability*. This development of mind is where the future of innovation begins.

The '4 Cs of Innovation'

The *Context* is society in general. The organisational *Culture* consists of self-organizing social processes. The *Capabilities* are structures, management systems, competencies etc. *Consciousness* is a meta-layer of learning; the key to adaptive innovation management.

We too believe that having a language around innovation is one of the preconditions for it to happen, and there are many more conditions that need to be met in order for innovation to happen. Arne has prepared the ground and outlined different layers of an onion that need to be considered for conscious innovation management. We have one more contribution in this section, included almost at the last minute and because we felt that this tool developed by Howard Smith and his colleagues might be one way of creating such a shared language, as well as a tool for visualisation, and a way to hold and represent opposing views. Let's read his story.

The Future of Innovation is on the Beach!

Name	**Howard Smith**
Affiliation	CSC
Position	Founder, and Global Lead, CSC Collective Intelligence
Country	UK
Area	Visualising and connecting innovation
Email	hsmith23@csc.com

**visual   Southbeach   language differences   conflict resolution
holistic approach**

The future of innovation lies on the beach! This is at least where I found it, together with a few colleagues (Southbeach, Miami, to be precise). We realised that in order for innovation to happen, and to happen smoothly, we must connect the pebbles we find. This is the ambition we have set out to achieve with Southbeach Notation (www.southbeachinc.com).

Everything that exists, or is yet to exist, is attended by an inseparable companion: an innovation shadow-self. To the untrained eye such phantoms, in reality abstract models of innovation yet to be performed, are dimly perceived, if perceived at all. To a skilled innovator, however, they become a dominating and pervasive presence in all creative work. The role of the innovator is to bring forth such apparitions from out of the shade and to subject them to a formal analysis, guiding improvement and transformation in products, services, processes, ideas and strategies.

Innovation demands a joined-up thinking – across processes, disciplines, organisations and markets. Future wealth creation is revealed by embracing multiple perspectives. We denude innovation of its power when we focus too closely on one area of the business or one area of expertise. The *process* of innovation must clarify *related problems* blocking progress wherever they lie. Our methodology must untangle conflicting causes and effects at all touch points in the customer value chain.

A universal visual language is required – one that can be embraced by any business, engineering or scientific discipline. The *language* of innovation must be capable of representing and aligning diverse *perspectives* and *roles*. Companies need this visual language to express complex multifaceted ideas – scenarios of their current and future challenges. We felt that once digitised, innovation would spring to life – and point to prototypical solutions incorporating new (to them) ideas, systems, processes and trends. It should be possible to draw on ideas in fields as far flung as finance, engineering, management, the law, global issues, education, marketing, the service economy, health care, information technology, strategy and politics.

For the word 'innovation' to mean anything, it must be defined as the reliable business process by which firms create value from all sources of creativity and knowledge - employees, customers and partners; it must connect visual notations, tools and methodology – semantically and organisationally; the supporting tools must be *collaborative*; companies ought to be able to join up their innovation ecosystems not via discrete silo applications, but by rich visual content and the associated meta-data.

Building viable new product or service opportunities rests on analysis: mapping, visualising and resolving the inherently complex organizational or engineering tensions and contradictory requirements. Companies must be empowered to align perspectives on the most promising directions. They should be able to do so taking into account both the technical and human systems involved – inside the firm, between partners and as a result of societal and regulatory trends.

The future of innovation is visual and plays to pervasive societal themes. Focus areas will include corporate sustainability, the engineering of the customer experience, climate change, biodiversity, resource utilisation and the green agenda. Try it out at www.southbeachinc.com.

Part IX will explore in more detail what needs to be considered in order to create an innovative organisation. By the way, we would just briefly like to elaborate on the difference between an organisation that is good at innovation, and an innovative organisation. Let us explain: the former is an organisation that might be quite good at the development of new products and services. If you walk into such an organisation and ask, 'Who is responsible for innovation?', the answer you will generally get is, 'The marketing department', if it is a fast-moving consumer goods company; or 'The R&D department', if it is a more technology driven company. Such organisations have structures and processes in place, and they tend to be rather good at the more incremental type of innovation. If, on the other hand, you go into an organisation and the same question is answered, 'We are all responsible for innovation here', you are much more likely to face a truly innovative organisation, and an organisation that is more likely to come up with a radical or business model innovation.

May we also point out that we believe that in economic difficult times an organisation that is good at innovation is more likely to cut back on innovation budgets and cancel innovation projects than an organisation that is truly innovative. In the former it is more about 'keeping up with the Joneses' than it is about finding your own path.

With this in mind, what observations have our contributors shared about creating conditions in which innovation thrives, and that make for a truly innovative organisation? We thought this sounded rather promising, and just the thing that might help consider context, deal with opposites and paradoxes, as well as facilitate a more holistic, systemic approach. We will watch the space with interest!

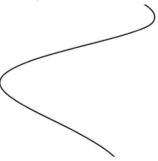

PART IX
General Conditions in Which Innovation Thrives

Much has been talked about conditions for innovation in general and in detail in the literature, demonstrated through case studies. Companies such as 3M, BMW, Proctor & Gamble and IDEO have been written about extensively and many of the insights around innovation have been formalised in frameworks and models, and provide some guidance to those who seek to understand innovation and its management. Yet still there seem to be some secret ingredients missing, leading to people in many organisations being rather dissatisfied with their organisation's innovation performance.

We believe that the 'wrong kind of mindset' has much to answer for, and, as you have seen in Part VIII, many contributors too share the view that the future of innovation requires a different mindset.

In this section we would like to give voice to a number of contributors who provide some additional insights into the kind of conditions in which innovation thrives, and what the elements are that are worth considering.

Joe Tidd starts us off by pointing out that some of the fundamental understanding of the considerations for innovation might have to be revisited, also connecting us back to Part III, 'Innovation, but not as you know it'.

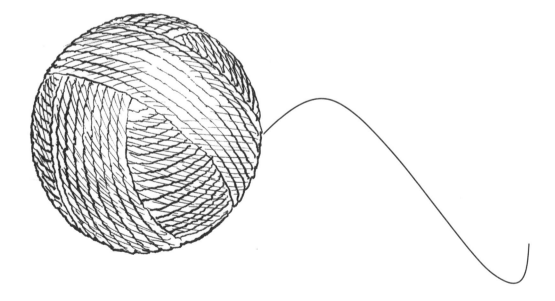

The Future of Innovation is the Basis for Social and Economic Change

Name   **Joe Tidd**
Affiliation SPRU, University of Sussex
Position   Professor, Technology and Innovation Management
Country   UK
Area   Innovation leadership
Email   j.tidd@sussex.ac.uk

development   leadership   risk   social change   sustainability

The future of innovation demands that talented managers and researchers engage with the more fundamental economic and social challenges, rather than being confined to less pressing issues such as new product and service development.

Historically, innovation has been associated with optimism for the future, contributing to both social and economic progress. However, this is no longer the case. Innovation is not fully exploited to tackle issues such as sustainability and development. Instead, the emphasis is on the role of institutions and regulations, and in many cases innovation has become crudely linked to unbridled capitalism and consumption, i.e., part of the problem.

Innovation must again become central to meeting such challenges. Innovation policy and management need greater integration. Policy-makers need to understand how technology, markets and society co-evolve through a process of consultation, negotiation and experimentation. This demands a better appreciation of how innovation works, and how different interests and stakeholders influence the rate and direction of innovation. We need to find ways to re-engage the energy and commitment of individual entrepreneurs and innovative organisations.

Engagement demands that someone has the interest, influence and imagination to search for novel solutions and to implement these. *Interest* requires motivation and commitment to work on a challenge, and implies an emotional and affective attachment beyond a professional or intellectual interest. *Influence* means having an appropriate level of authority, responsibility and resource to tackle a challenge. *Imagination* implies a readiness and competence to develop a new and desired future.

This will demand a new cadre of innovation leaders and managers in the private, public and third sectors, with radically different roles and capabilities. The kinds of challenges faced will be more ambiguous, ill defined or fuzzy, rather than clearly structured or well defined. The potential solutions and ways of solving them will be complex, unknown or untested, rather than known, predetermined or simple. The outcomes and results will be new, requiring discovery and invention, rather than simply applying something that already exists.

Part of the required change is the attitude to risk. Innovation is inherently risky and will inevitably involve failures as well as successes. However, risk has become a negative term, something which should be minimised or avoided, hence the 'precautionary principle' in policy which promotes caution and inaction. But this view perverts the nature of risk and opportunity, which are central to successful innovation. The term 'risk' is derived from the Latin 'to dare', but has become associated with hazard or danger. We must also consider the 'risk' of success, or risks associated with *not* changing.

Successful innovation management requires that managers and organisations be prepared to take risks and to accept failure as an opportunity for learning and development. Leaders and managers must provide the climate, time, tools and training to encourage others to use these resources at appropriate times and on challenging tasks that promote innovation and change.

For us one of Joe's key messages is that if innovation was always understood to involve risk, uncertainty and fuzziness, this will only increase in future. Going along side this is his call for new roles and capabilities, and a different perspective on what we consider to be 'risk': the risk of not innovating might be greater than the risk of innovating; a fundamental mindset change.

Another aspect that has not been taken into consideration sufficiently and that is close to our heart is that of a need for a holistic approach. It somehow is one of those things that seems only logical once you have thought about it, but this is not quite as apparent before someone has made it explicit. Of course, a holistic view is closely linked to a systems approach. The fundamental premise is that you cannot change part of a system without this having an effect of the rest of the system. We sometimes liken this to a mobile: if one part of the mobile is moved the rest will change their position. If this is not happening, if the other parts are held in place, it will result in the changed part breaking off. Think about how the introduction of teams was executed in many organisations. People were told that 'from now on you will work in teams' – but more often than not no training to help with dealing with diversity or conflict management would be offered, and rewards and remunerations tended to remain aligned to individual performance.

If creating and sustaining innovative organisations is about nurturing certain behaviours and mindsets then, clearly, the context in which this takes place has to change too. This includes hard factors, such as structures, roles and processes, as well as softer factors, such as leadership behaviours values, reward and recognition schemes as well as training and recruitment agendas.

It is these soft aspects that Julian Birkinshaw emphasises as an essential part to look at if we are to create a more innovative future. By the way, it was interesting to observe that in a recent review of papers for the innovation track of the 2009 European Academy of Management conference a larger number of papers than ever before focused on behavioural and mindsets issues. The awareness that innovation success depends on people (stupid!) and values and behaviours and mindsets is certainly spreading.

The Future of Innovation is Overcoming the Design Flaws in Management

Name   **Julian Birkinshaw**
Affiliation London Business School
Position   Professor and Deputy Dean, co-founder of MLab
Country   UK
Area   Management innovation
Email   jbirkinshaw@london.edu

management model   management innovation   design flaw

Innovation will continue to be one of the key strategic imperatives for commercial and not-for-profit organisations through the downturn and for the years ahead. I see two important trends. One is a much greater emphasis on the 'soft' side of innovation management – the skills, values and culture that support new product or service innovation. Decades of research has shown there is no silver bullet, no formula for success. Formal structures for managing development projects can help, but they can also drive out genuinely new ideas. Access to seed funding, and slack time for working on new projects, can be a blessing or a curse depending on how they are offered. Incubators designed to protect new business ideas often become orphanages for unwanted ventures.

This research has led me to realise that innovation management is an oxymoron. You cannot manage innovation any more than you can force a person to succumb to a religious belief. Rather, the challenge is one of managing *for* innovation. If the right set of conditions is put in place and sustained over a period of several years, the odds of generating worthwhile innovative outputs go up dramatically. So it will be the firms who build the appropriate skills, values and culture that will be most successful.

The other important trend is a broader perspective on the nature of innovation. Many managers view innovation narrowly in terms of technological advances, new product introductions or process improvements. But research is increasingly showing the value of a broader definition. For example, one line of research has shown how business model innovation can generate firm-level competitive advantage. Another, of great interest to me, is the increasing interest in *management innovation,* defined as the implementation of a management practice, process or structure that is new to the state of the art and is intended to further organisational goals. Well-known historical management innovations include Du Pont's development of capital budgeting techniques and Toyota's investment in the problem-solving skills of its line employees. More recent examples are Procter & Gamble's 'Connect and Develop' open innovation model and Motorola's Six Sigma quality methodology. Because of its systemic and hard-to-copy nature, management innovation offers firms the potential for competitive advantage in ways that product and process innovation do not. Indeed, it has been argued by Gary Hamel that 'over the past 100 years management innovation, more than any other type of innovation, has allowed companies to cross new performance thresholds'.

Research conducted by myself and my colleagues at the Management Innovation Lab (MLab) shows that management innovation is difficult to do. We are all prisoners of the same calcified management systems that shape the way we behave and even the way we talk, so it is hardly surprising that we find it difficult to imagine an alternative set of structures, tools or techniques that might replace them. To make matters more challenging, there is no play-book, no clearly understood rules for management innovation. But our research suggests there are several vital ingredients that always come together when management innovation happens. These include: a distinctive and novel point of view on the future, a clearly articulated problem or challenge that needs resolving, a core group of heretical thinkers and action takers who push the new idea through the organisation and a deep understanding of the traditional orthodoxies that need to be overcome. By bringing together these ingredients, companies can increase the likelihood that they will accelerate the process of management innovation.

So it's about the soft aspects, and about a broadening of understanding of innovation. Can we observe another of innovation's warps developing? Or is it indeed a new fabric we are beginning to weave? If it is we surely need to carefully unravel the old fabric and take a close look at which threads are still needed and which we might have to let go.

Perhaps one of the threads we need to let go off is that of believing that we can 'manage innovation'? We somehow like the distinction Julian makes when talking about an impossibility of 'managing innovation' but 'managing for innovation'. When we first read 'innovation managing is oxymoron' we wanted to rebel, but when we read on it made sense, entirely. This is probably why this section is called 'General conditions in which innovation thrives' rather than 'How to manage innovation'. 'Managing for innovation' has a much more rounded, holistic tone to it than 'managing innovation'.

The concept of a holistic approach to innovation is also the connecting piece to our next contribution. So, enough from us; let's see what Tom Hulme of IDEO has to say on this topic, and what his thoughts on realising a holistic approach to innovation are.

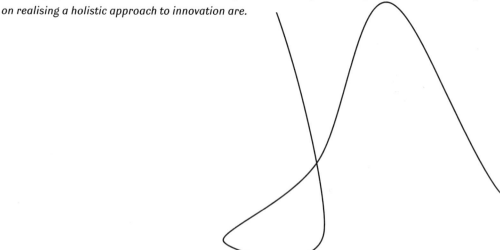

The Future of Innovation is Holistic and Networked

Name	**Tom Hulme**
Affiliation	IDEO
Position	Business strategist
Country	UK
Area	Innovation and design
Email	thulme@ideo.com

collaboration   competitive advantage   network   holistic   wisdom of crowds

Innovation can be fragmented. Inside organisations, there is a tradition of different departments working in isolation behind closed doors, with varying degrees of empathy for the needs of their consumers. That kind of scenario is changing fast as the line between the consumer and industry blurs. For it to flourish, innovation's future lies in a less disjointed approach – we're already seeing signs of it becoming more holistic and collaborative.

A more holistic approach is now crucial because it's increasingly difficult to create sustainable advantage without aligning every aspect of a consumer offer. An interesting example is Apple, which is often cited as a world-class product developer. However, Apple's *potency* is the fruit of its innovative approach to *an ecosystem of* product and service design, retail, marketing and manufacturing – it certainly didn't invent the MP3 player and arguably didn't build the most innovative one at the time. Its dominance is ongoing proof that holistic business ecosystems deliver the greatest competitive advantage.

This holistic perspective also *needs* a lateral vision. As great ideas can be discovered in diverse and unexpected places, we need to collaborate in new and surprising ways. We believe that the best ideas come from crashing, combining and contrasting disciplines and perspectives, and technology is enabling us to do this in very different ways. At IDEO, we often involve disperse and eclectic networks of consumers and experts in creating and evaluating ideas. The effect is sometimes fusion, and sometimes fission, but the results are always fruitful. In particular, it has proved to us the value of seeking, as well as expert insights, the wisdom of the crowd.

Close collaboration with the consumer can give rise to *remarkably effective and powerful* business models. A particularly successful example can be found where the public intersect with the TV and record industries. *X-Factor* is a UK TV talent show (the US version is *American Idol*) in which viewers vote for the performers they like best. The format has transformed a business expense (record companies searching for fresh talent) into a revenue source (viewers pay to vote). Because singers are only launched on the market when the viewers have made it clear they will buy their music, risk for the record company is mitigated.

And it's becoming clearer and clearer that consumers want to be involved. The popularity of Starbucks' Mystarbucksidea.com, which allows consumer to create and rate new ideas and keep up with developments, is a case in point. Opening direct communication with consumers globally, at relatively low cost will soon become the norm.

The future of innovation is where big impact comes from applying *a holistic approach and building a portfolio* of innovations rather than one hit wonders; it will be where wisdom of the crowd is the first port of call rather than the last resort.

If we have talked about the structures inside an organisation that need to be aligned to create an innovative organisation Tom goes beyond that, applying the same view of embracing a more holistic approach in its consideration about products and services, taking a systemic approach when considering the entire offering – as well as with regards to who is involved in the development.

A holistic approach is also one that moves away from an approach based on 'either or' – we have already elaborated on this point in Part III on 'The winds of change'. What are some of the 'ands' that need to be addressed for the future of innovation?

The first of our three contributions on this topic is Petra de Weerd-Nederhof, focusing on operational effectiveness and strategic flexibility.

The Future of Innovation is Organising for Strategic Flexibility

Name	**Petra de Weerd-Nederhof**
Affiliation	University of Twente
Position	Professor of Organisation Studies and Innovation
Country	The Netherlands
Area	Innovation management
Email	n.c.deweerd@utwente.nl

**organising innovation   strategic flexibility   operational effectiveness
creativity   innovation performance**

The future of innovation requires the proactive balancing of multiple innovation performance requirements. Striving for sustained innovation and longer-term competitive advantage implies a continuous confrontation between today's work and tomorrow's innovation in the organisation of innovation efforts. The readiness to adapt to, anticipate or create future innovation performance requirements is labelled *strategic flexibility*, which in fact is a prerequisite for future *operational effectiveness* of the innovation efforts (the realisation of innovation goals).

Striving for strategic flexibility contributes to both incremental and radical innovation. In order to shape a sound basis for future innovations and business success, companies need a strategically well-chosen 'flexibility mix'. Operational effectiveness, requiring operational flexibility in terms of, for example, being able to gather and rapidly respond to new technical and market knowledge as a project evolves, should go hand in hand with strategic flexibility to create room for new strategic options in future. Achieving strategic flexibility particularly also requires flexibility in different organisational functions, for instance in human resources policy and in product and process design.

Creativity and innovativeness are rooted in highly competent and committed employees. But, to be innovative on the level of a project team of an organisation or on the inter-organisational level of co-maker relationships, supply chains and networks, and in an open innovation setting, adequate organisation design and leadership fitting to the situation is also needed. These organisational and managerial capabilities are a substantial part of companies' competence base and are also the subject of processes of innovation and learning. *Organisation of innovation* therefore has to go hand in hand with *innovation of organisation*.

The need for strategic flexibility implies dynamics from within the organisation: a firm's goals and strategy may be changed proactively and with considerable frequency to improve performance, based on the development of (new) core competencies and the better development of key resources. Strategic flexibility as a prerequisite for operational effectiveness in the (near) future underlines the importance of searching for flexible organisational forms (innovating the organisation), especially when looked upon from a social dynamical viewpoint.

Given the need to perform under high time pressure, concerted action is required. This implies a framework of performance measurement embedded in effective feedback mechanisms. The design and implementation of such performance management is a difficult task in an environment characterised by creativity and professionalism. It can only be successful if it is based on a good insight in, and understanding of, social dynamical processes, stressing room for creativity and learning, the importance of an innovative climate, professional autonomy and shared leadership, collective mind and personal development. Designing the organisational structures and management systems must go hand in hand with functional interaction patterns and style of leadership. Organisational solutions can and will be found in the employment of ambidextrous organisational forms and semi- or quasi-structures, as well as in the deployment of dynamic capabilities which reflect an organisation's ability to achieve new and innovative forms of competitive advantage.

What Petra talks about is the need to balance the today with the tomorrow, elaborating on strategic flexibility as a tool to facilitate this. Balancing today and tomorrow, balancing operational efficiencies with innovation excellence – this comes back again to the issue of 'and' instead of the seemingly easier 'either or'. Of course, a term has been coined for 'the management of both', and the term is the 'ambidextrous organisation' Petra has just mentioned it, did Paul Matthyssens much earlier on in Part II. We found that Ulrich Weihe also had some nice thoughts to offer on 'balancing' and ambidexterity as well as being a proponent of a holistic approach.

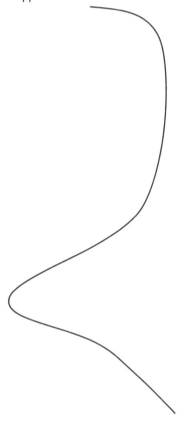

The Future of Innovation is Dependent on Craft and Art

Name	**Dr Ulrich Weihe**
Affiliation	McKinsey & Company, Inc.
Position	Engagement Manager
Country	Germany
Area	Innovation management, innovation process
Email	Ulrich_Weihe@mckinsey.com

innovation engine   craft   art   commercialisation   ideation

Growth and Innovation

Most companies that demonstrated over-proportional growth over an extended period of time showed superior *portfolio momentum*. Besides focusing on the right market segments, innovation is the key to maintaining portfolio momentum. However, many companies struggle to innovate continuously and successfully at scale. Many executives actually still perceive innovation as somewhat of a mystery. Indeed, it is very complicated to excel at innovation and it needs to be tackled holistically by addressing many levers. Actually, McKinsey research in the chemicals industry has shown that > 40 per cent of businesses investigated have failed to create value from their innovation investments in the past five years – a more than alarming sign.

We are convinced that innovation is most successful in a 'craft and art' approach.

- *Craft* means getting the basics right. Install disciplined process management throughout the innovation process. Conduct rigorous analytics before starting the journey since success depends on systematically generating insights with the right tools and frameworks along the way. However, craft alone will not ensure success.

- *Art* means getting the magic to work. The truly successful innovators among companies foster creativity and routinely break company orthodoxies. They challenge and enrich ideas and plans by bringing in the 'street-smarts' of experienced managers. Art means to systematically build commercial judgement across the company, particularly in R&D department where a focus on technologically driven innovation and 'push' to the market is still all too abundant.

The most successful innovators integrate 'craft and art' along the entire process of innovation management and set up a well-functioning *innovation engine*. Starting from setting an aspiration on what they want to achieve with innovation, they systematically translate these aspirations into a strategy with suitable focus areas or search fields, which are both intrinsically attractive and suitable for the company's own capabilities (technically and financially). From ideation through commercialisation, many best practices of innovation can help companies tackle the difficulties of becoming a successful innovator.

Reaching Beyond

A notion which is still not very common in many industries is collaborative and open innovation. Reaching out beyond your own R&D department and – more broadly – beyond your own capabilities, making use of the knowledge of others has proven tremendously valuable in the consumer goods and high tech area. Several examples immediately come to mind such as Procter & Gamble's 'Connect & Develop' platform, the 3M Lead User Approach, and Lego's Mindstorms. Some examples also exist in the basic materials sphere already. Goldcorp successfully employed open innovation to discover new sources of gold on their mining territory. However, almost 90 per cent of managers in the basic materials industries (energy, metals, mining, chemicals, construction industries) indicate that collaboration with academic institutions on specific projects and R&D partnerships/alliances/joint ventures between companies are still the predominant models they apply. The biggest concerns about using open innovation models are around the integrity of intellectual property. However, several models exist of how open/mass innovation can be used and basic materials companies should think intensively about how to most effectively leverage the vast ideation and problem solving potential outside of their own firm.

Getting a well-functioning innovation engine to work is difficult, no doubt. However, innovation is and will continue to be one of the most critical growth drivers of our industries and companies are well advised to further build innovation capabilities. This is particularly true during the economic downturn, when the basis for future success will be laid.

There you have it: being well balanced and open, are the key cornerstones of the future of innovation. We do not mean to be flippant here; it sounds so simple yet reality indicates it is not, otherwise more companies would have achieved it by now – and Ulrich has commented on the fact that, despite the desire to become more innovative, it remains quite a hard thing to achieve. It seems to us that most organisations seem to be better at the craft of innovation than its art. Would your senior management be comfortable with the word 'magic'? Do not most – perhaps even us reading the book – still want proof, facts and figures, certainty?

Let us hear from our third voice calling for balance, Kathrin Möslein.

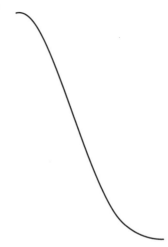

The Future of Innovation is Hopefully More Like its Past!

Name	**Kathrin M. Möslein**
Affiliation	CLIC – Centre for Leading Innovation and Cooperation
Position	Professor
Country	Germany
Area	Innovation and value creation
Email	moeslein@hhl.de

**balanced innovation   sensemaking   openness   ambiguity   open-i
munich airport**

While in recent years 'innovation' has became one of the most popular buzzwords worldwide among academics, business people, consultants and politicians alike, the current financial and economic crisis might help us to find our way back to the roots and to the essence of innovation. This will be necessary to drive the field forward. Therefore, we call for balanced innovation!

Being paradoxical by nature, innovation fascinates most in its extremes, but flourishes the most in balance. There are many examples to illustrate this paradox. Today, companies and customers alike get enthusiastic about openness in innovation, while most innovations that managers and markets value most stem from closed innovation processes. Innovators call for leadership, but excel best in democratic settings. Creativity, ideas and knowledge – the ingredients of innovation – reside in widely distributed actors and locations, while decision makers expect to see highly focused, well-integrated and closely connected innovation systems that can be evaluated on the basis of productivity and performance.

The consequences of this constant misfit of experiences and expectations in innovation programmes, projects and processes are widely visible and well known, but rarely understood. Corporations start open innovation initiatives and invite their customers to contribute, but often forget about their own employees as important innovators. Academics explore the absorptive capacity of a firm in order to foster open innovation and the firm's ability to innovate, but forget about the interactive nature of openness and the necessary balance of give and take that drives voluntary contributions in the long run.

In order to better understand this constant quest for balance in innovation activities we have set up a very hands-on research project, called *Open-I* (www.open-i.eu). *Open-I* sets the focus on open innovation within the firm and explores the tensions organisations face when opening their innovation processes to new key actors, like external innovators outside the traditional organisational boundaries or peripheral innovators inside the organisation , but outside the core innovation unit. The project allows us to run field experiments with leading innovators, like

Munich Airport (the most innovative airport in Europe and one of the top innovators worldwide), DATEV (an extremely innovative software and IT service provider for tax consultants, lawyers and companies in general) and innovative micro organisations with global reach. The field experiments are real 'eye openers' with regard to the need for balance in innovation in many dimensions: balance between openness and closedness, continuity and discontinuity, closeness and distribution, local practices and global reach, individual ideas and collective commitment – innovation as usual and innovation as unusual.

Faced with these tensions and ambiguities, we noticed how much we can learn from and with Karl Weick's work in the field of 'sensemaking'. Sensemaking is often characterised as the ability or attempt to make sense out of ambiguous situations. To put it more exactly, we could see sensemaking as a process of creating situational awareness and understanding. It is most needed in situations of high complexity or uncertainty. In these kinds of situations people have to create sense in order to be able to act and to decide. In organisations that strive for innovation, it is a key task of leaders to create sense and to reduce ambiguity for their employees and teams – and for themselves. To create the future of innovation out of a situation of global crisis will call for exactly this: sensemaking and balance.

The point Kathrin makes about inviting suppliers and customer to collaborate – and forgetting the people inside the organisation resonates with us. A comment from a workshop on Open Innovation run by the Innovation Leadership Forum early 2008 was, 'It is quite interesting to note that we seem to have much fewer problems with external collaboration; collaboration internally is much more fraud with difficulties.'

Have you noticed how much talk there is about the need to understand and making sense? The emphasis on people, mindsets, the way the brain works? This understanding can no longer come from books, as Julian said, there are things to be understood and grasp that we did not need to go into in the past. The increasing complexities, the speed of change, the 'undeniability' of the systemic nature of our existence require that we go deeper in our understanding than before. That we understand connections, the implications of connections and the consequences of changes in part of the system on the whole. Experimentation, trying things out, exploring different avenues, in controlled context is one way of reaching such understanding. Has that not been the approach of science over generations?

David Bennet too writes about experimentation, or to use his words, 'playing with ideas', and shares his thoughts on what the elements and process are that make innovation happen.

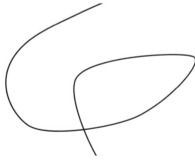

The Future of Innovation is Creating Innovation From the Inside Out

Name	**Dr David Bennet**
Affiliation	Mountain Quest Institute
Position	Co-Founder
Country	USA
Area	Innovation management, critical success factors
Email	dbennet@mountainquestinstitute.com

**knowledge   take effective action   critical success factors   question and assess
culture of the team**

First some definitions: learning is the creation of knowledge; knowledge is the capacity to take effective action; and innovation is the creation and application of new or unusual ideas and/or products. Second, the fundamental learning cycle of learning, knowing and doing sounds simple, but can be quite challenging to implement. From a systems view, the major subsystems are the learner, the environment and the learning process. Each of these needs to be optimised for maximum payoff of creativity and innovation.

What are the *critical success factors* (CSF) leading to successful innovation? Consider the innovation process starting with the information, knowledge, experience, theories and goals of an individual or small group. The next step is to expand that knowledge base through a learning process. This process takes information in through experience, reflects on it, and through abstract conceptualisation creates understanding, meaning, insights, judgement and the ability to anticipate the outcome of actions. CSFs would include: communicating with your unconscious and listening to its ideas; working with your emotions to enhance awareness and utilisation of ideas through playing and excitement; building the right content of information; working in an enriched environment, playing with ideas; exploring and dialoguing with two others; and a willingness to risk being wrong. Use exercise and good nutrition to keep your mind/brain healthy.

There is more: manage your stress level so that it creates strong arousal and interest, but not so strong as to create fear and stress. Question and assess the importance of what you learn in terms of its relation to the objective. Be aware of your own theories, beliefs, frames of reference and have the ability to shift them at will. Recognise the plasticity of your mind and the control you have over it through your willpower, unconscious and ability to influence your own genes through Epigenetics. Seek the meaning of your learning by asking, and answering, how and why questions. And spend time reading and studying other disciplines close to your expertise to generate creative ideas from the connections and potential synergy from the interface between disciplines.

Given a creative idea, it must then be converted into a product. This is best done by an integrated product team, where a spectrum of expertise is available. Examples include design and development engineering, test and evaluation, quality control, logistics management, financial management, cost estimating, market analysis and sales. The critical success factors would be the depth of expertise and the ability to manage and integrate these experts to ensure an integrated approach during the development and production processes. Team-members must listen, learn, understand and collaborate to ensure a high-quality, robust product. The team leader would facilitate, create a common language via team collaboration, and use a systems approach with continuous learning. When successful, these become the culture of the team. The innovative product will be capable of adding value within a broad range of context variability – ensuring its market acceptance.

Again we hear about learning, about collaboration, about experimentation. The third aspect of David's system, the learning process, makes an important link back to Part VI, 'The roles of Big Brother and education'. How we are learning is perhaps not changing – has it not always been thus, as the ancient Chinese proverb indicates, 'Not hearing is not as good as hearing, hearing is not as good as seeing, seeing is not as good as mentally knowing, mentally knowing is not as good as acting; true learning continues up to the point that action comes forth'? (Well, this is a slightly more elaborate version we preferred rather than the commonly used one which goes, 'What I hear I forget, what I see I remember, what I do I understand.') We may just have forgotten that the doing, the experimentation are critical aspects of learning, and essential if one wants to go beyond learning (in the sense of memorising) and move on to understanding.

If we want to prepare our children for the future we need to move away from learning as memorising and move towards learning as experimenting and understanding.

Matthew Kingdon is someone else who has identified three drivers of what he calls 'innovation energy', which is not miles from what David was talking about.

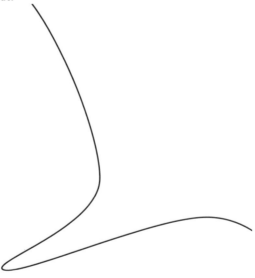

The Future of Innovation is About Creating Innovation Energy

Name	**Matthew Kingdon**
Affiliation	?What If!
Position	Chairman
Country	United Kingdom
Area	Innovation
Email	suzi.stephenson@whatifinnovation.com

ideas   energy   behaviours   innovation   insight

As we move into an increasingly uncertain future, innovation is more important than ever. As the economies of the world change the fallout is felt in households all over the world. Customers are changing and faster than anyone predicted or any market research company can keep up with. As the tide goes out so many companies are being caught swimming naked!

Given the new world reality we're going to have to reassess what 'risk' means in a company. We have no option but to be more audacious. We need to be closer to consumers and customers. Out go lengthy product and brand development projects and in come innovation projects that hit the bottom line very quickly. New ideas that drive sales, ideas that make organisations more nimble at work, ideas that connect companies to customers and weld steel into their backbones – this is what innovation is going to look like in the future.

Successful innovation is always (and will always be) characterised by motivated people, great teamwork and organisations that get out of people's way. We call this 'innovation energy' and it's a powerful strategy that works in any size organisation. Its effect is to strip away wasteful working practises and quickly engage project teams in a practical and inspiring way with customers.

There are three key components to the innovation energy equation:

1. *Right innovation attitude*: This is about having enough people in an organisation who believe that innovation is important, are confident they can do it and who care enough to stretch themselves in order to make it happen. Organisations can help to foster the right attitude in a number of ways: they can refocus their teams with a consumer perspective, create a crisis and embrace it and provide innovation skills training. In short, innovation energy demands that individuals give a damn and that they can answer the question: why should I bother to put my head above the parapet?

2. *Great innovation behaviour*: Innovation behaviour is an exciting concept that releases companies from the tyranny of process and bureaucracy. Over the years ?What If! has identified a number of behaviours that have been distilled into simple concepts such as: freshness, the practice of looking externally for inspiration and deliberately breaking age-worn patterns of exploration; greenhousing, the behaviour of building an idea, it involves 'leaning in' to an idea and blocking out ideas about why it won't work rather than why it might; and realness, the antidote to 'office-think', it involves mocking up

and prototyping – anything that conveys the idea in the same medium that the consumer consumes. Successful innovation teams practise these behaviours until they become habitual.

3. **Supportive organisations**: For innovation to happen it needs an organisation that at the very least doesn't get in its way and at best accelerates it. Creating a supportive organisation isn't an issue for middle management; it's a top leadership challenge that requires a long-term approach and a committed top team. Top teams within supportive organisations give their people 'freedom in a gilded cage' – they give them a single clear direction and leave them alone to get on with it; they innovate with innovation looking at structures they could put in place to make innovation inevitable; and they tell stories that engage their people around innovation at an emotional level.

The human element in innovation is the key to innovation energy, not structures or process. At the confluence of these three components exists a powerful innovation sweet spot – this is innovation energy and it's the future of innovation!

If David and Matthew spoke about a threesome, each in the context of creating systemic innovation, Rolandas Strazdas has identified four aspects that he considers critical to the future of innovation. You may recall us talking earlier about Bettina's research into Innovation Best Practice and Future Challenges and the shift in attention from processes to people. It is as if our understanding of innovation had to move up something like Abraham Maslow's hierarchy of needs!

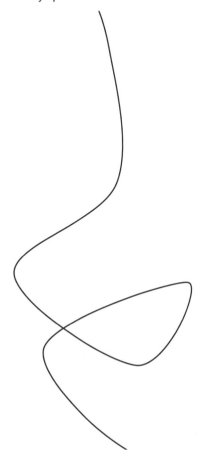

The Future of Innovation is Pragmatic Arguments

Name	**Rolandas Strazdas**
Affiliation	Vilnius Gediminas Technical University
Position	Head of Industrial Enterprises Management Department
Country	Lithuania
Area	Innovation management, creativity stimulation
Email	r.strazdas@takas.lt

pragmatic arguments   needs for innovations   resources for
innovations   environment for innovations   innovation development

The future of innovation is very positive. Usually I like emotional arguments, but here I will try to present my findings very pragmatically. To my understanding the future of innovation development depends on four elements which are crucial, namely: *the need for innovations; available resources; environment; knowledge about innovation development.* Let's discuss each of these elements:

- *The need for innovations* is very important for the innovation development. If there are no needs – there are no innovations. It is clear that needs for innovations are growing due to the growing population and the increased number of social, environmental, technological and political problems. We need to solve problems related to the global warming, ageing, energy, food and etc., so there are no doubts that it will require more creativity and entrepreneurship. Even if some of these problems are solved, human beings are created in such way that new and even bigger problems and challenges will be raised. Even if we satisfy some of our needs, new hidden needs will emerge. It is like in the fairytale about the dragon: you cut off one of his heads – but several new heads grow up in its place.

- *Resources* that are necessary for innovation development are growing. If you want to do something, you have to have resources (i.e., time, people, material, place, finance and etc.). Governments, companies and even families are allocating more and more resources for development of innovations. This trend is so obvious, that mental activities take over physical ones. One fine day 'smart' machines – robots – will do almost all physical activities, so people will have more and more human resources and more and more time for mental work – i.e., innovation development.

- *Environment* is also very important for the innovation development. If we look through our history, it is obvious that creativity and innovation development directly correlates with the development of freedom and security of the society. The environmental differences between the Dark Middle Ages and the Renaissance are clear. The history of the Renaissance (14th–17th centuries) evidently demonstrates that liberty was precondition for innovation development. I assume that our society becomes more and more liberal. I see more liberty in families, companies, countries, so the background for the future innovation development is very favourable.

- *Knowledge on innovation development.* Our understanding about how to develop innovations now is more comprehensive than it was 10 years ago. Just look at the number of books on innovations (including this) that have been written during the last 10 years. Hundreds of creativity stimulation, new product development, innovation management tools and methods were developed. I think it is very important to deepen our knowledge on innovations. I am also sure that in next 10 years our understanding and knowledge of innovation development will dramatically increase.

Summarising I must say that we never had such a good background for the innovation development and I am strongly believe in the future of innovation.

We thought it quite interesting that while other contributors discover emotions in the context of innovation Rolandas feels he needs to move towards the 'pragmatic'. The four aspects he identifies definitely provide organisations that want to become more innovative – or shall we say, in light of what Julian has said, create better conditions for innovation? – with useful starting points: innovation requires a purpose or need, resources to achieve the purpose or address the need, freedom of expression and an understanding of how to go about it. While many contributors alert us to the things we need to learn, know and understand, we also found it quite reassuring that Rolandas reminds us that there are things that we know already, and that we have come far over the past 10 or so years.

If Rolandas puts a need at the starting point for innovation, Lars Kolind reminds us that innovation is key driver for the creation of value. Let us see what other advice he has for companies who would like to improve their innovation performance.

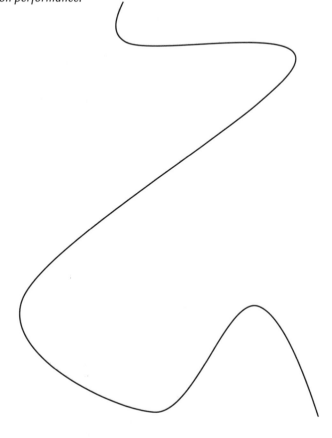

The Future of Innovation is Exciting

Name	**Lars Kolind**
Affiliation	Grundfos Foundation
Position	Chairman
Country	Denmark
Area	Innovation management
Email	lars@kolind.dk

innovation   meaning   purpose   partnership   collaborative organisation

It's exciting because innovation is becoming the key to creating value – just like productivity has been for the last 100 years. In the 20th century, the winning formula for business was to deliver products that were *good enough* at the *lowest possible cost*. Today, and indeed tomorrow, everybody can deliver good products at a low cost. So the challenge of tomorrow becomes to deliver the best product at a cost that the customer is willing to pay. In other words: the *best product* at a price that is *good enough*.

That makes innovation key.

The bad news is that innovation doesn't flourish in most companies today. Innovation just doesn't happen frequently in conventional hierarchical organisations that focus on shareholder value, which is what most businesses are today.

The good news is that is not impossible for a conventional, hierarchical company to transform itself into an innovation powerhouse. It isn't easy either, but the recipe is simple:

1. Make the business meaningful, i.e., take down shareholder value from its present position as the business mantra. In tomorrow's innovative business, shareholder value is no more the ultimate goal for a business, it is the consequence of doing the right things right. The purpose of the business should be to do something that has significant value to customers and to society, i.e., the meaning. The meaning of a mobile phone manufacturer is not to sell mobile phones; it is to connect people. And all innovation that company does, should be focused on connecting people better, faster and cheaper.

2. Build win–win partnerships in all areas, i.e., stop considering employees as employees – they are partners or associates. Stop looking upon customers as buyers – they are partners in value creation. Stop looking for ever-cheaper suppliers – they are partners in building better solutions. Innovation flows if partners have a common goal, which is the meaning of the business.

3. Transform your departmentalised, hierarchical organisation into a collaborative organisation, i.e., a (virtual) place where everybody can work with, communicate with and innovate with anybody. Eliminate management levels and forget titles. They were great in 19th- or 20th-century bureaucracies, but they are superfluous today. Connect everybody with everybody and let everybody work where they want, when they want, with whom they want and on which task they want. You will be surprised how things start to get done, faster, better and more creatively than you imagined.

4.   Embark upon a new way of management: value-based leadership instead of the power-based management you practise today. Why is it that your employees can buy real estate and take loans when you don't allow them to buy a new desk for the office without some 'responsible person' countersigning the purchase order?

Innovation happens when employees (associates) are happy, empowered, committed and liberated. You will never get to that point if you continue to run your business as if we were still in the 20th century.

Just do it!

'It isn't easy, but the recipe is simple.' It is simple because it is about connecting people, but just that is not as easy as it sounds. Does not the saying go, 'Everyone in the world is quite mad, except for me and thee; and sometimes I even have my doubts about thee.' Somehow this makes us think about the fact that we talk about change and the need for change – and always seem to be pointing towards others. Later on one of our contributors will refer to this quote by Gandhi too, and a fundamental truth really is: you have to be the change you want to see in the world. You are the only 'thing' you can truly change – though in changing yourself you may cause ripples in the pond of life that may well be far reaching.

Robson Luiz Schiefler points out – in his own words – that the number of ponds in which we can cause ripples (or not) is endless, and that it is our choice, or even responsibility, to choose ours and start making a big splash!

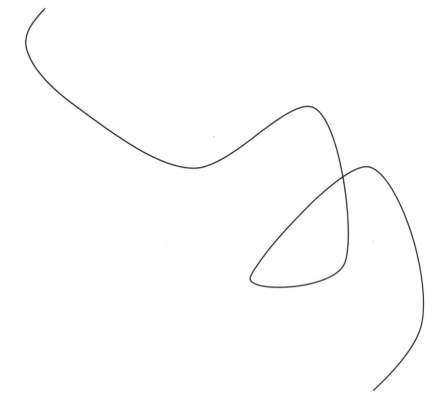

The Future of Innovation is Unpredictable!

Name	**Robson Luiz Schiefler**
Affiliation	COPEL – Companhia Paranaense de Energia
Position	General Assistant
Country	Brazil
Area	Electrical engineering
Email	robsonl@copel.com

challenge   routine   uncertain   crise   spirit

The future of innovation is unpredictable. Innovations can lead us to an infinite number of scenarios, and this infinite number of scenarios is the prize for everyone who decides to get involved.

The cyclic crises which periodically engulf our planet demonstrate that only countries, companies or individuals with the aptitude to innovate are able to manage a scenario where the set of variables is immense and the correlation between them is sparse.

The learning provided by the consistent steps on the innovation path is the support for those who, on a day-to-day basis, face the challenges of unpredictable.

The previous statements lead us to a positive convergence: people, challenges and environment.

Each one of these factors can foment the rising of initiatives focused on innovation, but only foment. To uphold an entire culture of innovation, a lot more is needed.

To keep the basics in focus, these are what's needed:

- people with a natural vocation for results, especially new ones, are an inestimable asset;

- the right challenges with the right amount of difficulty and potential of reward;

- the maintenance of a positive environment where ethics, good will and knowledge flow smoothly is the final key factor.

These three factors together can lead us to the future of innovation, which is unpredictable.

The unpredictable is not a frightening reality; it is just a myriad of scenarios, which are feasible.

The present uncertainty is calling for action!

The absence of action leads to no scenario.

The action starts a journey ...

This journey, with the right resources, must be via the innovation route, which is the only one which can lead us to, at least, one bright scenario.

Innovation is more than a state of mind – it is a state of spirit! Take your passport, not to travel but to the future!

The three factors highlighted by Robson resonate strongly with Rolandas' and Lars' comments: it is about people, it is about having a worthwhile challenge, and it is about providing a supportive context. Let us see what Ruth Thomson has to say about what might be involved in creating such a 'supportive context.'

The Future of Innovation is the Fundamental Human Nature of Ideas

Name	**Ruth Thomson**
Affiliation	Kodak European Research
Position	Innovations Leader
Country	UK
Area	Early stage ideas management
Email	ruth.thomson@kodak.com

ideas management   human   champion   black hole   software

We will always need new ideas and innovation. This is as true today as it ever was and will be true in the future. However, the way we choose to manage ideas has changed over time, influenced by studies and new schools of thought, as well as the increase in the use of software systems.

Computer systems help us streamline, simplify and organise many activities but I feel that there is a huge danger that, when setting up a new system, we increasingly set about developing a software solution without due consideration of the implications on the 'people' aspects.

This is particularly important for ideas systems. Our ability to create, evolve and develop ideas is a fundamental part of what makes us human, ideas are personal to us and it is critical that the 'people' aspects are central to how we approach ideas management going forward.

For example:

Minimise the Barrier to Entry

All ideas should be captured and shared (socialised). Don't pre-judge! Initial weak ideas might spark another thought or could be combined with something else to become stronger and grow. People have new ideas all the time but often these are lost. If this loss is due to a high barrier to entry to an ideas submission system then it is failing. Is the database difficult to navigate to? Is the champion faced with a dry, complex ideas submission form? A successful ideas system should make it as easy as possible for people to participate. Consider ... Does it *really* need to be on a computer system? Could you have a 'post-box'? Or an ideas board where cards are physically put on the wall for everyone to see and discuss?

Recognise the Value of the Contribution of an Idea and the Progress

People need feedback and recognition, it makes others want to join in and encourages you to participate again. Feedback on the progression of an idea feeds everyone's interest and helps us learn for the future. If a submitted idea disappears into a 'black hole-like' software system, possibly sending you an automated 'thank you' note, then that is a huge missed opportunity.

The Importance of a True Champion

The ideas that will turn into successful innovations do not necessarily start from the best ideas, but you can guarantee that behind every really successful venture there is a true champion; someone who really believes in the idea, and is determined to make it work. Clearly decisions on the resourcing of new projects must be taken in a rational and objective manner, but I believe that a key question to consider when assessing ideas is 'is there a true champion?' These examples demonstrate the importance of the consideration of the 'human' element that should be at the heart of any successful ideas management system. In the future I hope that we will be able to combine and balance the convenience of software whilst keeping true to the fundamental 'human' nature of ideas.

Ruth points out some fundamentals on conditions for innovation: if you say you want more innovation, and if you say that innovation is your future, you need to enable people to contribute! But make sure there is someone to read or listen to the ideas. We are sure that many of you will be familiar with the cartoon where a notice says 'Suggestions' above a letterbox which has a rubbish bin underneath it on the other side of the wall? That's not the way it is supposed to work. Someone, with understanding and care, needs to read the suggestions made and the ideas brought forward. It is also important to make it easy to bring up ideas, and to make it easy to share them. You need to provide people with evidence that you are serious about the importance of innovation. That involves listening to ideas; even better, you should go out and seek ideas! And yes, while it is probably part of an employee's role to help create a future for the organisation, it might not go amiss to thank them for their contribution and acknowledge their effort. This does not have to mean monetary rewards. Intrinsic motivation, pride and sense of achievement cannot be bought with money but instilled through praise, recognition and even a simple 'thank you!' (as long as it is heart-felt).

Since we have spoken quite a lot about emotions and behaviours let us no longer hold back the contribution of Franc Ponti who shares with us his seven strategies for achieving behavioural change.

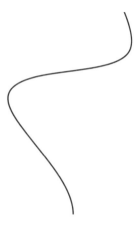

The Future of Innovation is Through Seven Strategies

Name	**Franc Ponti**
Affiliation	EADA Business School
Position	Professor of Innovation
Country	Catalonia – Spain
Area	Innovation
Email	fponti@eada.edu

strategy   open   zen   po   emo

Innovating means being able to address complex problems in a different and original fashion, contributing value in the process and achieving successful results. Innovation is therefore the outcome of combining creativity and change management. Having said this and leaving definitions aside, it is essential to have an associated behaviour model which is capable of transforming people and organisations and achieving real changes. This model is comprised of seven different strategies which are outlined below.

ZEN

It is not possible to innovate if we don't devote enough time. Innovation demands a different rhythm that enables us to reflect upon the future, study trends and see things from a different perspective. However, most companies state that they 'don't have time' to innovate. This big contradiction and the inability to overcome it is one of the keys to managing innovation.

PO

Innovation involves provocation, a constant challenging of conventionalisms and dominant ideas. If we don't dare to change the way we are then it will be hard to come up with truly creative ideas. Thinking PO is thinking disruptively, breaking brain patterns which prevent us from accessing groundbreaking ideas.

OPEN

Where is there more talent, inside your organisation or on the rest of the planet? You are the only one who can answer this question by conceding that no matter how much intelligence is locked up in your company, there is much more talent out there. Thinking OPEN means making a constant effort to incorporate the collective intelligence that surrounds us: customers, suppliers, experts, enemies, admirers, critical consumers, etc.

FLOW

Knowing how to think creatively is key to achieving innovation processes. It is essential to generate large quantities of ideas that are as daring as possible (divergence) and to know how to evaluate them, select them and come up with prototypes and innovation projects (convergence). However, there are a lot of barriers which often prevent teams from being sufficiently creative: self-censorship, pre-judging, the 'egos' of participants, etc.

EMO

It is hard to innovate without emotions. Organisations that are really able to innovate are those that connect emotionally with their customers because they know how to tell stories that appeal and seduce. To motivate emotions is not the same as manipulating. It means to succeed in getting a product, a service or a strategy to make someone live a different and emotionally gratifying experience. Consequently, it is of vital importance to transmit values that go beyond the intrinsic characteristics that define what a company does. In short, to enrapture.

HAPPY

You can do things with just professionalism or with a real passion. Undoubtedly, it is very difficult to orchestrate an innovation culture if we don't have people with a passion, who live the each day as an adventure and a challenge.

TEAM

In order to innovate we need to replace the attitude of blind competition that is still widespread in many companies with one of intelligent collaboration. To understand that cooperation within diversity and the setting up of creative debate platforms are much more effective than the irrational struggle between departments or senseless competition.

In your organisation, or the organisations you know, how many of these seven strategies are put in place to support innovation? Do you believe it can happen without them? Without all of them? Is there anything you, in your personal or professional life, can do to start implementing Franc's strategies? What happens if you follow your emotions, your passion and start cooperating in different ways? May be it's easier to imagine what might happen if we share the story of someone who has done just that: followed their own heart and their passion, and started 'living dangerously'!

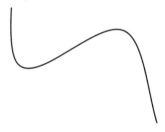

The Future of Innovation is Opening With a Story

Name	**Lekshmy Parameswaran**
Affiliation	Fuelfor Design and Consulting
Position	Co-founder, Innovation Design Consultant
Country	Spain
Area	Health care innovation, design
Email	lekshmy.parameswaran@fuelfor.net

health   experience design   boundary-breaking   complexity   partnership

The future of innovation begins with a story. 2008 was my year of 'living dangerously'.

I left a comfortable yet challenging job as innovation design director in the health care team of a large multinational corporation. I had clocked up a decade of experience in using design to change the strategic course of a 'super tanker'! Seeking a change, I followed my head and my heart to move to Barcelona and set up an innovation design consultancy together with my partner. We are called fuelfor and we specialise in health care innovation.

In writing this article I realise the significance of this moment; my experience of innovation inside a 117-year-old corporation is still fresh in my mind, as is my recent foray into innovation entrepreneurship as fuelfor takes its first steps in the world. It is an ideal vantage point from which to speculate on the future of innovation ...

The Future of Innovation Lies in ...

Seeing beyond existing boundaries

Opportunities for innovation lie in the cracks. In a corporate setting, innovation often required connecting skills and knowledge across disparate and rigid business divisions, or establishing entirely new business lines just to nurture an innovation. Stepping outside the commercial health care context I now see opportunities between the fragmented public, clinical and personal health care contexts. As fuelfor we decided to actively consult clients in all three contexts, offering a 360° view on health as a means for them to access innovation within their blind spots.

Feeling comfortable with complexity and mess

Once you step beyond existing boundaries, you soon discover how complex and messy the world really is! This need not be an obstacle, in fact when things are no longer black and white there is more room for creativity! Health care is one such complex territory. It is fundamentally a human experience, subjective and emotional, but incorporating science, technology and economy. One of the reasons I love working in this field is the chance to make sense of this rich complexity; it poses me a creative challenge. Design thinking and skills such as empathy, visualisation and experience design are entering the lexicon of business innovation as tools to tackle such complex problems.

Creating your own models of partnership

Tackling complexity works well when you bring diverse experts to think together. But I like how a multidisciplinary approach also forces each discipline to sharpen its individual contribution. Good partnerships bring out the best in each partner. At Fuelfor we seek partners who excel at complementary aspects of health care innovation. In doing so, our assumptions about competition, ownership and identity are being healthily challenged. We feel a need to define bespoke models of collaboration to give and learn the most from each relationship.

It's exciting to see that today's business, design and engineering schools are redesigning curricula to equip graduates with the practical skills needed for boundary-breaking, messy, multidisciplinary innovation! I look forward to learning from this new breed of innovators and discovering what future they will lead us towards.

If 'living dangerously' and creating your own innovation bubble sounds just that little bit too scary, take heart: there are organisations out there who do their best to create such innovation bubbles inside organisations too, fostering them so that they eventually encapsulate the entire organisation. To convince you this really is worth a try we would like to call on Werner Bernard to share his experience next.

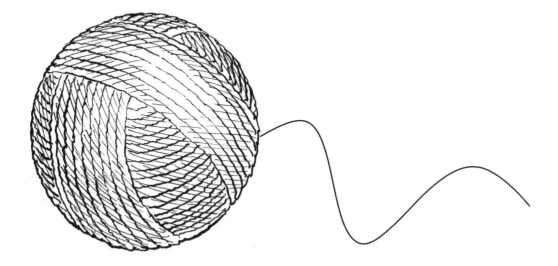

The Future of Innovation is Dependent on How Efficiently Intellectual Resources can Be Used

Name **Werner Bernard**

Affiliation Aerospace Industry

Position R&T Manager Innovation & Intellectual Property

Country Germany

Area Innovation management

Email werner.bernard@airbus.com

**access to information   creativity tools   individual/collective innovation
systematic innovation   recognition**

The future of innovation in an engineering-centred organisation such as the Airbus Centre of Competence (CoC) Flight Physics, is a question of how efficiently intellectual resources can be used. Innovation is the 'natural' output of approximately 930 highly qualified engineers employed in this CoC. With processes in place which support the transition of innovative ideas into real products, CoC Flight Physics, among other engineering centres, contributes to the success of our products. However, there is room for further improvements.

Here are some measures taken in CoC Flight Physics to stimulate and promote innovative thinking.

Information

Knowing that information stimulates innovation, we have ensured that the most recent technical developments now are just one click away. On the centre's internal network pages, several links to information sources were placed including those to internal libraries, patent publications and pertinent publications. Not only is the state-of-the-art technology easily available now, the links also help to understand the intellectual property situation, which is becoming more and more important.

Innovation Workshops/Creativity Tools

An organisation which wants to actively shape the future of its innovations, needs to consider both individual and collective innovations. It is essential to find ways of combining individual innovation ingredients, such as richness of ideas, creativity, dedication and enthusiasm, with a team approach, multiplying the innovative spirit. In this sense, a team may actually be part of an organisation or be only virtually bonded together by common interest.

Innovation workshops are an appropriate means of encouraging this. They have been developed to make the best out of individual creativity and the innovative dynamics of teams and use a set of creativity tools, which are applied in a process of 'systematic solution-finding'. The participants, usually from different neighbouring departments, collectively work out the 'real case' statement and the solution(s). The feedback from the innovation workshop is quite positive for both the workshop facilitation and the creativity tools applied. Better solutions can be found much faster using this kind of workshop, where all stakeholders contribute their ideas and knowledge to the real time solution. Alongside this, the participants learn how to use the creativity tools in their day-to-day work environment.

Recognition/Motivation

The 10 most outstanding innovations in CoC Flight Physics are celebrated in an 'innovation recognition event' where developers have the opportunity to meet with senior or top management. The combination of speeches, presentations and having lunch together results in quite sustainable motivation, much more than monetary rewards.

So, what comes next?

Innovation workshops have proven to be a very efficient means to promote collective innovation. This kind of workshops will step by step be opened to universities and R&D institutes where long-term relationships and contracts with Airbus already are in place thus minimising the implicit risks of opening to a broader community (e.g., IP issues, contract issues, piracy).

Online forums and open calls to contribute to discussions about 'disruptive solutions' will follow.

All the before mentioned measure are promoting innovation. However, the future of innovation remains dependent on the richness of ideas and the creativity of people.

One strand that almost all contributors in this section – if not the book – have emphasised is the need for and importance of collaboration. So, let's move to Part X where we explore in much more detail what all of that is actually about.

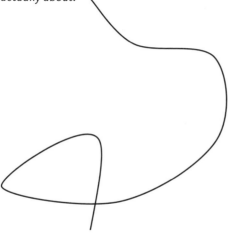

PART X
Let's Get Together

The issue of collaboration, whether internal or external to the organisation, has come up time and again in the contributions. To understand better the issues, ingredients and challenges of collaboration as well as share some leading edge thinking on this topic is the purpose of this section.

Sherrie-Lee Samuel reminds us just why collaboration is the only way forward.

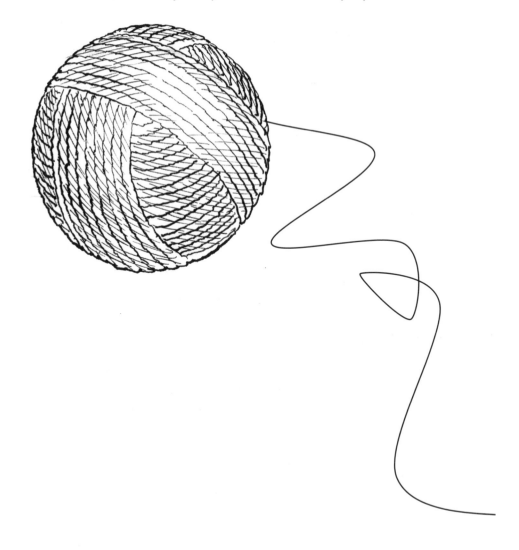

The Future of Innovation is Global Collaboration on Global Challenges

Name	**Sherrie-Lee Samuel**
Affiliation	Science and Technology Facilities Council
Position	PrepSKA Project Manager, Astronomy Division
Country	UK (Trinidad and Tobago)
Area	Challenge-led innovation
Email	sherrie-lee.samuel@stfc.ac.uk

**collaboration   global challenges   challenge-led innovation   global partnerships
grand challenges**

The 21st century has seen the advent of unprecedented global challenges that are increasingly placing pressure on the ability of mankind to cope. With foreboding predictions of rising temperatures expected to create a global food crisis by the end of the century and oil reserves estimated to last just 41 more years, it is no longer sufficient for countries to tackle major global crises alone.

Ideas often sparked from the creativity of individuals are rarely implemented as a result of the efforts of that one individual alone. And in global challenge-led innovation, this has never been more true. Global issues often require embarking on mega projects that demand the involvement of experts worldwide to share and build on existing research on the journey to minimising the impact of such challenges. Global challenge-led innovation therefore encourages commitment from science and research infrastructures worldwide, governments and the public to cooperate to face the problems head on. Thus, collaboration creates exciting opportunities for ideas to be analysed, improved and shaped into a workable solutions. Working together with a sense of purpose to achieve a common goal is a stimulating and essential motivator in the sharing of knowledge and securing involvement in global partnerships. More importantly, what makes collaboration so effective is the contributions and experience of diverse groups who can commit the often substantial resources necessary to sufficiently tackle major global issues.

Collaboration in challenge-led innovation however is not without its own challenges. Mega projects with extended timelines tend to call for hefty financial investments and resource commitment. As the funding cycles of countries vary so too does their science and innovation budgets as commitments are made to the country's own activities. International collaboration too is often fraught with legalities as countries enter into agreements that are necessary for ensuring continued involvement. As global agreements like the Kyoto Protocol have demonstrated, the process of negotiation tends to be lengthy, taking years to scope and indeed start. More interestingly, in spite of the altruism of a greater sense of purpose in tackling the world's grand challenges, worldwide collaboration is not without its critics.

So, *is* collaboration the best way forward? The question is not around a justification for the benefits of collaboration but about the availability of alternatives in addressing global crises that impact all nations. If not an international endeavour, then what? In the latter, nations stand alone, resources are stretched and the knowledge that comes with true partnership is lost.

Collaboration is an essential ingredient in attempting to address these growing global crises and it is only with commitment across borders that nations can begin to protect the future now. Whilst it is true that there is still a long way to go, countries with the resources necessary to mobilise quickly and effectively continue to be models for the role of collaboration in the future of innovation. My best guess for the future of innovation driven by these global challenges rests in the ability of countries to collaborate and to collaborate well.

If Sherrie-Lee has been, while firm, quite gentle in her call for collaboration, Edna Pasher is more forthright, exclaiming, 'It will take all of us to save us!'

The Future of Innovation is Innovating for Sustainability

Name	**Dr Edna Pasher**
Affiliation	EPA (Edna Pasher PhD & Associates)
Position	President
Country	Israel
Area	Innovation management, sustainable development
Email	edna@pasher.co.il

innovation   sustainability   knowledge management   learning   collaborating

Only innovative thinking and innovative doing will make it possible for our civilisation to survive. In these turbulent times it is clear that we need to re-invent our organisations and our businesses and our economic systems in order to survive.

Big problems need a very high level of innovation in order to be solved. A high level of innovation cannot be achieved by individuals. *It will take all of us to save us!* It takes collaboration at a level we have not seen before. 'The tragedy of the commons' can only be stopped through win–win solutions – where everybody understands the gains through the new way of doing things right. ('The Tragedy of the Commons' by Garrett Hardin, first published in the journal *Science* in 1968, describes a dilemma in which multiple individuals acting independently in their own self-interest can ultimately destroy a shared resource even where it is clear that it is not in anyone's long-term interest for this to happen.)

For too many years we have left the economy to be led by 'The Invisible Hand' which has become very greedy and corrupt because of lack of effective rules. We need to invent new rules and keep them! ('The invisible hand' is a metaphor coined by the economist Adam Smith who argued that, in a free market, an individual pursuing his own self-interest tends to also promote the good of his community as a whole through a principle that he called 'the invisible hand'.)

We must and we can stop 'the tragedy of the commons' and the greed of 'the invisible hand'! With information and communication technology (ICT) we have really become 'a global village' (a phrase first coined by Marshall McLuhan) and it really takes a village to raise a child. We can no longer afford to just make sure that our children get the proper education but not a promise of fresh water and clean air! Innovative solutions will emerge out of 'conversations on questions that matter' in 'world cafés'. (The world café is an innovative yet simple methodology for hosting conversations. These conversations link and build on each other as people move between groups, cross-pollinate ideas, and discover new insights into the questions or issues that are most important for them. The world café makes visible the collective intelligence of any group, thus increasing people's capacity for effective action in pursuit of common aims.)

My vision for the future of innovation is that it emerges out of multiple perspective conversations in conversing families, conversing organisations, conversing communities, conversing cities, conversing region, and a conversing world! Some conversations will be conducted face to face and others will be online dialogues. But *they will all focus on how we can save the planet for future generations!* This is the future of innovation worth inventing! Let's behave as a real global village and re-invent the village conversations for sustainability. And where there is a will there is a way!

Collaboration, like it or not, has no alternative if we want to address today's challenges. Collaboration in and between families, collaboration in and between companies, collaboration in and between nations; collaboration that creates a global village where we all share the same ambition: to create a future that is worth inventing.

Let's then turn to some of the consequences of such collaboration, drawing on Venky Rao's insights first.

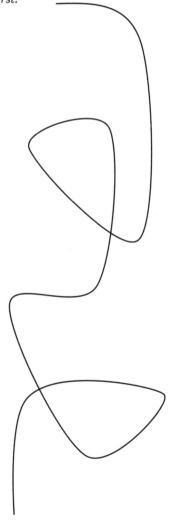

The Future of Innovation is Harnessing the Creative Capabilities of Global Ecosystems

Name	**Venky Rao**
Affiliation	Satyam
Position	Senior Vice President
Country	India
Area	Innovation management
Email	Venky_rao@satyam.com; venky_kovuru@yahoo.com

ecosystem   globalization   knowledge   virtualization   innovation networks

The future of innovation will harness the creative capabilities of the entire global ecosystem. While in the short to mid-term the current economic and geopolitical issues will likely dictate the global trade and how the different geographies play a role in the introduction and success of innovative products and services, the future will belong to those innovators (individuals, organisations, countries and regions) who understand and tap the virtualisation benefits that involve global trade in the flat world. With the increase in global trade as a percentage of world GDP, lots more traditional services and products across the agriculture, manufacturing and services industry will become potential sources of virtualisation to reach, respond to and reap the benefits for producers and consumers across the world. A good chunk of these virtualisable options will act as a wellspring of innovative ideas that usher the world in the future.

Innovation networks will effectively tap into these opportunities by delivering results much beyond what traditional product and process innovations have often produced. They optimise the entire global ecosystems including partners, suppliers, customers, government agencies and non-governmental organisations. As the parties to the innovation process extend beyond the four walls of an enterprise, devices, approaches, revenue models, delivery channels and profitability can be transformed in ways that no individual can achieve working alone.

Another important aspect will be that innovations may potentially destroy the traditional 20th-century supply chains (both in products and services). Emergence of new players from the outside and at times unrelated industries bringing in new business applications may potentially destroy the original paradigms and unseat the traditional players. Perhaps the economic challenges witnessed in the later part of 2008 will essentially provide this breeding ground though the possibility of tougher government interventions and rules may scare the new entrants and hinder them in the short term.

The future of innovation will not only involve traditional engineering and marketing disciplines, but increasingly will call for better negotiators with cross-functional visibility. The organisational locus will change from traditional R&D and lines of business to something that is more of an extra-enterprise as ecosystems drive the new business models. The innovation of the future will not only be measured simply in terms of patents and new product launches but more importantly by market growth and relationship capital, notwithstanding the fact that protection and respect of intellectual property will become an important theme.

The future of innovative networks taps into much richer idea pool of an extended enterprise than of today's traditional boundaries, and ensures risk reduction with global partnerships tapping and relying on each player's strengths. The future will see a sea change in the knowledge management by ensuring it focuses on building insights which are converted into an innovative idea pool. It will employ social networking and crowd sourcing to tap into larger creative capital. Innovations will take place where rubber meets the road bringing in new ways of forging partnerships and value creation in the new flat world.

Venky argues that to deal with the challenges as well as make most of the opportunities, networks are necessary. Not only that, he also sees new organisational forms emerging as a consequence of it. Boundaries will become permeable, hierarchies will flatten, power relationships shift and traditional functions will morph.

Mo Degen is another of our contributors who sees the emergence of new organisational forms. Let's read her perspective.

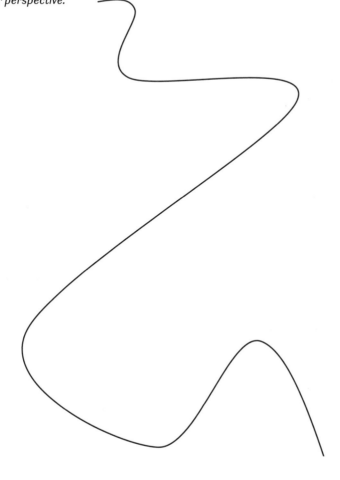

The Future of Innovation is a Team Process with Holistic, Subversive, Innovative Thinking

Name	**Mo Degen**
Affiliation	ChangeAgency Network
Position	Head of Transformation Management at Deutsche Telekom Kundenservice GmbH
Country	Germany
Area	Transformation, change and knowledge management
Email	info@changeagency.de

system thinking   team systems   holistic view   team language   creativity

The future of innovation in an increasingly complex (working) world will depend on whether and how companies and employees of all levels, functions and teams manage to think and act as a system, identify problems, take decisions and transfer these into adequate solution and work strategies; this and the following thoughts are the conclusions from the many discussions and collaborations with my colleague Fritz Rainer Pabel.

These processes not only require a combination of individual competences and expertise, but also meta-competencies such as imagination, fantasy and creativity. These competencies are required as 'system integrators'; the individually received and accumulating new input is transformed and consolidated within the team system as an integrated, subversive and innovative thinking process. This results in the birth of a 'new' language, or rather the team system's 'native' language, which is formally expressed as, for example, a product that has been developed as the solution to a task. When taking a look at the relevant literature, it has been shown that the successful completion of projects can no longer be regarded as a linear production process. The problems posed by work demands have become so complex that they cannot be solved without the help of complementary structures on an organisational and working level. Project-oriented, interacting team systems present such structures.

The benefit of team systems with a systematic network structure is their holistic thinking process, which integrates individual thought patterns and applies the complexities of today's working demands to individual competencies.

In order to be able to function, a team system needs a meta-language that is developed through the imagination, fantasy and creativity used in project communication. The creation and use of this communication is a prerequisite for successful task completion as well as the ability to socially interact. This is by no means commonplace; the managers and employees of most companies have been socialised according to the laws of the globalised market jungle and only collaborate when it is in their individual interest. The generation of solutions to increasingly complex problems in highly complex projects, however, requires a level of teamwork that matches such complex work demands. Individual interests, for example, would hinder successful teamwork of this nature; individual interests have a different quality and are required elsewhere. The teamwork required to complete a complex task is not the sum of individual competencies or effort, but rather the result of the work of a real entity; a system that thinks, decides and acts as a whole.

To develop such innovative team systems in organisations, continual consideration of the following topics is essential:

1. **The organisational form of a company and its relation to the environment:** What structure should a company adopt in order to effectively deal with increasing complexity?

2. **The work structure including the flow of operations and processes:** How should work and processes be structured in order to cope with increasingly complex demands?

3. **The employees' key competencies, as employees also need to be able to master complexity:** Social skills and the ability to imagine, fantasise and be creative are becoming increasingly important.

4. **New leadership requirements:** A move away from controlling and directing to the management of self-direction, self-organisation and learning.

Don't you just like the idea of imagination, fantasy and creativity as mega-competencies? And that these are the competencies on which to build effective communication between highly diverse individuals? Could it be that the days of the memo are over? What exciting prospects.

It seems that Mo is not the only one thinking along these lines, of finding new ways to communicate, and about thinking more deeply how the so much talked about teams can work together better, especially in the context of innovation. Let's see why Anne-Katrin Neyer believes that the future of innovation will be colourful.

The Future of Innovation is Going to Be Colourful

Name	**Anne-Katrin Neyer**
Affiliation	University Erlangen-Nuremberg
Position	Assistant Professor
Country	Germany
Area	Innovation teams, sensemaking
Email	anne-katrin.neyer@wiso.uni-erlangen.de

innovation teams   sensemaking   team dynamics   communication   prototyping

Whereas one might think that the current financial and economic crisis will make the future of innovation dark, I believe that the situation of 'managing the unexpected' offers the possibility to more consciously use the various aspects of human beings' innovative potential.

In recent years a lot of research has been done to understand how individuals shape innovation. The simple conclusion is: two are better than one if the atmosphere among the two is nurtured by trust, cooperation and shared understanding. The pressing issue is: Does this also work when one is required to innovate in times characterised by pressure, cost-cutting and fear to become redundant? I don't think so.

Successful innovation teams are in most of the cases defined by the following terms: openness to experience, openness of individuals to get questioned by others, openness to realise that initial ideas might not good enough and openness to challenge one another. Using my metaphor of colours, one could say that successful innovation teams are full of warm colours.

While such multifaceted openness is clearly key, we tend to ignore some very important – but highly feared and thus not openly communicated – realities: such openness is difficult to live; it often includes a lot of (painful) learning experience and sometimes the wish to send the other team members to the moon (or beyond …). These very human feelings have nothing in common with the widespread success stories of strong innovation teams characterised by 'two is better than one'; they are characterised by subdued colours rather than by warm colours. However, looking beneath the surface of these success stories we find that the success of strong innovation teams is not grounded in the creation of a country club atmosphere. In contrast, these teams have mastered the creation of what one might like to refer to as the 'good guy–bad guy' dynamics. In the words of my metaphor: successful innovation teams use the full palette of colours available. Such teams operate on a foundation of a highly trusting atmosphere (the 'good guy' dynamics) which is the basis for openly communicating and discussing any uncertainty, ambiguity and bounded rationality (the 'bad guy' dynamics). The balance of the two inherent dynamics allows successful teams to manage the unexpected. In order to so, there are tools available that help to make the future of innovation colourful: storytelling and prototyping are methods and tools that will allow innovation teams to balance the 'good guy–bad guy' dynamics.

To conclude, the future of innovation is not black or white, it is not about being well behaved or being socially desirable; it is about creating the innovation team's dynamics characterised by the overall chart of colour range.

The key words that stand out for us from Anne-Katrin's contribution are 'trust', 'stories,' and 'openness'. And will you be surprised to hear that others have picked up on these topics too?

Trust, such an elemental and fundamental pre-requisite for all open and honest exchanges; trust that we are not being laughed at when coming up with a 'crazy' idea; trust that our idea will not be hijacked and sold on as someone else's; trust that the idea will not be used against us. Kirsimarja Blomqvist even goes so far as to say that 'the future of innovation is powered by trust'.

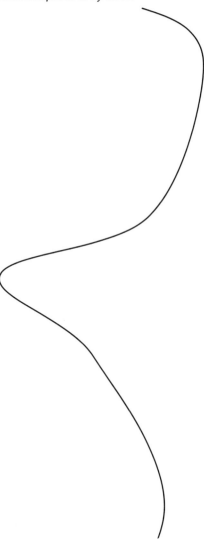

The Future of Innovation is Powered by Trust

Name	**Kirsimarja Blomqvist**
Affiliation	School of Business, Lappeenranta University of Technology
Position	Professor of Knowledge Management
Country	Finland
Area	Trust, networks
Email	kirsimarja.blomqvist@lut.fi

trust   innovation   collaboration   knowledge sharing   diversity

Trust is an all-encompassing force making innovation possible. It works for innovation at all levels, from individual's self-confidence to macro-level institutions supporting intellectual and economic exchange. For people to be willing to share their knowledge, and to participate in implementation of other people's ideas, trust matters.

Innovation is a social activity that knowledgeable individuals with different ideas, skills and knowledge make happen. They come from various backgrounds that differ in work practices and culture. By nature innovation is characterised by information asymmetry and complexity. Trust acts as a threshold condition making it possible to accept the risks and vulnerability involved. It is relevant in all phases of the innovation process, from brainstorming and R&D to experimenting and launching new products. It is vital for leadership, cross-functional and virtual teamwork, selling innovative services and products, consulting, change management and alliances. The higher the risk, the higher the need for trust is.

Basically trust is a threshold condition for any effective communication and cooperation. At its simplest, trust is the willingness to accept vulnerability. In the innovation context it can be defined as actor's cooperative behaviour based on expectation of the other party's competence, goodwill and self-reference. Relevant competence (substance knowledge, skills and know-how) is a necessary antecedent and base for trust in innovation, where the complementary knowledge and resources are key motives behind cooperation. Signs of goodwill (moral responsibility and positive intentions toward the other) are also necessary for the trusting party to accept the risk involved.

Innovation demands also an ability to see the value in other people's ideas. Sharing and synthesising non-redundant knowledge and diverse views is necessary for innovation. A strong self-reference (identity) makes it possible to connect at a deep level with those different from oneself.

Competence, goodwill and self-reference characterise trustworthiness both in individuals and organisations. At organisational level clear values, strategy, structures and fair processes provide the complementary mechanisms for stronger trust combining both interpersonal and impersonal trust. At an inter-organisational level, trust complements contracting and provides the flexibility and commitment needed. At macro-level trustworthy institutions, such as the legal system, monetary and political institutions support the intellectual and economic exchange.

In contemporary knowledge-based network economy trust is critical yet an intriguing and paradoxical issue. Levels of trust in large organisations and institutions have decreased worldwide. Trust is valuable, increasingly rare, and in innovation it is non-substitutable. For those able to build – and increasingly also re-build – trust, trust gives a competitive advantage.

The future of innovation is in trusting networks of knowledgeable individuals coming from different professional backgrounds, organisations and cultures. Trust makes it possible to share and create knowledge and simultaneously build norms and contracts that make fair value creation possible.

Whom do you trust, and who trusts you? Is the role and importance of trust understood in your organisation? What is done to 'earn trust', especially by senior management? Why should employees trust their bosses with their ideas? Why should they trust them when they hear: 'This time we are really serious about the change initiative we have just started', or 'This time it will be truly different'? Kirsimarja's arguments are difficult to refute, as is her statement that levels of trust have decreased – and not only in large organisations. What can we, what can you, individually and collectively do to get trust levels out of the doldrums?

A second issue that was raised in Anne-Katrin's contribution was that of storytelling which, again, we find resonating in other contributions. First we have Jeff Butler who talks about the role of fiction, followed by Juha Kaario who talks about 'serious fun' and telling jokes.

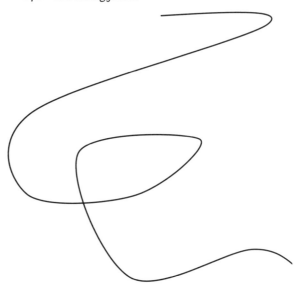

The Future of Innovation is the Role and Roll of Fiction

Name	**Jeff Butler**
Affiliation	Manchester Institute of Innovation Research, Manchester Business School, University of Manchester
Position	Research Fellow
Country	UK
Area	Innovation fiction
Email	jeff.butler@manchester.ac.uk

history   imagination   opportunities   ethics   children

The history of innovation is an interpretation around concepts, processes, systems and situations. The future of innovation is an opportunity space where we exist in the present and where we write history. The future of innovation in 2009 can be appreciated via fictional perspectives taken from the convenient dates of 2020 and 2090.

Innovation opportunity space is a knowledge-time-conceptual 'universe' in which imagination, intelligence and information combine. We try to understand and control the conditions which encourage and induce useful combinations of ideas, investments, opportunities and requirements. By 2020 the aspiration to control innovation is abandoned.

In 2020 in our knowledge-intensive societies, innovativeness has replaced productivity as a measure of 'economic' vitality. 'Economic' pressures mainly emphasise significant or transformative innovation. Cumulative incremental innovation is taken for granted. Research rekindles the criticality and circumstance of apparently random and serendipitous events. Policies try to emulate conditions and increase event probability. A powerful search engine probes the meaning and depth of randomness.

The ethics and philosophy of innovation lead indirectly to the intrinsic appreciation of innovation as an expression of human endeavour and purpose. Art and fiction stimulate and support innovation and form a symbiotic relationship. Innovation inspires art and fiction and between 2020 and 2090 innovation managers and entrepreneurs are gradually superseded by innovation artists. By 2090 the word 'economy' has disappeared from use and we refer to the vitality of innovation and art and happiness in our society without resort to measures and indicators.

2009 innovation types included intangibles such as managerial, organisational, service, 'business model', user-inspired and design-driven innovation. By 2020 the conceptualisation of innovation types and processes was exhausted. A new science and technology of innovation started to emerge. Service science was renamed as value science. By 2090 value science and technology was creating new 'services', 'systems', 'landscapes', 'novels' and 'canvases' as metaphorical expressions of imagination and innovation value. Innovation space is navigated precisely using intellectual and value coordinates. Images of innovation potential (value streetscape) are generated instantaneously from every position and conceptual framework. Innovation fiction media allow workers to plug into a genetically and psychometrically personalised system which allows travel through this streetscape and motivates enthusiastic work and play. Originality workers genuinely believe that they originate and champion their own work.

Children amuse themselves with comedy archives of innovation mythology and mycology. Mycology mushroomed just after 2030 when digital social networking and innovation profiling migrated to organic materials. Spores and viruses replaced radio frequency identification (RFID) tagging and could attach to ideas and knowledge.

Frustration, uncertainty, risk, anxiety and stress are captured in works of art and fiction to make innovation a vivid and unavoidably satisfying experience. Work, travel and play in the innovation universe are seamless, inexpensive, environmentally safe, emotional yet perpetual. Expertise, experience, enthusiasm, energy and elaborate explanation are heavily expended in fictionalising the 'future of innovation'. Entertainment innovation theory accepts that there will always be some too late for the future of innovation and some too early for its history.

The unimaginable of today will be tomorrow's old story that surprises no one any more. There will always be those who declare that 'There is no reason anyone would want a computer in their home' (Ken Olsen, President, Chairman and Founder of Digital, 1977) and believe that 'Everything that can be invented has been invented' (Charles H. Duell, Commissioner, US Patent Office, 1899). Are you one of those? Is your boss? The boss's boss? And if so, what are the implications for innovation? Or, perhaps more importantly, how can you circumvent the consequences such attitudes have for innovation?

And have we not talked about different ways of learning and education before? So what do you think of Jeff's 'enter-edu-innovo-media'? It's less of a joke than you might think – it is most certainly not a joke if you follow Juha Kaario's argument.

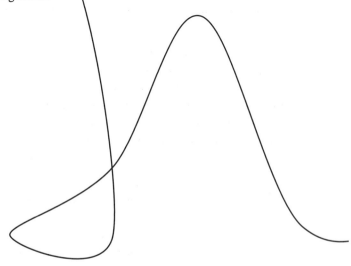

The Future of Innovation is Serious Fun

Name	**Juha Kaario**
Affiliation	Nokia Research Centre
Position	Manager, Business Validation
Country	Finland
Area	Mobile communications
Email	juha.kaario@nokia.com

humour   storytelling   marketing   consumer information   expectations

A successful innovation tells a story that helps people to see the benefits they will get. In the same way, a successful joke manages to create an atmosphere where listener can relate to the situation and is surprised in the end by uplifting or unsuspected twist.

A good joke contains four universal story elements. The first element is an introduction that relates a joke into a setting of which the listener has prior knowledge. Next the joke introduces key actors, who should be familiar to the listener. The two elements create together the emotional attachment, which creates the core for a successful joke. The next element is a narrative, which merely explains what is happening to the actors and leads towards the last element – the punch line. The punch line always includes an element of surprise, which manifests the category of humour the joke belongs to. For example, the surprise can be based on context deviation, exaggeration or irony. The key in the delivery of the punch line is an unexpected narrative twist in the familiar emotional setting.

Explaining an idea is like a delivering a joke. An idea becomes an innovation when it is successfully shared and used by others. All too often we fell into love with our original ideas and cannot see alternative paths to success. This is like a joke that only makes one person laugh. An innovation needs to contain a storyline that resembles that of a good joke.

Like a joke, innovations have four basic elements. An introduction relates the innovation to the competencies a company and its customers have. This defines also what opportunities there are to meet the customer competencies to, e.g., is the setting in business-to-business or business-to-customer markets? The key actors are the technologies or application features that make clear sense to the expected customers. The customers are the ones with competencies to operate in the introduced settings, not a specific segment or user group. In fact, the introduction and key actors define the emotional attachment that should be tested to gain a deeper understanding of who the customers might be. The next step is a narrative that defines how innovation is explained to the customers, e.g., the marketing message, user interface or service interaction style. The narrative needs to be clear and easy to understand, but it will not be sufficient if there is no prior emotional attachment. Finally, the innovation needs a punch line that differentiates it from the competition. Like in jokes, the punch line is a surprising twist in the narrative within the premises set in the emotional attachment. It also defines the category of the innovation. Some alternative innovation punch lines are novelty, cost efficiency, natural extension and vertical opportunity.

Innovations do not always have to be funny in a way that jokes are, but it often helps if they are. For example, the demand for green innovations to fight the looming environmental problems is evident, but mostly the sustainable development is driven forward in a serious tone appealing more to reason than to feelings. A simple acid test is to think of the last time you laughed at a beer commercial and whether you have ever laughed due to a recycling advertisement? Even in the serious areas innovations can be fun and uplifting, if one just avoids certain types of dark humour like irony or sarcasm. The best innovation makes people laugh with you, not at you.

Blimey, innovation as fun; innovation through jokes … how does that sit with today's organisational reality? But think about it! How do we come up with something truly new? How do we solve with impossible problems? Let us tell a story. The Canadian Electricity Board faced the same big problem every winter: every year snow would bring down their power lines somewhere, causing power cuts and triggering an extensive and expensive search for the breakdown point. So the company arranged a brainstorming session to figure out what they could do about it. One participant had a brilliant idea: 'How about if we put a pot of honey up the electricity poles? That would attract bears, the bears would climb up the pole, this would shake the power lines, and the snow would fall down.' Now, how would you react to someone suggesting such an idea? Would your response be, 'Don't be ridiculous, we have a serious problem to solve', or would you say, after the laughter had died down, 'Hm, an interesting thought! What use can we make of that?' In fact, the reaction in this story was the latter, and the team started to think about different ways the power lines could be shaken to prevent the snow from bringing them down. The solution they came up with was to fly helicopters over the power lines: the vibration of the rotor blades would cause the snow to fall down. This was much cheaper than trying to locate and repair the breakdown! So, serious fun for innovation is not such a joke …

Another thing that is required to accept such ideas is openness. Openness to things that seem impossible, openness to things we cannot prove, openness to people who are different to us. Openness is what Antonio Messeni Petruzzelli believes represents the future of innovation; let's read why.

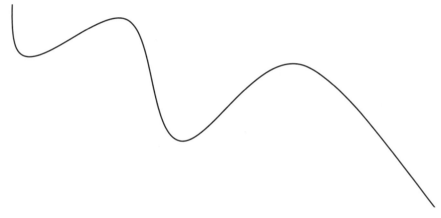

The Future of Innovation is Open Your Strategy

Name	**Antonio Messeni Petruzzelli**
Affiliation	Politecnico di Bari
Position	Research Fellow
Country	Italy
Area	Innovation management
Email	a.messeni.petruzzelli@poliba.it

innovation   openness   exploration   search   external sources

I believe that the future of innovation is represented by openness. Nowadays, firms are becoming more and more specialised in a single field of knowledge and rarely have all required heterogeneous resources internally; therefore to successfully innovate they need to acquire technical knowledge from external sources, such as customers, suppliers, institutions (chambers of commerce, trade associations, etc.), research organisations and universities, competitors, consultants and affiliated firms. This idea is well described in the 'open innovation' model, which suggests that the advantages firms may gain from internal R&D activities tend to decline. Therefore, to innovate they have to draw in knowledge and expertise from a wide range of external sources. Being too focused internally may lead firms to miss a number of opportunities.

An example of this open innovation model is represented by the Procter & Gamble (P&G) approach to R&D. In fact, in order to ensure greater exploitation of external ideas and actors, P&G shifted its R&D strategy toward 'connect and develop' rather than focusing on internal R&D. The 'connect and develop' model is based on the idea that external sources of ideas may often be more valuable than internal ones. Accordingly, open innovators are those that integrate these external sources into their innovation processes and competitive strategy.

Similar strategies are adopted by other organisations, especially in the software industry. For instance, JBoss, IBM, MySQL, MySpace and YouTube are all examples of successful firms that have based their value creation strategies on community-driven process, rather than on in-house activities.

The relevance of openness is also highly related to firms' capability to explore new potential solutions and introduce breakthrough innovations. In fact, creating breakthrough innovations is often a function of the external knowledge that a firm can access. External knowledge may allow the firm to overcome 'competency traps' and 'core rigidities' that limit the firm's ability to access and build on new paradigms. Such knowledge is vital to firms in industries characterised by dynamic and complex technological environments, where individual firm capabilities are limited in being able to guarantee firm success.

An open organisation is an organisation that constantly spans its technological, organisational and geographical boundaries, in order to reach and capture new information and pieces of knowledge. This permits to move beyond a 'local search' and increases the ability of a firm to create new knowledge through the recombination of knowledge across boundaries. To achieve this goal, firm members may attend conferences, browse patents, read trade and scientific journals or reverse-engineer competing products.

A further example of such an approach can be seen in Microsoft's development of the Windows user interface, built upon knowledge developed first at Xerox PARC and subsequently at Apple.

Openness may also represent an important solution to face the current crisis, since it may allow firms to discover new business opportunities. This is especially true for mature industries, which have already started their decline. Exploring new knowledge domains permits the development of novel capabilities, through a learning process entailing variation and experimentation, and involving a shift towards new technological trajectories that may represent an effective solution for re-inverting the declining phase.

Antonio talks about the openness that has become known as 'open innovation', an awareness that 'not all the best people are working for us' and that we need to find ways and channels to engage with them. In fact Part XI, 'Innovation from everyone, everywhere', delves deeper into that topic. But it ain't the end of Part X yet and we would like to hand over to Yoshihiro Tabira who elaborates further on the concept of open innovation.

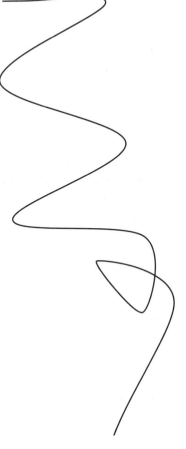

The Future of Innovation is Dependent on Open Management

Name	**Yoshihiro Tabira**
Affiliation	Graduate School of Technology Management, Ritsumeikan University
Position	PhD candidate
Country	Japan
Area	R&D management, organisations, product development
Email	yoshihiro_tabira@yahoo.co.jp

openness   environment   language   interaction

The future of innovation may depend on using an open style of managing technologies and strategies. Therefore the keyword of innovation in the 21st century is *openness*.

There are many ongoing studies about the open innovation process, which promotes a certain innovation process by widely utilising internal and external resources. However, the open innovation process is not only about gathering or combining technical ideas which exist inside and outside a corporation, but also about exploiting strategic ideas both within and without the firm; at the same time in the open innovation process, technical ideas and strategic ideas are made to fit together like the parts of a jigsaw puzzle.

On the other hand, the open innovation process can be viewed from the organisational evolution process, where technical and strategic ideas which exist inside and outside the corporation involve based on variation-selection-retention process.

Such open innovation process is not limited to companies: public, private research and development organisation that provide technologies and ideas to companies should also openly exploit technological and strategic idea which exist inside and outside the organisation. Already there are some R&D organisations that license their own R&D results to companies and at the same time in reciprocation they receive companies' researchers. What this implies is that the technical manufacturing information required for product commercialisation and the knowledge of the market which is known by the company, shifts to public and private R&D organisations. This can create an enabling environment for inducing the innovation process of public and private R&D organisations, and also of companies. At that time, a prototype for an application is an effective tool and acts as a common language between companies and external R&D organisation. However, this situation will require the external R&D organisation to acquire new skills. External R&D organisations should develop new skills to make such a prototype for an application.

And there are many sources of innovation, such as users and suppliers. So, in order to facilitate the innovation process, a company should facilitate the exchange of ideas through interactions between public and private R&D organisations, users, suppliers and the companies in question.

Of course, in this open innovation environment, scientists and engineers need new skills, but they should not only merely combine ideas but also exhibit some originality. This interaction should preferably be with scientists and engineers who have wide scope of the market in mind, and they should also have the ability to fit together technological and strategic ideas. Thus innovation will be made possible through the integration of the technical ideas and strategic ideas that are dormant within the scientists and the engineers.

Yoshihiro brings together several threads we have come across before: openness, the use of prototypes to create a shared understanding and an interdisciplinary approach where the total should be more than the sum of the parts.

We have mentioned diversity being one of innovation's strong warps several times before but now is a good place to let the voice of those of our contributors be heard who made it the central argument of their contribution. We would like to start with Dianka Zuiderwijk who believes that the future of innovation is for those enterprises that 'understand that innovation lies on the boundaries between disciplines'.

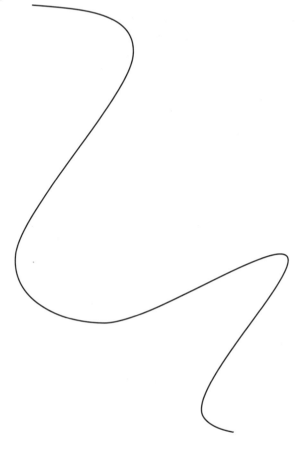

The Future of Innovation is Within Your Reach

Name	**Dianka Zuiderwijk, BA, MSc**
Affiliation	Lloyd's Register
Position	Oil and Gas Business Assurance Manager
Country	The Netherlands
Area	Innovation climate, diversity management
Email	dianka.zuiderwijk@lr.org

diversity   system   organization   management   capability

In today's volatile business environment, sceneries change at a dazzling speed. Survival of the knowledge-based enterprise is determined by its ability to change at the same rate or faster. This requires equally challenging management formats. What we need is management ability to respond to changing competitive environments and the courage to branch away from entrenched routines.

The knowledge provider of the future is polymorphic, adjusting itself continuously, while connecting its elements through a shared capability platform with its core values as its principal guidance. It is organised as an open system, allowing it to reach out to elements outside of its network on many different 'terms of engagement', while continuously grouping and regrouping existing and new capability in combinations the environment demands tomorrow. The scope, scale and pace of the various organisational elements will not fit a one-size-fits-all solution.

Managing this complexity requires dynamic systems to connect to domestic as well as to more 'alien' elements that exist at varying levels of organisational maturity and service complexity. The knowledge enterprise of the future does not have strict organisational boundaries, it does not spend time on suffocating control systems dragging trenches through its organisational landscape and, rather than wasting its energy on making new clones of itself, it cherishes diversity in its elements.

These enterprises understand that innovation lives on the boundaries between disciplines, on the interfaces with clients and on the outer edges of the space in which the organisation resides. They adopt performance metrics that drive future rather than historic value, and manage delivery based on a light but robust risk-management framework, anchored into each of its element's operational systems, embracing, protecting and supporting them rather than disrupting the systems that were carefully shaped to suit their specific business and client needs. These enterprises know that the opportunity cost of innovation is extremely worthwhile, for it creates the business of tomorrow. But at the same time, they carefully balance their innovative activity with their core capabilities; generating today's profits with yesterday's exploration.

Innovation cannot be managed. It is rather a consequence of organisational climate. This climate can be nurtured by putting conditions in place that provide room for shared thinking in cross-functional and cross-business relationships. Innovation will come naturally once the silos have disappeared and relationships based on mutual trust and respect have had a chance to grow.

Keeping the innovative spirit in a knowledge-based enterprise at times of economic downturn requires courageous leadership and a shared precociousness. The best reason being the fact that the services valued by clients today would not have been there if the organisation had not displayed this courage in the past.

Like Julian Birkinshaw earlier, Dianka states that innovation cannot be managed but that it rather is a 'byproduct' of organisational culture, a culture that thrives on trust and is characterised by high levels of diversity. To innovate it is essential to bring people from different backgrounds together, to engage with 'aliens' and find new combinations in the different skills sets, and most of all, have the courage to pursue the wild ideas that that arise out of such diversity.

One other aspect that keeps being mentioned, but that is not really at the core of any of the contribution, is that of leadership. Greg Rivera too believes that the future of innovation lies with diversity though with a different twist.

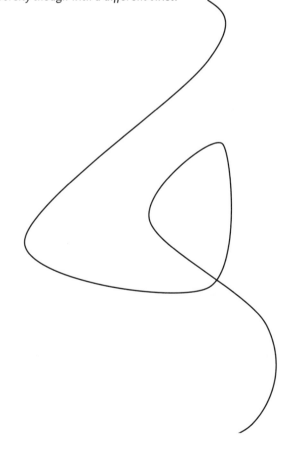

The Future of Innovation is Dependent on Cultural Intelligence

Name	**Dr Greg Rivera**
Affiliation	INNOVALAB Bilbao
Position	Director
Country	Spain
Area	New media, innovation strategy, art and science
Email	grivera@bib.coop

**evolutionary innovation   integral culture   evolutionary system design
artscience   social design**

The future of innovation is the artscientist's capacity to integrate the diversity of critical and creative expression without boundaries. Emerging practitioners are at once embracing both the arts and sciences. These transdisciplinary creators are building an integral form of culture – artscience. Artscience is a synergetic culture re-emerging in an integral form.

The sciences are transforming receptively with new information from the relationship with the arts. In this dance, innovation is emerging from the relationship between nature, history, media and culture in communities throughout the world. The transformation of art and science practice is becoming an integral culture. Buoyant with the human will its creators build capacity through critical and creative systems. We have the capability to continuously enrich the places we live through conscious reflection and action. In essence we are nurturing innovation to prosper.

In a new trajectory of sociocultural development the arts are entwining with the social sciences, physical sciences and technologies. I present a strategy for a conscious sociocultural evolution to build evolutionary learning communities to create the conditions for innovation cities and regions. An interrelated view of the major cultures of the arts and sciences emerges *in-forming* villages, towns and cities within potential innovation regions. Influencing the transformation of the arts and sciences are ancient and contemporary world cultural belief systems flowing into one another. Roy Ascott perceives the overall system: 'While traditionally focused on the appearance of things and their representation, art is now concerned with processes of interaction, transformation, and emergence.' Despite more than a century of influence, Eastern philosophies and ancient ways of knowing from other parts of the world continue to be provocative in the West. People are reconsidering their relationship with nature and each other.

Attuned to the need for human unity, contemporary artscience intermingles two broad streams of culture – the arts and sciences. Present-day artscientists seek life-affirming and life-nurturing practice. Contemporary artscientists create a benign relationship with human systems and nature by working in aesthetic, collaborative, creative and sustainable modes. In essence they are paralleling nature's creativeness.

The ancestral knowledge of discovery, invention and innovation continues in contemporary learning communities. These coherent patterns of collaboration are social and evolutionary learning in the present and future times. Ancestral knowledge emphasised the creative process in various critical ways of knowing in its originating sources. Present emphasis should be on the critical understanding of the consequences of future systems. Beyond (but inclusive of) specialised disciplines individuals, communities and organisations can be richly informed by transdisciplines including (a) psycho-personal/sociocultural interpreters, (b) bio-physical pattern witnesses, and (c) process-structural innovators. I speculate these characteristics can be mindfulness of nature's spirit and self-organising laws of ethical and transparent behaviour. An ethical social behaviour may reflect the human and nature's symbiotic relationship. The future unfolding and endurance of human and social development can continue to form into an emerging integral artscience.

Greg sees a new type of person emerging, a person that encapsulates diversity in him- or herself, a balancing act not at the organisational but the personal level. Another case where diversity is held within one person is when two national cultures come together in one person. This experience has led Meltem Etcheberry to believe that the future of innovation lies with diversity.

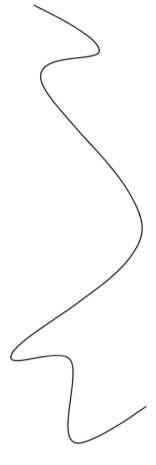

The Future of Innovation is About Diversity

Name	**Meltem Etcheberry**
Position	Interior Architect
Country	France
Area	Innovation and diversity
Email	meltem.etcheberry@wanadoo.fr

innovation   diversity   children

Innovation is an open door to a new world of experience. A world full of surprises, questions and challenges ...

It all begins with a wish or a need to be fulfilled: 'I lack something.' 'How can I do it?', 'How can I get there?' are questions underlying any project or idea. They pave the way for creation!

The next step is to think another way and change the rules: 'What can I do with this?', 'Can I do it differently?', 'Can this be used in a new fashion?' These questions pave the way for innovation!

In a word, innovation derives from all kinds of ideas, different viewpoints, the search for doing better and of course curiosity.

To see and use potential resources in ourselves and in the others; an open mind that leads you beyond the limits, towards unknown roads, towards new ideas and people. It is the way for moving forward!

Moving Forward for Diversity!

My private and business lives allow me to experience exciting and challenging management tools.

At a private level, I love watching my 10-year-old son's behaviour. He has a double identity thanks to his parents originating from two different cultures. He is bilingual, thinks both ways and understands the complexity of the world. To tackle an issue, he considers alternatives, uses one or the other way and finally often makes up his own, original way that neither of us could have thought of!

At a business level, I work with a team made of people originating from all over the world. They bring their identities, their cultures, their ways of thinking, their experiences, their lives. This environment is incredibly rich: together, we find very efficient business solutions.

This mindset requires a capacity to adapt to others, requires a good level of understanding, an open mind and tolerance to other people's viewpoint and references. It slowly changes you: you get to see that no issue has one single solution but a variety of ways to tackle it!

You think and talk differently: innovation begins with diversity!

Diversity for Innovating!

I am convinced that to move forward and innovate, we need to welcome new ideas, concepts, as well as new ways of thinking and doing business. They come from different horizons and can deeply challenge us. They allow us to see various perspectives and dimensions in our undertakings.

Diversity is an asset that deserves being fully discovered: it is an open door to a world of innovation!

Is diversity an open door in your organisation? Is it a door people can see and through which they are willing to go? Diversity driven by different cultural backgrounds is also close to the heart of Elisabeth Plum.

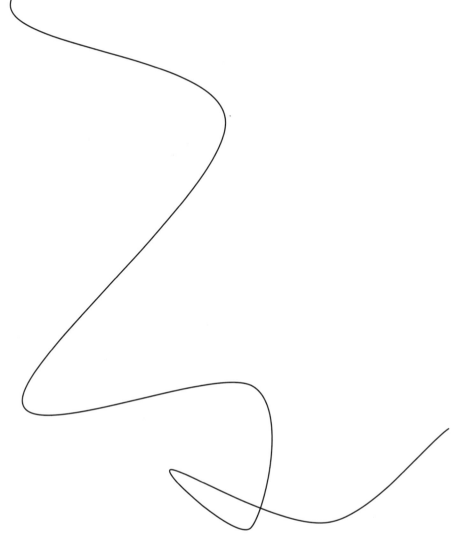

The Future of Innovation is Dependent on Cultural Intelligence

Name	**Elisabeth Plum**
Affiliation	Plum & Co ApS
Position	Director, PhD
Country	Denmark
Area	Innovation management (or rather, leadership of innovative processes), cultural intelligence
Email	ep@plum.co.dk

cultural intelligence   homogeneity   irrational reactions   cross-cultural communication   cross-disciplinary collaboration

The future of innovation looks bright if we succeed to develop our cultural intelligence so we can optimise the creative collaboration between people who think and act differently.

Groups who are innovative consist of people from different backgrounds that allow different knowledge and perspectives meet and be confronted to create something new. Unexpected questions and disagreements within a group can spark off the questioning of usual thinking and practice and lead to innovative ideas. But differences within a group do not automatically lead to new thinking. Whether they do depends heavily on how group members experience and handle the cultural complexity in the group.

Our cultural backgrounds influence the way we think and act and the way we interpret each other's contributions. We don't only have one cultural background. We all have a multiple cultural identity consisting of our nationality, gender, profession/education, age and organisational function (R&D, technical service, HR, marketing and sales), and all of these differences can be sources of new ideas.

If an innovative group chooses the 'nice and easy' way by seeking harmony in their group relations and level out their differences, this will destroy their creative potential. The homogeneity of the innovative group needs to be continuously confronted and stimulated. But at the same time we know that people need trustful relations. It's a well-known fact in psychological theory that we need to feel heard, listen to and understood by other people in order to be able to unfold our full professional and personal capacity. If we don't find these conditions we tend to defend our own unique points of views and nobody really listen to each other.

Leading an innovative group thus requires finding ways of balancing acknowledgement and use of the differences with building a trustful common ground, and the new concept of cultural intelligence (CI) can be an important competence in innovation management.

CI is the ability to create a fruitful collaboration in situations where cultural differences play a role. CI consists of three interdependent dimensions focusing on respectively the emotional, the cognitive and the practical dimensions of cross-cultural encounters.

Members of an innovative group need to pay attention to the various professional and personal competences that they and others bring into the situation and they need to develop tools that invite constructive confrontations between their different knowledge and points of view. But what is often underestimated or avoided are the irrational end emotional dimensions of the encounters in the homogeneous group. This dimension is the 'touch paper' – the thing that changes fuel into fire and contains both the creative potential and the 'danger'; the positive driving forces and the stumbling blocks that can destroy or enliven the contact.

CI gives us a framework and a language to understand and capitalise on the differences in the innovative groups rather than tolerate or ignore the potentially creative friction caused by difference.

One of the things we take away from Elisabeth's contribution is that a desire for harmony, a tendency to level out differences and achieve a shared ground – generally at the lowest common denominator – is the death of all potential that lies in diversity. Rather than trying to 'equalise' we should strive making most of the differences, relishing their richness and colour. However, that does not come without effort, which is one of the points that Petra Köppel makes in her contribution.

The Future of Innovation is Building on the Success of Intercultural Collaboration

Name	**Dr Petra Köppel**
Affiliation	Synergy Consult
Position	Proprietor
Country	Germany
Area	Innovation by cultural diversity
Email	info@petra-koeppel.de

intercultural leadership   diversity   corporate culture   global mindset   learning

Global competition does not only force companies to innovate, but also delivers potential for new solutions. In international cooperation within and across companies people with different cultural backgrounds, genders, ages, religious beliefs, education and social status get and work together. Creativity research tells us that learning takes place if differences meet – so you don't learn by meeting someone similar, but you learn by interacting with someone different. This is the secret of why multicultural teams can be more creative: members contribute different ideas, perspectives, knowledge and methods and therefore are able to analyse a problem more comprehensive. In addition, they can pool their resources to find the way that fits best or can develop a complete new solution by combining and developing existing approaches.

The problem lies in the fact that people are attracted by similarities and have a natural dislike of anything different or unknown. So it is a question of changing attitudes within a company: a corporate culture of openness, curiosity and appreciation must be established. People slowly learn first to be aware of differences, second to accept them and third to appreciate them. In the final stage, they know and respect cultural and all other work-related differences and use them constructively. This is most relevant for all problem-solving tasks, like research or product development. On the operative level, the leader of a diverse team needs to dedicate enough time in detecting all resources (like culture-specific and personal skills and knowledge) available in the team, establish common ground for cooperation and settle the processes for exchange and communication. This includes both emotional aspects like trust and liking and task-related aspects like rules and techniques.

A perfect example of how intercultural cooperation fosters innovation is the car-making company Tata Nano. The decision-makers selected not by accident but by pure intention team members of different cultural origin. So developers from India, Germany, Austria, Italy and other countries cooperated and shared their ideas – be it the market knowledge of the Indian partners or the high-technology expertise of Western engineers. Together they built a low-budget car that is a true innovation and feeds exactly the demand of the market. It is difficult to imagine that a homogeneous team would have been able to achieve this result.

In the future the success of companies will depend on their ability to innovate in management, processes or products. Until now only a few have unleashed the potentials of intercultural cooperation; most managers still see differences as barriers, try to level them and not surprisingly struggle with intercultural conflicts. Companies must build a global mindset, i.e., the understanding of global interrelations and the skills to interact with people around the globe. It is up to the management to introduce a global mindset to their corporate culture by adapting structures and processes (e.g., decision-making processes or human resource practices) and by developing the competencies of their workforce especially including intercultural leadership.

How right Petra is. There are not many of us who enjoy the company of people who are very different, who challenge the way we think, question what is dear and important to us, or to whom we constantly have to explain in a different way what we have just said. But the issue is, unless we do have exchanges with people who are very different from us our views remain narrow, we only see one side of the coin. The fact that most of us have been through an education system that trains us to believe that there is a right and wrong, and a true or false, does not make accepting different positions any easier. If there is a right and wrong then, if I am right (as I would be) the other person must be wrong, and is therefore not worth listening to.

Anni Roolf picks up the point that we need strong individuals – and that they need to be open and encouraged to cooperate.

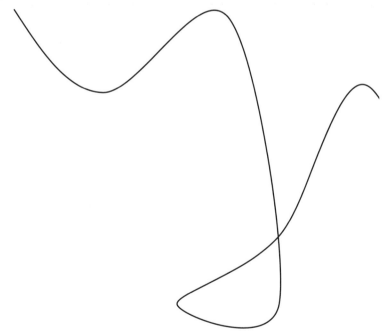

The Future of Innovation is About Nurturing the Breeding Ground

Name	**Anni Roolf**
Affiliation	Forum for Business Design and Creative Leadership, Zollverein School Alumni Association
Position	Vice-President
Country	Germany
Area	Boost of innovation and creative leadership in practice, education and research through a hub for public dialogue
Email	anni.roolf@zollverein-school-alumni.org

cultural richness   corporate social vision   social reforms   recruiting   diversity

The future of innovation will be more characterised by the interaction of organisation and society, and therefore by fundamental social, cultural and political issues. Organisations are no self-sufficient spaceships, which are able to optimise their ability to innovate just on the organisational level. The breeding ground for vitally needed people and ideas is a society which is cultivating strong individuals, their curiosity, creativity and social mobility and which is training openness and cooperation by encounter with the different.

The goal of recruiting of an innovative organisation is to involve the perspectives of people with different cultural and social backgrounds. A socially and culturally rich environment enables the recruiting of such employees, who can advance innovation. The more strong individuals will be integrated into the organisation, the easier it is to retain strong individuals for innovation's sake. An open encounter with the unknown is part of innovation: this comes naturally to employees in an organisation of diversity. They observe their surroundings and know where to look for intensive encounters, and this leads to ideas, insights for future requirements, strategies and partnerships. The less monocultural these surroundings are, the richer the inspiration for the organisation.

For the very reason that it is in the organisation's self-interest to get employees and ideas from a prolific environment, it seems to be logical to nurture one's own breeding ground. As part of their visions organisations will develop their own vision of society, that will define which social breeding ground is needed to extract the resources for the organisation to innovate. Concrete projects in the organisation's surroundings will be deduced from this social objective. On the one hand the organisation will support in the external society what it needs internally, and on the other hand it will give something back to society in exchange for what it has taken.

Such activities could be located in the fields from which innovative organisations benefit. The sector of education and research will be reformed in that strong individuals, curiosity, creativity and courage will be rewarded within it. In order to support openness and new ideas it would be fruitful to create possibilities and procedures in all fields of society, which would enable people of different disciplines, nationalities, social backgrounds and moral values to meet each other. Such 'social tourism' would have to be an integral part of education and job requirements. This higher collective knowledge of one another would increase enormously the ability of society and its organisations to innovate, because needs and suggestions of others would be transparent. Furthermore, the social question is also relevant for innovation, as the emergence and enforcement of new ideas depends on the social mobility of people and their creative leeway in powerful positions.

The implementation of these points means enormous reform efforts in many fields, in which innovative organisations will participate actively in the future. The leaders of the future have understood that innovative organisations are embedded in an innovation-supporting society and that attention for social developments and interaction with their surroundings are in the very own organisational interest.

Another powerful argument for diversity, and the emphasis on a wide range of aspects that have to be re-aligned in order to enable us to make use of that diversity. Leadership is most certainly one of the key elements. We take the cues of what is and isn't acceptable from our 'leaders', people we admire or people we work with or for. By the way, we believe that if we succeed in educating stronger individuals the influence of 'leaders by power of position' will decrease. Leaders will no longer be able to rely on 'you do so because I tell you so.'

Another field for rich interactions – or the potential of it – is the interface between academia, industry and consulting. More often than not, we stay in our professional boundaries, surrounding us with like-minded people where explanations are not necessary and we can probably finish each other's sentences for each other. Innovation conferences attended by innovation specialists, marketing people from and for marketing people. Where is the tension in that? Where are the benefits and the stimuli? The benefits of diversity do not drop into our laps, we have to make an effort to bring the potential to fruition. In order to benefit from diversity better communication is requires, new ways of communication are required; and it requires bringing these different bodies of knowledge together in the first place. Iain Bitran is one of those who makes the effort to establish some bridges.

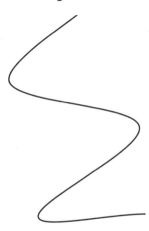

The Future of Innovation is
One in Which Academics and Professionals Speak the Same Language

Name	**Iain Bitran**
Affiliation	The International Society for Professional Innovation Management
Position	Executive Director
Country	UK
Area	Innovation associations, conferences and networks
Email	bitran@ispim.org

conferences   events   networks   innovation   associations

If, as various gurus say, the future of innovation is an open one where diverse parties collaborate to make the world a better place, then where do innovation conferences fit in?

Consider for a minute the two extremes on offer today. On the one hand, we have corporate conferences where delegates pay top-dollar prices to listen to some innovation guru 'live by satellite' (presumably via YouTube), are fed mushroom vol-au-vents for lunch (for some inexplicable reason these conferences never include evening social events ...) and then have to listen to presentations on how successful the presenter's company is (the 'rah rah' presentation) or on Henry Ford, the Walkman and the iPod (the 'Innovation for Dummies' presentation)! On the other hand there are serious academic conferences where everyone is far too clever and cannot communicate without the aid of some complicated graph or other.

I propose that a successful future is one where academics and practitioners can meet, speak the same (or at least similar) language and learn. To make a genuine difference beyond their own 'worlds' i.e., in a genuinely open future, then this is what must follow.

When I say meet, and we are talking of the future, I do mean meet in a physical sense and not in the world of Facebook, MySpace, LinkedIn, Xing, Second Life, wiki this and blog that. Of course technology has a role to play and has innumerable benefits but we must harness technology without succumbing to the temptation of believing in a purely technology driven future. Just as the PC never delivered the paperless office, Second Life *et al.* will not deliver the 'personless' conference.

It is the reliance on the human need to interact that is shaping the International Society for Professional Innovation Management (ISPIM) conferences. ISPIM membership and attendance has grown by 25 per cent every year for the last five years. Its message is clear: we have fun running ISPIM and we want people to enjoy our events. Enjoyment is the strongest stimulant for networking, shared experience and creativity that exists.

So what does that actually mean? Well we need good quality content with a stimulating structure during the day. We are getting there. Now fewer than 60 per cent of abstracts that are reviewed are presented in the final event, and we will be raising the bar every year. We have restructured sessions to be shorter, snappier, with much greater interaction and facilitation. And of course our social events, the ISPIM trademark, will continue to be of the highest quality, formal and informal and creating experiences for delegates that they could not have as an individual or as a tourist. It is important to us that delegates experience the 'wow' factor as this is something they can take away with them and share with others. Oh, and we will never increase the conference price to beyond its current level compared to other events.

So, if ISPIM is right, the future of innovation conferences is one of open borders where people connect through shared experiences that lead them work together on innovation.

Watch this space ...

As Iain points out, we need to leave old patterns of behaviour and assumptions behind and find new ways of interacting, of mixing different domains of knowledge together. Having been to, and in fact having met at, one of ISPIM's conferences we have had an opportunity to witness the richness and stimulating effects of such events first hand. It is not least due to the ISPIM conference in 2008, or rather the title chosen for the conference in 2009, that seeds for this book were sewn (as we shared in the introduction).

If conferences that bring practitioners, academics and consultants together seem already quite revolutionary, what then will you make of Lawrence Dooley's prediction that the future will hold collaboration, even with your competitors?

The Future of Innovation is Collaborative

Name	**Dr Lawrence Dooley**
Affiliation	Management and Marketing Department, University College Cork
Position	College Lecturer
Country	Ireland
Area	Innovation management
Email	l.dooley@ucc.ie

collaborative innovation   knowledge creation networks

Organisations must continuously innovate in terms of product, process, market and business model to remain sustainable. They innovate to enhance competitive advantage over other organisations and improve profitability. However, the paradox is that these organisations may need to collaborate with competitor organisations in order to successfully innovate. The desire to develop radical innovations that occupy 'new' market space often requires an organisation to move significant distance from its existing competencies and capabilities. As this distance increases so does the risk of failure in undertaking the prospective innovation. This has led to a shift in innovation perspective from concentration on developing internal organisational competencies to support innovation, to the 'new' perspective of inter-organisational collaborative networks and collaboration.

Future organisational innovation activity will be exemplified by continuous innovation, achieved by inter-organisational networks exploring opportunities through horizontal and self-managed systems. The trend towards inter-organisational collaboration is driven by increased global competition and shortening product lifecycles, increased complexity and cost of the innovations being undertaken and a more discerning market. The model of collaborative innovation allows an organisation certain advantages such as access to deficient internal skills and capabilities, distribution of the associated risks and costs across the network partners and ultimately the enhancing of their ability to deliver the innovation to the market. To date, the majority of innovation networks have concentrated on areas such as technology transfer and collective commercialisation of technology. However, future networks will see their locus of concentration move to earlier phases of the innovation process as they endeavour to achieve better alignment of the discovery phase output with their collective commercial interests. Knowledge-led innovation networks can engage university and industry partners in the national innovation system, offering a mechanism for leveraging the university sector's research capability to contribute to the development of both industry and the knowledge economy, while still maintaining the university's core missions of education and fundamental research.

This shift towards collaborative innovation disrupts the traditional routines of the innovation process and requires the organisation to develop new skills and competencies if they wish to continue to innovate. The relevance of the organisation's technical competence is a fundamental qualifying criterion for their participation in the network. The 'new' skills centre on the organisation's ability to interact with other partner organisations, share knowledge and collectively manage the networked innovation process from beginning to end. Capabilities such as partnering and integration of organisational cultures, effective collaborator selection and protocol routines, building trust amongst network partners, clarity of purpose regarding objectives, intellectual property rights and strong project management skills all influence the organisation's collaborative capability. Rarely does an organisation or the network possess all these capabilities at their origins; however, successful innovation networks will nurture the development of these abilities over time to enhance their innovative capability. The presence of these factors allows networks achieve the required knowledge exchange and commitment amongst participating organisations to facilitate innovation development. As we progress into the future, the importance of these skills and capabilities will increase as collaborative innovation becomes the norm.

So far we have talked about the importance, richness and value of diversity, but have said little explicitly on how and where to find it! Of course, we have individuals who hold diversity in themselves such as Greg's artscientists or Meltem's son. Lawrence has pointed us to another source of diversity, beyond competitors (who may well have the same mindset as the people in our own organisation, at least when it comes to assumptions about our industry): inter-organisational networks. Seeing tremendous potential in such networks Lawrence also points out that new and different skills and perhaps even roles will emerge to benefit from them.

What skills might we be talking about? We felt that Tomasz Kosmider is providing some useful insights on this.

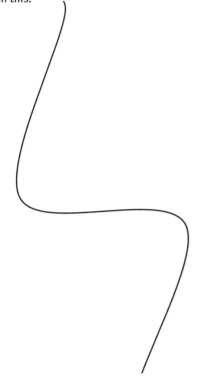

The Future of Innovation is
Dependent on Present Education,
Communication and Exploitation Activities

Name	**Tomasz Kosmider**
Affiliation	Technology Partners Foundation
Position	President
Country	Poland
Area	R&D management
Email	Kosmider@ibb.waw.pl

knowledge communication education research partnership

The future of innovation will mainly reflect our present activities in the following areas:

First, *education* – not only in development of the abilities to innovate but also the abilities to manage innovation processes. Innovation is changing. What used to be a clearly defined process in which companies developed knowledge and used it to create products to sell, is being replaced by *open innovation*: complex relationships that bind companies to competitors, commerce to academia, business and scientific disciplines to one another. A particular challenge is posed by managing across partnerships. An increasing proportion of European research is done through partnerships, for example through alliances between firms, through industrial contracts with research and technology organisations (RTOs), through industry–university links, and through consortia of various kinds including in particular those within the EU Framework Programmes. Managing partnerships takes special skills. Europe lacks enough of these skills and, moreover, this skills gap is limiting Europe's ability to adopt partnering and open innovation as effectively as it could.

Second, *communication* – not just to inform about innovation, but communication which develops a synergy of actions leading to innovation through a dialogue among all actors who contribute to innovation. Communication is an especially critical issue in research and technology development (RTD) partnering and open innovation. RTD partnering is increasing across most industry sectors and between the private and public sectors. The days when companies needed and could afford to maintain all their RTD resources in-house have gone. There are also enormous differences between organisations in their understanding and adoption of research management processes and best practices, and a frequently poor understanding of the behaviours necessary for successful partnering. These are major barriers to collaboration, since they increase business risk. Sophisticated firms are reluctant to collaborate with prospective partners that appear unprofessional or naïve in the way they do business – even though their technological skills may be ideal. Unsophisticated organisations may feel diffident about entering into partnerships, for fear of being exploited by 'smarter' organisations or becoming trapped into dependent relationships.

Third, *exploitation* – innovation cannot deliver the benefits that Europe needs without management of the results. Improvements are needed in several areas:

- The desire and capacity of industry to absorb research results.

- The ability of firms, RTOs and universities to work together, in particular to manage their often conflicting needs regarding intellectual property.

- The ability of a university or public sector research organisation to exploit its research.

Where a university does research as part of an established relationship with an industrial firm, the route to exploitation of the results is usually clear. A greater challenge is to exploit results created by a university or public sector research organisation on its own. Academic results frequently do not make it through to commercial application due to a lack of focus on supporting industry, inadequate funding for spin-outs and other forms of exploitation, or simply insufficient staff skills and motivation. The notion of industrial support as the 'third leg' of a university's mission (alongside teaching and research) is gaining ground in Europe and is to be encouraged; today, there are positive examples in France and the UK but, generally, this is still weak.

Tomasz brings universities firmly into the diversity mix, arguing from an open innovation point of view what needs to be considered. Universities' contribution to the future of innovation is also close to Mark McBride's heart, though he also identifies some areas that need to be addressed to derive all possible benefit from collaboration with universities.

The Future of Innovation is the Commercialisation of Academia and the Rise of the Sleeping Giants

Name	**Mark McBride**
Affiliation	Pharmalicensing Ltd
Position	Director
Country	UK
Area	Open innovation for life sciences
Email	mmcbride@utekcorp.com

academia   technology transfer offices   Brazil   China   India

I see there being two key trends in motion which will significantly affect the future of innovation.

For many years I have watched a quiet battle fought to encourage academic researchers away from an old-fashioned research-for-research's-own-sake mindset. I have always canvassed that there should be consideration of the broader economic benefits of ongoing and potential future academic research projects, issues that necessarily lay outside the protected environment of the university's walls.

Academics and university managers have occasionally appeared to be oblivious to the nature and sheer speed of commercial technology developments and therefore failed to create as much new knowledge as perhaps could have been expected, inadvertently compromising the evolution of new products and services.

Ultimately the responsibility for such subtle shift of mindset to embrace the requirements of the external whilst making a balance with the internal, must rest with the university's own technology transfer officers, and this is where I see an important changes occurring, the first of my trends for the future of innovation.

The second I see relates to geography, recognising that we are now part of a global economy.

It is clear that the creation of many of the most innovative products of the last half century was in some part due to the close proximity (both in terms of geography and of goal) of high-quality research-based universities to high-technology businesses (just think of the clusters of innovation that surround Harvard, Princeton, Berkeley and MIT in the United States, or the many science parks around Oxford and Cambridge in the United Kingdom). The link is clear and should continue to be encouraged and driven by relationships developed between high-tech industry and local academic technology transfer offices.

Such geographical relationships must not, though, be allowed to become a hindrance to the exploitation of broader sources of intellectual property (IP). In this internet age, whilst mutuality of goal must remain, the boundaries of geography must be allowed to stretch, whereby industry can seek far and wide to source the most appropriate IP to drive the innovation of the future.

Nowadays universities located in countries where their role is seen as a key component of national research and innovation policy, work with well-funded technology transfer offices in environments conducive to strong academic/commercial ties. These ties are driven by clear and transparent policies of global knowledge transfer, research collaborations and mutually beneficial licensing agreements.

Those universities in countries where government are now developing policies as outlined above, including the 'sleeping giants' of Brazil, India and China, will start to discover the benefits of increased links between their research groups with their extensive untapped IP portfolios, and the IP-hungry commercial organisations elsewhere seeking to explore and ultimately commercialise that IP.

Of course, this dynamic must not be one-way, where the IP from the academic groups in the developing countries simply flows to the developed world's industry. It must be two-way, with IP flowing back to help drive new projects and the development in turn of more innovative technologies in those developing areas.

Of course, geographical dispersion of knowledge and IP will play its role, and will bring with it additional benefits as well as additional hurdles. While especially Iain has argued for face-to-face meetings – which we happen to believe in strongly too – we cannot at the same time deny the power and importance of virtual networks. While the joke goes that British people will not even speak to someone face to face unless properly introduced (well, we guess that joke is a little dated, but still ...), we now find ourselves collaborating and exchanging views and knowledge with people we have never met – this book is living proof of that! It is interesting to observe how trust seems to be granted by proxy. Social networking sites work like that: you are more likely to connect to someone who knows someone you know and trust than to someone with whom you do not share any connections.

Trust and respect are the foundations on which collaboration can be build. What is happening in your organisation to foster them?

We said earlier that diversity brings with it its own set of issues, and perhaps requires the creation of new skills and roles. That this is not only theory but that new roles are actually being created is evident in the experience that Hanna Lehtimäki shares with us.

The Future of Innovation is in Multi-Voiced Business Competence

Name	**Dr Hanna Lehtimäki**
Affiliation	Life Works Consulting Ltd
Position	Finnish Foundation for Technology and Innovation (Tekes) Programme Coordinator
Country	Finland
Area	Innovation management, business innovations
Email	hanna.lehtimaki@lifeworksconsulting.net

**co-innovation   networks   multivoiced   innovation funding
business competence**

I am currently working as a coordinator for a programme called Innovative Business Management run by the Finnish Foundation for Technology and Innovation. My duties as a coordinator for the programme are to build networks and create collaboration between managers and business researchers in Finland and internationally. My duty as an innovation catalyst is to bring parties from different institutional and cultural backgrounds to meet and discuss with each other and to create new ways of collaboration between researchers and business managers.

The Finnish Foundation for Technology and Innovation emphasises that expertise in technological innovations alone is not enough in guaranteeing Finland's international competitiveness in the future. The foundation has successfully funded technology innovations in Finland for 25 years. For the past three years business development and service development have moved into the focus of innovation funding. The increasing pace of change in the operating environment requires that enterprises are continuously able to reinvent themselves. A stronger emphasis on commercialisation of innovations is needed.

Creating business innovations is all about co-innovation: bringing business managers, researchers and governmental officers together to enthusiastically create novel solutions to business management. The challenge is to identify issues and topics in which each of these three parties find something interesting for themselves. All of these parties continuously express their interest in the views and understandings of the other. However, finding fruitful working solutions is not all that simple. There are differences in the time span, expected results and willingness to invest into novel working methods. Thus, another challenge in creating innovations is to identify practices that attract each of the parties and lead to fruitful collaboration.

Thus far, the programme has funded 56 research projects and 36 company development projects. The vision is that in 2010, at the end of the five-year programme, the renewed and internationally networked Finnish business sector and universities know how to anticipate opportunities, take advantage of innovations and develop new cooperation models between enterprises, universities and research institutes. In Finland we believe the future of innovation lies in multi-voiced business competence. It means the ability of researchers, business managers and government officials to co-innovate novel solutions for innovation management.

We are certainly looking forward to the insights generated from the project Hanna describes. We know we need diversity to innovate, and we know that successfully drawing on diversity is rather tricky. So nothing more worthy, in our view, than to attempt to develop tools, approaches, techniques that enable us to draw on the 'multi-voiced business competence' that is needed to truly innovate.

Dusan Schreiber too argues the benefits of collaborative innovation, emphasising that such networks of innovation will span geographical as well as cultural and language boundaries. He, too, argues for collaboration that does not only span business boundaries but becomes an effort to which science, technology, society, economy and politics are all working together. As Edna said earlier, 'It will take all of us to save us.'

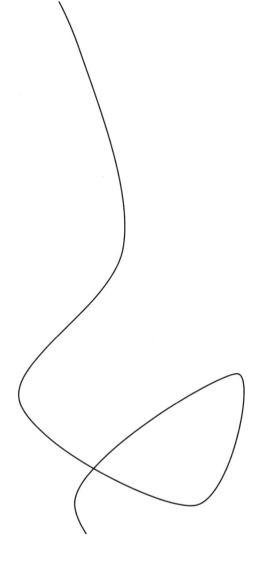

The Future of Innovation is in Collaborative Networks

Name	**Dusan Schreiber**
Affiliation	UFRGS
Position	Doctoral Student
Country	Brazil
Area	Innovation management
Email	dschreiber@ea.ufrgs.br

innovation   collaboration   networks   collective learning   social development

The future of innovation will be focused on collaborative innovation, based on collective learning and management of shared knowledge, due to the high degree of complexity of science and technology which requires increasing investments in innovation. This new scenario requires analysing contexts, studying trends, visualising new paths and solutions; what is technically and economically viable and viability will be achieved through collaborative efforts.

It's important to understand that the profile of innovation is tied to context, to the stage of development of the society either technologically, socially or economically. Innovation should be interpreted as a continuous process in the permanent state of construction and transformation, supported by the work of many professionals of different types of knowledge and skills. This diversity of knowledge, skills and competencies will allow different approaches to the same problem or scientific challenge, generating a variety of ways to be analysed and a conceptual richness which will enable new ideas.

These cooperation networks for innovation will surely pass over the geographic, cultural and language divisions, uniting people from different nationalities, focusing on the combination of skills and competencies in order to achieve the goals in the scientific and technological areas. Efforts will be more and more concentrated on the identification of the most skilled people to contribute towards the innovative processes and projects, regardless of their origin, nationality, religion, gender or race.

Different settings and formats will characterise these networks of cooperation in innovation, being established between governments, universities, firms and their customers; between firms and their suppliers; and between governments and independent researchers and independent laboratories or private ones, public or non-profitable organisations, in several ways of partnerships and cooperation agreements.

Networks, systems and organic approaches will be adopted as patterns not only in science and technology but in all segments of society, exerting great impact and influence on social relationships, demanding from society a change in terms of concepts, perception of the world and interpretation of social relations and environments. This will surely change the self-perception of human beings and their place in the world, as individuals and as part of society, which will lead to resistance, rejection, anger, alienation, radicalisation, among other social phenomena.

A regulatory action will be demanded from governments to minimise possible distortions in the exploitation of the benefits generated by innovations and reduce the inequality of the opportunities for scientific and technological development and its application to the benefits of its citizens. The non-profit transnational organisations will assume the role of monitor in this process.

Concluding we can say that the future of innovation will depend on the combination of science, technology, society, economy and politics – allowing working in a collaborative way and sharing knowledge and benefits worldwide.

Dusan sees the future of innovation as people from different fields working together globally. The challenges we are facing are truly unprecedented. Were you aware that global GDP, which has grown steadily and even exponentially over the most recent 200 years, has come to a halt (you might want to watch an eye-opening presentation by Umair Haque on http://vimeo.com/3204792 [accessed 09.04.09])? It truly does need all of us. It seems that our next contributor, Geoff Carss, has already a term for such collaborations: value webs.

The Future of Innovation is About Innovation Value Webs

Name	**Geoff Carss**
Affiliation	Imaginatik plc
Position	Vice President – Professional Services
Country	UK
Area	Collaborative innovation
Email	geoff_carss@imaginatik.com

value webs   stakeholders   involvement   open innovation   networks

The future of innovation will be defined by our appetite to create new models for innovation, demonstrate leadership and find new ways of extending the enterprise to include other stakeholders.

Multinational companies realise they employ world-class expertise and need a way of engaging them in the innovation process on a large-scale, sustained basis to help solve material business problems. Enlightened large companies have taken this one step further and understand that there is significant insight, creativity and ideas in the extended enterprise – including their suppliers, customers, consumers, business partners, academia and alumni networks.

One model which I believe will start to emerge over the next few years is that of collaborative innovation value chains or value webs. While the concept of value chains has been around for some time the idea of a company recognising it can create an innovation value chain as a means of creating sustained competitive advantage is quite new.

Most models for open innovation typically have a large company drawing insights, ideas and innovations from smaller companies with only one level in the network (although I appreciate there are a number of exceptions to this).

The collaborative innovation value chain can be described as follows:

- A multinational company identifies the need for diverse collaboration to solve complex business problems.

- This set of business problems are not easy to solve, and solving them will create significant business value, and may take some time.

- The ultimate beneficiary of any new solution may not be the direct customer of the multinational but may be a consumer who will pay a premium.

- The multinational recognises that bringing together a diverse but complementary set of organisations over a period of time will create a significant barrier to entry.

- The company also recognises that there needs to be some form of differentiated relationship with members of the value chain such as minority equity stakes, shared IP development, exclusive relationships etc.

- While the multinational may sit at the centre of the value chain/web (as it has the capacity to invest and direct) it may need to influence its suppliers and customers to adopt similar approaches for them to be able to contribute effectively.

At Imaginatik we are seeing some companies reaching out to suppliers, customers and consumers with some 60 per cent of our customers involved in some form of collaborative innovation programme.

To engage a number of these groups at any one time, to solve complex and material business problems, will require new models of governance, ethics and alignment of business goals.

I believe the potential benefits of collaborative value chains or webs are so significant, due to the potential for competitive 'lock out' as well as well as profit increases, that we will see examples of these appearing in the next one or two years.

If you aren't innovating with your suppliers, customers, consumers or business partners then be assured that your competitors are – it's an arms race.

Is your organisation engaging in this kind of innovation process? Where does your organisation go when you have a problem you seem to be unable to solve? If you do engage in this kind of innovation, have you got the appropriate ethics and governance models in place?

In our final contribution in Part X we would like to give voice to Sally Davenport who alerts us to the fact that for the future of innovation we are no longer talking about collaboration as a 'contact sport' as she calls it; and that the way we are collaborating, will see its own innovation too.

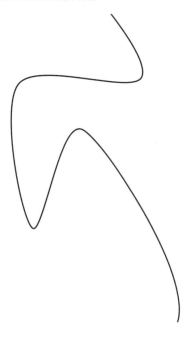

The Future of Innovation is Rewriting the Rules of Contact

Name	**Sally Davenport**
Affiliation	Victoria Management School
Position	Professor/Head of School
Country	New Zealand
Area	Innovation and distance
Email	sally.davenport@vuw.ac.nz

geographic proximity   cognitive proximity   internet   oral culture

The notion that innovation is a contact sport, that personal interactions and relationships are essential, is a legend that permeates our understanding of how to nurture successful innovation. That may be fine for our generation but what about for those that are following closely behind for whom interactions and relationships are ephemeral and ethereal when mediated through social media such as YouTube, Facebook and MySpace. Those participating in an interaction may never meet face to face in the same place (literally not virtually) so what does this lack of close proximity mean for the future of innovation?

That geographic proximity is important for innovation is a theme that grew out of observing the success of regional clusters and now the 'power of place' underpins many a public policy designed to build communities of innovation. More recently, the notion of open innovation has recognised that knowledge and innovative ideas can be sourced from network constellations external to the firm. However, even in this literature, it is assumed that knowledge flows are magnified by geographic proximity and that arm's length transactions are likely to be problematic.

Being close by, geographically, is only one type of proximity. You can perceive yourself as close to someone who is not located nearby and this type of proximity is more cognitive in nature. The relationship exists because those involved believe that the relationship exists and this type of cognitive proximity is what underpins interactions in the social virtual environment that is the internet.

A recent piece by *New York Times* writer Alex Wright talks of the internet and its user-generated content as being an oral rather than literate culture. Building on some earlier work by the linguist Walter Ong, Wright describes an oral culture as additive, aggregative, situational, participatory and empathetic. A literate culture, in which most organisational and innovation processes would currently sit most comfortably, is subordinate, analytic, objective, abstract and distanced. An oral culture, he says, fosters 'a collective, highly social way of understanding by building consensus over time, though iterative dialogue and, at times fostering antagonistic views' which, if it wasn't about oral culture, could be a description of the ideal creative process!

We know that social media tools are an outlet for the spirit of fun and irreverence that are so fundamental to creativity and innovation, so from this angle, the cognitive proximity that underpins virtual relationships should be a great boost to innovation. Of course, the whole notion of ownership of ideas created in the midst of such communities of unrelated people who contribute content for reasons other than pure financial gain (as evident in open source software), is paradoxical to some of our more traditional innovation concepts including intellectual property regimes. Understanding how and why the YouTube generation participate and more importantly contribute will provide the necessary *gestalt* in the way we think about 'managing' innovation in future.

So will innovation still be a contact sport in future? Yes – but only if we change our understanding about what we mean by 'contact'!

Whatever you thought would stay the same, think again. The future of innovation requires us to revisit all that is familiar, and accept that innovation will be from everyone, everywhere.

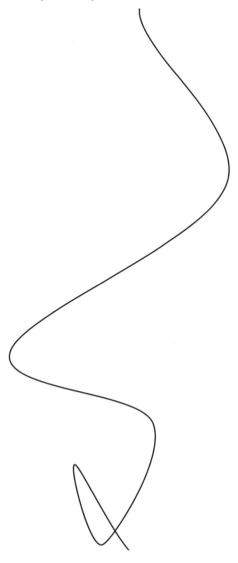

PART XI
Innovation From Everyone, Everywhere

'Open innovation' – is there any person in innovation management milieu who has not yet heard, read, used and even experienced this notion? Hardly! Open innovation is not another kind of a buzzword; it is the name of the new era we have entered long before the very notion was introduced. Many companies have already been practising open innovation for years without operationalising and interpreting their efforts as such. Jeff Butler, from whom we heard in Part X, has once most eloquently explained why open innovation as a 'neat concept' is welcomed by governments, companies, universities, scholars, conferences: 'Managers might be happy enough that Henry Chesbrough, of the Haas School of Business, University of California Berkeley, has effectively consolidated and interpreted this momentum of observations and has given it more relevance and significance and popularisation'.

The degree of openness has increased continuously over the decades. To put it into historical perspective we would like to cite from an article by David J. Teece from 1989 (incidentally also at the Haas School of Business) on the inter-organisational requirements of the innovation process the conceptualisation and the emergence of technology collaboration for innovation:

> The manifold benefit from broad-scale collaboration activity have been recognised abroad, and more recently in the United States as well. One assessment of the United States is that until now, however, we have taken it for granted as an article of faith that no co-operation should be permitted, that it is best that we keep companies apart from one another. Meanwhile, other countries have adopted different models. For instance, Japanese co-operative activity is ubiquitous and is not only in the form of R&D joint ventures but also R&D collaboration ... In order to capture value from the innovation it may be necessary for a number of firms to collaborate, with different firms being responsible for different activities. In some cases these firms may be horizontal competitors and antitrust may block desirable collaboration.

In the 1990s the notion of a 'strategic alliance' suddenly became popular when companies that began to cooperate with other organisations could produce significantly more technological developments and commercial results than those adhering to 'going-it-alone' strategies.

We have undertaken this historical excursion to give yet a further indication of how rapidly the world is changing. What was unknown yesterday, odd, obscure, dubious, vague, irrelevant and a remote and distant possibility, has become the standard today; it even makes us smile, amused and bewildered, that such level of collaboration was once banned. Today it seems like a strange dream, doesn't it?

'Innovation from everyone, everywhere' is the section that elaborates on the future of open innovation and crowdsourcing. We discuss novelties in professional competencies, collaborative settlements and interaction inevitability. We are delighted to commence this part of the journey with the story from Dwayne Spradlin who draws on his experience of putting the open innovation paradigm into practice.

Dwayne leads into his contribution by emphasising the need for taking stock and rethinking in organisations. On our journey towards open innovation across the globe a lot remains to be done, understood and realised. With an open mind we have to look at innovation processes, innovation strategies, innovation cultures, corporate cultures, strategic developments, policy-making, effectiveness, efficiency, R&D capabilities, IPRs, new product development, profits, commercialisations. It is a discontinuity, a disruption, and a fundamental change for organisations and their surroundings.

Dwayne's second thread is the introduction of a new position, the 'citizen innovator'. To find out who the citizen innovators are, where they come from, what their principles are and why they are key to open innovation and its future, read on!

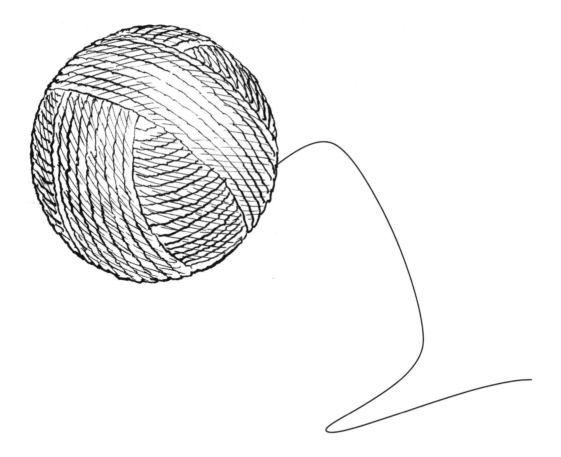

The Future of Innovation is Open Innovation and the Citizen Innovator

Name	**Dwayne Spradlin**
Affiliation	InnoCentive
Position	President and CEO
Country	USA
Area	Prize-based open innovation
Email	dspradlin@innocentive.com

citizen innovator   open innovation   InnoCentive   intellectual property

The most successful organisations in the 21st century will be those that realise that real sustainable advantage is not a product of the inventions themselves, it's in building organisations that know how to repeatedly harness innovation inside and outside their organisations, and on a global scale, regardless of its source. We call the practice of systematically supplementing internal innovation efforts with access to the world's vast reservoirs of creative, intellectual, and inventive talent 'open innovation'.

Requiring organisations to think very differently about the innovation process, internal rewards systems, organisational structures, and intellectual property, this approach represents a step change improvement over the 100-year-old innovation status quo of today.

For businesses burdened by increasingly costly innovation efforts and high failure rates, this means new ideas, faster solutions, and cost efficiencies. For foundations and government, channelling the world's innovation capacity towards important problems means an unprecedented opportunity to impact public good.

Organisations with the courage and discipline to embrace this change will fundamentally change the effectiveness and efficiency of their innovation efforts, some becoming the new innovation leaders in their spaces. Much more than an extension to the 'business as usual' innovation approaches of today, it is in fact a fundamental rethinking of innovation and is vital to all our innovation futures.

This brings me to a term I used earlier this year: the *citizen innovator*. Highly creative and inventive individuals have had monumental impacts throughout history; the likes of Leonardo da Vinci, Benjamin Franklin and Sir Isaac Newton. Often considered giants in their day, these are the archetypal citizen innovators, often the beneficiaries of great patronage, with resources and substantial freedom to roam in creative circles, these individuals have inspired many ... they were also few in number.

With the convergence of technology (internet, social networking, communications), increases in standards of living and education, and a more global awareness than at any time in history, I believe there are now legions of citizen innovators around the world ready, willing and able to invest their relevant experience, knowledge, creative talents and hunger for problem-solving toward the important challenges of our time. Some will engage simply to make a difference, others for financial gains. But make no mistake, they are changing the way we innovate, from corporate research and product development to improving the human condition and re-inventing government. This is an empowerment movement and represents the most democratic of ideas: that we as individuals have a necessary and vital role to play in shaping our world – and in some cases an obligation.

In closing, open innovation and citizen innovators are principal actors in the structural evolution of innovation as we know it from the status quo of the past to an open, global, and vibrant innovation platform for the future. Whether it's the need to get new products to market sooner, improve medical treatments or address climate change, this approach changes everything.

Are you a citizen innovator?

Sylviane Toporkoff is also sure that some problems are really 'too big for an individual brain', like this book on the future of innovation. We could not but agree that globalisation should be widely used to create opportunities. Are you enjoying it in this very book at your hands? Thank you, Sylviane, for writing that 'the future depends on the ability to create a culture that supports and promotes innovation'. Let us start this culture here, right now, right at this very moment. It is time to be brave! Brave in many fields – are you ready for that?

The Future of Innovation is a Key Opportunity for Europe

Name	**Sylviane Toporkoff**
Affiliation	Institut d'Etudes Européennes Paris 8 Université
Position	Professor
Country	France
Area	Economic development: innovation and ICT/ shaping the future
Email	stoporkoff@items-int.eu

convergence   Europe   globalisation   innovation   SMEs

The future of innovation is crucial in many fields among others health, food, energy, environmental issues, quality of life ...

Innovation is changing rapidly, in response to globalisation increasing complexity and growing awareness that new ideas can come from anywhere.

Collaboration, convergence and interdisciplinary research are the future of innovation. The problems to solve are just too big for an individual brain! See the success of open-source software development.

We understand in Europe that it is impossible to compete with countries like China and India on cost alone. Innovation is the key and should be based on originality, quality, service, safety, environmental responsibility ...

We should turn the challenges of globalisation into opportunities and in these days of economic crisis there is a common understanding that innovation is the key.

Innovation should not only happen inside organisations but also be a collaborative process including the end user and anybody who can add knowledge.

A new culture should be developed in order to foster innovation continuously. Among others, in such a complex system of cross-licensing and alliances a serious question should be raised; i.e., will patents still be relevant?

We all know that stockholders focus on investing on short-term transactions only at the expense of building for the future. We need change!

If we want a future in our society, especially in Europe, we should boost innovation with real finance. It is crucial to create investments by the private as well as the public sector on a long term in particular for small and medium-sized enterprises (SMEs) that very often are the most innovative actors.

It is important to understand that innovation in all sectors of our societies is more than just the result of research and development. It also depends of the capability of creating new ways to think and very often SMEs are more appropriate to create the proper environment to do so. Of course it requires among other challenges to get rid of bureaucracy which is time-consuming and destructive to creativity. There is no future for innovation as long as bureaucracy will slow down so many intelligent initiatives.

Today, the future depends on the ability to create a culture that supports and promotes innovation including a change in education. Political leaders should be more aware of this.

The future of innovation requires new skills. Will the education system be able to provide them?

We need a high quality of education at all levels. Not only in management, finance and marketing but also in science. Investment in human capital is more and more important in order to create a knowledge-based economy. It is especially important to invest and give continuous support (companies as well as governments) in young minds (including women), i.e., even before university, and introduce them to science and a new creative way to think.

Pop and football stars have international recognition, people who innovate should get the same!

As Albert Einstein said, 'The important thing is not to stop questioning. Curiosity has its own reason for existing'.

Maybe the citizen innovator Dwayne has been talking about is one of the solutions? Perhaps the new skills and roles proposed in earlier sections might help ...

Wim Vanhaverbeke leads our mission into the open innovation and its future. Like Dwayne, Wim goes into details of why open innovation is the new mainstream, the direction where most industries are progressing. Wim adds to our current understanding by sharing with us his taxonomy, some leading attributes and archetypes of open innovation. A pivotal force, a breakthrough power, a striking constituent to the understanding of open innovation in Wim's prescription is its seamless integration into the 'corporate growth strategies'. Does the organisation you are a part of possess this quality?

The Future of Innovation is Open Innovation

Name	**Wim Vanhaverbeke**
Affiliation	Hasselt University
Position	Professor
Country	Belgium
Area	Innovation management
Email	wim.vanhaverbeke@uhasselt.be

**open innovation   theory of the firm   R&D internationalisation
external venturing   alliances   spin-in and spin-out**

Traditionally, large innovating companies relied mainly on internal innovation to develop new products. Chandlerian economies of scale and scope in R&D explain why large-scale internal innovation was effective. Chesbrough and other scholars analysed why this 'closed' innovation dominated for more than half a century, and why closed innovation is nowadays more and more replaced by open innovation. More and more firms switch to an open organisation of their innovation activities in response to the increasing costs of R&D, the shorter product lifecycles, the growing technology clout of suppliers/customers, the growth of venture capital and the globalisation of knowledge.

Open innovation has proven to be a viable way to manage and organise innovation in firms. However, the long-term success of open innovation as a new trend depends on its applicability to different firm and industry contexts. This, in turn, depends on the development of a useable taxonomy that is embedded in sound theories. This taxonomy should broaden the applicability of open innovation, which has been applied originally to new product and new business development in large industrial companies. This also explains why open innovation scholars have been preoccupied with technology-driven ventures, which prevented them to consider other sources of innovation. In my view, the following dimensions are central in the taxonomy:

- **the level of analysis:** open innovation is mainly studied at the firm level. Other levels of analysis are the individual, departments and divisions in organisations, bilateral ties between firms, innovation networks and national systems of innovation;

- **technology lifecycle:** technology can be developed to a particular stage. Open innovation strategies are different in an early, pre-competitive phase to those in a stage where products are ready to go to the market;

- **sources of innovation:** scientific and technological breakthroughs, design, customer insight, market intelligence, etc. ...;

- **type of partners:** upstream/downstream partners in the value chain, eco-system partners, technology partners, etc. ...;

- **internationalisation:** large firms are almost always multinational enterprises (MNEs). How to integrate the geographical dimension into open innovation?

This is not an exhaustive list and the different dimensions are of course not orthogonal to one another. They have to be taken together leading to some archetypes of open innovation.

Developing stronger ties with existing streams of literature is a direct consequence of the taxonomy and the broadening of the application areas of open innovation. The refreshing insights of open innovation are derived from careful observations how contemporary companies innovate. There are, however, several existing theories that can be brought in line with open innovation. I cannot go into the details here, but the benefits and managerial challenges of open innovation can be clarified in terms of real options theory, the relational theory of the firm, the resource and resource dependency theory, the transaction cost and transaction value theory. Furthermore, I am convinced that these theories have to be recombined and integrated to deliver a full theoretical explanation of open innovation. Moreover, open innovation requires the integration of innovation management and strategic management. The search of firms for external technology and external pathways to the markets can only be explained when the role of business models and strategy in open innovation are fully analysed. Similarly, one can only understand open innovation when it is seamlessly integrated in corporate growth strategies.

In the context of open innovation Dwayne has proposed a new role and Wim has provided us with a taxonomy; Ron Dvir will follow with describing a physical context in which open innovation can take place. 'Future centres', as Ron calls them, are outlook posts, labs, incubators, tornados, bridges, arenas for making innovation happen. Though Ron describes them in monstrous shapes and colours, they seem extremely friendly habitats for innovation. You may say 'What? Another practical mechanism? How many more can we want?' Well, without innovating innovation we will not be able to create a sound future of innovation! More experiments, more experience, and constant exploration are the only path to better and better open innovation paradigms.

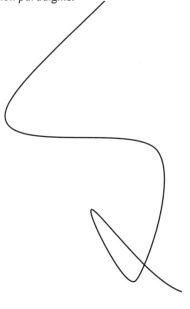

The Future of Innovation is Co-Creation, Contactivity and Co-Futurising

Name	**Dr Ron Dvir**
Affiliation	Innovation Ecology
Position	Director
Country	Israel
Area	Future centre
Email	rondvir@innovationecology.com

future centers   innovation centers   open innovation   co-creation   futurizing

The current innovation paradigm has the shape of a pyramid – at its top, few 'creative people' come with some brilliant ideas; at the second level, a larger proportion of the population develop these ideas; then, we have even a larger group that bring that implement them; and finally, most of us consume the output – be it a commercial tangible product, an art object, a political decision. This is the case in most organisations and communities – commercial, political, social. What if such organisations 'squared' the pyramid and many of the stakeholders participated directly in the upper level of the innovation pyramid? Take the city, for example. What if a large proportion of all citizens sectors would be involved in inventing the future of the city, and inventing new ways to develop it and solve its main problems?

How can this vision be realised?

In the last decade, the idea of 'open innovation' attracted academic research and visionary manifestos and, more importantly, it became a practical and effective way to integrate sometimes thousands for brilliant brains in the innovation process. The way the LINUX operating system was developed by a virtual network of thousands of programs is a powerful example of effectiveness and impact of such approach.

In the recent years, more than 30 'future centres' were established in a variety of private and public organisations. These are organisational, physical, mental and methodological spaces for collaboratively exploring future challenges and developing solution. Metaphorically, they are used as *outlooks* for the future, *innovation labs* for solutions, *incubators* for entrepreneurship and intrapreneurship, *tornados* of creative energy, *bridges* between perspectives, disciplines and stakeholders, and *arenas* for purposeful innovative dialogues.

A future centre (FC) is made of a set of interlinked building blocks: a clear vision (why and for what for it is set up), a portfolio of services that translate this vision into value to the founding organisation and wider community, a dedicated team of innovation facilitators, a core process for looking into the future and then addressing it in a practical way, a toolbox of innovation and futurising methods, a sustainable business model, an attractive physical space that enables different kind of thinking and collaboration, a virtual environment that complements the physical one, and a clever organisational positioning.

In the research project 'Open Futures' an international research and development consortium explored this emerging approach and developed an operating system for future centres. I think that in the coming years we will see many FCs, perhaps using different titles, in multiple domains. There will be urban FCs, regional FCs, national FCs, FCs of specific organisations and FCs of a cluster of enterprises in a specific area.

Why? Because the future centre is a practical mechanism to practise the paradigm of open innovation and realise, collaboratively, the suggestion of Alan Kay: 'The best way to predict the future is to invent it.'

It seems that Ron envisages innovation strategies at all levels and for all kinds of organisations – and what is more, he envisages innovation strategies for entities that today would not be considered to be 'organisations'. We believe that the open innovation movement together with stronger individuals who feel loyalty to a cause (or vision) and their own beliefs will create some interesting challenges for our current understanding of 'organisation' and 'organising'.

Matthias Kaiserswerth continues the story of open innovation by sharing a story from his experience at IBM Research. We can't help agreeing with him that, 'Making the world work better is an ambitious goal. Working together on a "smarter planet" brings the realisation of this vision within reach, and innovation to the next level'. Are you with us?

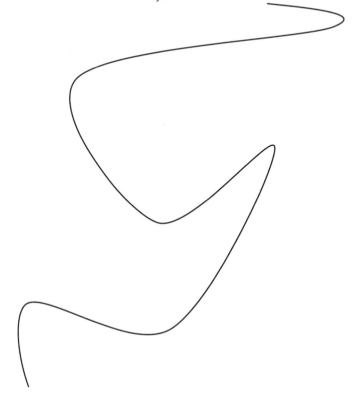

The Future of Innovation is Open and Collaborative

Name	**Dr Matthias Kaiserswerth**
Affiliation	IBM Research
Position	IBM VP and Director of the IBM Zurich Research Laboratory
Country	Switzerland
Area	Research
Email	kai@zurich.ibm.com

smart   collaboration   intelligent   global   nanotechnology

The future of innovation is open, multidisciplinary, global and collaborative. And it offers real benefit to society. In a world that is becoming smaller, flatter and more interconnected, enterprises and even countries can only thrive on sustained innovation and the adoption of new innovation models.

The nature of innovation is changing – in a radical and fundamental way. To develop technologies just for their own sake or for business reasons will no longer suffice: it will become increasingly important that new technologies be easy to use and of real value to the individual and to society at large. To be successful in tomorrow's markets, companies will have to live up to these expectations by creating truly smart solutions.

Accepting the grand challenges of our world requires the joint effort of the best minds and a synergistic blending of diverse perspectives. Therein lies the true power and value of collaborative innovation. At IBM Research, we work with academia and other public and private research institutions as well as with clients and business partners across the globe on a broad range of topics.

We pursue, for example, three dozen research projects within the framework programmes of the European Union. One of them is called 'HERMES Cognitive Care for Active Ageing'. In this project IBM researchers collaborate with 15 European partners in an effort to help older people counteract the weakening in their cognitive capabilities, thus helping them lengthening the stage of independent living. The researchers create easy-to-use and intelligent technologies that help train or assist one's memory. The project includes a special focus on developing an interface that will be comfortable for technology-adverse users, which requires new concepts and diverse skills. Therefore, the HERMES consortium brings together experts ranging from gerontology and speech processing to hardware integration and user-centred design. Their joint promise is to let forgetting become a distant memory.

Nanotechnology is another area where open and interdisciplinary research efforts will bring about cutting-edge solutions that will make the world work better. Tiny structures – 10,000 times smaller than a human hair – could spark advances in various fields such as nano-electronics, information and communication technology, health care and life sciences, as well as energy and environment. Nanotech applications in the energy sector could, for example, lead to more efficient use of solar energy, or new ways of purifying or desalinating water, and thus may even help tackle some of the biggest challenges of our time. Nanotech solutions heavily depend on interdisciplinary expertise, sophisticated tools and ultra-sensitive research environments. An excellent example is the new nanotech centre, a private/public partnership of IBM Research and the Swiss Federal Institute of Technology, which is currently being built on the campus of the IBM Zurich Research Laboratory. The two institutions join forces to conduct research into new atomic and molecular-scale structures and devices for future supercomputers and other breakthrough innovations.

Making the world work better is an ambitious goal. Working together on a 'smarter planet' brings the realisation of this vision within reach, and innovation to the next level.

Are you finally with us? We believe you are! Then, let us think on making our planet smarter! Paul Hissel seems to have a clever plan for that: an integrated, virtual innovation chain. Does that sound feasible to you? To add to Dwayne's idea of 'citizen innovators' Paul proposes another role: the 'Innovation Chain Master'! How do you like that? Imagine that you are being asked, 'What do you do?' and you reply: 'I am an Innovation Chain Master!' Does this sound good, respectful, mysterious, intrigue, agreeable, and attractive enough for you? We wonder how many business cards with 'Innovation Chain Master' will soon appear.

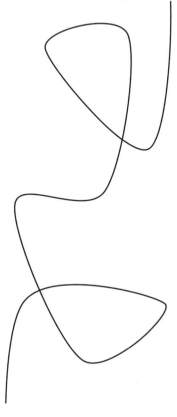

The Future of Innovation is Innovation Chain Masters

Name	**Paul Hissel**
Affiliation	Philips Applied Technologies
Position	Senior Consultant Innovation Management
Country	The Netherlands
Area	Product innovation, innovation management
Email	l.h.hissel@philips.com

**coordination   alignment   collaborative value creation
rewarding/fair value appropriation   virtual value chains**

Innovation in the future will be far more global and based on multi-party collaboration than today. The main benefits are clear: providing more flexibility to build, adapt and optimise the innovation chain together with other (unique or very capable) parties (the virtual innovation chain) instead of having all competences in-house (the integrated innovation chain) and sustaining them at world-class level.

The concept of open innovation points in that direction, but is insufficient as the integrating and leading element is missing. Somehow bringing innovation partners together does not automatically result in effective and efficient innovation: on the contrary! Future innovation chains will have to be linked together and include the (strategic) alignment of the entities in the chain, similar as in a full value chain.

However promising virtual innovation chains may look, there are some serious flaws that have to be taken into account. Additional (and certainly not trivial) efforts are required for:

- building the innovation chain (scouting, selecting and involving the innovation partners), linking the entities and sustaining the chain;

- managing the processes in the innovation chain: these will run less smoothly and efficiently than integrated chains because of differences in processes, terminology, culture and systems, and the element of mutual trust;

- management of the alignment and stability of the chain as all entities will have their own agenda and might participate on a quite opportunistic basis. Besides negotiation will be required for coordination and management of the chain instead of hierarchical control;

- taking the lead to boost the output of the chain: the 1+1=3 effect. Virtual chains in themselves lack clear internal coordination and so an entity that takes the lead is necessary. It is obvious that this entity and its role will have to be accepted by all parties involved;

- rewarding value appropriation. In integrated innovation chains all entities contribute in a coordinated way to the total innovation output. Value appropriation (sharing) over the contributing entities is no issue because the value is consolidated at the integrated chain level. But when the jointly created value including IP must be shared over the virtual chain, collaboration can get tougher! Concepts for rewarding value appropriation will be needed, taking into account the value and uniqueness of the contributions, dependencies and independencies (substitutability of entities), level of risk taking ... Virtual innovation chains will work more randomly: sometimes they will work and sometimes they will not meet up to expectations for the total chain or for any of the entities.

In the future there will be a clear need and opportunity for Innovation Chain Masters, consciously taking care of above points. The future of innovation is these Innovation Chain Masters.

Without this role virtual innovation chains might be less successful in the end as fully coordinated integrated chains. In this respect it is interesting to observe the Toyota model and the relation with its suppliers: a virtual implementation of a fully integrated and tuned innovation chain (under the undisputable leadership of Toyota).

While it may sound a little outlandish at first we quite agree that there is a need for someone to coordinate and orchestrate virtual collaboration chains. Bettina, a lover of classical music, recently listened to a concert without a conductor. While the performance was nice she somehow felt that it was lacking passion and the extra sparkle that differentiates an average from an outstanding performance. Thinking a little about it she concluded that it is the conductor who awakens and amplifies the passion of the orchestra, it is he (or she) who brings those along that might be flagging, it is he (or she) who quietens those that might be too loud, it is s/he who knows whom to put into the limelight, and who creates the vision and direction for the team. Innovation teams are a bit like an orchestra: individuals can and will perform without a passionate leader, because they are professionals, take pride in a good job and are passionate themselves. But a passionate leader can elevate them to the extraordinary. That triggers us to ask you, 'Do you choose innovation leaders based on availability or passion?'

But back to the story ...

It's incredible, how alike we think (now, is that a good thing, after what we have heard about mindsets that think alike and the role of diversity in innovation?)! Paul finishes his statement with Toyota case; Fernando Ozores starts with a Toyota example. We have interspersed too much of our thinking between these two contributors already, so let us ponder no further and hand the baton to Fernando!

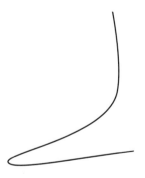

The Future of Innovation is Common People Becoming Extraordinary

Name	**Fernando Ozores**
Affiliation	Buenaidea
Position	Director
Country	Spain
Area	Open innovation, personal creativity
Email	fernando.ozores@buenaidea.es

open innovation   creativity   people   globalisation

Below I outline my vision of the future of innovation in five assumptions and one thesis.

Assumptions

1. Being creative is inside the DNA of humans, being innovative is inside the DNA of organisations

Some people are more creative than others; some companies are more innovative than others. However, all individuals and organisations are always capable of performing certain levels of creativity and innovation.

2. Innovative organisations exist because they have extraordinary processes and/or extraordinary people

While Toyota has managed to beat its competitors by basing its processes on a lean management discipline, Google is enticing talented people from around the world. Both of them are making extraordinary things every day.

3. The extraordinary processes are not linear any more

Manufacturing based in Taylorism, Fordism or post-Fordism is still convenient in many industries, but they do not make a difference any more, even when offshoring. Leading companies as Procter & Gamble[1] have understood its business as an open platform for developing its markets. What makes the difference is the ability to distillate inputs from different sources. Recalling the Cluetrain Manifesto,[2] markets are conversations, and they are not linear at all.

4. Extraordinary people are able to recombine existing knowledge and technologies in a creative way

Diversity and personal experience are some of the most powerful ingredients that foster creativity. In this sense, the polymath (e.g., Leonardo da Vinci, *Homo Universalis*) has a competitive advantage

---

1 'Connect and develop: the practice of accessing externally developed intellectual property in your own business and allowing your internally developed assets and know-how to be used by others' (www.pgconnectdevelop.com).

2 The Cluetrain Manifesto can be found at: www.cluetrain.com.

when trying to solve a challenge in a creative way. The more diverse skills, interests and experiences, the more extraordinary results will be obtained.

5. Today it is easier for any individual to be extraordinary

Globalisation and digitalisation have brought a plethora of valuable resources that facilitate the development of the *Homo Universalis*. For the first time in history, any individual can learn astronomy, photography or philology anywhere, any time. It is only a matter of will and determination. Anyone can easily obtain professional results with digital cameras and Photoshop, be a DJ with iTunes, become a video producer or create a new TV channel.

Thesis

In the light of these facts, the future of innovation is providing an exciting opportunity for individuals, especially those who feel themselves extraordinary or do want to feel themselves extraordinary.

For example, consider this fictitious scenario:

- IKEA communicates its challenges to millions of consumers from around the globe.

- People provide their concepts by using smart software (everyone can be an industrial designer).

- IKEA chooses the idea from a policewoman in Las Vegas.

- One studio in Buenos Aires performs the fine tuning for industrialisation.

- IKEA publishes bills of materials, standard costs and auctions for manufacturing.

- A shoemaker in Barcelona discovers how to simplify the production of certain components and gets a contract for one year.

200 years after the Industrial Revolution, the specialised single-skilled job is condemned to extinction. Organisations need individuals who are somehow polymaths and the world is starting to procure them now. The challenge for the organisations is how to orchestrate these contributions when they are not linear.

Fernando's proposal that the future of innovation can be summarised in five assumptions and one thesis reassures us that Mark McBride was right to believe that 'One of the strengths of the book as it will deal in conclusions rather than waffle!'[3] Indeed, building on concise and succinct suppositions and assuming their validity Fernando offers a 'fictitious scenario'. His assumptions and his scenario will seem fictitious to some – but only too real to others! It all depends where you come from, and what your 'normality' is.

To believe in Fernando's future of innovation, to believe in open innovation, to believe in collaborative innovation – trust and keeping 'the lawyers out of the room' is essential. This is indeed the opportune moment to introduce David Simoes-Brown, and hear his thoughts on the future of open innovation.

---

3   Please see p. xxii in the Introduction.

The Future of Innovation is Together

Name	**David Simoes-Brown**
Affiliation	NESTA
Position	Head of Corporate Open Innovation
Country	UK
Area	Corporate open innovation, collaborative innovation
Email	david.simoes-brown@nesta.org.uk

open   corporate   collaborative   together   trust

Drivers and the Driven

Let's ignore the difficulties and problems of collaboration for now. There are many factors driving businesses large and small towards corporate open innovation (COI) at the dawn of the 21st century: Innovation is expensive and outsourcing promises lower overheads; innovation is now global and even the largest multinational corporations (MNCs) realise that their knowledge has limits; innovation is slow and often incremental and MNCs are attracted by the possibilities of quickly side-stepping disruptive competition or colonising new markets in a kind of corporate lateral thinking; innovation is a group endeavour and some businesses have been quick to recognise the potential of the new web-based networks as humanity wires itself together.

It is fair to say that most writing on COI is from the MNC standpoint. Most small companies are not familiar with COI as a concept and don't know where to start or how to engage with MNCs even if they do. From the perspective of small and medium enterprises or start-ups the motivations are quite different. NESTA's P&G Open Innovation Challenge has shown us that what many small businesses need above all is a customer. And if that customer is also a business or development partner rather than a pushy venture capitalist who insists on owning a large chunk of the business, so much the better.

Trust in the Future

So what about those difficulties and problems? The solutions to the problems of intellectual property are almost as numerous as the business partnerships themselves. One solution NESTA noted in its Corporate Connections programme was to 'keep the lawyers out of the room' for as long as possible. This approach resulted in a profitable and unlikely partnership between McLaren and NATS and contrasts with the 'sign first, ask questions later' approach of most MNCs. For more unequal 'David and Goliath' partnerships, more creative approaches to intermediation can be beneficial as can the plethora of web-based idea-matching services that is now emerging. The one common element here is that establishing trust among actors in the innovation process will become a much more deliberate part of innovation strategy. A side effect of this will be the necessity for more empathy between very disparate organisations. Partnerships will only succeed if everybody can answer the question 'Why bother innovating?' on behalf of their external partners.

Extreme Collaboration

Just as the extreme sports such as wingsuit flying or BMX racing are more exciting and rewarding than their more conventional counterparts, extreme collaboration can get you further, faster. NESTA and Virgin Atlantic's current experiment in user-led innovation in which we are encouraging users to take a stake in the outcome is in stark contrast to the usual situation in which companies get away with paying nothing for ideas. Initial indications are that this approach is paying off and that treating customers as potential business partners can work. Of course with conventional companies this sort of innovation is tough. A recent paper from Cambridge's Institute for Manufacturing notes that implementing an open innovation strategy presents many challenges for management. Many MNCs have a decent strategy but are struggling with attaining the more operation capabilities to match. Some large companies will also have to be culturally reprogrammed in order to enable openness and cooperation rather than encourage secretiveness and competition. They will have to look hard at how they achieve the high levels of personal commitment to a project that open innovation requires.

Innovation is the New Marcomms

To conclude, I feel excited about this new phase in innovation. As open innovation moves from the margins to the mainstream it has the potential to reinvigorate all R&D and NPD (new product development) activity in companies. If you're old enough to remember how marketing became essential in the boardroom in the 1980s then perhaps like me you'll predict a similar resurgence as innovation gets a pace a top table.

What we particularly like about David's contribution is that he not only talks about the importance of open innovation, and the role of trust within it, but that he also has some real-life examples of where open innovation has worked well, and where lawyers were not dominating the relationship. We also found it quite reassuring that innovation in general and open innovation in particular are not facing a unique challenge: David reminds us of the struggle of marketing to gain attention some decades ago – and may we add quality here too? Both disciplines struggled at the outset and no organisation today would assume it could do without it. So, are you old enough to remember how marketing, co-creation, internationalisation, globalisation came onto the scene? An even more intriguing question arises: what is it that the generations to come will push into the boardroom?

Do you remember FedEx employee Chuck being left Cast Away *on a small island after a plane crash?[1] When, after five years of isolation, he finally returned home he was unable to adjust back into daily life. This reminds us of our Part VIII, 'A question of mindset'. It is much more difficult yet much more important for people to re-align their mind. Compared to that, aligning processes and organisations is easy!*

We are not quite sure whether this challenge is made easier or more difficult by the scope that Dan Himmerich foresees: 'five billion problem-solving minds across the globe.' How to change the mindset of five billion people to embrace open innovation? Let's see what Dan suggests.

---

1   Robert Zemekis' film *Cast Away*, 2000, by DreamWorks Pictures and Twentieth Century Fox.

The Future of Innovation is Collaborative Problem-solving on a Global Scale

Name	**Dan Himmerich**
Affiliation	Richworth Enterprises
Position	Principal Consultant
Country	USA
Area	Innovation management, discontinuous innovation
Email	Dan_Himmerich@hotmail.com

problem-solving   collaboration   global   crowdsourcing   open

The future of innovation will be defined not by the formal processes and methods so prevalent in organisations today, nor by individual models and theories proposed by the research community. Instead, the future of innovation will emerge from the confluence of social spaces and the active involvement of five billion problem-solving minds across the globe. In commercial software, we have seen the beginnings of a transition from tightly controlled intellectual property to software invented, enhanced and transformed by large communities of 'open source' participants. This industry is beginning to realise that a single R&D lab cannot possibly compete with the collective creativity of thousands of insightful, active contributors in the open source environment.

Imagine what will happen when manufacturing, aerospace, architecture and design, and other industries embrace this approach – no longer will small groups of engineers or market researchers guide the emergence of the next generation of goods and services – instead, the communities who consume these products will collaborate to invent, enhance, adapt and transform them at a pace and in ways that no single organisation can possibly hope to match.

As the scope of innovation efforts expands, so too will the complexity of managing the people, processes and outcomes of global collaboration efforts. We can anticipate that '360-degree problem solving' will emerge as an effective tool in optimising the problem-solving/innovation process. As organisations seek to maximise their potential to innovate at scale, it will become increasingly necessary to understand how different people connect with innovation differently, and how we each solve problems differently. Managing diversity in problem-solving style will become as important to organisations as recruiting, organising and optimising diversity in technical or domain competence. Problem-solving teams – particularly teams collaborating on a global scale – will find that knowledge of their preferred style of problem solving, in the context of their collaborators' styles, will greatly increase the speed and effectiveness of the problem-solving/innovation process.

Bravery will be required by those organisations visionary enough to break with their historical business models to harness the creative diversity of motivated consumers – everywhere.

Skill in navigating the complex path to effective global innovation and problem solving will force the creation of entirely new organisational, motivational and leadership disciplines. Global innovation is not simply ideation at scale, nor broad customer sampling. Rather, this approach puts problem identification, solution design, prototyping and even production tooling in the hands of networks of problem solvers.

The ability to manage problem solving and innovation on a global scale will define the next era in management, and in management of teams. Those organisations that can harness the chaos, diversity and speed of global social networks will be the ones who thrive. Those who cannot will find themselves falling – in the words of Leon Trotsky – 'into the dustbin of history'.

How many organisations do you know for which you can already see the march to the dustbins? How many which you can see retrenching into cost cutting and redundancies rather than investigating and seeking a way into the future? No doubt, not falling back into accustomed patterns requires bravery, just what Dan calls for. Turn the page, it is time to be brave! Perhaps it only requires a few of us to be brave and the others will not be able to resist the pull. Perhaps we only need to get some opinion leaders – even better celebrities – on board, and perhaps we can achieve a tipping point.

Cheryl Perkins' view is perhaps a little more down to earth, reminding us that we should achieve a balance of a strong emotional devotion for the result with efficiency of the implementing processes.

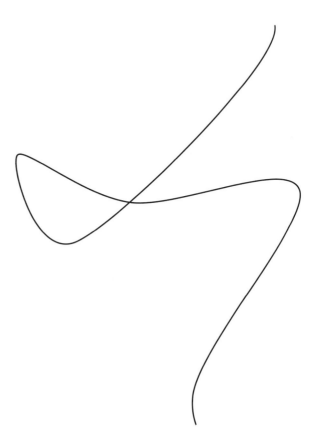

The Future of Innovation is Personal Passion and Strategic Collaboration

Name	**Cheryl Perkins**
Affiliation	Innovationedge
Position	Founder; President
Country	USA
Area	Innovation management and growth strategies
Email	cperkins@innovationedge.com

**crowd sourcing   open innovation   strategic partners   collaborative networks
innovative passion**

The future of innovation involves a balance of personal passion and strategic collaboration. Most people, like myself, have personal passions that influence their business goals. If you're in charge of your company's innovation strategy and creating a culture of innovation, it's especially important to do what excites you. It's true what they say: 'You'll be most successful when you're doing something you feel strongly about.' It's that passion that drives persistence, resilience and the desire to collaborate with others to make a change.

Which bring us to one of the most powerful ways to keep your innovation circuit running with new ideas: *crowdsourcing*. This new form of open innovation uses the power of inspired user groups to accelerate innovation while utilising virtual volunteer consultants.

One way to do this is to start by identifying potential strategic partners and/or companies that will help your business and/or ideas grow. Target the decision-makers within those organisations, such as marketing people or innovation leaders, who likely have expansive networks of important contacts. The power of your network, or 'crowd', can open the doors of opportunity, stir innovation and pave your way to progress toward your business goals.

Ironically, some businesses are actually created from the power of the crowd. For example, iStockphoto.com began as an image-sharing network used by a group of designers, but grew to revolutionise the field of stock photography by offering the work of tens of thousands of contributing photographers at much lower fees. Many companies use their own customer base as a valuable source of input and new ideas. Some even open up to opportunity for customers to vote on certain plans or ideas. Many websites and blogs have become a more dynamic, 21st-century version of the traditional 'suggestion box'.

The concept of crowdsourcing is expanding into another, somewhat unexpected area. In a *BusinessWeek* article called 'Crowdsourcing Customer Service' (September 10, 2007), Kerry Miller examines a company called Get Satisfaction which offers what they call 'people-powered customer service'. The author explains:

It works by allowing anyone to ask a question, submit an idea or complaint, or just 'talk,' all of which gets posted ... for everyone to see. Companies can participate directly ... but other users can chime in with answers of their own. A rating system pushes the best ones to the top.

A growing number of organisations are using services like this or a similar format of their own to cut down on traditional customer-service frustrations and expenses, while increasing customer satisfaction and providing better insight into customer needs.

As with any new idea that so dramatically changes the traditional way things have been done, crowdsourcing has its critics and can present some problems. However, if it's properly managed, the ability to develop new solutions, streamline the R&D process and tap into the creative power of the masses will continue to make crowdsourcing an interesting new tool for innovation in the future.

Isn't it amusing how a crowd, more likely to be associated with an assembly of persons or things in close proximity, densely packed together with a lack of order and loss of personal identity, when used in the context of innovations can suggest a scenario of perfection? A highly desirable state: using crowdsourcing to power 'five billion problem-solving minds across the globe'.

Francesco Sandulli picks up the issue of crowdsourcing and proposes that crowdsourcing and open innovation will have a particular role to play within the service industries – while exposing that we still have a way to go!

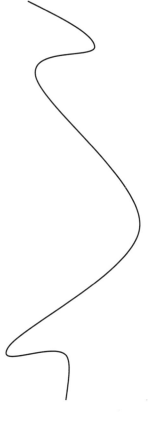

The Future of Innovation is Grasping the Potential of Open Innovation in the Service Industry

Name	**Francesco Sandulli**
Affiliation	Universidad Complutense de Madrid
Position	Codirector of the UCM Chair on Information Society
Country	Spain
Area	Open innovation
Email	sandulli@ccee.ucm.es

platforms   services   intellectual property   crowdsourcing   knowledge

The future of innovation will be tightly related to the growth of the services industry and the spread of open innovation. Firms have started to systematically use external knowledge to accelerate their internal innovation. In the next years we will see a strong trend of open innovation in services, and not only in the services industry but also in the manufacturing industry, as the bundle of products and services is becoming more common every day among manufacturers.

Since its conception the open innovation paradigm has been mainly focused on and implemented by the manufacturing industry. Just recently firms in the services industry such as telecom companies, hotel chains, internet firms or banks have become aware that the open innovation paradigm may also be successfully applied to their operations. But, why will open innovation be an especially valuable paradigm in the services industry?

First, open innovation promotes crowdsourcing and collective innovation. These concepts are easier to implement in the services industry where the customers are used to playing a more relevant role in the creation and delivery process of new products. Moreover, the intangibility of services also makes it easier to increase the scale of the innovation system from a few innovators to a multitude of innovating agents. Second, open innovation may solve the problem of a lack of distribution channels for innovation. A huge amount of firms that develop new services have limited success due to difficulties and the costs in accessing distribution channels. Open innovation creates new distribution channels to service innovators: for instance, the most important telecom companies in the world are opening their voices and data networks to the distribution of services created by a third party; banks have also started to use their ATM and branch networks to distribute new services not invented by them. Third, open innovation accelerates time to market, so it could increase the firm's competitiveness in the services industry where time to market is already typically much lower than in the manufacturing industry.

However, there are some questions related to the open innovation paradigm in the services industry that still have to be solved in the future. For instance, innovations in services have a significant component of tacit knowledge, especially in the case of process innovation. We still don't have open innovation mechanisms that solve the delicate issues related to tacit knowledge sharing.

Perhaps, some of the current innovation brokers such as InnoCentive or Innovationexchange may redefine the knowledge exchanges beyond the current IP-based exchange system. In fact, intellectual property rights are enforced in the services industry with greater difficulty, since many innovations in this field cannot be patented. When deciding the degree of openness of research projects, one of most common problems of open innovation is correctly assessing the innovation capabilities of your partners. The tacit knowledge component and the still unstructured innovation process in many services firms make this task even harder.

Open innovation has the potential to radically change the way we think about services competitive dynamics; however, it is still a run into the night where management commitment and common sense will be needed.

Was there ever a greater challenge than appealing to people's 'common sense'? Looking at what is happening around us we sometimes wonder how common common sense really is! Will we be able to develop the skills required to survive and thrive in this brave new world? Will we not need yet another new skill set and profession? Perhaps Robin Spencer's human – rather than technical – integrator, the 'web-footed boomer', might be able to help? Human integrators' – we believe that the sooner they come to the scene the closer to the future of open innovation we will be.

The Future of Innovation is the Rise of the Web-Footed Boomer

Name	**Robin W. Spencer**
Affiliation	Pfizer Inc.
Position	Senior Research Fellow, Innovation and the Idea Farm
Country	USA
Area	Innovation management, demographics, roles
Email	robin.w.spencer@pfizer.com

demographics   baby boom   internet   complexity   skills

We can name some of the driving forces for innovation in the near future. As Thomas Friedman puts it, the world is increasingly hot, flat and crowded, which is to say that climate change, electronic connectivity and the growth of tropical megacities will impact everything. Because electronic communication is now global, instant and essentially free, change will continue to accelerate and see its swings exaggerated. Our grandparents saw just one or two Schumpeter technology cycles in a lifetime, now these cycles arrive and pass at a rate of three or four per career: the pace of change has increased to the point where it is visible to everyone, and many would say disruptive. The swings are not just faster but also wider: the late-2008 financial meltdown is a stark reminder of the amplifying domino effect of our connectivity. These will be the pervasive forces calling for innovation: faster, wider, chaotic change against a backdrop of unprecedented global climate and demographic shifts. There will be no lack of problems crying for new solutions.

At the same time, the same electronic connectivity is opening the gates to truly universal participation. Billions of people with cell phones or commodity-priced computers connect to each other, for entertainment, family, social and business reasons. They use their phones for price optimisation in villages in India, and to reshape participative democracy in choosing American presidents.

What will the future look like then? Huge, complex, urgent problems, and billions of connected people, many willing and wanting to make their lives better. A necessity facing an opportunity.

But there is a gap in the middle, and 'interface mismatch' if you will. Millions of people can blog all they want about their ideas for cheaper energy, accessible health care, carbon footprints or political change. But the solutions will be complex, multidisciplinary and fiercely detailed mixtures of politics, economics and technology. This will give rise to a new species, the *web-footed boomer*.[1] These professionals, with a career's worth of technical and professional experience, a sudden personal economic imperative and the connectivity of the web, will become an army of 'human integrators'. They will place themselves to face large, complex problems (with which they

---

1   As in 'baby boomer', because professionals with science and technology skills are now retiring from their primary careers at a rate far above the Wests replacement capacity. Polls show that many boomers will retire from their primary career in their late 50s (not always by choice!), but expect (and need) to keep working to their late 60s. This is the decade of their opportunity.

are familiar from their traditional careers), and at the same time, because they are working alone or in small organisations, they will turn for support to the global electronic network to amplify their effectiveness. Under consultant-type contracts from sponsoring organisations, they will be catalysts for innovation by approaching large complex problems by integrating of hundreds of micro-sized pieces of solutions, gleaned from millions of participants on the web.

Robin brings us back to human beings and their, still, crucial role in the innovation process. With all the technology, and all the new possibilities and opportunities it brings, the role of the 'human integrator' is still a critical one in the future of innovation; and it is one that embraces and builds on our increasing global, virtual environment, even thrives on it; the human integrator is needed as 'connector', translator and communicator.

Robin's contribution provides us with the perfect link into Part XI which will start off by investigating the role of communication in the context of innovation – internally as well as externally – in much more detail.

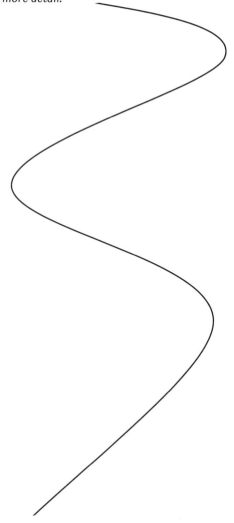

PART XII
This is All You Ever Wanted ...

With all the fantastic opportunities that arise in the open innovation sector we still see one potential obstacle: that of translating all those wonderful ideas from everyone and everywhere into action; in short, of creating innovation out of invention and creativity.

Where is the problem, you may ask. Well, think about it. Have you ever tried to 'sell' something entirely new to someone? Are we not only too familiar with stories such as the ones about the telephone (American President Rutherford Hayes said, 'An amazing invention – but who would ever want to use one?'); personal computers (Kenneth Olsen, co-founder of Digital Equipment Corporation, is quoted to have said, 'I see no reason why anyone would want a computer in their home.') and copy machines (the inventor of the Xerox machine, Chester Carlson, had great difficulties interesting anyone in his invention. Only after eight years, and having been turned down by IBM and the US Army Signal Corps, did he find an investor in the Haloid Company, later to become the Xerox Corporation). Imagine trying to explain a microwave to someone from the Middle Ages. Imagine explaining a laptop or one of today's mobile phones to someone from your great-grandparents' generation. Not easy. As Henry George, American writer, politician and political economist said, 'The march of invention has clothed mankind with powers of which a century ago the boldest imagination could not have dreamt.' – and that was over a century ago. Definitely not easy to sell the new – particularly not if you only use words, rather than words and pictures – or even better, prototypes.

So if you (individually or collectively) come up with 'the next best thing since sliced bread' you need to be able to communicate the concept to others, to enthuse others about your idea, to get their buy-in and their support and, finally, their money.

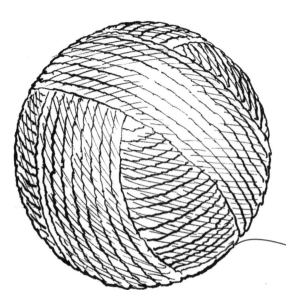

In the closing of Part XI we raised the issue of changes in market needs and wants. Thinking up great things in one's garage and creating new markets is great, for sure, but in most instances even those ideas are based on the observation of a need, a want, a desire or a shortcoming. This is what Stefan Fazekas picks up in his contribution – let's see what he's got to say.

The Future of Innovation is Starting with More and Better Listening

Name	**Stefan Fazekas**
Affiliation	Management Consultant – Project Relations
Position	Owner
Country	Austria
Area	Project management services, process/organisation consulting and interactive future search
Email	stefan@fazekas.at

listen   information   knowledge   dialogue   internet

The 'free flow of information' has proven to be an excellent means of organisational effectiveness, especially when implemented as the antithesis to 'Keeping back information increases my power'. Of course it may lead to information overload, especially when supported via intra-, extra- and internet. It still is easier to produce and spread data, which hopefully have the potential of becoming information to the reader, than it is to digest them.

Even looking at the amount of data available on the web, accessible on a global scale – as long as political barriers don't block it – and readable in intercultural regions – as soon as language barriers don't hinder the free flow of information – no single person has a chance to make use of all the data published, even within their specific areas of interest, during their whole lifetime.

Search engines and Web 2.0 initiatives are supposed to address this issue in order to help transforming data via information to (applied) knowledge – and sometimes wisdom. Now, this is not to blame the data hype in the virtual space; it is great that humankind achieved this and many of us – including myself – would not like to miss it for anything in the world.

Actually we don't need to discuss the web and the communication processes it supports. Let us just focus on interpersonal communication behaviours. Observing them highlights that we are running into the same problems, whether we are using the internet or engaging in any verbal information exchange between human beings.

We constantly tend to (over)inform our communication partner – or shall I say: receiver?! – without allowing sufficient time for questions, feedback, asking for feedback, recapping and so on. Our rationale is that we have less time than ever, everybody keeps telling us so, and that everything is moving faster. But perhaps it is that we adults have unlearned active listening – yes: unlearned? Just remember telling stories to your children, or when you were a child yourself.

What is happening is that many are talking, more or less unidirectional, and many aren't really listening, most likely because they are already thinking about what to talk about next.

One cent per word spoken and unheard in public and commercial organisations and there would never ever be a financial crisis in this world.

Needless to say (or is it?), that in communicating about the current economic crisis – and any other kind of crisis – there lies a chance of managing it. It is a pity that negative news receives much wider coverage than good news – that's why PR experts coined the phrase 'Only bad news is good news'. So how about an Austrian newspaper publishing only good news, throughout the entire paper, on 1 January, 2009? Wow!

It commands respect to read that the new American President establishes a Chief Technology Officer (CTO) in order to make further use of the internet, which he had already used in a highly professional manner during the election phase, in order to enable the dialogue with the wider population.

Dialogue is also the buzzword for interpersonal communication. Perhaps it might be better to say less but at the right time and to the right person, not only to have talked together but also do have done things together.

Dialogue forms the basis for innovations, which – sometimes – are fuelled by ideas.

How about a web service that we could selectively allow to monitor our written and oral conversations with the aim to improve them? A basic set of functionality could compare quantities – the number of written words or the duration of air time – per candidate and apply voice and pattern recognition via an algorithm watching for commonly used words, phrases and tonalities – i.e., distinguishing between *making statements* and *asking questions*. Of course the functionality would expand over time. However, rather than waiting decades for the full scope of functions to emerge while being developed by a small expert community, a much better impact could be achieved by rolling it out on a global scale as soon as possible. Centres of education and learning might be a good starting point.

Much could be written about such enhancement as computing capacities, speech-to-text and text-to-speech capabilities improve and as it becomes possible to address more human senses in communication such as colours and smells.

However, will this piece even be read, exceeding as it does the given word limit ... will it be accepted and printed?

Well, Stefan, we guess you have your answer – at least to the last question. We so much agree, innovation cannot happen if we broadcast, if we hold forth monologues. Innovation happens through dialogue, it happens by asking questions, and by listening. In your organisation, what is the ability to listen like? Are people listening, do they really hear what is being said – or do they have effective filters that tune out the bits they do not like to hear?

Communicating innovation is also at the centre of Cees Jan Mol's contribution – read on!

The Future of Innovation is Going to be Communicated Differently

Name	**Cees Jan Mol**
Affiliation	Pluscomm
Position	CEO
Country	The Netherlands
Area	Communication of innovation
Email	ceesjan@pluscomm.biz

communication   content-perspective   habit-orientation
participative production   sackboy

The future of innovation will become the playing field of a new communications approach: one focused on habits rather than on content. Why? Because 'Sackboy' has entered the living room.

Sackboy is a funny little creature and the main character in *Little Big Planet*, a new hit on the Playstation3. Vital to the success of *Little Big Planet* are the thousands of players building new levels all other players can enjoy. With *Little Big Planet*, 'participative production' has spread its wings beyond open source and now progresses from the PC game of *World of Warcraft* into the living room via *Little Big Planet*. Living room TV entertainment is no longer only broadcast. The paradigm of communication as a linear form of content transmission has reached its limit.

How will this change in communications approach help innovations be communicated better? The old 'transmission model' (characterised by questions like 'What is the right channel?', 'How do I get my message across?') is 'content-centric': it zooms in on the message transportation. If you study it more closely, in communicating innovations such an approach is actually not particularly helpful.

When the Dutch multinational Philips Electronics attempted to change its culture in the early 1990s, a logo 'customer' (customer u me) was created to focus on the customer. Message-wise that communication was effective. Three 'Customer Days' were organised in the course of five years: global gatherings of all 160,000 employees, sitting down to increase their customer focus. Message-wise, the need to focus on customers more was again effectively transmitted. The President of Philips at that time delivered a great speech on the topic, stating that, 'As of now we will become customer-oriented. Based on these great products!'

Effective transmission of content does not necessarily communicate your innovation. When innovations like customer-centric behaviour or instruments for it are launched, a habit-orientation to communication would suggest a different criterion for assessing effectiveness: 'Does the "new message" constitute the "new reality"?'. As seen from the example above, a content orientation easily leads to a default execution in which the content of the 'new message' actually remains (too close to) 'the old message'. What a content perspective obscures and a habit orientation would highlight, is that 'you' and 'me' aren't customers, we are colleagues. If you want to focus on customers, why not invite them to your Customer Day? How can you become customer-oriented with 'great products' (should the president be the judge of that?)?

This is why an effort like the 'Innovation Framework for Sustainable Development' of Philips Research is an interesting experiment (see Dorothea Seebode's contribution Editors comment: which you can find in Part V). It serves for more than conveying content; its action-oriented purpose is also to rally and direct. It works by asking 'How have I been understood?', 'What is the "takeaway" I have just passed on?', 'What have you just told me that makes this framework stronger?'.

In the habit-oriented approach, effectiveness results from constituting what is common, realising the innovation as communication takes shape. Thank you, Sackboy!

As Stefan and Cees argue, change – innovation – can only happen if we are able to communicate appropriately, if we can create arguments that others can understand and buy into, and if we approach the change with a systemic perspective. We must develop the ability to engage with the non-linearity and the systemic nature of communication. What we say and how we say it will have an effect on others. We need to be aware of these effects and take them into consideration. If we want our messages to be understood we need to learn to communicate them in a way the intended recipient can understand. If we are talking about things that do not exist, this ability becomes even more important.

Do you know the classic film 12 Angry Men, *starring Henry Fonda? Another of our recommended 'understand innovation' films. Let us explain why. A jury of 12 is sent to find the verdict of whether or not a young man has killed his father. The evidence seems damming, and 11 out of the 12 decide at once that he must be guilty. Only one of them, Henry Fonda of course, has his doubts. He enables his fellow jurors to share his doubts by relating bits of evidence to them that have meaning for them personally. Let us share an example of this: one of the jurors is wearing glasses; one of the witnesses who had claimed to have seen the murder through his window from his bed, straight after having been woken up from sleep, wears glasses too; the glasses-wearing juror is asked, 'Do you wear your glasses when you sleep at night?' That was all that was required: to the glasses-wearing juror it was clear that the witness could not have seen without glasses who actually committed the murder. Needless to say in the end the verdict is 'not guilty' due to a lack of evidence, and of course the young man is not guilty. To us the film is a masterful illustration of how you need to find points your communication partner can connect with. Without it getting an understanding for your idea, which is a pre-requisite for acceptance, you will face an impossible challenge. Just broadcasting does not lead to anything, least of all understanding.*

This seems quite an appropriate moment to hand over to Chris Harley-Martin.

The Future of Innovation is Selling Ideas to Sceptical Audiences

Name	**Chris Harley-Martin**
Affiliation	GSK Nutritional Healthcare
Position	Vice President
Country	UK
Area	Product innovation
Email	chris.harley-martin@gsk.com

sell   validate   plan   critical   entrepreneur

The future of innovation relies on our making significant improvements in the articulation, validation and planning of business ideas prior to execution; how we plan and sell our ideas to a sceptical audience of investors is a critical factor in future success.

As innovators, we can no longer complain about a lack of ideas or access to consumers but there is still 'many a slip 'twixt cup and lip' that could be avoided with an increased capability in planning and selling our ideas.

Creating and executing business ideas that create positive change relies on three main steps: idea creation, planning/development and execution.

We have started to resolve issues of idea flow and creation through movements such as open innovation and there are now fewer barriers to execution because of the disintermediation of access to consumers, especially through the growth of the internet (although this does not necessarily guarantee that anyone will buy what we have to sell). However, we continue to have issues in the planning/development of ideas, and in particular the articulation, validation and business planning of ideas that make money for the organisation.

In short, the entrepreneurial mindset and skill set of the organisation falls short when we have to 'plan and sell' our ideas to a sceptical audience.

Although I believe this shortfall is generally true, it is particularly true for ideas that sit 'outside the norm', the kind of ideas that are left limp on discarded Post-it notes when we are asked to 'prioritise' after a day's brainstorming. I am sure you know the ideas I mean; they are not particularly well articulated but seem to touch a chord, it is never very clear how we will use our existing research tools to 'prove' they will make money and they are often tricky to execute with the existing attitudes and resources.

In my experience, these discarded ideas often represent the real opportunity for sustainable growth but even if they survive prioritisation then they will fall victim to our lack of skills and discipline in articulation, validation and planning.

There is not the time or space in a short article to describe the multiple tailored interventions in culture, process and resources that could deliver the necessary improvements but even a few simple questions such as, 'How does my organisation make money and how does my idea help us do this?' together with structured support from experienced business people can have dramatic effects in helping us plan and sell even these 'hard to do' ideas, provided there is an environment that encourages and rewards growth through innovation and ideas.

The future of innovation relies on us building the competence and skills to improve the articulation, validation and planning of business ideas; in the right environment, some simple improvements in our approach to concept expression, using real-world experience to validate ideas and a commitment to business planning disciplines we can secure the future for ideas that make money. Just ask the successful entrepreneurs in *Dragon's Den*.

How about if we bring Stefan's request for better listening and Chris's suggestion for better communication together? It is not as easy as it might seem. We believe we can safely assume that all of you have been part of a brainstorming session. We don't know about you, but we can certainly recall occasions when what we believe is a fantastic idea comes to our mind early on in such a session. So enthralled are we with our own idea that we are unable to listen to what everyone else is saying, closing our minds to new and different opportunities, just waiting for a gap in the conversation so we can bring forth our marvellous idea. Have you ever been in such a situation? Yet at the same time innovation depends on individuals being passionate about their ideas, about believing in their ideas with a passion that is not defied by objections and rejection (nor by people's unwillingness to listen).

By the way, did you know that even the way you phrase a question, particularly if it is about asking someone to choose between different options, can influence the outcome? A piece of research conducted by Robert Dew (whose contribution is in Part VII) presented at the 2008 ISPIM conference was an eye-opener to us. While the focus and context of the paper were slightly different, the bit on 'framing effects' is in our view highly relevant in the innovation (and decision-making) context. What Robert found in his research that the same basic facts can receive a positive or a negative response, depending on how the options are phrased – or framed as he calls it. This basically suggests that most decision making is non-rational, and that decisions will depend on the reference point that is given to us in the way the information is presented. In case this sounds a little abstract let's share the example Robert gave in his presentation. In both scenarios people were asked to choose between two outcomes that would be the result of vaccinating 600 people. Scenario 1: (a) when using vaccine 1 200 people will live, (b) when using vaccine 2 there is a 1:3 chance that 600 will live, and a 2:3 chance that 0 people live; the majority of people went for option (a). Scenario 2: (a) 400 people will die; (b) there is a 2:3 chance 200 people will die and a 1:3 chance no one will die. Even though the basic facts here are the same as in the first scenario the decision was entirely reversed! So the way we present our facts and information will have a critical influence on the response. Something worth knowing, don't you think?

How we package our message, how we present its opportunities and downsides and its value is critical. Which leads us into Georg Obermaier's contribution, in which he emphasises the personal communication of values in the context of innovation.

The Future of Innovation is the Personal Communication of Values

Name	**Georg Obermaier**
Affiliation	Institute for Microstructure Technology, Karlsruhe Institute of Technology
Position	Research Associate
Country	Germany
Area	Innovation process, innovation management
Email	georg.obermaier@imt.fzk.de

non-technological insights   communication   values   richness   personality

We have just passed a critical milestone in the age of biophotonics, tissue engineering, grid computing, nanotechnology and other emergent key technologies. We now have sophisticated knowledge to stimulate a new market revolution in which we will achieve a higher level of mastery in the generation, control and use of novel key technologies that will be fully exploited to establish a broad range of innovative market applications. However, now that we have the technological means and insights to enhance the quality of tomorrow's daily life, we lack competences to utilise our technological skills for innovation. Since the main drive for innovation is not just technological knowledge but also non-technological insights, we are strongly convinced that such non-technological insights are the future of innovation. To clearly specify these soft innovation drivers we have to return to the original roots of innovation, pointing out its behavioural aspects.

Innovation is something new and useful. It originates from society and is dedicated to society. Hence, the nature of society forms the character of innovation, which in turn implies that social cohesion plays an important role in creating and establishing innovations. Social cohesion here is nothing but social interaction based on the principles of social communication. Communication is thereby recognised as a process by which we assign and convey sense and meaning. The attempt of communication is to create a shared understanding, implying that if there is no communication there is no innovation. The power of communication brings people together, gathers individualists into becoming partners, converts talks into dialogues and turns transactions into relationships. That's why we believe that in future innovation will be achieved through social interaction which itself depends on social communication.

However, communication is complex, multifaceted and inhomogeneous, meaning that different ways of communicating exists. As already mentioned, innovation originates and is dedicated to humankind, implying that communication is a skill of human beings. One can say that personal communication is the most efficient and richest form of communication because it is immediate, individual and fast. It avoids discrepancies and disagreements, it reduces uncertainties and equivocalities, and it is expressed in signs, symbols and voices. Thus, personal communication generates and provides the kind of value and richness that is necessary to meet the needs and expectations of innovations.

Finally, and to conclude, the crucial element for the future of innovation is personal communication – the personal communication of values.

We believe that there are a number of important points here, points that can at the same time be stumbling stones for innovation. Georg brings us back to the importance of the individual person in the play of innovation, connecting it to an ability to communicate which, so he argues, depends on a shared language and understanding. This need for a shared language and understanding is undeniable; at the same time we have to watch out that this shared language is not the result of a shared mindset! As American architect and journalist Walter Lipmann once said, 'If we all think alike no one thinks very much.' Indeed. Diversity is critical yet diversity needs special consideration when it comes to communication; with that we mean that we need to find ways to communicate across mindsets and enable people with different starting points to share in the same vision or end-point (as have discussed in more detail in Part X, 'Let's get together'). While personal communication is the most immediate form of communication, we would still argue that there is plenty of scope for miscommunication and misunderstandings within it.

Georg places an emphasis on personal communication; despite and because of the virtual worlds that have become part of the innovation game we too believe that personal interaction has a crucial role to play – as does Joanne Lawrence.

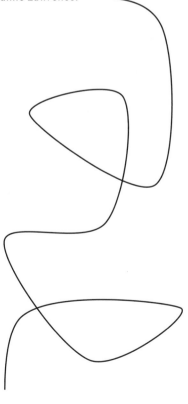

The Future of Innovation is the Disappearing Water Cooler

Name	**Joanne Lawrence**
Affiliation	JT Lawrence + Company
Position	Managing Director
Country	USA
Area	Organisational and e-communication
Email	JTL@jtlawrenceandco.com

**communication   culture of innovation   digital communication
organisational communication   trust   safe environment**

What effect will the way we communicate in organisations today have on our ability to innovate in the future?

Innovation is about taking risks, about generating seemingly crazy ideas that just might work. Innovation thrives in environments where new ideas are welcomed, cross-fertilised and encouraged without fear of reprisal or ridicule; a place where innovators are secure and confident enough to nurture their ideas to fruition and everyone feels that 'it is better to have tried and failed than never to have tried at all'.

With proliferating virtual offices and fewer people gathering around the water cooler, are we deconstructing that environment? Are we eliminating the spontaneous social interactions and serendipitous conversations that often lead to the next great idea?

As much as communication technology may be linking us globally, it may also be isolating us from our colleagues next door. With exponential use of mobile phones, text messaging and overflowing inboxes, we are in constant touch, yet may be growing increasingly out of touch. We transmit information in the shortest sentences possible: messages are to the point, nearly anonymous and starkly devoid of emotion (unless you count smiley faces). Even when we are present, we're absent. How often do you find yourself communicating via email to the person in the next cubicle, or texting during a meeting?

Perhaps we need to rethink e-communication, viewing it not as a replacement for communicating, but more as a tool for continuing the face-to-face exchanges that sustain a creative organisational culture.

Organisational communication is a strategic enabler: it aligns employee behaviour with visionary goals – such as innovation – supporting their realisation. It is both a managerial competence and an investment, and requires time, thought and energy to yield results.

Real communication inspires, informs and involves an organisation. It is as much about content as process: *how* we communicate is as important as *what* we communicate. It is more than sharing knowledge or data: it is sharing stories that motivate, experiences that teach, and creating relationships that build trust. It is providing opportunities up, down and across an organisation that encourage conversation, are personally engaging and create a culture of belonging and with it, the safety to take chances.

Digital communication, on the other hand, is a *tactic* for transmitting information. It can support, but not substitute for the emotional and mental connections made at a cross-departmental meeting or chance hallway encounter. Over-reliance can potentially undermine the creativity often implicit in direct communication. E-communication's main attributes – speed and brevity – are almost antithetical to innovation. Words without context can be misunderstood, terseness can be interpreted as uninterest, and fewer words mean fewer chances to trigger creative associations and new perspectives. Subtle clues evident in face-to-face interchanges are missing, leading to distrust and self-doubt. The creative energy that arises naturally from a spontaneous interaction and the time needed to explore ideas are lost.

Innovation thrives where trust abounds and colleagues co-create in a supportive culture. To sustain such cultures, we need a more thoughtful, holistic approach to organisational communication, with e-communication playing an important, but less primary role.

In short, we still need water coolers.

Are you too living in a country where smoking inside an organisation is forbidden? What has that got to do with anything, you may ask … Well, if you do, you may have noticed that the 'smoking room' – which generally means a point outside the side entrance – has become the new water cooler where people from different parts of the organisation convene, joined together by a shared passion, smoking. And when people share a passion they talk, and when people talk ideas bubble up. We know senior managers who regular visit the 'smoking corner' even though they don't smoke, just to keep up with latest gossip and developments in their organisation.

Whether it is the water cooler or the smoking corner, Joanne reminds us of the importance of such gathering points, and of the importance of storytelling. By the way, storytelling is also a great way to create bridges between different mindsets! Stories help to make sense; they help to create and share meaning. Joanne reinforces the need for personal, face-to-face communication in the context of innovation.

Using metaphors and analogies is another useful tool in the context of innovation. Have you heard of Toyota's use of the metaphor 'rugby player in a dinner suit' for the development of its Honda some years back? Does the metaphor not convey a powerful picture in your mind? Does it not help to create a shared vision for people from different background?

Anja Maier uses the analogy of jazz to illustrate her perspective on communication in the context of innovation.

The Future of Innovation is Orchestrating Ideas

Name	**Dr Anja Maier**
Affiliation	University of Cambridge, Engineering Department
Position	Research Associate
Country	UK
Area	Orchestrating ideas through communication
Email	anja.maier@cantab.net

communication   idea implementation   jazz music   structure   improvisation

In large organisations people generate many creative ideas, but often these vanish soon afterwards and rarely translate into the very innovations that these organisations ask for. Why do ideas vanish? It is because ideas are not followed through. It is the 'following through' that needs attention and support. Identifying, developing and nurturing ideas is a far greater challenge for innovation in an organisation then coming up with those ideas in the first place. Therefore, we need to focus on the post-idea-generation phase: orchestrating ideas through to performance in front of an audience – the market.

'Orchestrating ideas for innovation' means marrying ongoing routine operations (the support structure) with non-routine and uncertain elements (the 'experiment'). Are they incompatible? On the contrary, they are mutually dependent and mutually beneficial.

As an analogy, take jazz music. It has structure and it is improvisation, a fluid join between converging and diverging. Jazz ensembles vary in style, size and instrumentation. Yet, there are uniting elements on which musicians need to agree, such as chord progression, rhythm, improvisation, lead and ending. Within that frame, jazz musicians collaborate with each other, compose when playing, throw in ideas, pick other ideas up and extend them. Jazz musicians answer calls from their fellow players and inspire them through their response.

Compositions may well never be played again, yet ideas have been followed through. Communication is a vehicle by which ideas are followed through. This communication is often unspoken, coming from a clear understanding of each others' roles and intentions and the willingness to let others take the lead. In a similar way, ideas need to be orchestrated through communication.

Orchestrating ideas for innovation through communication is the subject of our research. We emphasise the importance of communication for improving the new product development process. Our empirical investigations indicate that many non-technical problems in organisations are – mostly unintentionally – labelled communication problems. Which, upon scrutiny however, appear to be caused, for example, by misaligned perceptions of factors, such as 'roles and responsibilities', 'autonomy of task execution', 'leadership', 'application of corporate vision', 'goals and objectives' and 'overview of the sequence of tasks in the process'.

In such situations, a communication problem might be the outcome rather than the cause. We argue that factors influencing communication provide levers through which communication can be improved. To address this, we have developed an assessment method of communication in new product development. The Communication Grid Method exposes differences in expectations and perceptions at team interfaces with respect to a variety of factors influencing communication, such as the ones mentioned above. It is able to show important gaps between the current and desired states of factors as perceived by the people collaborating. Factors can act as enablers and barriers. Take 'leadership', for example. To stick to the analogy with jazz music, there might be a superstar soloist inspiring all other players, setting a standard that lifts everyone's game, yet even that star might behave in a way that might diminish the will of the other players to perform well.

In sum, consideration of these factors should be integral to managing any new product development process. It provides the structure within which ideas for innovation can be orchestrated through communication.

Have you noticed Anja, like Chris before, mentions the enthusiasm with which we generate ideas – just to leave them unused in a drawer or on a wilting Post-it note? We have already looked at the need to be able to communicate such ideas and to get buy in, and in Part IX we have talked about a need for a systemic approach. Anja has built on this by offering the analogy of jazz music.

Have we mentioned before how delighted we are at how well questions asked by one contributor seem to find answers or at least starting points for answers in another contributor's thought? We feel that Anja and her colleagues have started to develop a tool that will help to identify communication gaps, and thereby start to facilitate better communication across diversity.

If we have talked about getting acceptance for and developing an idea in the first place, Federico Frattini alerts us to another communication hurdle: that of selling our idea outside our organisation, and creating acceptance of our marvellous idea in the marketplace.

The Future of Innovation is Managing the Fuzzy Back-end of the Innovation Process

Name	**Federico Frattini**
Affiliation	Politecnico di Milano – Department of Management, Economics and Industrial Engineering
Position	Assistant Professor
Country	Italy
Area	Innovation management
Email	federico.frattini@polimi.it

**diffusion of innovation   customer acceptance   early adopters   market launch
fuzzy back-end**

The technological innovation process can be roughly conceived as composed of two major phases: a first one which is aimed at identifying and developing a new or improved product or service, and a second stage where managers struggle to successfully commercialise and establish that product or service on the market. It is fair to say that innovation management scholars have directed their attention much more to the first stage of this critical process so far. They have in fact largely studied how to develop a firm's capability to identify the most promising ideas for new products and services, how to effectively seize and incorporate the needs of extant and prospective customers into its innovation efforts, how to better organise and manage engineering and development projects. Far less attention has been devoted instead to look into the diffusion processes of new products and services, to understand the reasons underlying different levels of customer acceptance and, consequently, to devise appropriate methods to manage the critical interface between the innovation process and the market. These issues have been the exclusive domain of bordering albeit distinct scientific disciplines such as marketing, sociology and economics.

In my opinion a number of evolutionary trends are currently in place that, in the near future, will make it easier for a firm to generate and successfully develop new products and services:

- The opportunity to more easily tap into the diffused creativity of dispersed and skilled individuals, enabled by low-cost, web-based platforms and intermediaries (e.g., innocentive.com or designboom. com).

- The overarching diffusion of new digital communication paradigms (e.g., Web 2.0 and online communities) that will allow to more easily involve the final users into a firm's innovation process.

- The growth and diffusion of innovation intermediaries (e.g., new product development service companies, contract research organisations, technology brokers), that allow a firm to more easily access missing pieces of technical competencies and knowledge.

If it is true that these dynamics will demand some changes in the management of the generation and development of new products and services (how to cope with crowdsourcing?), they will unavoidably improve the chance of a firms to succeed in the earlier phases of the innovation process.

At the same time, the market acceptance of new products and services will become an even more critical process to administer:

- The pervasiveness of communication networks will magnify word-of-mouth, imitation, bandwagon and social contagion dynamics, with significant (both positive or negative) effects on the acceptance of innovations.

- The growing interconnectedness of high-technology markets will make it harder and harder to successfully establish a systemic product on the market, especially when it substantially undermines the status-quo.

- Ethical and social concerns, and other forms of intangible benefits, will become more and more decisive in determining the market success of new products.

I believe these trends will shrink the success rate for fully commercialised new products, notwithstanding the higher number of high-quality ideas and innovation opportunities available to a firm. I expect therefore that, even in high-technology industries, competitive advantage will be more and more influenced by marketing and commercialisation skills rather than mere technological prowess, as some authors have already noted.

The main challenge for innovation management scholars will be therefore to integrate established concepts and interpretative models belonging to traditionally distinct disciplines, i.e., innovation management, marketing, economics and sociology, to gain a better understanding of the dynamics underlying what could be called the 'fuzzy back-end' of the innovation process. This is a pre-requisite for addressing some questions that will be of paramount importance for the success of a firm's innovation efforts: how to manage the innovation process in order to elicit a positive attitude toward the new product among its early adopters? How should marketing instruments be employed to streamline the acceptance of highly radical innovations? How to coordinate the market launch of a new product with concept generation, engineering and development activities, so as to stimulate and harmonise the behaviour of the different players of the value network?

Our immediate (and lasting) reaction is, great! It will become increasingly difficult to pull wool over consumers' eyes with marketing gimmicks and false claims. Perhaps the new forced openness, created by consumer power and geographical, instantaneous connectedness, will help to shape the new kind of morality we were calling for earlier?

It will certainly drive organisations to get a better understanding of true customer needs and wants. This ambition, as Svend Haugaard argues, needs to be deeply rooted in every aspect of an organisation. To find out what that might look like, read on!

The Future of Innovation is Uncertain

Name   **Svend Haugaard**
Affiliation   Danfoss A/S
Position   R&D Project Manager, MBA
Country   Denmark
Area   Innovation strategy
Email   svend@haugaard.mail.dk

big thoughts   risk   open innovation   lead users   change

The future of innovation belongs to those who deeply understand how to formulate, execute and live a strategy for tapping into customers' unfulfilled but yet unknown needs while delivering true beneficial changes to their markets and industries.

Business strategy has been studied for decades by academicians and industry professionals who have formulated a plethora of tools, tips and tricks for analysing an organisation's external opportunities and threats, internal strengths and weaknesses, for laying out possible scenarios of the future and for successful strategy implementation.

To gain competitive advantage a strategy process demands creativity and mental space for big thoughts, which however exposes the organisation to risk of failure – the 'new strategy' may be wrong (only the future can tell, and for sure it will), may be deemed to have shortcomings, may lack flexibility or it may be impossible to implement. Real life often mixes these issues so business strategy is no easy task.

A starting point should be to recognise that in business the future per se is uncertain no matter how many business school tools are being applied to the strategy process and how much effort is put into it, so an organisation must be flexible to adapt its strategic direction to whatever comes around externally or internally to the organisation. Keeping track of the future becomes more important than ever before due to decreasing product lifecycles and increasing globalisation – what is launched on the market today may be difficult to sell tomorrow because customer habits change rapidly or because some remote and rather unnoticed competitor made a better offer on the marketplace.

How then achieve sustainable competitive advantage when the future is more unpredictable than ever before?

A possible answer is that future successful organisations must live by the strategy and values of open innovation in close cooperation with lead users of attractive markets. Management and employees alike must accept and appreciate that their organisation has no full control of the innovation process, that game-changing innovations inevitably will occur outside their command

and control (this is already happening today, in case you hadn't noticed it) and that there are always more subject matter experts outside the organisation than inside it, no matter how big an organisation is. These experts may reside with competitors, suppliers or customers or in other industries outside the organisational scope of business. Organisations must also face that attractive lead users may be someone else's customers in an industry where the organisation has no presence and no strategic intend to enter.

The concepts of open innovation and lead users are still fairly new and are poorly understood by the bulk of innovators, and they to some extent still need to prove their value. Nevertheless, they should be considered carefully as a path for future business success.

Organisational attitude is bound to change and we are all a part of the game, which starts with a simple question: how will we compete in the future marketplace, where industries and markets can change at the speed of light?

So we are back to open innovation and crowdsourcing, which need to be brought into the core of organisations. We have talked a fair bit about that in Part XI, so let's rather connect with Svend's opening statement which was about identifying unfulfilled customer needs. What then might be a good way of identifying winning ideas? Michael Simpson shares his experience with us.

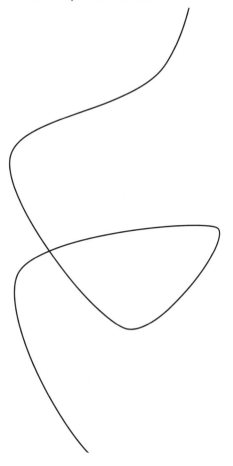

The Future of Innovation is How Smart Companies will Generate Winning Ideas

Name	**Michael Simpson**
Affiliation	Ideas First
Position	Managing Partner
Country	United Kingdom
Area	Insight and idea generation for global FMCG companies
Email	msimpson@ideasfirst.net

global   ideas   insights   virtual hothouse   innovation

Identifying winning insights and producing winning ideas are critical steps in the innovation process for any successful organisation. These steps will become even more essential as organisations respond to the toughest economic recession for a generation and begin in earnest to make the changes required to meet climate change commitments. From my practical experience of running more than 180 ideation projects with global FMCG brands, I believe that 'smart companies' will focus in three particular areas to generate winning insights and ideas over the next five to ten years.

First, history has shown that smart companies gain strength by staying focused on generating new ideas that meet consumer demand for innovation, particularly during an economic downturn. This approach paid off for companies such as L'Oréal and Procter & Gamble during the last significant recession. They grew market share by maintaining investment in innovation research for priority projects, and by investing in the launch of new products, taking advantage of relatively low media costs. However, given the economic pressures and greater levels of consumer austerity, it will be critical for smart companies to ensure that their ideation efforts are clearly focused on real consumer needs, driven by perceptive insights and creating true market opportunities.

Second, smart companies will exploit new virtual technologies to generate insights and ideas from a broader pool of creative talent in a faster and more cost effective way. New 'Web 2.0' technologies now provide the platform for smart companies to expand the idea- and insight-generation process beyond typically small and centrally located innovation teams. This approach is one of the winning philosophies expounded in Karl Albrecht's *The Power of Minds at Work*, and was practically demonstrated in a recent global innovation project for Johnson & Johnson that used a new online tool called the virtualHOTHOUSE™ to engage with a large innovation team in 14 priority markets to generate new product ideas for the Johnson's Baby® brand. Smart companies will also use these virtual tools to 'outsource' insight and idea generation to global trend experts, social networks and creative consumer panels, or in direct partnership with small technology companies. This 'outsourcing' approach is widely used by Procter & Gamble and it is the driver of Dell's IdeaStorm® process. In addition, smart companies will exploit the proliferation of smart-phone technologies to communicate with target consumers, as a way, for example, of quickly testing the potential of new product concepts.

Third, smart companies will focus insight- and idea-generation efforts on meeting the challenges of climate change. As worldwide political consensus for change grows, neither organisations nor consumers will be able to avoid their environmental responsibilities. Despite economic pressures, smart companies will see climate change as an opportunity to focus on insight and ideation activities to re-engineer all aspects of their businesses, including product development. An excellent example of this has been the Japanese car industry's ability to consistently outperform the 'big three' American manufacturers to produced more advanced and energy efficient cars. The innovative approach of the Japanese has been significant in reducing the big three's share of the US market from 74 per cent to 44 per cent over the last 12 years. This environmental 'watch out' applies equally to other industry sectors and underlines the urgent need for all manufacturers to apply new thinking and new processes to generate ideas that will both meet the short-term needs of consumers and help counteract the longer-term threats of climate change.

Michael draws the strands of consumer focus, open innovation and sustainability together, providing a framework that organisations can use to guide and focus their development efforts. Does your organisation have a clear reference framework for selecting – and deselecting – ideas? Some overarching values or guidelines that help people in your organisation navigate the labyrinth of possibilities? That such guidance or perhaps some other kind of framework can be rather useful is the belief of Nikolai Khomenko.

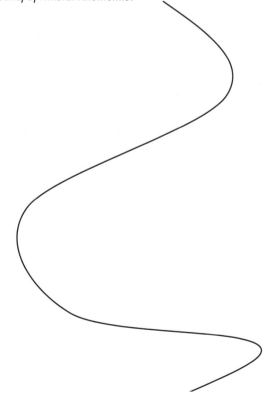

The Future of Innovation is a Practical Tool-box for Sustainable and Systemic Innovation

Name	**Nikolai Khomenko**
Affiliation	Insight Technologies Lab.
Position	Director
Country	Canada
Area	Management of innovation, systematic innovation, OTSM, classical TRIZ
Email	Nikolai.Khomenko@gmail.com

OTSM   TRIZ   sustainable innovation

As usual, to understand opportunities for future we should analyse trends from the past through the present into the future.

But first we should clarify what we will call *innovation* in context of this short analysis. Our PhD student spend almost an entire year looking for more or less widely accepted definition of what innovation is. So we provide here our understanding of what innovation is, and will consider the situation from this standing point.

First, each innovation contains some idea on changing an actual situation, i.e., no change – no innovation. It means we need powerful instruments for getting innovative ideas.

Second, an idea becomes an innovation only when we successfully implement it. So we need instruments to maintain the process of innovation.

Now, what can the past tell us about these two components of an innovation?

1. For hundreds of years people got innovative ideas and implemented them by chance or by trials and error. To understand what the future of an innovation will be like we should analyse what could be done to get and implement innovative ideas using instruments. In the 1940s a Russian scientist undertook a great piece of research into the history of systems evolution. Based on this analysis of real-life experience of innovators throughout history and around the world he came up with certain conclusions and, based on these fundamental ideas, developed the theory on how to develop instruments to obtain effective innovative ideas in an effective and systemic way. Altshuller named it TRIZ (Russian acronym for the Theory of Solving Inventive (Innovative) Problems). Later he transformed TRIZ into OTSM (Russian acronym for The Theory of Powerful Thinking).

2. During the last decades of the 20th century American scientist John P. Kotter undertook great research into the history of implementation of innovative ideas, resulting in his 8-Step Model of an effective process of implementation of innovative ideas. Integration of Altshuller's and Kotter's approaches allowed getting innovative ideas and implementing them more efficient than before.

3. Above all we can see that competition in the world market increase dramatically and became global.

Now we could foresee some of the future of innovation. On the one hand instruments to produce and implement innovative ideas became more and more powerful. On the other hand, the real world and markets demand innovation more and more often. These two trends lead us to a conclusion that to be an innovation leader in the future companies and organisations should use concept of a *regular, sustainable system or chain of innovations*. In other words, to be successful in innovation it will not be enough just get one single innovation and implement it properly, but leaders of organisations should develop systemic chain of innovation. As a result demand for integration of powerful tools for innovation will grow up dramatically. Integration of OTSM-TRIZ and the 8-Step Model seems to be rather promising for creating a much more powerful approach for sustainable and systemic innovation.

The desire to understand the future is important – and funnily enough, it often helps to look back in order to look forward. This is what Nikolai suggests. While too strong an anchoring in the past is often seen as an obstacle to innovation, it does not have to be! Understanding the past is one thing, believing that it determines our future is another. Try introducing something into an organisation without understanding what has happened before, without understanding the culture which is the result of what has happened before. Chances of success will be based primarily on luck. Innovation is not something we should leave to luck and chance. We should drive it forward, drawing on all the tools, understanding and insights available to us. Understanding the past is part of it. Not to be used as a constraint but as a springboard and accelerator.

Of course we could also not agree more with his call for a systemic approach to innovation. Unless we organise and manage for innovation it will never happen.

But back to a call for a focus on the customer; let us hear three more voices on this topic. We would like to start with Paul Sigsworth who brings together the call for new consumer research methods with a demand for a truly integrative and systemic approach to innovation – in short, he calls for bravery in order to achieve sustainable innovation.

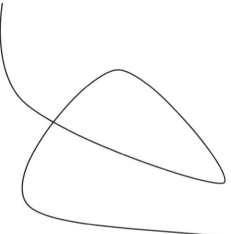

The Future of Innovation is Putting the End at the Beginning

Name	**Paul Sigsworth**
Affiliation	Nestlé
Position	Learning and Development Specialist (with subject matter responsibility for innovation)
Country	UK
Area	Innovation capability and HR aspects of innovation
Email	paul.sigsworth@uk.nestle.com

execution   commercialisation   risk   durable   business models

The future of innovation will be extensively shaped by an increased focus on the execution of ideas that have been validated. Businesses have become acutely aware of the cost of capital over the last decade, well before the current financial crisis struck. In innovation this has meant increasingly sophisticated techniques to address the 'fuzzy' (yet actually not very difficult) front-end, and enormous rigour over prototyping, testing and stage-gate management. It is deeply ironic that innovative ideas that have survived this Darwinian assault course can then be thrown into the business's routine machine for commercialisation where they have to compete with everything else that is going on. The most they can often hope for is a few short moments in the limelight in the first three to six months of their delicate lives. The reason is clear. There is often an organisational disconnect between development teams and commercial streams. Yet even when these streams are involved early, it is mainly directed at getting buy-in to the concept and often feels very token.

In future the innovation world will see that playing 'safe' at this stage is counter-productive. More attention will be paid to innovating in execution. How would it be if we developed and applied consumer research methodologies that were projective rather than retrospective? If we developed launch media strategies based around attitudinal clusters rather than the common groupings so loved of media owners and their planning systems? If we considered radically different routes to market, sampling, merchandising and customer relationship programmes? Of course these exist in pockets, but the execution of innovation is rarely systematised in the total innovation process. Innovators generally have permission from their shareholders and stakeholders to take risk and have become much better at managing risk in the development stages of products and services until they are sure they have something that offers a relevant difference. Let this risk principle, and all the safeguards that go with it, spread into the final lap of the race and compound difference of product with difference of execution to create a durable hero in the consumer's mind.

This has major implications for how innovators operate. It implies creating the willingness of stakeholders and shareholders to imagine different business models. It implies a shift from bringing in members of the commercial team (who may have limited innovation capability) at a middle stage and essentially asking them to graft the innovation onto their existing approach, to running an integrated execution stream from the very beginning. It implies a shift from a bravery/ timidity model to a bravery × bravery model that seems paradoxical in tough times, but which may well represent a rich future seam for innovation.

Did we not hear about the need for bravery before? Well, we guess the future of innovation is not for the faint hearted. The future of innovation is for the courageous, brave and imaginative! Don't forget that these are not traits we are necessarily born with. These are traits that we can encourage and nurture.

Our second voice is that of Mark Richardson who, like Nikolai earlier, emphasises the need for a definition and links that definition to a customer focus, ending with a call to identify those who are truly close to the consumer.

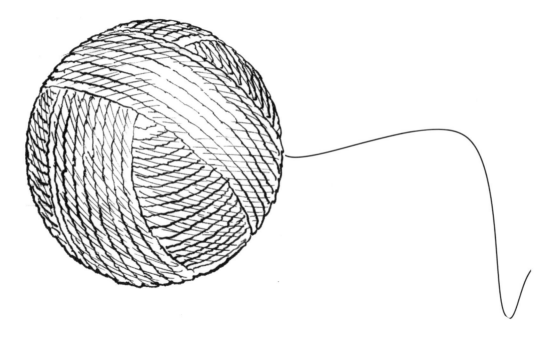

The Future of Innovation is in the Hands of the Customers

Name	**Mark Richardson**
Affiliation	Smith and Nephew Wound Management
Position	VP Research and Technology
Country	UK
Area	Open innovation
Email	mark.richardson@smith-nephew.com

customer needs   technology push   unmet   needs

Before giving a view on the future of innovation it is important to first of all define what it is! To me, it means successfully bringing something new (novel or creative) into the hands of the user or customer which they will value. This final delivery to the customer or user is important – ideas alone are not innovation, inventions alone are not innovation – they must transfer through to the market in some way. So where does its future lie?

Innovation is a messy process and it can be hard to nurture, manage and grow – in fact some would say the more you try to manage or control it the more elusive it becomes. However, I feel innovation can be most successfully achieved if you have access to both parts of an important equation.

So here is the recipe! Take an unmet or poorly met customer need and add a unique (or first ever) way of satisfying it and you have a good chance of delivering a successful innovation.

Few would argue that these ingredients have a place in the mix of successful innovation but to my mind the future must surely lie in the hands of those people, companies and organisations that best understand the needs of their customers (current or proposed) – these needs are the route to commercial success. Such organisations love their customers and this love is reciprocated. This gets beyond the transactional to the emotional. Gets beyond neat technology to products or services that WOW people even if the technology is old (Apple did not invent the MP3 player – but they understood what experience the majority of people needed to have in order to adopt the technology in their millions and move it into the mainstream).

Of course we do need new technology, services and ideas. But these alone, however clever, will fade and die if they don't strongly resonate with a customer. In my mind technology push is futile. Yes we need to master the technologies important to our business and improve and develop them but if you come up with a neat idea and then hope it just might be viewed as good by customers then you should surely fear for your own future and that of your organisation.

The future of innovation is in the hands of those who own the customer relationship and can develop a deep understanding of a chosen customer or market. If you don't have that the connection with the end customer then find companies to work with who do have that link – they can tell you in an instant if you are on the right track. Once you know what the customers want (or what the relationship owner *knows* that the customers want) and *why* they want it (even better than they know themselves) *then* go and invent or find the winning product/service. You may find it already exists in a different field or industry. Also be prepared to take risks in this process and to fail (often) but with the customer needs as your guiding compass you are on the way to being the most innovative provider in the eyes of your customer

How do you go about understanding customer needs? Are you satisfied with what they tell you or are you aiming to go deeper and figure out what might really benefit them, but they are not quite aware of it themselves? In our view there are far too many organisations around who still hold the view: we know what's best for you!

The last of the threesome is Carol Oman who continues the argument, asking for a new 'consumer insights tool-box' and suggests that empathy is a key ingredient for gaining success-promising consumer insights.

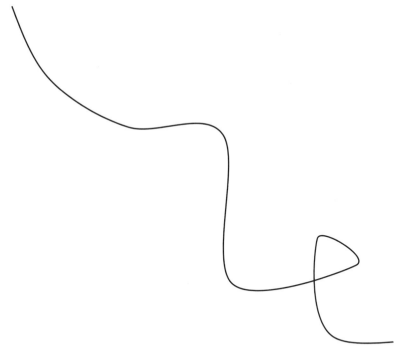

The Future of Innovation is in Sight, Through Clear Insight

Name	**Carol Oman**
Affiliation	Kraft Foods Global Inc.
Position	Senior Scientist, Consumer Innovation
Country	USA
Area	Fuzzy front end
Email	carol.oman@kraft.com

consumer insight methodology online research

The future of innovation is the advanced integration of a dynamic and vital consumer insights tool-box. The current qualitative and quantitative methodologies must adapt to increased technology access, breakthroughs, shifting attitudes and differing behaviours, on a global basis. Enhancements of traditional methods will comprise new technology, increased expertise access and better user interfaces. The fuzzy front end will become less fuzzy – the term will seem antiquated. Innovation truly involves a reduction rather than elimination of risks, so consumer research is necessary. Satisfying project requirements is more than marrying research needs with technology to obtain meatier results. To get those precious 'aha' moments, methodologies must consider the new input. Although the majority of 'new tools' will be old tools with new labels, a few truly distinctive and practical techniques based on sound research and scientific principles will emerge.

Customisable, collaborative tools are instrumental in product development, affecting company and consumer interactions, and modifying the flow of information. Such phenomena seem space age, but are significant to those who have mastered the intricacies of online services. The influence of early adopters is undeniable – and as with shifting paradigms should be carefully observed – because the autonomy introduced by personal devices and online exchanges can improve respondent engagement. Free-flowing information is a double-edged sword, however – witness a recent backlash in the pain reliever category to an ad with a misinterpreted insight. A boycott hastened by a social networking site taught a serious lesson: don't underestimate the power of internet connections.

Interactions have gone beyond simple search engines and video sharing. As social networking expands, other forms of transformational internet communication will continue to appear. On the trail of online do-it-yourselfers, the innovators of the internets will develop new ways of communicating, creating more well-defined, yet overlapping communities. Electronic voices are more conversational in tone, making them more accessible and knowledge more ubiquitous. Not all applications may have staying power though. Micro-blogging is a potential source of tedium and ennui.

'Insight' is overused and frequently associated with simple observances. It's important to develop methods to advance the field and obtain more veritable insights. An insight is an elegant summation of behaviours and attitudes on a deeper, emotional level. When the insight is right, it is recognisable and can be felt viscerally. Because most insights are improperly packaged, related to difficulties in need articulation, increased consumer interaction will be at the heart of tool-box renovation. Innovative online research techniques will allow for faster data collection and richer insights due to larger sample sizes, increased computing power and more robust designs.

New thought leaders will emerge from the evolution with a well-defined vision: empathy that inspires communities is the foundation for sustainable, best research practices. Challenging conventional wisdom for valuable additions to methodologies will lead to success when there is consistency, appropriate analytics and diligent research. In the changing arena of consumer science, collaboration skills will be vital.

Have you ever thought about user involvement as a way of reducing uncertainty at the fuzzy front-end? May we just put in word of caution? It is not any odd user you want to involve in innovating. Did not Henry Ford once say, 'If I had asked people what they wanted they would have told me: faster horses'? Asking consumers what they want is not quite enough. What you want is imaginative, engaged, forward-looking and demanding customers who drive your thinking forward (even though they may also drive you a little mad in the process ...).

By the way, we thought it quite interesting that the three contributions emphasising a need on concentrating on the customer come from practitioners; strong and passionate arguments for customer focus and revisiting existing approaches. However, this is not to say that academics think differently here, as you will find out when reading John Bound's contribution.

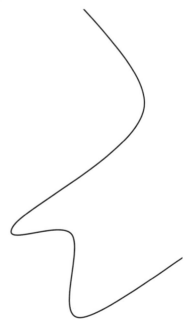

The Future of Innovation is Revolutionising Marketing Research

Name	**John Bound**
Affiliation	London South Bank University
Position	Visiting Research Associate
Country	UK
Area	Marketing modelling
Email	jbound@onetel.com

marketing   mining   neuroscience   observation   qualitative

As with much else consumer marketing research has changed a great deal in the past few years and many old techniques have been discarded. New approaches to gathering information from consumers are being developed all the time and it is fairly predictable what will happen. What paradigm changes will take place is another matter.

Typically marketing research – I will spare you text book definitions – data have been collected by either asking a few people questions in such a way that the answers could be counted and taken to represent the whole market or by stimulating individuals or groups to talk about products. People were talked to face to face. Less satisfactorily, they were persuaded to write answers.

Now such information is collected by talking on the telephone or responding to questions and other stimuli on the web. Much larger samples may be contacted cheaply and in many ways may be more representative. Data gathering techniques using mobile phones and the web are being rapidly developed. This is predictable.

The problem remains that the responses are dependent on the stimuli. For example, even small variations in question form or presentation, such as previous questions make big differences.

Administrative databases also offer great quantities of data for data mining. This developing technique is again predictable. Linking databases within data protection limits is possible. There is therefore a big agenda already written for marketing research techniques.

I now suggest two completely new areas. The first is cognitive neuroscience – in effect seeing which areas of the brain light up when something is going on either internally – thought – or some stimulus is received. The patterns of activity elicited by quite simple situations are highly complex and little understood though now they may be observed. I speculate that these patterns will be partially understood and what people buy related to their previous and current experience. Both observational and experimental data may be available. The process of getting people to verbalise will be thus short-circuited. Psychology will be revolutionised just as molecular biology has been.

The second technique which is already being examined is observation of what people post publicly on the web. Watching people as they shop in a store or pass a display is done already, again within data protection limits. On the web a vast amount of material on every imaginable topic is posted. The problem will be how relevant data may be extracted and evaluated.

Software to analyse qualitative data – that is conversational type data – already exist. Development of this though predictable. Body language remains as a challenge to software writers.

There are of course other developments imaginable. A new society may prohibit all these techniques and indeed forbid the whole practice of marketing. One thing seems clear: the development of existing quantitative data from samples of respondents may be refined but is a dead end.

Don't you just love it? Now John has made the connection between costumer focus, new approaches to market research and understanding the human brain for us. We somehow feel a little nervous though: will these new methods be used to develop truly needed and wanted products and services, or will they be tools to manipulate us into wanting more things we do not need? Is the increasing role of the consumer that George Priovolos foresees a possible driver of greater responsibility and concern for the wider good, or will it merely increase a focus on the 'me'?

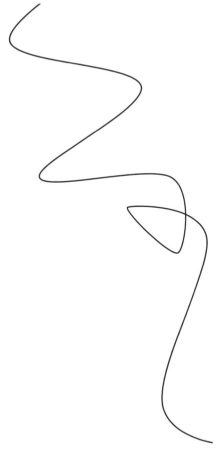

The Future of Innovation is the Consumer Firmly in Command

Name	**Dr George V. Priovolos**
Affiliation	Iona College
Position	Marketing Professor
Country	USA
Area	Innovation in the service sector; cross-cultural diffusion of innovations
Email	gpriovolos@iona.edu; gpriovol@yahoo.com

innovation   new product development   micro-design   micro-production virtual intermediaries

Innovation, in the future, will be driven by an emerging consumer ethic that emphasises freedom and choice in the production as well as the consumption process.

Increasingly, people will evolve from mere contributors of information used in the development of new product/service ideas to *micro*-designers and even *micro*-producers of original products and services themselves.

Helped by 'smarter' electronic devices-personal assistants, which can unobtrusively and in 'real-time' collect information about their owners' activities and revealed preferences, consumers will be able to get intimately involved in customising products and services to fit their precise needs and wants.

The same 'smart' personal assistants will provide consumers with continuous access to a wide variety of virtual exchanges where new product/service ideas may be traded. New virtual intermediaries will be needed to make these marketplaces of ideas more efficient e.g., by facilitating the generation, refinement, 'packaging' and initial assessment of creative concepts.

This new market architecture will force traditional 'producers' (i.e., product manufacturers and service providers) to radically change their *raison d'être*: their first and foremost concern would be to efficiently and soundly 'co-produce' (with interested buyers) the product/services demanded.

To this end, their core operations will likely entail 'making' the various parts (elements) that will be subsequently compiled into final products/services as desired by individual consumers. Since the latter will ultimately combine parts from various sources in numerous different ways to create unique end products/services to satisfy their individual needs, part compatibility would be a major opportunity for establishing a competitive advantage – it will undoubtedly be a major challenge from a technical point of view as well.

As a result of increased scarcities of natural resources, producers of the various product/ service constituent parts will also be expected to use efficient production methods utilising – to the extent possible – renewable materials and energy sources. Consumers with an ownership stake in the design and production processes would demand higher levels of accountability and transparency in this regard.

When consumers are in partial control of the design and production processes, the nature and scope of customer service will need to be redefined, too: the degree to which producers enable the consumer to participate in these processes in a mutually beneficial way and the ability to supply the necessary 'infrastructure' for converting ideas to desired products will ultimately determine whether consumers view a particular vendor as a 'quality' manufacturer/provider.

In this new paradigm, certain aspects of new product/service marketing and branding will be initiated by the consumer him/herself. Much like uniquely mixing and matching parts to produce an exclusive end product/service, a firm's individual customers will probably desire to put together their own stories and images that make what they are about to consume distinct from (and presumably superior to) the competition. In fact, given their substantial and substantive role in the product/service development process, it may be only fair that they become the brand themselves.

The question remains open: do the new possibilities create a new sense of morality and responsibility or merely facilitate even greater egotism? Let's hope that all of us want to be responsible, sustainable and caring brands!

Perhaps we should read closely what Gunter Ott has written as he proposes that innovation without sense (and meaning) is a wasteful use of resources.

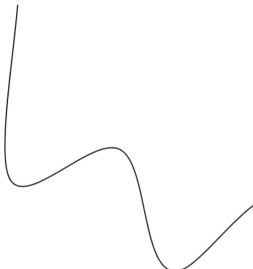

The Future of Innovation is Dependent on Our Ingenuity

Name	**Gunter Ott**
Affiliation	Siemens AG, Industry Sector, Drive Technologies Division, Industrial Automation Division
Position	Director, Design Management
Country	Germany
Area	Industrial design, product design, brand management and innovation
Email	gunter.ott@siemens.com

**industrial design   product design   user interface design   functionality
user experience   specific use of aethetics**

Industrial design and the future of innovation will basically depend on ingenuity. Senseless innovation is a waste of resources. Companies that do not succeed in finding innovative products (hardware, software, services) to provide an additional or new use in their specific context for their customers will not survive on the long run. Almost every company claims that its products are 'innovations'. Does this mean that these products provide a completely new function? Or an unusual combination of formerly known techniques? Or does the product or its function support a formerly unknown customer advantage? Sometimes the marketing idea is regarded as the 'innovation', not the product itself. The word 'innovation' is therefore used in abundance but rarely in the right context. The original meaning of the word describes something completely new without any former example, something that has not been seen or experienced ever before.

Something new needs to be explained. Its function needs to be perceived at first glance, operations must be easily comprehensible and inner logic has to meet the user's experience in such a way that people *desire* to use it.

Normally scientists and engineers encode their ideas extremely, so that normal people have problems to understand them and thus don't like to use them. This is where the designers (industrial or product designers) come into play. It is their task to analyse the specific innovation and come up with an understandable and usable form. To do so they use traditional or unknown formal languages, quote known designs or come up with new archetypes. They provide the key for the decoding of the product by the specific use of Aesthetics, i.e., *Gestaltung*.

More and more industrial designers account themselves as the sole innovators in a company – the only ones that dare to think unconventional ideas and transform them into products.

I am not convinced of that, because true innovation distinguishes itself primarily by technique and by the useful effect of an idea. First aesthetics are not important for innovation, but they are a strong differentiator and therefore an important success factor in a saturated market.

Industrial designers used creative techniques very early to generate innovative ideas. Engineers closely working with industrial designers appreciate their approach, their way to query things and to form a 'creative climate'. Industrial designers should support the development of innovative products especially in capital goods industry as integrated part of the development process. Their skills help to develop innovations to market release just by translating the abstract image of an idea into a format that can be comprehended by all decision makers.

Industrial designers play a supportive role within the innovation process. They care for representing the idea in a way that decisions can be taken and that innovations can be used.

Additionally they are predestined for taking over the role of brand management. Each product is a vital and direct contribution to a company's brand – more direct and more valuable than any high glossy brochure, any advertisement or any TV commercial. The aesthetics of each product contributes directly and long-ranging to the brand's account – like function, technique, quality and price.

Innovation has to be perceived as part of the self-image of a company that changes its recognition of industrial designers. They are no longer the ones that spice the products up. They are the ones that give benefit to innovations, differentiate products by their aesthetics and manage the brand by product-aesthetics.

By the way: this is why brand management is not to be done by the marketing department.

We have talked about the desire for experiences, for the consumer to be involved. At the same time we talked about the need for sustainability, and to be able to communicate our ideas. Visualising ideas is an essential part of communicating. Designing innovative products and services in such a way that they can be understood without lengthy manuals or explanations considerably improves acceptance rates. Gunter emphasises the role of designers in creating and visualising ideas as well as in translating novel concepts in a way that makes them easily accessible. Perhaps then designers are a good lot to get involved and, indeed, the notion of the designers' valuable contribution in the context of innovation is one for which the future is hear already today.

At the same time Gunter cautions us not to believe that designers are innovation's panacea; while they clearly have an important contribution to make, so do a number of other players.

Let us give the word to Christiane Drews who focus on 'design thinking' rather than designers per se, and explains how design thinking can also help to facilitate what we have identified as one of the future of innovation's big challenges: the meaningful involvement of and communication between a number of different communities (or disciplines).

The Future of Innovation is to Make Design Thinking Interdisciplinary

Name	**Christiane Drews**
Affiliation	Virgin Atlantic Airways
Position	Aircraft Interior and Product Designer
Country	UK
Area	Design thinking, product innovation
Email	drews-c@gmx.de

hope   design thinking   interdisciplinary   stakeholders

My personal hopes for the future of innovation is build on conversations I was lucky enough to have with people like Bettina von Stamm, Mat Hunter from IDEO, Kevin McCullagh from PLAN or John Bates from London Business School. It implies that a greater variety of disciplines will understand the benefit of using design methods or what is talked about as design thinking used in new contexts. The user-centric orientation of design thinking will help to create new products, services and business models, which have more meaning for the consumer and the marketplace. Other characteristics of design thinking could also be important for the future of innovation. Namely:

- Experimentation at early stages of a project to engage as many stakeholders as possible in the discussion stages of a project and therefore constantly refining ideas into concepts, and finally into real products and services.

- Keeping a wide perspective on the project at all times, even when working on details of the solution, helps taking into consideration the environment a service, product or business model will sit in.

- The ability to accept ambiguity during the process and take it as an opportunity that there is not one right or wrong answer. This mindset might just lead to multiple concepts that can benefit from each other in the end.

- The orientation from the future backwards rather than projecting what is and what has been into the future.

Innovation is only possible when challenging the norm and questioning a brief one has been given; innovation becomes integral part of work when you are trying to find the best possible answer to a problem. More precisely, when opportunity finding becomes more important than problem solving – which leads to answers that were not apparent or existing before – this is where designing is related very closely to inventing.

Nurturing the right breeding ground for design thinking will make it necessary to overcome hierarchies between disciplines and to fully embrace the symbiosis of engineering, finance, operation and design; all disciplines needed during a project to guarantee a successful outcome.

The recognition of the need for joint efforts on an equal level is important not only for product but also for service and business design. The basis for this level playing field must be laid early on in primary education to prevent stereotypes from building up, it then needs to be strengthened in secondary education and built and expanded on in graduate and postgraduate courses.

Again a focus on meaning and user-centricity, and Christiane has kindly shed a little more light of what is actually meant by 'design thinking' and why it is important in the context of innovation. But not only that, she has emphasised the need for diversity, and for the openness to benefit from all that has to be laid early on in life: through and during and beginning with our first education.

If Christiane closes her contribution with emphasising the need for creating appropriate conditions for innovation and design thinking, Sabine Junginger uses them as opening statement. Let's hear where it takes her.

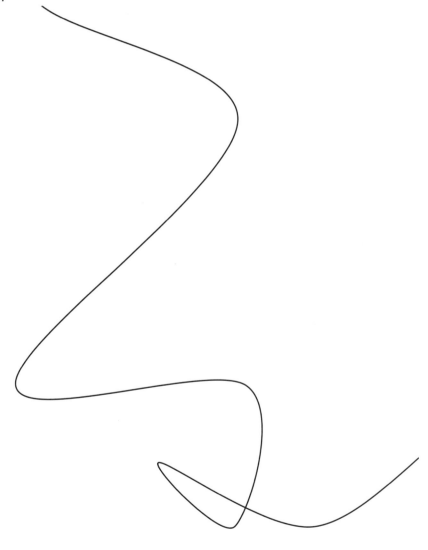

The Future of Innovation is as Change in the Making

Name	**Sabine Junginger**
Affiliation	Lancaster University
Position	Lecturer Design
Country	UK
Area	Product development/organisational change
Email	sjunginger@mac.com

people   designing   changing   managing   organising

When I think of the future of innovation, organisations and their abilities to limit and nurture innovation come to my mind. Organisations, one might say, provide the framework for the kinds of innovation that can take place within its boundaries and on their fringes. For long, it has been accepted that fundamental assumptions, values, norms and beliefs held by people within an organisation have to change in order for the organisational framework to change. Yet, only recently have design thinking and design methods been linked to planned organisational change. We now see many different design areas emerging that specialise on this key ability of design to effect changes in how people perceive of things and problems and as a consequence, how they behave and act accordingly. These include service design, transformative design and design thinking. I argue that across all these emerging (and existing) design specialisations, it is product development based on specific human-centred approaches that is the key to suspending existing organisational values, norms and beliefs – which often form the barriers to innovation. I am saying product development because no matter what the aim is, no matter who engages in it, no matter when or where it takes place: design is always engaged in the conception, planning, making and delivering of a product in one form or another. Once we are clear that a product is synonymous with the outcome of a deliberate design inquiry, it is no longer of importance what this product is – a technology, a system or an object. Instead, we can focus on why a product comes into being, for whom it is intended and how it aligns with an organisation's vision and purpose (or does not!).

Most people recognise design as the art of change and we tend to view the design outcomes (products) as manifestations of these changes. What we have not paid merely enough attention to in the past is how the activities of designing themselves allow people to uncover fundamental assumptions so they can be examined and challenged if necessary. If we were to understand product development as a core design activity and if we were to shift our notion of product from a good for sale to the outcome of a deliberate design enquiry, we would not only open the boundaries of innovation but we would likewise bring in design thinking and design methods in areas we have yet to discover their applicability. We would think of a product no longer as the end or the answer but as the starting point that generates the questions we need to ask to arrive at future innovations.

Sabine, like Christiane, highlights the role of design thinking in the context of innovation and organisational change. We find her redefinition of 'product development' quite refreshing as it opens up new perspectives and possibilities. Don't you think that this view allows a shift in focus and understanding – of product development as well as change? If we were to apply design thinking, as introduced by Christiane, to the process of problem solving it would be less about 'right and wrong' and more about the exploration of different possibilities, and about finding one with the greatest benefits combined with the fewest downsides. We also like the idea of the outcome as starting point rather than being an end point. What would happen to our understanding of innovation if we took on this new perspective? Would it lead to what Robert Logan and Greg Van Alstyne call 'designing for emergence'?

We would like to call on Robert first and allow him to introduce the concept of 'designing for emergence'.

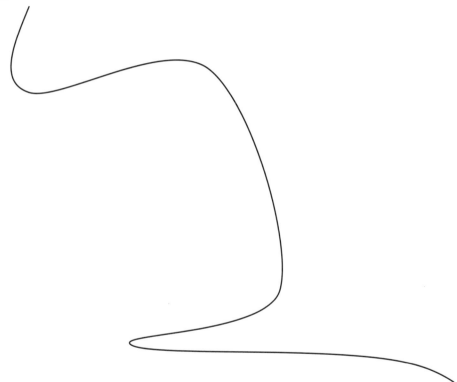

The Future of Innovation is an Emergent Phenomenon

Name	**Professor Robert K. Logan**
Affiliation	Strategic Innovation Lab – Ontario College of Art and Design
Position	Chief Scientist
Country	Canada
Area	Design – emergence
Email	logan@physics.utoronto.ca

design   emergence   foresight

I am a physicist and the Chief Scientist at the Strategic Innovation Lab (sLab) in the Faculty of Design at the Ontario College of Art and Design, Canada's oldest art and design university. At the sLab we believe that the introduction of a technology is not sufficient to enable new possibilities. What's necessary is our readiness to perceive that technology's value and meaning within our lives. We believe that true innovation occurs by matching breakthroughs in science and technology with the needs, desires, expectations and latent behaviour of potential users.

We make use of the concept of strategic foresight, which involves thinking about, debating, planning, shaping and ultimately designing the future. It requires understanding the available choices and then choosing among them while at the same time anticipating change. Strategic foresight begins by recognising emerging signals from science and technology and aligning them with newly emerging behaviours in the sociocultural domain as well as in the marketplace among potential competitors. It also requires an honest appraisal and evaluation of the capabilities of one's organisation so that one's insights can be converted into opportunities for innovation and success.

Greg Van Alstyne and I discovered the surprising and counterintuitive truth that the design process, which leads to new products, services, methods and systems is not always, in and of itself, on the forefront of innovation. Design is a necessary but not a sufficient condition for the success of new products and services. We intuitively sense a connection between innovative design and emergence. Emergence refers to the process by which a higher level of organisation arises through the aggregation and interaction of lower-level components, revealing new behaviours or properties not associated with the lower-level components as exemplified by the emergence of life and the process by which nature creates new organisms in the biosphere. In other words the process of the innovation of human artefacts parallels Darwinian evolution in nature.

Design, emergence and innovation are interrelated. We suggest that design must harness the process of emergence; for it is only through the bottom-up and massively iterative unfolding of emergence that new and improved products and services are successfully refined, introduced and diffused into the marketplace.

In our 2006 paper *Designing for Emergence and Innovation: Redesigning Design*, Greg and I develop the notions that:

- An innovative design is an emergent design.

- A homeostatic relationship between design and emergence is a required condition for innovation.

- Since design is a cultural activity and culture is an emergent phenomenon, it follows that design leading to innovation is also an emergent phenomenon.

To conclude we would suggest that the future of innovation lies in making use of strategic foresight and in the harnessing nature's process of emergence and evolution through the bottom-up process of understanding human needs and desires and then matching them with the appropriate technologies and scientific insights, rather than starting with technological breakthroughs or scientific insights and trying to commercialise them.

Now, don't you think that 'designing for emergence' is another interesting notion? Complexity theory has been valued in the context of innovation for a while now – particularly in the context of understanding discontinuous innovation. Of course, emergence is a concept closely linked to complexity theory. Without further ado we would like to pass the baton over to Greg Van Alstyne who elaborates further on the concept of 'design for emergence' and explains its role in the co-creative future of innovation.

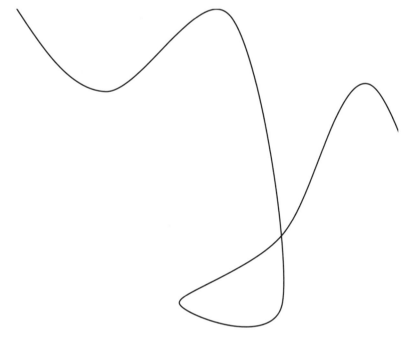

The Future of Innovation is Design as Catalyst, Not Control

Name	**Greg Van Alstyne**
Affiliation	Strategic Innovation Lab (sLab), Ontario College of Art and Design
Position	Director of Research
Country	Canada
Area	Designing for emergence
Email	gvanalstyne@faculty.ocad.ca

design   emergence   co-creation   complexity

To apprehend the future of innovation, we need to better understand both the increasing ubiquity and the dawning limits of design. In my research I'm seeking to articulate the role of design in the new, complex spaces of co-creation, where outcomes are the result not of direct specification and control from the top down, but of indirect forces that must be elicited, harnessed, or induced to emerge from the bottom up. I believe we are witnessing a paradigm shift from a top-down, centralised model of design to an increasingly bottom-up processes of creation and development.

As a result innovators must learn to *design for emergence*. I first articulated these views in *What People Want: Populism in Architecture and Design*, proceedings from the 2004 DOM Conference in Linz, Austria. This enquiry continues in Toronto at OCAD's Strategic Innovation Lab, through a series of papers in collaboration with physicist and media ecologist Robert K. Logan (also a contributor to this volume).

Designing for Emergence (D4E) re-envisions the responsibilities of the designer and the mechanics of the innovation process in these new models of co-creation, in which many agents provide input. D4E supersedes the inherited legacy of modernism, with its overt ideology of domination and mastery. In this new, systems-based model, intended benefits and other consequences are appreciated as effects and patterns that emerge through complex interactions among these agents and their environment, in a model analogous to that of biological self-organisation and evolution.

In ecology and biology, the ceaseless co-evolution of organisms with each other and their environment is accepted fact. In the social sciences, language, culture and behavioural interaction may clearly be understood as the product of emergent processes. For business, industry and design, however, the co-creation/co-evolution model of innovation has yet to acquire this mature status: while it gains relevance and popularity in practice, theory races to stay abreast. Yet once we look for evidence we find it in abundance. One can examine past examples, as Dr Logan and I have done, from the tool making of early humans to Gutenberg's printing press. Our contemporary awareness of D4E arises from the increasing power and importance of contemporary techniques such as the collaborative filtering recommendation system used by Amazon.com, Google's much-admired PageRank algorithm, the rise of the open source movement and wider application of genetic algorithms.

Those who have chartered this terrain from different perspectives include Dee Hock, who founded Visa and the Chaordic Commons; Tim O'Reilly, who coined the term *Web 2.0*; and Norman Packard, who pioneered complexity studies at Santa Fe and went on to synthetic biology. While I don't know of many others who are articulating the shift in the same terms that Bob Logan and I are using, nonetheless we are clearly witnessing a tectonic shift from nouns to verbs, from products to services, from making stuff to making sense, from controlling and specifying to enabling, inducing, influencing and inspiring. This is the biggest and most interesting future wave in the innovation ocean.

Co-creation and emergence – how does that sit with still dominant management models of strategic planning, control and uncertainty avoidance? If innovating in itself becomes an experience, are we then closer to an even higher level of 'experience innovation' than the one called for by Joseph Pine II?

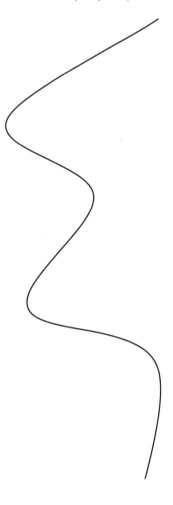

The Future of Innovation is Experiences

Name	**B. Joseph Pine II**
Affiliation	Strategic Horizons LLP
Position	Co-Founder
Country	USA
Area	Experience innovation, offering innovation
Email	bjp2@aol.com

goods   services   experiences   Starbucks   policy

A few years ago I gave a boardroom talk in Milan, Italy, to a number of executives from different companies. One was the Vice President of a global coffee manufacturer, who said something that floored me: 'There's been no innovation in the coffee industry in 15 years.' I responded: 'Have you never heard of *Starbucks*?' This gentleman could only conceive of innovation in physical *goods*, not in *experiences* – a particularly ironic stance given we were in one of the foremost coffee meccas of the world, the city that inspired Howard Schultz to create the Starbucks coffee-drinking experience.

The Experience Economy

That is what we desperately need in business today: experience innovation. Why? Because we are now in an experience economy, where experiences – memorable events that engage people in inherently personal ways – are becoming the predominant economic offering. It supplanted the service economy that flowered in the latter half of the 20th century, which in turn superseded the industrial economy, which itself displaced the agrarian economy. Experiences are what people want, and therefore what companies must offer.

And yet, governments still shovel money at farmers to subsidise their crops and their way of life. They shovel money at universities for research into more and more goods while protecting manufacturing jobs, reducing the economic dynamism that will create new experience jobs. And now, with a global financial crisis in full boil, we see governments doing everything possible to protect financial services. As my partner Jim Gilmore likes to point out, most all the recent innovation in financial services has served to prop up goods (primarily houses and cars) in lieu of financing true economic growth through innovation in experiences.

The Path Forward

Let us stop. Not stop innovating goods and even services, for they will always be necessary parts of the economy. But let's stop favouring them over experiences. Governments should stop protecting the old while slighting the new. Companies should start looking to experiences for growth. And consumers should just keep on doing what they've been doing, seeking out new experiences, forsaking old goods and services and rewarding those companies that give them what they want.

We need more countries like New Zealand – a fount of new and wondrous experiences, including bungee jumping, Zorbing and canyoneering – and which even created a cabinet-level position to leverage the tourism possibilities flowing from Peter Jackson's *Lord of the Rings* movies. We need more companies like Apple, which realised that the best innovation in goods should be about enabling great (computing, music-listening and communicating) experiences while the marketing of those goods would best be done inside engaging retail experiences. We need more experience entrepreneurs like Howard Schultz, Chip Conley (founder of Joie de Vivre Hospitality) and Robert Stephens (founder of the Geek Squad). And we need more innovators like Tim Berners-Lee, Wil Wright, Philip Rosedale and Jane McGonigal who recognise the almost infinite possibilities inherent in digital technologies for creating the new, the wondrous, the engaging.

So how about you. Are you ready to pioneer such experiences?

Could we all become pioneers of experiences if we embraced Sabine's redefinition of product development and accepted that we are on a never-ending journey? Can we embrace design for emergence and go with the flow rather than wanting to control and dominate? What if we accepted impermanence as a fact, and that we are on a continuous journey, never reaching the end? Hey, if things change all the time and nothing is for ever, why not try out a few things along the way? But perhaps we should be less flippant. How about, then, putting it in the words of 'Steps', Bettina's favourite poem by the German novelist and poet Hermann Hesse?

Steps

How every flower wilts and every youth

Makes way to old age, blossoms each step of life,

Each wisdom too and every virtue

At their own time and cannot last for ever.

At each step of life the heart must be

Ready to say good bye and start again

To give itself with courage and without mourning

Into different, new commitments.

And within every new beginning lies some magic

That protects us and helps us living.

Cheerful we are to move from room to room,

Attached to neither as to a home,

The world's spirit does not want to tie or narrow us,

Step by step he wants to elevate and broaden us.

As soon as we are comfortable in one circle

And settled in, decay is looming,

Only those ready to depart and travel

May escape paralysing complacency.

Perhaps even the hour of death

Will send us afresh to new spheres,

The call of life will never cease.

Well them, heart, bid farewell and recover!

Life's call to us will never cease, we will never reach the end point; we are on a continuous journey. The sooner we can embrace that thought the sooner we can reduce our fear of change, and the sooner we can embrace experimentation and ambiguity as a way of life.

This might sound like the end – but fear not, there is still some way to go! Of course we could have ended here, and wrapped up with our Part XIV 'Famous last words' – yet there were so many more wonderful contributions that emphasised a particular industry's or country's perspective that we decided to dedicate a section just to giving voice to those. So, please read on and find out what the future of innovation looks like when seen through 'A particular set of lenses'.

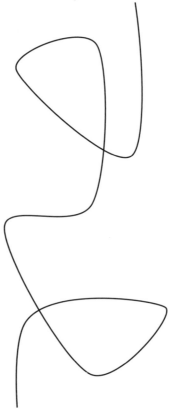

PART XIII
Innovation Through a Particular Set of Lenses

'The Future of Innovation' journey is something that amazingly reflects three realities of the present; they are openness, global collaboration and diversity. Indeed, 'open doors' are not only drivers and enablers of innovation and its management, but have become part of good practice. In fact, global collaboration is one of the 'decencies of mankind': everybody is welcome, no more conflicting opposition nor incompatible confrontation in developed versus developing world – we all are one universe. Another truth is, innovation management is boundless, multidimensional, and everybody looks at it from a different perspective. This section proves it yet again.

'Innovation through a particular set of lenses' is an exploration of mega-, macro-, meso-, and micro-level nuances, distinctions, features, contrasts, details, indications, evidences, signs, implications, hints, suggestions, schemes, ideas, outlines, proposals, instructions, recommendations, implications and knowledge for making innovation happen in different companies, in different industries, in different countries, but always as part of one global community.

This section has two main parts: the first looks at the future of innovation from a particular industry's perspective, the second from a particular geography's point of view.

The major message from it is clear: management of innovation around the globe and across industries has as many differences as it has similarities. Insights from insurance and health care, charity and energy indicate an approach of inter-industrial and international collaboration with an underlying attitude of, 'together, we can make the future of innovation achieve its major goal: make people happy with their living environment, nature, food, air, water, health ... lifestyle. To do that we have to open our heart to all positive emotions, thoughts, moods and spirit!' Quite right we say, it is a known fact that if negative emotions capture a nation it is hard to produce anything creative, constructive or positive.

After reading the following chapter, we believe you inevitably come to realise that the desirable 'Future of Innovation' depicted in this book by more than 200 bright contributors from more than 50 countries is of paramount importance for us, and we believe that you will be inspired to start such a thoughtful, considerate, open, all-embracing and sustainable future today, here and now.

We begin by looking at the future of innovation from the perspective of different industries, with representatives of the energy, chemical, telecoms, service, insurance, health care, media, FMCG, charity industries sharing their thinking. We will hear about links, ties and connections between industries that are to be developed (further). From an industry-specific focus we move on to size, to small and medium sized companies – or SMEs – to use a well-known term, depicting their strategies and global role. We will hear what the future has in store for SMEs, the perpetual motion, engine, driver, source and spring for innovation, closing by mapping innovation challenges and a set of objectives for our 'global village'.

Industry Contexts

A backdrop against which the major challenges and thinking in industry can be understood better is painted by Tessa van der Valk, Langdon Morris, Leon Pretorius, Axel Thallemer and María J. Nieto.

Tessa shares some observations such as outsourcing and collaboration, leading to the 'blurring of organisations' boundaries that will be even greater impact in the future. In Part II, 'The winds of change', John Bessant used the term 'knowledge spaghetti' for a scenario in which relevant bits and pieces of information can no longer be found in one place, and need to be hunted down in different knowledge domains, countries and industries.

Have you ever imagined that a 'small dedicated biotechnology' firm could be a good example of an organisation that, constantly and deliberately, weaves and recombines its connections and technologies to succeed in a competitive marketplace? If not, perhaps you might like to start thinking about it now.

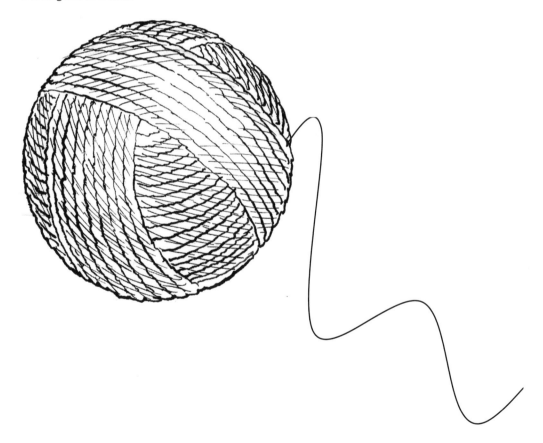

The Future of Innovation is a Blurring of Boundaries

Name	**Tessa van der Valk**
Affiliation	Innovation Policy Group of TNO
Position	Researcher
Country	The Netherlands
Area	Networks of innovation
Email	tessa.vandervalk@tno.nl

networks   open innovation   boundaries   business models   organisations

In several technological fields, an increased level of outsourcing by organisations is observed. This tendency is fuelled by an increasing technological complexity, an increasing speed of technological change and a scarcity of resources. The coinciding tendency of specialisation of organisations has made networking capabilities of vital importance to their survival. This way of organising innovation has been a great challenge for organisations, and this challenge will only be greater in the future.

First of all, the number of different types of organisations or other actors to interact with is increasing. For instance, in several industry sectors, intermediate as well as end users are becoming more and more important in innovation. This growing diversity of partners will place an ever higher demand on the collaborative competences of organisations, most notably their ability to select partners and subsequently manage these relationships effectively.

Furthermore, the tendencies sketched above will require organisations to constantly reconsider their boundaries and reposition themselves within their technological field or market. The ability to organise innovation in new ways will be increasingly important. In this respect, developing and employing innovative business models will be one of the primary sources of competitive advantage. Correspondingly, it will be those organisations which are able to make innovative connections between other specialised organisations that are most likely to be successful in the future. In other words: the highest profits will be achieved by those organisations that are able to efficiently organise their internal activities and manage the boundaries of their organisation, but are also well aware of what happens beyond these boundaries.

An illustrative example for these developments can be derived from the life sciences sector. Small dedicated biotechnology firms are constantly looking for ways to enable earlier commercialisation of their competences, in the light of a decreasing availability of funding. By providing R&D services and out-licensing technology platforms these firms employ hybrid business models in an attempt to finance their product development. These firms are also increasingly looking for niches that are not perceived to be lucrative by large established organisations, such as medicines targeting relatively small, highly specific patient populations. And these small firms will be particularly in need of sustainable relations with patients and their representative organisations.

The implications of these developments are not static; they require constant, deliberate management efforts. Counter intuitively, these efforts should thus be aimed at effectively blurring the boundaries of the organisation.

Organise, re-organise. Take nothing for granted but keep what works, at the same time be willing to let go if the next scenario demands this. How does that fit into strategy and planning cycles?

Langdon Morris delves even deeper into the current complexities, describing them as a 'mess'. We felt somehow reminded of an old Indian tale where a grandfather talks to his grandson about the two wolves that live and fight inside each and every one of us: one is good, the other is evil. When the grandson fearfully asks, 'But grandfather, which one will win?' the grandfather looks at him and says, 'My dear grandson, whichever one you feed.' We feel that the fear to acknowledge and embrace the complexities is the bad wolf, and that understanding the necessity to seek global change and embrace the complexity with courage is the good wolf. Indirectly, Langdon warns us about feeding the bad wolf and as a remedy against it suggests the application of 'disciplined innovation methods'.

The Future of Innovation is to Change the World

Name	**Langdon Morris**
Affiliation	InnovationLabs LLC/www.innovationlabs.com
Position	Partner
Country	USA
Area	Innovation purpose and methodology
Email	LMorris@innovationlabs.com

complexity   methods   methodology   energy   quality of life

The world, you have undoubtedly noticed, is in quite a bit of mess right now.

Let's see ... Oil and coal power the global economy, but the pollution and climate change that they produce causes increasingly difficult and challenging problems for all of us. The global economy is in a period of crisis, and there are many wars and other violent conflicts occurring around the world. A huge wave of retirees is about to burden the pension funds of the industrialised nations, while the divide between rich and poor is widening. Health care for many is inadequate, and for many more it is nearly non-existent.

Etc.

Yes, we face lot of challenges, and they become even more difficult to deal with because they are intertwined, interconnected, interlinked. The complexity of 'retirement' and the complexity of 'health care' aren't separate issues, but two sides of a single coin. The complexity of 'energy' and of 'economics' are not separate issues, but two aspects of a single phenomenon.

Complexity itself may be the biggest problem.

So we ask, naturally, 'How will we get out of this mess?'

My answer is that we will apply disciplined innovation methods that engage the creativity and intelligence of millions of people in order to master today's unprecedented complexity, and to design solutions that will lead, eventually, to a better world.

Hence, 'the future of innovation' is in helping to transform the global economy and global society. This is not a modest task, but it is *the* necessary one.

What, specifically, will 'innovation' help us *do*?

Properly applied innovation methods will help us to ...

... accomplish more work with less energy by making products and machines more energy efficient.

... develop new sources of energy to replace hydrocarbons and nuclear sources.

... substitute 'intelligence' for 'mass and energy' in all the products we consume, making them lighter in weight, and more efficient in operation,

... understand human needs, and meet them. It will help companies to be more attentive and caring, and less abusive, so that they manage and operate with more empathy and less abuse.

... to clean the air and water so we can breathe, drink and eat, improving the quality of life for billions of humans living in substandard conditions.

None of these will be simple accomplishments, but all of them are necessary.

Innovation *methods* will help us understand what is real and important, to know what we must do and how to do it; it will help us focus on the real, underlying problems of human society rather than the superficial and trivial ones.

Because the future of innovation is not about making and selling more stuff: it's about shifting our focus from quantity to quality.

Without 'innovation,' practised at the highest levels of effectiveness, the ultra-complex problems we face may not be solved.

So 'the future of innovation' is to change the world.

Langdon emphasises the need to shift from quantity to quality which we believe is also a shift away from the promotion of constant and relentless consumption to a mindset driven by sufficiency. This indeed would change the world.

That the whole world is connected, and that we hence need to seek to connect different parts of the world in our search for solutions, is a key argument presented by Leon Pretorius. He shares a nice example of intercontinental collaboration in the field of 'engineering technology and innovation management' and gives some clue into the African context of innovation.

The Future of Innovation is a Socio-technical Systems View

Name	**Leon Pretorius**
Affiliation	Graduate School of Technology Management, University of Pretoria
Position	Professor
Country	South Africa
Area	Systems and innovation management
Email	leon.pretorius@up.ac.za

systems   global village   teams   culture   innovation

The future of innovation will be determined by the current and future users of technology. A systems view on products and technology can enhance new innovations. Current products and systems are the incubators for new innovations. However, the mind can also be constrained by current world views and technologies. The power of simulation and cyberspace should not be underestimated in positioning new innovations in the global context.

Remember, innovations diffuse into some market that may be the global village. The fact is, the world is connected. International teams can therefore contribute meaningfully to innovations at all levels of the organisation. Innovations will come to fruition and diffuse in this interconnected world where multicultural approaches are the norm not the exception.

All species on planet earth are linked by one common drive for or dependency on energy. Innovations focusing on sustainable use of energy should for the foreseeable future be in great demand. An approach to research in innovation that links or integrates the concepts of systems energy and innovation through *inter alia* the management of technology may prove useful in future.

A sound basis in engineering and technology management may prove essential in the next thrust for enhanced innovation in the global village. More young bright minds taking on the challenge to do useful research in engineering technology and innovation management is the next barrier to improved innovation in the future.

Increased collaboration efforts on innovation research between East, West and Africa are essential. An example may be collaboration agreements between University of Pretoria, South Africa (as a hub), University of Johannesburg, South Africa, University of Ravensburg, Germany, University of Singapore and University of Hefei, China, with whom the author has contacts in the field of engineering technology and innovation management. These collaboration efforts need to be extended in future.

Further to this, real innovation will have to focus on organisational issues including entrepreneurship and intrapreneurship. Dedicated efforts in the fields of spin-offs from research institutions as well as spin-ins towards technology business will have to be nurtured especially in the South African context, which houses many multinational organisations.

A realisation that the future, and therefore also innovation, is not static but depends inherently on the one thing that marches on without regard, namely time, is truly necessary. The congruence of systems dynamics and innovation management may also be necessary in the greater scheme of things. A firm realisation is required that innovations depend on people that are part of populations dynamically changing in various regions of earth. The socio-technical context of innovation is of ever increasing importance for the future of innovation especially in Africa with its many demographic challenges facing it.

Connections between continents, connections between organisations, driven and enabled by a group of people with a particular skill set: intera- and entrepreneurs.

The penultimate sketch for shaping the future of innovation in the industrial context is provided by Axel Thallemer. In Part IV, 'The good, the bad and the ugly', we have already discussed the detrimental powers of innovation. In this section we are sharing some alarming facts from a particular industry's perspective. Axel makes us think of innovation not only from a novelty perspective but encourages us to ask wide-ranging questions about context, implications and the integrity of a new creation. Good parents feel responsible for their children; why does this sense of responsibility seem to lack in so many innovators? We are used to speaking about the effects of innovation in terms of their commercial and business impacts, rather than in terms of its impact on humanity and humankind. We are used to specifying innovations as continuous or discontinuous, process or product, for local or global market, cradle-to-cradle or cradle-to-grave design. Should we not rather talk about innovation in terms of sustainable, recyclable, energy-saving, eco-friendly and other notions that help to juxtapose human-minded and profit-oriented innovations? Should we not begin to demand ambidexterity of innovation, offering sustainability as well as profitability? Let us look at Axel's insight.

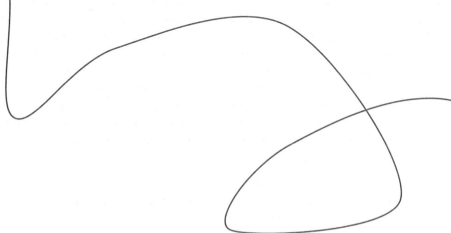

The Future of Innovation is in the Industrial Context

Name	**Axel Thallemer**
Affiliation	Airena®!
Position	President
Country	Germany
Area	Product development process, industrial capital goods
Email	gestalt_ung@yahoo.de

control energy mobility nature styling

There is no new product development without raising new questions to (un)known problems. By analysing weak points balanced with strengths, new opportunities are being discussed against impending risks. Answers are less important than the right questions. From those scenarios possible fields of innovations may be claimed. These fields have to be compared with competitors' products or components in the business areas targeted.

Innovation is not comprising new looks for old technologies. Styling appearances for the mere sake of continuing the sales support of marketing or advertising departments does not belong in this category at all. Currently this may be perfectly experienced in car industry. A product which does not constantly renew itself fades from public interest. Platforms and components are widely shared between products, leaving the product as mere embodiment of the brand. The only real differentiation is the car's look, since its functionality and reliability are no longer distinctive features. We can apply this situation to consumer goods. Coffee machines, toasters and juicers for instance all rely much more on styling and brand than on actual innovation. The criteria of the proper use of the term 'innovation' has to be measured by new scrutiny.

Is the new product, component or service doing something better than a previous solution? Is it more complicated to achieve this goal? Is it reliable and showing long-lasting performance? Is the whole process around it sustainable? Are the materials recyclable? How much energy in total is being used – lost – for manufacturing? How much energy is incorporated in the material chosen? (Think of ecological and social side effects of harvesting diamonds, gold, silver, plastic or uranium ... aluminium – the latter is solidified electricity!) The proper material has to be chosen to suit the purpose of the product, which shall incorporate the intended innovation. Both materials and processes predetermine the looks of the product or component. Materials as well as processes have to be selected also on criteria of sustainability and recyclability. Relatively late in new product development under the scope of innovation, the shape is coming into the process of determining the artefact. Predefined processes, environmental concerns and technological constraints are driving the look of the newly created object. No shape is distinct of purpose, nature of innovation and its inherent materialisation. Real innovation – as defined here – very rarely occurs. Mostly one is dealing with styling existing technical packages under the auspices of brand or no-brand! Future innovation has to start with critical questioning and questioning over and over again before one even thinks of giving any answers. After thorough analyses purpose-driven *gestalt* materialised via processes and environmental technologies will shape future innovation. Since humankind is based primarily on energy, mobility and control, gaining inspiration from nature inductively – not for copying role models – will be of the utmost importance for future innovation!

Does your organisation ask such questions? Are long-term effects and systemic consequences considered? Or does the excitement about what is (technically) possible override all challenging voices?

One final contribution then before we move on to industry specific contributions. Maria J. Nieto looks at the future of innovation through the particular lenses of high-, low- and medium-tech industries, calling for a different approach at all fronts: academic, scientific, policy-making and managerial. Indeed, there are rather a lot of aspects where an approach that works perfectly well for an elephant can be used with equal success on a mouse. It sees that attention to developing contingency approaches has only entered people's consciousness quite recently. Only recently have we started attempts that develop different approaches for 'small and fast' versus 'big and slow'. Do you think about the context for which a programme, approach, framework or tool was developed before applying it in your own, specific context?

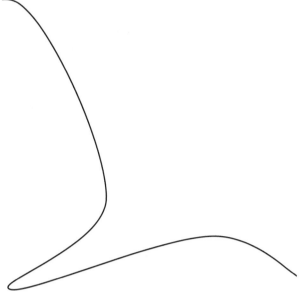

The Future of Innovation is for All Industries

Name	**María J. Nieto**
Affiliation	Universidad Carlos III de Madrid
Position	Associate Professor
Country	Spain
Area	Innovation in low- and medium-tech industries
Email	Mnieto@emp.uc3m.es

**innovation process   low and medium technology industries
non-R&D innovation activities   incremental innovations**

The ability to develop and implement innovations is increasingly important for firms in all industries to survive in markets that are ever more global and competitive. Traditionally, however, there has been more interest in studying the innovation behaviour of the so-called high-tech (HT) industries than the low- and medium-technology (LMT) industries.

This interest appears disproportionate given that mature LMT industries still make up the largest part of the manufacturing industries in OECD countries and that their preponderance is falling at a very slow rate. The innovation process is often misunderstood as something that is not embedded in the whole economic environment of firms. The behaviour of LMT industries is an important indicator of the rate of investment in the economy in general. LMT industries are not only generators of innovation, but also key users of innovation generated in HT industries. In fact, LMT industries are often the best customers of HT industries and the levels of performance of LMT and HT industries are heavily interdependent because of exchanges of knowledge and the interconnection between industries.

Recent studies have revealed some key aspects that help bridge the cognitive gap between the innovation process in LMT and HT industries. Innovation in LMT firms is not usually based on the latest scientific or technological knowledge, but often involves internally experimenting with and adapting technologies and learning that are not necessarily rooted in formal R&D components. There is, though, no reason to believe that LMT firms are less likely to be able to face the challenge of innovation than R&D intensive firms are. The key point implies to recognise the essential sources of innovation. Innovation processes in LMT firms are not primarily based on systematic R&D development, but on practical, experience-based, learning by doing, by using, by searching or by interacting.

Previous considerations reveal the importance of analysing and understanding the innovation behaviour of LMT firms from and academic and scientific point of view. Moreover, a challenge for policy makers and managers also exists.

Research and technology policies have usually been too focused on HT industries. More of policy makers' attention and efforts, however, should be oriented to develop and sustain development in LMT industries. The more visible nature of radical innovations has been largely responsible for shifting policy making in favour of HT industries. Most firms, however, do not make radical innovations but all can and should make incremental innovations and adopt new products and processes first made by others. Furthermore, the economic importance of incremental innovation is extremely high. Products and processes are usually changed considerably during the diffusion and adoption process and gains in productivity are very high in this stage.

From the point of view of LMT firms' innovation management, the recommendations are straightforward. LMTs should recognise the great importance for innovation of other related activities and sources which are not exclusively R&D-based. Innovation could take place through acquisition of tacit and practical knowledge, and through formal and informal diffusion between firms. In these industries, improving the adoption and commercialisation of new technologies requires initiatives that go well beyond the boundaries of conventionally defined science and technology policy.

The energy sector is clearly a key driver in today's economic scenario. We will hear from its representatives, Juan Matthews, Jorma Nieminen, Steffen Kammler and Imad Rherrad, that they believe as much as Leon and Axel that our survival and continued existence in this global village will, first and foremost, depend on energy. We all have experienced emergency shutdowns, a sudden disconnection of electric power. In these moments of de-energisation we feel disconnected, frustrated, devastated, powerless, helpless and lost. It is often only then that we realise how much we rely on easy access to electricity, how entirely dependent we are in our daily life on energy!

Internationally, after water, energy is perhaps the most urgent issue which needs to be tackled by the development of alternative fuels, new means of generating energy and improved energy efficiencies. A challenge lies in the complexity and multitude of energy options including hydrogen, solar energy, wind energy, wave energy, biomass, geothermal energy as well as traditional coal, hydroelectric and nuclear energy. It does not help that there is little agreement as to which energy source to bet on.

Without question, what we do today to develop renewable energy sources, to encourage green technology and eco innovations, and to connect energy consumers with energy providers to solve problems will directly affect the quality of life of the future generations.

Industry – Energy

It is a truism that universal challenges such as pollution, dwindling natural resources and climate change can no longer be set aside for future generations to deal with. Juan Matthews reflects on the adoption of new energy sources from macro and national level, going further to mega and international levels. He speculates on the issues of introducing renewable energy and non-fossil fuels along with consequences of further automation in the labour market. If you are interested in the future of innovation from the angle of the crises in energy or demographic change, here you go: Juan gives you his thinking.

The Future of Innovation is Determined by Global Warming and the Ageing Population

Name   **Juan Matthews**
Affiliation   First Circle Ltd
Position   Managing Director
Country   UK
Area   International technology business
Email   juan.matthews@ntlworld.com

ageing   global warming   investment   demographic   energy

The future for innovation is linked to the two main issues that face the world – the crisis in energy as we move from fossils fuels; and the demographic changes in the largest economies.

Targets to reduce carbon emissions will require the adoption of new energy sources, the rapid closure of fossil fuel power plant and a move to electric or biofuelled transport. This has to be achieved in the next 20 years. Market forces, as fuel prices increase, will open opportunities for renewables but also drive the undesirable innovation of production of lower-grade fossil fuels like tar sands. The rapid growth of emerging economies may eliminate the reductions in carbon emissions made in developing economies, unless they can be enabled to skip current practice and introduce clean technologies. The question is how can the introduction of renewable energy and the use of non-fossil fuels in transport be accelerated? For example, the use of electric vehicles will require a complex infrastructure and a set of agreed standards for access. Technology challenges also remain in areas like efficient electricity and hydrogen storage, as well as tapping renewable sources. Getting solutions from the laboratory bench to the production line has always been difficult. Closed research in companies has not always been optimum though duplication and failure to agree standards. These issues are beyond the market and will require intervention not only at a national level but globally.

Meeting the costs of coping with the ageing society will be made more difficult by reduced savings and a smaller workforce. This demographic crisis will sweep most large economies in the next 30 years starting with Europe, Russia and Japan but impacting on Korea and then China by 2040. The United States will suffer less than most but even there there will still be some effects. Without continuing economic growth, pressure will increase on the shrinking workforce to meet the demands of an increasing burden of pensioners. Immigration from developing countries will inevitably be used as a means of offsetting this but skilled labour is required and it will drain resources from these countries and limit their potential. Continued economic growth is a priority and that can only be met by innovation. Innovations will be required not just for technology solutions but also in new financial structures for regulating energy use and paying for pensions. Reductions in the workforce through automation will need to take place for both manufacturing and labour intensive services like health care.

The financial problems that emerged in 2008 have shown that regulation has to be improved and government intervention is inevitable. A lack of investment funds always accompanies a recession but we cannot afford to lose the impetus of creating new companies and developing new technologies that provide the solutions we need for our future. As well as supporting research governments may also have to provide funds to take the place of venture capital and private equity. The skills for managing investment projects lie in the private sector and ways need to be found of using these skills even if projects are publicly funded.

What kind of energy is used in the processes of your organisation? What are levels of awareness around the three steps towards sustainability: recycle, reuse, reduce? Do these principles influence the design and development of new products and services?

Let's move on to our second thinker in the energy space, Jorma Nieminen, who takes a look at the paramount energy challenge through a number of different lenses: securing global energy supply, reducing greenhouse gases, using a low-energy industrial process, all the while maintaining a healthy economy. In fact, can we have both – a healthy economy and a healthy environment? Jorma attempts to find a way to address this quandary.

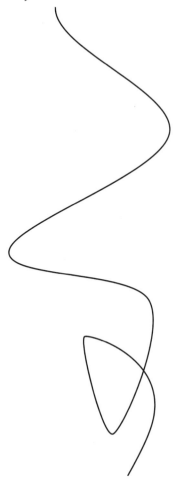

The Future of Innovation is Guaranteed by Compelling Global Problem-solving Needs

Name	**Jorma Nieminen**
Affiliation	Turku School of Economics
Position	Doctoral student
Country	Finland
Area	Global innovation future roadmap
Email	jorma.nieminen@benefon.fi

**global challenges   problem-solving   compelling innovation needs
zero-emission energy sources**

The future of innovation seems guaranteed with the world facing tremendous challenges. This article views some particularly important innovation domains defined by conspicuous global problems. Supply of energy, drinking water and food must be met while simultaneously reducing greenhouse gas emissions and keeping the economy in shape enabling continued improvement of living conditions, health and education. A related problem in many countries is excessive population growth while in others it is the collapsing birth-rate and fast-ageing population, disturbing demographic structures and economic balance. Security of people implies a need to pre-empt, contain and manage conflicts, terrorism and crime within democratic frameworks. Obviously, described challenges, standing for many, can be overcome only by massive array of innovations spanning several research fields from 'hard-core' natural sciences to 'softer' social sciences.

The focus here is the paramount challenge of securing the global energy supply while reducing greenhouse gases and maintaining a healthy economy. Per capita energy consumption can be reduced most effectively by innovating low-energy industrial processes, smart location-optimised zero-energy buildings and re-engineered energy-optimised transportation systems. Regarding transportation, energy efficiency can be improved greatly by an optimised role-division between public and private transport, and with the eventual results of the ongoing race between competing vehicle propulsion concepts in oil-based fuels, grid electricity and hydrogen. Sophisticated vehicular multi-sensor control and communication systems lead evolution towards automatic highways. By employing super-broadband services in the emerging ubiquitous optical networks, interconnecting buildings globally, we can innovate enhanced-functionality virtual activities in businesses, public sector, culture and private life that now need individuals' physical presence and travel, with energy and time usage. To manage this all globally, we need innumerable interdisciplinary innovation teams of varying scale and broad competence ranges.

To minimise our carbon footprint, we need increased production of zero-emission energy, including solar, wind, hydro, tidal and geothermal power, but also nuclear power – fission now and fusion when available. Indeed, we cannot exclude nuclear energy if we are serious about climate control! Incremental innovation improves techno-economic performance of traditional zero-emission sources. Radical innovation is in sight for low-cost massive hydrogen production by using photosynthesis with cyanobacteria, studied in several universities, including University of Turku. Presently rather low efficiency of such hydrogen production may be greatly improved by genetic re-engineering of the used cyanobacteria, for instance. An ample supply of low-cost hydrogen will enable practical zero-emission motor vehicles.

The future innovation activity is not only about inventing new solutions but also about diffusing them successfully to bear on the targeted problems. For many serious global problems, there are good solutions that, for varying reasons, have not been implemented everywhere. In such cases, diffusion research may provide clues for how to innovate around such implementation barriers. Innovation has been the main carrier of human progress since invention of language, cutting stones and fire, and will remain so until our sun goes red and dies some five billion years from now. The real innovation challenge is well before that date when we need to find ways of moving humankind to a planet that circles some younger star in our galaxy.

We believe that Jorma makes quite an important point when emphasising that all the good new stuff can only fulfil its potential when disseminated! In many cases possibilities and alternative solutions are out there, but there is a lack of appetite from the users/consumers side, be it for cost reasons or for the sheer fact that a deeper understanding is lacking. We are talking of a lack of understanding of the severity of the current situation, a lack of awareness of alternatives and possibilities and a lack of understanding of the consequences of certain choices.

Concerns over climate change and rising oil prices have made reducing energy consumption and emissions a priority for governments and businesses around the world. To name just a very few:

- The European Commission has proclaimed '20 20 by 2020', an action plan to solve climate change via reducing carbon emissions by 20 per cent and getting 20 per cent of all energy from renewable sources by 2020.

- Toyota Motor Corp. has announced its action plan for contributing to a low-carbon society at the 'Toyota Environmental Forum'.

- Wal-Mart has declared that it will be 100 per cent renewably powered and is installing solar panels on roofs.

- Wall Street has commenced its 'green' revolution through a growing number of firms implementing initiatives to decrease their carbon footprint.

Solar energy clearly has the most amazing potential – if only we can find economic ways of harnessing it. Perhaps we are closer than we think? Let us see what Steffen Kammler has to say on the solar energy.

The Future of Innovation is Sustainable, Affordable Energy for All

Name	**Steffen Kammler**
Affiliation	City Solar Power Plants AG
Position	Founder
Country	Germany
Area	Renewables, solar energy
Email	steffen.kammler@citysolar.de

energy   solar   sustainable   collaboration

Fossil fuel supplies are running low while worldwide energy consumption is drastically on the rise. The World Energy Council predicts an increase of nearly 60 per cent in annual demand to 220 billion megawatt hours by the year 2050.

Efficient use of solar energy can simply and effectively meet long-term supply gaps and replace fossil fuels.

The sun is a giant, inexhaustible source of energy. The fact that the sun radiates more energy towards Earth in two days than could be obtained from the entire crude oil and coal deposits on the planet is reason enough to utilise this enormous potential effectively. For this reason solar energy is, in my view, one of the key technologies of the third millennium. My goal is to use the power of the sun to make the future safer and worth living for everyone.

In the light of growing environmental awareness and rising oil prices, we are convinced that this technology will prevail over the coming years – the cost of energy generated with the power of the sun in Italy, Japan and the US state of California is now at a similar level to production with natural gas or nuclear energy.

Large solar plants, which feed power into energy providers' grids and could successively replace coal-fired or nuclear power in the future, only exist in limited numbers across the globe thus far. We are convinced that the efficiency of photovoltaic (PV) modules will increase in the coming years to the extent that renewable energy will partially or fully replace fossil fuels.

We are enthusiastic about the fact that the generation of solar power unites and harmonises man with his environment and with nature. Ethics and ecology are of particular concern to us as we wish to pass an intact environment onto future generations.

The raw material silicon plays a key role in the production of solar modules. The effectiveness of the solar module primarily depends on the quality of the solar silicon or on the percentage of solar radiation that can be directly converted into electrical power. In the field of PV plants this is currently 15 per cent. But it is an upward trend. In order to further increase power yields in future, researchers are working across the globe on new technologies to produce alterative semi-conductors. City Solar Power Plants AG regards itself as a pioneering innovator that focuses predominantly on its own research and development. It has come up with a new process to produce ultra-pure silicon, which it is on the brink of transferring to industrial use. Our new process requires significantly less electrical energy than conventional production processes and is thus more cost-effective. This enables us to make an important contribution to further lowering the production costs of solar power and helping the technology to break through.

If more power is generated during peak times than can be consumed, the question of durable and environmentally safe energy storage comes up again and again. The demand for cost-effective and efficient reservoirs arises particularly with solar energy, as this can only feed power into the grids during periods of sunlight. To provide supply independent of the sun and operate the grids outside of periods of sunlight requires efficient bulk energy storage. Working in collaboration with the Chair of Inorganic Chemistry at the University of Frankfurt, we believe that we are on the right track. The Director of the Chair, Professor Norbert Auner, has managed to use H polysilane (HPS) for hydrogen storage. The HPS, which releases hydrogen when water is added, only leaves SiO_2 and simple silica sand as residual substances of the chemical reaction, the latter of which can, in turn, be reused as a starting product for the production of HPS and silicon. As 'white coal', HPS can be stored, transported and handled for any length of time. It can easily be produced from an intermediate product of silicon production. It is not linked to carbon or carbon dioxide in the energy cycle. Thus HPS provides completely CO_2-free energy supply. This is, in our view, a pioneering success, which will drive forward the development of new forms of energy and will sit in harmony with the environment instead of destroying it. This is, in my opinion, the future of innovation.

Now how about that? Does that not sound rather promising? Have you noticed the level of collaboration, and drawing on different areas of expertise that has made this advance possible, and the willingness to challenge existing assumptions? Let us keep our fingers crossed and let's hope that the cost of solar energy will come down to affordable levels, soon. Indeed, studies are showing that there is going to be a crossing point on the cost of solar versus regular energy by around 2015.

Imad Rherrad is our last voice in the foursome on energy, providing a thoughtful outline of possible focal points of the future of innovation in energy.

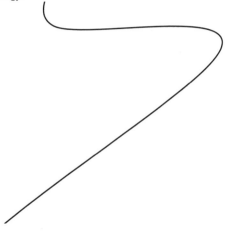

The Future of Innovation is Innovative Thinking

Name	**Imad Rherrad**
Affiliation	Government of Québec, Canada
Position	Economist
Country	Canada
Area	Evidence-based view of knowledge transfer; humanities and social sciences in R&D
Email	imad.rherrad@mcccf.gouv.qc.ca

innovation   clean and green energy   technologiocal path   technological divide

The future of innovation will focus on green and clean energy, its production and use. The recent UN experts' reports, the increase in oil prices, the 2008 US elections and presidential debates show the urgency of finding new ways to produce and use this kind of energy.

It was brave of Barack Obama, the 44th President of the United States, to admit that the US cannot continue to use energy as they actually do and it is time to invest in clean renewable and non-renewable energy solutions. However, it is important to remember that environmentally friendly solutions consist of more than just clean energy sources, and should also cover consumption behaviours and technologies on which they are based.

We believe that the focal points of future innovations in energy will focus on:

1. Advanced technology to produce green, clean, affordable and reliable energy based on wind, solar, hydropower and ocean energy, geothermal energy, biomass, etc.

2. Higher-efficiency residential appliance and commercial equipment that can help reduce energy waste and pollution (zero waste solutions). Currently most of our activities, such as washing our hands, cooking food, running washing machines, charging our phones and computers, etc., consume more resources than they ought to!

3. The incorporation of humanities and social sciences into research and development in the field of energy for a better match between clean technologies and users' behaviours. The issue here is more than just technical feasibility of green and clean solutions, technological change and users' needs, and should also focus on the social and ethical dimensions of future solutions and innovations in the matter of energy. The recent history of nanotechnology and genetically modified foods is a good example to illustrate and understand these issues

4. Finally, new incentives to promote environmentally friendly lifestyles and high energy-efficiency products (taxation incentives, green insurance system, pricing reforms, etc.).

In this way, the future technological path in the energy sector should be similar to that of new information technologies:

1. significant public investment in basic research and applied technologies;

2. commercial transfer of quasi-transversal technologies;

3. the first mover advantage in patenting and commercialisation of clean technologies.

The unequal access to new solutions in the matter of energy should be another point of similarity with the new information technologies sector. Indeed, the emergence of the new technological path in the field of energy should certainly raise the question of a possible 'green and clean divide' between developed and developing countries. In this context, two issues should be addressed: to what extent the 'green and clean divide' will be different from the so-called digital divide? And, of course, how will we bridge the technological divide separating developed and less developed countries?

Finally, whatever the trends in the field of energy, unexpected events should certainly play a major role in this sector. Therefore, it would be interesting to know how and to what extent the future of innovation in this sector will surprise us.

Imad is right, it would be interesting to have an inkling of what the energy sector has in store for us with regards to the development of alternative fuels, new means of generating energy and energy efficiency.

The field of 'green technology' is enormous and encompasses a continuously evolving set of methods and materials, from techniques for generating energy to non-toxic cleaning products, driving to a healthy environment and a healthy economy. Here, too, we see a more holistic approach emerging, as Green Technology, a non-profit initiative designed to inform government efforts toward sustainability, providing a forum in which government officials can communicate with those in the private sector who are developing and distributing green technologies, demonstrates (www.green-technology.org). Here you can find information on energy conservation, renewable energy sources such as solar and wind power, as well as recycling, water purification, sewage treatment, air pollution control, environmental remediation, green buildings, and many other technologies.

While energy is clearly a major factor in the sustainability debate, there are also other relevant industries such as chemistry and biotechnology which apply their thinking to conserve nature and even reverse harm already done. That is what is our next section is about.

Industry – Chemistry

The invention, design and application of chemical products and processes to reduce or to eliminate the generation and use of hazardous substances, is known as green chemistry.[1] Biotechnology as a research domain opens the way for new applications in health care, agriculture, food production, new scientific discoveries and environmental protection.

Rob van Leen sees the future of innovation through the combination of chemistry and biotechnology. His understanding is that such a union provides business opportunities, preserving a safe and sound planet.

---

1   Adopted from www.green-technology.org

The Future of Innovation is Addressing the Challenges of Climate Change and Clean Energy

Name	**Rob van Leen**
Affiliation	DSM
Position	Chief Innovation Officer
Country	The Netherlands
Area	Innovating for a more sustainable future
Email	rob.leen-van@dsm.com

chemistry   biotechnology   energy   climate change   chemical industry

Chemistry and biotechnology will play a major role in addressing the challenges of climate change and clean energy, actually they already do. Life sciences and materials sciences specialist DSM has built its 'Vision 2010' strategy on addressing these challenges.

The chemical industry has long been perceived as part of the problem instead of the solution. The 'average' global citizen considers the chemical industry to have only limited relevance to improving society. The time has come for a fundamental perception and paradigm shift, since I firmly believe that chemistry, especially based on its more recent fertile marriage with industrial biotechnology, is well positioned to get a firm grip on the challenges posed by climate change and the quest for clean energy. Climate change, greenhouse gases and dwindling oil and gas reserves call for a transition to the use of renewable resources. Innovative solutions through a combination of biotechnology and chemistry will lower costs, reduce CO_2 emissions and provide for new functionalities.

Don't take only my word for it that the chemical industry will deliver on its promises. Just take a look at the increasing number of innovative breakthroughs that have been launched by our sector. The number of products already on the market is quite impressive, varying from 'green' waterborne resins, energy transmission improving coatings, biopolymers and bio-fuels, to a wide range of polymers and lighter materials which e.g., improve the fuel consumption in automobiles and aviation. These are not only examples from DSM, but also from our colleagues. And they only mark the beginning of innovations in this field.

From a technology point of view, we are initiating new developments at the crossroads of life sciences and materials sciences. Currently some 20 per cent of DSM's €8.8 billion turnover is related to biotechnology and the activities and opportunities in this field are rapidly growing, due to recent technological breakthroughs. In addition, the awareness of the advantages in terms of costs and environmental impact is rapidly increasing. DSM's White Biotechnology programme is focused on (biotech tools for) bio-fuels, bio-based chemicals (such as succinic acid and bio-butanol) and bio-polymers. Because we believe in the power of open innovation, in all these areas we cooperate with customers, competitors, research organisations and governments (such as the US Department of Energy). For example, by the end of this year we will open, together with one of our partners, the world's first demonstration plant for the fermentative production of bio-renewable succinic acid, which will be used to produce bio-polymers, but also numerous 'green' derivates. Fermentation processes yield energy savings of 30–40 per cent compared to a typical chemical process, both reducing CO_2 emissions and saving on a company's purchasing bill. In the case of succinic acid, CO_2 is even consumed in the production process!

Innovation through the combination of chemistry and biotechnology will make a marked difference for our future and will not only provide business opportunities, but perhaps more importantly will be an expression of the chemical industry's responsibility in helping to preserve a safe and sound planet for the generations to come.

Did we not talk about awareness earlier? Would you, like we ourselves, rather not have prejudices against the chemical industry? How are we, as users, meant to be able to make decisions about what a most sustainable choice might be when we walk through the supermarket or garden centre? How are we to know, which of the products will be least harmful over its entire lifecycle? It is constantly suggested to us that we ought to buy a new, more energy efficient car. But think about it. How many resources go into the production of a new car, how much energy? How long could we continue driving or slightly less environmentally friendly car before one catches up with the other?

From the greening energy and chemistry industries our journey takes us to the field of telecommunications where Vish Nandlall paints a colourful picture of disruption.

Industry – Telecom

Vish Nandlall takes us into the future of telecommunications via hard lessons from the past. He recalls some classics such as 'Microsoft did not invent the iconic computer user interface' and 'Google did not think up the internet'. From today's understanding Vish shares with us the disruptive tomorrow of telecommunications with an expanding set of players and business models.

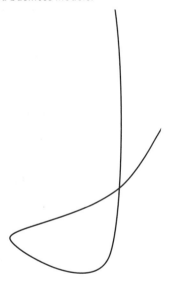

The Future of Innovation is in Our Past

Name	**Vish Nandlall**
Affiliation	Nortel
Position	CTO Carrier Networks
Country	Canada
Area	Innovation management
Email	vnandlal@nortel.com

Nortel   XA-Core   Sunday afternoon parking lot phenomena   telecom changing the world

I have found over the maturing years of telecom that we have relegated innovation to the thought clutter closet, and it is a shame. We stand today on the precipice of new disruption, and I am hopeful that it will provide the tipping point that ushers a renewal of the research ethic that has made the leap from stringing cable to pumping bits over the air.

I am reminded of the final push in digital telephony switching, which resulted in Nortel's parallel compute engine triumph: XA-Core. While the surface motivation was to deliver a high-capacity voice-switching system, our true purpose was to show the world that it could be done. It was during this time that I first noticed the 'Sunday afternoon parking lot phenomena' at Nortel's Carling facility: in stark contrast to neighbouring firms, ours was full. This was to become a regular bellwether for innovation across the years. The inspiration that filled our parking lot on Sunday was driven by a 'change the world' spirit, which is not always appreciated in the hardened world of quarterly focused boardrooms.

What gets lost in translation? Invention typically reveals itself as an 'engineering fetish', which may not coincide nicely with the practical application of net present value analysis. But this is because we require imagination beyond the innovation itself, the will to 'change the world' not just through manifesting the invention, but also through innovating the market.

Microsoft did not invent the iconic computer user interface and Google did not think up the internet, but both came up with the business-model innovations required to profit from those marvels. The joint calculus of the inventor and the visionary market model can elevate the idea from zeitgeist to new industry.

This lesson is hard won. In the mid 1990s, Nortel had pioneered a personal business communicator called the Orbitor. Near the validation phase of the design, there was an internal trial period, where Nortel employees acted as test subjects to work out the bugs in the system – it was an object of envy to parade with this shiny toy, blasting chat messages to other members of the trial elite, enjoying the benefits of simultaneous ring to your office number or editing your emails as you shuttled between meetings. This was not only inspired design, it was a fundamentally new way to interact and manage your time: here was a device that could change the world.

Sadly, the business case could not reconcile these innovations with the existing industry models, and so the project was abandoned. A few years later, Palm was soaring high on the strength of an emerging personal data appliance (PDA) market. The revolution had come, and we were left with a new tale of the 'one that got away'. These industry fish tales are manifold, the most legend of which is Xerox PARC's personal computer vision 'borrowed' by Microsoft and Apple. It is correctly assessing the market context which is the art of innovation.

I can state without a doubt that the telecommunications industry is poised for great disruption: from the expanding set of players and business models, to the transition from of an internet of linked documents to one of communities and activities. I still see a world that can be changed and new ways that people can become connected – and it is this thought that will keep the parking lot full next Sunday and forge the disruptive opportunities of tomorrow.

Have you looked at your own industry with an out-of-space perspective? What disruptions might be on your agenda? What would be things that could derail the smoothly running train of today's operations? And, with the current economic crisis in mind, what could you do about it?

Industry – Service

Moving on to the service industry we find that both our contributors here, Sandro Battisti and Diane Robers, make a nice connection for us. Sandro is first with his expectations that telecommunications will play a significant part in the development of new business models in service industries.

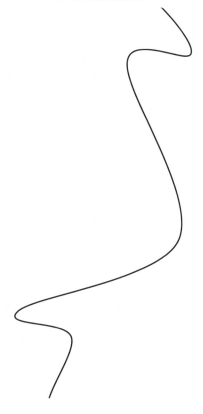

The Future of Innovation is Services Based on High Technologies

Name	**Sandro Battisti**
Affiliation	Politecnico di Torino
Position	Student
Country	Brazil
Area	Innovation management
Email	sbattisti@neoset.com.br

**high technology   innovations in services   innovative organisation
emergent countries   commoditised services**

The future of innovation will come from services that are supported by high-technology solutions. To succeed organisations will have to know how to manage the complex integration of such technologies or systems in highly competitive environments. This will occur through the rendering of services, such as the supply of telecommunications and electric energy, into new alternative technical forms. These will be considered more efficient and economically more viable for the final consumer.

To rise to this challenge companies will have to understand the true dimensions of the complexities involved. In these highly competitive global environments the processes of technological innovation will involve diverse contingencies factors, specific to each organisations, which demand a new position vis-à-vis innovation. Thus, the factors driving the success of these innovative organisations will have to be based on a vision of efficient internal and external communication.

The approach to achieving innovation will definitely not be more the same any more. New external factors, such as the current worldwide financial crisis, will affect the approach to innovation. The increasing reduction of the investments in technology will cause a reduction of the potential innovations in high technology. The ever more competitive environment will demand of companies to develop new approaches that allow them to foresee the wants and desires of customers quicker than ever before.

The core of innovations in services will be based on technology being established in companies today whereby commoditised services will form the basis from which to drive cost reductions. The global demand for new commodities in turn will be raised, again driving further demand for the development of new services, creating a positively enforcing cycle. The efficient delivery of these services and allegiance to the customers will also be an appropriate short-term strategy for organisations to fend off competitors.

I believe that the future of the financial investments in innovation should focus on the development of new services in high-technology sectors. From a Brazilian perspective I would like to suggest that such positioning can be achieved mainly through the investment of international organisations. This will happen through the constant and global growth of merger and acquisitions of companies currently controlled through Brazilian shareholders. The result will be a consolidation of worldwide management models, drawing on the human as well as technological resources available Brazilians today.

Finally, I believe that a visionary book on innovation should include a suggestion for a definition for *the innovative organisation,* one that possess technological base available in emergent countries such as Brazil. Thus I suggest the following: *The innovative organisation of the future will be one that is capable of constant growth through the innovation in commoditised services, building on its established high-technology base.* This will be the dominant innovative positioning for the next decades.

Would you like to know what else the future of innovation might have in store for the service industry? Perhaps Diane Robers can help us here. By suggesting what the future of innovation in the service industry looks like she simultaneously highlights the areas for further research in the service innovation. Very appropriate of her to call on the education sector to pay attention to setting the agenda for training 'service entrepreneurs'. Are you ready for that, Professor? We come back to this thought-provoking question again with Paul Coughlan, further on in this chapter.

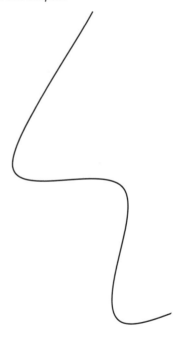

The Future of Innovation is in Services

Name	**Dr Diane Robers**
Affiliation	PricewaterhouseCoopers AG WPG
Position	Head of Innovation Competence Centre
Country	Germany
Area	Service innovation
Email	diane.robers@de.pwc.com

service innovation   business model   success factors

- Innovation in services becomes standard;

- service innovation will drive product innovation;

- a new profession will emerge.

Whereas innovation in services today is still in the early stages – despite the service sector's contribution to GDP – the 'industrial' future will be driven by service innovations. This will affect the business-to-customer and the business-to-business sectors. The obvious driver for new services is (IT) technology, where new forms of customer interaction occur. We will see more forms of customer-driven innovations leading to new services, e.g., in the automotive aftersales market. Former 'product'-oriented industries like energy or building and construction will transform more and more into service providers. Business models like pay-per-use will become standard for manufacturers, which look for new approaches in business innovation. Those service companies which just have begun to deal with the topic will be forced to handle new service innovations in a professional way, otherwise they will lose market share and potential growth.

In the next decade we expect to see a turnaround in innovation whereby service innovation will drive product innovation, and a new profession will emerge as standard: the innovation manager in the service industry – equivalent to the R&D manager for products. This does not diminish the achievements of engineering. Contrary, intelligent service innovators will learn from industrial processes and methods, adopting them where ever adequate.

As a consequence new forms of education will be needed as well as a new managerial ability to enhance service innovation success, involving actively the human 'entrepreneurs' of the firm. Service innovation success is determined by four factors:

- setting clear innovation goals;

- fostering innovation culture and entrepreneurship;

- providing resources and managing innovations properly;

- monitoring and measuring outcomes.

Each component needs specific skills, such as strategic thinking or project management or valuation skills. The most challenging one is the cultural part. Innovation culture means sharing knowledge and tolerating mistakes, open communication, composing interdisciplinary/international teams, rewarding efforts and increasing time and free space for creativity. Future education and training concepts will have to focus especially on how to set up a stimulating innovative climate within the firm. All this does not get past one fundamental reality, namely that the service entrepreneur is someone who has a strong belief in a new service business idea.

The decade of service innovation has only just begun. Let's get on with it.

Two perspectives from different sides of the world, both Sandro and Diane see a major role for ICT in the future of the service industry, predicting some changes that are facilitated through technologies many of which existing today already.

How do things in other service industries look like, say, for example in insurance? How about 'back to basics' as the latest trend in innovation? Well, that is what Anthie Zachariadou is suggestion, and we believe her. Do you?

Industry – Insurance

It might seem that Anthie questions innovation as the future of the insurance industry; however, read it carefully and you will find some true gems for the future of innovation.

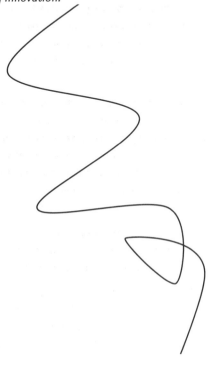

The Future of Innovation is Possibly Simpler than We Think

Name	**Anthie Zachariadou**
Affiliation	Royal Crown Insurance Company Ltd
Position	Director
Country	Cyprus
Area	Innovation in services
Email	anthie@spidernet.com.cy

insurance   policies   accidents   security   peace of mind

The purpose of insurance is to make people feel *safe!* Primarily, financially safe, because if they do have financial peace of mind they can carry out their daily activities, pursue their goals and achieve their ambitions without the constraints caused by money-related worries. The economic crisis has shaken people's core belief that they can obtain financial security simply by doing their job, or doing their job well, or working hard to obtain the qualifications that will lead them to a job that pays well.

For insurance-providing institutions, the 'mission' had never been to make profit simply by collecting vast amounts of money and distributing smaller sums to those that suffer a loss. Historically and philosophically the very existence of insurance companies has been to carry out a social and financial role – that of ensuring homeowners, merchants, businesspeople, travellers and generally everyone that is active in society, feels safe at all times. They will feel safe because there is a back-up in case something goes wrong.

Innovation in insurance will be in line with the 'back to basics' theme that is accompanying the current events in the financial world. Any new products will be innovative in that they will tend to the consumer's most basic needs. The need to develop insurance policies that are completely breakthrough and radical – e.g., 'StockPrice PLUS' or 'Comprehensive Tax Liabilities' or 'CyberInsurance', and the like – will take a back seat to enhanced simple policies for the home, the vehicle and the family. Innovation should not always mean original or avant-garde. In the case of insurance, it can mean finding new ways of satisfying the inherent needs of simple people, especially in the midst of uncertain times such as these.

Policies with fewer exclusions, less small print, wider covers and simpler procedures, policies with plain language that inspire trust in those that write them and produce a feeling of a security in those who read them – those would be innovative policies. Homeowners would not have to worry about what would happen should any rare weather phenomenon befall their house, or whether they will be able to afford a new television should theirs be stolen. Employers would not feel that their business is being threatened if there is a serious injury on their site to someone without a valid contract of service with them. Car owners would not pay for mechanical damage themselves. The point would be to unload people from financial anxieties, instead of implicating them in complicated procedures in case there is an emergency.

Everywhere we turn nowadays, we see that 'less is more'. Being innovative – that should not come with the 'more', but should adapt to the need for 'less'. Simple, clear, basic, pure, plain, unsophisticated, comprehensible – that is 'less'. Complicated, long, unintelligible, confusing may be more impressive, but it may conceal the bad behind 'more' trimmings. Innovation in this day is simple – to find the substance, to find good quality and integrity that may have been lost in the way of doing 'big' things. Innovation in insurance is as simple – to go back to helping people concentrate on doing what means something to them by easing some of their burdens. Making them *feel* safe again would be absolute innovation.

Here is a nice motto from Anthie: 'Innovation in this day is simple'. How about innovation to find the substance and to find quality and integrity, things that often got left behind in the pursuit of 'big' things. Indeed, life is so complicated that there is an ever increasing desire for simplicity, for a return to nature, a return to childhood. When you see today's manuals – be it for a washing machine, a camera or a mobile phone – don't you want to simplify them? Anthie says, 'Making them feel *safe again would be absolute innovation': how true. This could be applied not only in the insurance industry but also to transport, tourism, home, internet, medicine.*

Each industry must find the ulterior motive that drives its innovation ambition. This, clearly, means that innovation does not always have to be radical – on the contrary. But perhaps the 'breakthrough' lies in the way we think about it, and how we achieve it, while the outcome itself seems rather less innovative. The key to, and ulterior motive of, innovation is the creation of value. What is it in your industry that delivers the ultimate value to its customers or users?

And one more comment on Anthie's contribution as there is one more word that literally jumps out at us: 'trust'. Trust and safety, so we can get on with our jobs and lives (the purpose of which should be to create a better world for everyone).

We thought it was quite interesting how specific strands emerge from those writing on different service industries. We have already identified ICT as one of the key enablers of innovation in the service industries. Hearing Anthie talk about the insurance industry and Lynne Maher, who will be next, about the health care industry we find that they are talking almost about the same things and are thinking in the same direction. How so, you may ask? Well, read on!

Industry – Health care

For us individually, health is of one of the primary issue, literally a matter of life or death. It is inspiring to see the optimism with which Lynne Maher describes how health care in Britain is driven by innovation and co-creation. We just invited you to consider the kind of safety Anthie talked about everywhere, in transport, tourism, home, internet and medicine. Lynne builds on this and confirmation collaboration not only along the supply chain but also highlights the value of exchanges between industries.

As a matter of fact, co-creation is increasing its scope. Starting from cooperation between companies and end users it is now evolved into collaboration between industries. Lynn's words are inspiring not only for the health care industry but also for other industries and innovation management as a whole, as their focus is on the fundamental question of 'how to provide improved services'.

The Future of Innovation is Going to Transform Healthcare Services

Name	**Lynne Maher**
Affiliation	NHS Institute for Innovation and Improvement
Position	Head of Innovation Practice
Country	UK
Area	Innovation in the health service
Email	lynne.maher@institute.nhs.uk

mindset   exploration   connection   collaboration   celebrate

'None of us is as smart as all of us'.

Phil Condit, CEO Boeing

The future of innovation in health care is bright. In the UK's National Health Service (NHS) we already have much to celebrate in our 60-year history. Many traditional surgical methods have been replaced by less invasive keyhole methods, new diagnostic techniques even negate the need for surgery altogether. Information technology has revolutionised the use of data across the NHS and improvement efforts have led to massive improvements. Of course there is still more to do but I am optimistic because I see two big themes emerging strongly. One is an increased emphasis on innovation in healthcare *services* to match the focus on technology and devices. The second is recognition of the importance of a deliberate process for innovation that can be used by *all* rather than the assumption that innovation is a result of a few clever people who sit in an isolated room and come up with all of the ideas.

Both themes are connected. Tom Kelley from the design firm IDEO makes the point that 'companies that want to succeed at innovation will need new insights. New viewpoints. And new roles'. I would add: these in turn will bring new ideas about how to provide improved services. Most 'innovative' organisations do have a specific process, some quite defined and some less so but nevertheless embedded in routines. A common feature of innovation processes is to encourage exploration outside of traditional mindsets. This means making creative connections with other industries, some of which we would not usually associate with our own. This trend is increasingly being used in health care and we have found that ideas which may be commonplace in other industries can have a significant positive impact when applied in a health-care context.

One example of this is a recent collaboration between a cardiac team from Great Ormond Children's hospital and the pit crew from Ferrari, the Formula One racing team. By transferring knowledge about teamworking from one to the other of these completely different industries, there has been a radical improvement in the efficiency and safety of the transfer of children from the operating theatre to the intensive care unit (cited in *Thinking Differently*,[1] 2008). Lean processes traditionally used within manufacturing have been adapted for health care resulting in more effective and efficient services that have reduced waste and improved the level of value-added time for patients. Similarly our relationship with service designers has exposed the NHS to powerful tools and techniques which although commonly used within service design were new within the health service. One of these is the power of observation, not in the style that clinicians are expert in, where their skills are honed to link symptoms with diagnosis, but observation based on anthropological principles. This has helped teams to better understand what is really happening in the front line of care and is now resulting in new design solutions providing exceptional health service experiences.

Using a specific innovation processes which encourages us to look outside our traditional mindsets and make creative connections with other industries enable us to transform services for millions of patients.

Something occurred to us when reading Lynne's contribution: just as our morality and mindset have to catch up with technical possibilities so do the services and support that go alongside the technical developments. The more holistic approach we need to develop in the context of innovation in general applies equally to the need for a more holistic approach across the spectrum of types of innovation. What we mean is that when developing new products, new services and new business models we need to take a look at the wider picture and understand how they might affect other parts of the system. How do products affect services, how do business models affect the design of products and services, and so on.

But back to our topic, health care. Helen Baxter echoes Lynne's contribution, suggesting that we should 'deliver not only high-quality treatments but also high-quality care experiences'. Her insight that in health care services we should 'innovate in the design' is again one that is applicable to a multitude of industries. It is great to know that the end-user and customer focus, which originally was introduced in fields other than medicine, is now incorporating into health-care design, and that the needs of patients are co-designed between them and medical establishments. Even if it might be a little immodest to praise ourselves, we hope that with this book we might contribute to combining and integrating a wide number of views and perspective: business, government, consulting, and academia, individual, company and industry perspectives. For your collection of catch phrases, we suggest you add one of Helen's maxims: 'a stitch in time saves nine'.

---

1   Published by and available from the NHS.

The Future of Innovation is Working with Patients and Staff

Name	**Helen Baxter**
Affiliation	NHS Institute for Innovation and Improvement
Position	Associate – Innovation Practice
Country	UK
Area	Innovation in health care
Email	Helen.baxter@institute.nhs.uk

healthcare   innovation   experience   service   care

The question of the future of innovation in health care is influenced by the history of innovation in health care. Everyone can think of many innovations particularly products and/or technology, for example, penicillin and keyhole surgery, which have transformed health care. Although products and technology innovations are important and will continue to influence health-care treatment they can only be part of the solution, the real difference is our ability to deliver not only high-quality treatments but also high-quality care experiences. This will only be achieved if we innovate in the design of our health-care services. Using innovative service design techniques to challenge our current thinking and mindsets about health service delivery will lead to innovative, transformational solutions. One mechanism to challenge mindsets is the use of service design approaches to capture the real experiences of patients, carers and staff as they receive and deliver care. Within health-care improvement there have been substantial efforts to improve performance (functionality) and engineering (safety) of service delivery processes; however, there is a lack of consideration of the aesthetics of the experience (what does it feel like to receive or provide the care process?).

In truth this approach can be challenging to staff and patients. Traditionally it has been staff who interpret the needs of patients to make service improvements. Staff feel that they know what a patient's needs are and base this assumption on their professional training, this is further reinforced by our history which has supported the notion of a paternal approach to health care. The future of innovation in health care can be greatly improved through the delivery of high-quality health-care experiences which would complement any new technological advances. For this approach to work the relationships between patients and staff need to develop in a new way where they routinely listen to the each other's experience and work together to co-design high-quality care experiences.

If innovation is the successful exploitation of new ideas, it is important to have a robust process which allows the generation of lots of ideas in relation to a challenge/problem area, some of which are then developed and implemented to create the best solutions. Traditionally within health-care provision, there are two main routes to new service development; either an individual has an idea about how to change the service, or staff respond to a policy directive by thinking of an idea to comply with the policy. In both cases there is a tendency to quickly take forward the first idea without taking time to really understand the challenge and to develop a range of possible solutions. The rationale for our current approach of rushing in with our initial idea is often 'lack of time'. Action is applauded while thinking is considered to be procrastination in disguise. The future of innovation in health services might rest on the age-old saying: 'a stitch in time saves nine'. Let's make time to really understand the challenge and develop the right solution before we rush forward to implement the first solution.

We have talked about idea generation earlier (e.g., Svend Haugaard's and Michael Simpson's contributions to Part XII) but we would like to ask again, where do the ideas in your organisation come from? How far do you cast your net, and what criteria do you use to select the ones to take forward? And what do you do to ensure dissemination and engagement with the new?

Would you object if we suggested that TV should become a part of our health-care considerations too? We would argue that good and bad news impact upon our state of mind, our mood, spirit and, in many cases, dominate our leisure time. Can you imagine life without television? (Having said that, there has not been a television in Bettina's household for a rather long time and Anna has ceased watching television as she's 'sick and tired' of meaningless programmes, rumours, ads and 'much ado about nothing' on the screen!) Health care and television – the results of their collaboration could be utilised in any health-care establishment. It is known that negative emotions blossom disease, while positive fight it. Now happening without plan or indent, we see programmes or movies retelling miracle stories of recovery, the strong will of patients or their doctors' efforts. If done on purpose, health-care and TV collaboration could supply us with certain information, knowledge, understanding, comprehension, all provided interactively.

Industry – TV and film

Scott Larkin's predictions about the impact of the television industry, and the media industry more generally, on the future of innovation do not include the health industry – though taking his thinking further the potential might well be there! Read on and we will come back after his contribution to why we might think that might be.

The Future of Innovation is a Process-driven Extrapolative Continuum

Name	Scott Larkin
Affiliation	Advanced Systems, Incorporated
Position	Chief Operating Officer
Country	USA
Area	Process drivers for future innovation
Email	SLarkin@AdvSystems.com

possibilities   process   shocks   collaboration   extrapolation

The future of innovation has process drivers in cumulative experiences, education and exposure to visualisations that innovators receive during the formative stages of the creative cycle. For individual innovators, a continuum of creative influence spans the time leading to their productive efforts and is a valuable target area to focus influence. Governments, companies and innovative groups have the opportunity to achieve generationally inspired innovation through focusing the attentions of multiple innovators across a broader depth or source influence, and for greater time, leveraging emerging capabilities to enable the next-generation achievement of innovation in areas that would formerly have been impossible or impossibly expensive. Looking at possible timelines for innovations that result from the synergetic advances of envisioned breakout products enables innovative outcomes to exceed what was original intended for them. We saw this in the experiences shared by innovators who viewed the 1960s *Star Trek* television science fiction series depicting handheld mobile communication devices, and the far improved ear and eye piece blue-tooth mobile smart communications devices available today, as the outcome of that creative process. Other items featured in *Star Trek* are still being worked toward, such as the universal translator. Components such as voice recognition and language translation software, noise-cancelling headphones and miniaturisation and wireless communications to make such a device achievable are present. The innovative product device and service to integrate these capabilities has not yet been produced to capture significant market share, but is on the near horizon.

Potential areas for future innovation can be viewed through cataloguing envisioned possibilities that are tailored to audiences who are interested in using the anticipated solution outcomes and to those who are interested in developing the solutions as well as funding their development. Websites like InnoCentive[1] foreshadow possibilities in this area. Prioritising target areas for innovations and having a vision for where one should innovate can be driven by leadership, environmental and market forces.

Media influences future innovation through artistic expression and the speculative exploration of imagination. Innovation is more directly achieved as a response to forceful shocks to current

---

1   Editors' note: please see the article in Part XI, 'Innovation from everyone, everywhere', for insights on the future of innovation from Dwayne Spradlin, President and CEO of InnoCentive.

systems. The greater the shock the more rapid will be the influence of momentum towards specific goals. For example, shocks from attacks in the US caused innovation in privacy protections and transit system security.

Challenges exist in how to align those with needs, those with the vision for innovations, those with the resources to fund and develop innovations in a timely focused manner and those with the ability to effect shocks to the system that drive the immediacy of response. The specialisation of interest groups and the complexity of innovation design pathways can be self-limiting in the scope (knowledge, expertise, resources) of those able to respond. There is also value in dispersed collaboration where a reward incentive is an important factor in determining where innovators desire to focus their available time to work toward outcomes.

The future of innovation will benefit from framing goals in any endeavour where concepts born through imaginative extrapolation are visited and revisited. Interactive television will be here soon.

What are your thoughts on how health care and television could combine to drive the future of innovation? Our inspiration came when Scott started talking about Star Trek. *If you have seen the series, do you remember the healing chambers, and robots undertaking operations? Scott already pointed to futuristic films as a source for ideas for future innovations. Perhaps that is it, what about healing chambers? How could that be translated into reality, or what bits could be translated? Some interesting food for thought ...*

Duncan Hopper lifts the veil from the future of movies and elaborates on minicini (there is a new term for your 'innovation management glossary'!). In particular, Duncan elaborates on some radical changes in technology and marketing that will drive the development of minicinis. Let's ponder on that a bit. Technically the filming industry is becoming increasingly digital, and films are becoming available via internet and on mobile phones and the PC. Do you, too, believe that in a few years, with the digitalisation of our homes, movies will be digitalised too, and, as a result, we will no longer have to go to the cinema to see whatever film we like? Well, don't we? Modern consumers can manage and manipulate films as easily as they use 'my documents' folders. Unlike our ancestors, all of us do have the opportunity to experiment and play with and in the digital world. Not too long ago we were amazed at the boundless opportunities a 1MB flash-drive would offer us. Now we can have 2TB, that is 2000MB, at our service. What do we need 2TB of digital memory for? We humans seem to have an insatiable desire to possess and acquire things that are far beyond our actual needs. But soon enough we rather liked what was excessive and find a use for it – mobile phones on which we can watch movies, keep our photos and store our documents. With the digitisation of movies and the rise of minicinis, will we stay at home, and will the film theatre become an institution of the past? Welcome to the brand-new world of cinema as envisaged by Duncan.

The Future of Innovation is Minicinis

Name	**Duncan Hopper**
Country	UK
Area	Film industry
Email	duncanhopper@email.com

cinema future screen distribution films

Cinema and feature films have come a long way since the Talkies hit town but really until now the industry, dominated by Hollywood both in its studios, agencies and star system, although with a small but healthy independent sector, does the same thing it has always done. It produces an 'entertaining' piece of film work on celluloid for an audience that pays to come into a purpose-built cinema and watch it.

That is all about to change and the signs, as you start to see promotional clips on your mobiles and watch along with another million fans the latest hot short online, are all there. There is a revolution happening! Watch this or, come to think of it, any other space you care to name for the future. The drivers are in place now but they are not yet in fifth gear, more like second. They will 'movie on up' to coin a phrase. Let's briefly look at them.

Global product protection is the first and most essential. Everyone who makes films wants access to worldwide markets for the cost revenue advantages this brings. You want the latest James Bond? Well, control your fraudsters and you will get it! Global markets are great drivers. China has made great strides in this field: more to do elsewhere.

Technology is next. Digital cameras and digital films have been around for a while but the cost advantages of these, coming in with the existing and new mass markets for the products, mean high tech at low cost. Hand-held cameras with fewer crew members needed makes a huge difference to a film's budget. The cameras also now have new tricks, they 'do' substantially more: editing on the spot, zooms, wipes and reshoots all available. Translation costs are also way down as an enabler.

Cinema projection (that's an old word!) equipment is now so much smaller with more flexibility. That is to say nothing of the vast and booming home cinema kits. The net result is you can show in many more places with much lower costs. Minicinis will abound in the most unlikely or indeed obvious venues.

The biggest revolution, however, is with the consumer, with their new interests and consequent high demand. Despite freebies they will, studies show, pay for the right technology to suit their micro needs. If the costs of viewing, via internet, mobile phone and PC are there, and they are, then more and more people are looking at more and more films. Students rarely go to the old cinemas now: they watch online with friends.

New film makers are coming into the industry and making more and different films. Evidence, you ask? Well, look at how documentaries are now mainstream! New directors and actors are also appearing, and becoming more acceptable. Hollywood knows a winner when they see it! The internet and reality websites are the new breeding grounds for what I'd call the not an 'old rat pack,' but a new 'minicini guerrilla film army'.

So, when you sit at home in your own minicini or in one of the new cini bars having a drink and a meal and watching, or looking and listening at the wall in the railway carriage with your 3D cinispecs on, or wire-linked into your own I-cini, making calls at the same time, do you also catch a glimpse in frame, as one of the new movie makers gets a shot of you for his reality pic? Viewing is not going to be what it is, or used to be, any more. Welcome to the brave new movie world!

We find both Scott and Duncan talking about translation. While Scott Larkin earlier spoke about a universal translator in the context of interactive television, Duncan Hopper highlights the facilitating factor of cost effective translations on the film industry.

In the next contribution we will hear about a different kind of translation: Olivier Fleurot from Mars Petcare explains that the success of FMCG companies will depend on the successful translation of consumer insights into new products. How miraculously the language, the processes, the tendencies, the needs, the objectives, the strategies, the essence are correlated, united and are indispensably interchangeable with countries, companies, industries and humankind. Indeed, it is exciting, fascinating and charming how differently and similarly we see the future of innovation.

Industry – FMCG

Olivier Fleurot miraculously, in merely three paragraphs, summarises in an easy accessible way the most important aspects and the essential foundations of a FMCG innovation strategy. Read it carefully, however, and you will find that much of his thinking is equally relevant to many if not most other industries. (Some more thoughts on consumer focus and market research can be found in Part XII, 'This is all you ever wanted'.)

The Future of Innovation is Through a Technology Manager's Lens

Name	**Olivier Fleurot, PhD**
Affiliation	Mars Petcare
Position	Technology Director
Country	Germany
Area	Technology management
Email	Olivier.Fleurot@eu.effem.com

**disruptive innovation   technology management   science & technology
technology roadmapping   intellectual property**

The future of innovation will require organisations to find the optimum balance of effort between short-term needs for market successes supporting top/bottom line growth and longer-term ambitions to develop new technologies unlocking sustainable competitive advantage.

Innovation will still rely on translating business-relevant consumer needs into efficient product executions. However, bringing successful products to markets will become more challenging due to intensifying competitive pressures and need for shorter development times, combined with increasing cost, price and sustainability concerns. In this context, market winners will be those organisations that possess talented professionals, capabilities and processes to:

1. anticipate future consumer needs earlier than their competitors,

2. be most adaptive to rapidly changing business environments,

3. leverage science and technology available internally as well as externally to access best-in-class know-how and accelerate development times, and

4. leverage global scale to derive competitive advantage in local markets via tailored and speedy execution.

Successful companies will also adopt long term perspectives on science and technology, in full alignment with their strategic business agenda. This will enable them to devote time and resource to develop solutions to anticipated and key unmet consumer needs that cannot currently be met. A robust translation of a company's business and innovation strategies into its technology strategy component will be key to identifying as early as possible where science and technology efforts should focus as well as to building a sound intellectual property strategy. Technology roadmapping will greatly help build necessary programs (resource required, timeframes to deliveries, fit with strategy, etc.), identify internal technology gaps and external opportunities and ultimately ensure alignment between the science and technology programme and the innovation strategy.

The ability to secure intellectual property will provide sustainable competitive advantage when a disruptive technology offers an efficient breakthrough to unlock delivery of a new and relevant consumer benefit. To seek early access to such technologies and fast-track routes to market, companies will strengthen their open-innovation capabilities to build on external know-how and create win–win opportunities where benefits of market successes are shared. When existing technologies are capable of delivering new consumer expectations, operational efficiency and speed to market will be key drivers of market success.

Last but not least, talented and engaged professionals will be at the heart of the future of innovation, from identifying insights to unlocking technology hurdles and creatively and efficiently developing and manufacturing quality products. This will require a careful management of team compositions to foster cultural and technical diversity, and access a large pallet of cross-functional skills within teams. As the competitive demands for experienced professionals will continue to increase, attracting and retaining top talent will remain the most powerful enabler of success.

Have you noticed the emphasis on, and attribution of importance to, the alignment of business strategy, innovations strategy and technology strategy? Which then needs to correspond and responds to unmet consumer needs?

Comparison – is there anything else that can help us better understand the things? Tom Lewis Reynier, as Olivier Fleurot, focuses on consumer products, but from a charity fundraising perspective. In Tom's experience innovating charity products is 'a much tougher exercise'. Let us hear what he says and then compare his insights with those from the FMCG industry.

Industry – Charity

In this section we have already touched the innovation process in health care and learnt from Lynne and Helen that health services in the UK draw on insights and experiences from outside their industry. Did you know that charities are and will increasingly be using techniques such as crowdsourcing?

Tom assures that 'charities can provide what a lot of consumer products cannot and this is a sense of purpose, an undeniably meaningful impact. A life-changing opportunity'. We argue that 'a life-changing opportunity', is an innovation mission for many, if not all the industries. We all want to change our lives for better. As Arvind Srivastava, in Part IV 'The good, the bad and the ugly' eloquently explained it: 'The future of innovation ... it is our perpetual desire to become Good – Better – Best!'. What is best for charity can be best for health care, too. Let's see how.

The Future of Innovation is Charity Fundraising

Name	**Tom Lewis Reynier**
Affiliation	Charity Fundraising Consultant
Position	Fundraising Innovation Consultant
Country	UK
Area	Innovation management
Email	tomlewisreynier@hotmail.com

charity   fundraising   innovation   donor   communication

We still don't have a cure for cancer. Warfare pockmarks the globe and environmental catastrophes strike with increasing regularity. Now more than ever there's a need for charities, and charities need money to help those who can't help themselves. The challenge for fundraising in these charities is to innovate the propositions they take to their donors and to increase the share of wallet they can command. In this sense it's the same story as with consumer brands. Be relevant. Build loyalty. Increase market share. The purpose of innovation within this process is to develop new propositions or 'asks' that the charity can approach its donors with that generate this increase in revenue. These are a charity's fundraising 'products'.

But the difference between a consumer product and a charity's product is that you don't really *need* the charity product. It's not like toothpaste or 4X4 cars which are well established in the popular consumer psyche as conventional product categories. Charities are essentially trying to invent products that grab your attention from a standing start, with no historical equity in a product category. Consequently the innovation process tends to be more radical and less incremental than it is with the sorts of products you see in supermarkets and this is a much tougher exercise because there are fewer reference points.

But there's also an opportunity here for charities to have a real conversation with their donors. Charities have stories to tell. These stories are incredibly powerful. They can be compelling too, because they can be about how you as a donor can make a difference to change people's lives – and this is an opportunity that you don't get in a supermarket.

Donors like this because they feel engaged and empowered. They feel that they are having a positive impact. They like to have this impact measured and communicated to them so they feel good about what their money is doing. Charities can provide what a lot of consumer products cannot and this is a sense of purpose, an undeniably meaningful impact. A life-changing opportunity.

The boldest charities are taking up this challenge by welcoming donors in and giving them the opportunity to define the ways that they get involved – to spend their own money in the ways they want to spend it. Products can be developed through an innovation process that collaborates with the donor – builds communities of donors, networks people with similar values and interests, informs them and then allows them to customise the products they invest in. It's a form of open innovation delivered using the Web 2.0 tools of social networking and taking a pinch of mass customisation. The boldest charities are and will increasingly be using techniques such as crowdsourcing to plug their supporters directly into their work. Hopefully this will lead to a place where the product development and marketing expertise of the supermarket shelf will combine with the opportunity a charity brings to fulfil the consumer.

Storytelling, have we not heard about it before? Anne-Katrin Neyer, in Part X, 'Let's get together', emphasised its role in innovation. Here Tom outlines that charities have stories to tell, and that this represents an opportunity that you don't get in a supermarket. We would like to turn this around and ask: how can supermarkets benefit from telling their powerful and compelling stories? Might storytelling represent an opportunity for SMEs, too? As you might have guessed, we are moving on to another set of lenses, that of small and medium-sized enterprises, to explore the future of innovation from their angle, their perspective, their experience and their insights.

SMEs

Mridula Gungaphul provides an overview of the role of innovation in SMEs and, at first glance, does not seem to bring much new to the discussion. However, her realisation that even under the financial impediments often experienced by SMEs innovation is the only mean for survival, is crucial. Thus, we start the discussion on the future of innovation in SMEs with the sad understanding that innovation will either help us to live longer (one extreme) – or die sooner (another extreme).

Innovate or die – how many times we have heard this warning? Now we have to make it a reality, a daily routine, a life source, a set of exercises for an SME's muscles. SMEs, are you ready to re-examine your processes, people, culture, systems, technology and relationships with customers and stakeholders and think of innovation as a lifestyle? Please don't panic: have no worries, there are some insights in store for you, at hand, in this very book.

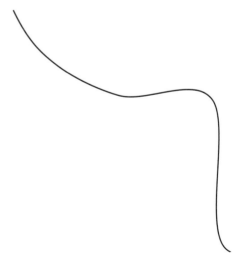

The Future of Innovation is in the Context of SMEs

Name	**Mridula Gungaphul**
Affiliation	University of Mauritius
Position	Senior Lecturer
Country	Mauritius
Area	Innovation and SMEs
Email	m.gungaphul@uom.ac.mu

innovation   SMEs   success   competitive   technology

One has to be able to adapt to a rapidly changing environment to be competitive and gain competitive advantage in a market. In a world that is changing faster than most of us could ever have imagined, creativity and innovation are vital to a company's success and survival. However, although innovation is commonly linked to technology it is not always only about technology. It is about new or modified ways of thinking and doing things, new or modified products, new experiences, new events, new or modified services, new brands etc. Thus, innovation is so pervasive in our day-to-day life, that it drives the way we live and interact with society and the environment in general. Innovation helps us to live longer (one extreme) or die sooner (another extreme).

Innovation is not only just for large organisations but also concerns small and medium firms as globalisation is affecting all businesses irrespective of size, sector of activities etc. In fact, innovation plays a very central role in the survival, success and growth of small and medium enterprises (SMEs). SMEs are recognised as the 'life blood' of modern economies and they are a major source of employment, wealth generation and poverty alleviation amongst other factors. Governments worldwide rely to a large extent on their local SMEs and are placing much emphasis on developing support systems to nurture these small businesses perhaps more so than large businesses. In fact, innovation often lies at the heart of small business's ability to compete successfully with their larger rivals. With increasing market pressure and fragmentation SMEs have no other option but to adopt the philosophy of continuous innovation. To develop, achieve and maintain competitiveness SMEs must re-examine its processes, people, culture, systems, technology, relationships with customers and stakeholders, etc. In doing things differently and in adopting innovative practices, these create added value to the offering and in turn influence profit and performance. The future of SMEs relies on innovation for a number of reasons. SMEs may not have the choice but to innovate to respond to innovation by competitors. They may also have to innovate to prevent competitors harming their own business. It may also simply be because they want to commercialise a new technology to take the lead before a competitor.

However, it may not be at all easy for SMEs to innovate as they have certain constraints. Their main obstacle is finance. Many of them operate on a low profit margin and may not have much to spend to develop innovative products, processes or practices. So what is the future of innovation in these SMEs? Simply, it is 'innovate or die'. However hard if may be, SMEs should develop a culture which encourages innovation and employees should also be involved in all innovative practices to ensure commitment. Businesses which are recognised as innovative in all sense of the word, ensure customer loyalty.

In today's highly competitive environment SMEs have to acknowledge that, *innovation is the future*!

Jose Albors-Garrigós observes four major challenges that are rather helpful to grasp and perceive 'a new era, where we must think creatively of new innovation paradigms, scenarios, products, sustainability'. Some challenges like, open innovation, can be converted into a strong advantage if we use it properly. Even in this chapter, with Scott Larkin, we have called for an already classic example of InnoCentive when open innovation paradigm is used as a business model. Let us change our mindset and think of challenges in terms of opportunities, a combination of circumstances favourable for the purpose, good chance or occasion to advance oneself – an opening rather than a closing circumstance. We come back to that with Ann Ledwith, right after Jose and his observations.

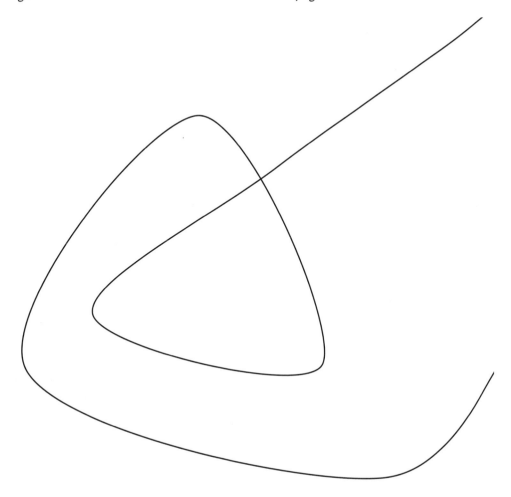

The Future of Innovation is its Challenges and Intermediate Regions

Name	**Jose Albors-Garrigós**
Affiliation	Universidad Politecnica de Valencia
Position	Professor
Country	Spain
Area	Technology and innovation management
Email	jalbors@doe.upv.es

innovation dynamism   SMEs   absorpotion capacity   innovation management
intermediate regions

The views I will share with the reader in this brief note must be considered in a context: that of an intermediate region or country in a critical moment a deep economic crisis that has challenged the economic growth paradigm of Spain.

From my point of view, and centred on the above context, the future of innovation is based on four basic challenges. The first is, how can we truly upgrade the innovative dynamism of the service industry, which is composed of a large mass of SMEs and of micro enterprises. Clearly, and based on our research, the new innovation paradigms such as open innovation, networks, clusters etc. will play a relevant role alongside the involvement and commitment of knowledge centres (universities, regional technology centres or RTCs) in their activities. Moreover, absorption capacity of these firms will have to be improved. A second challenge is to deal with traditional industry, which has lost its leadership as a consequence of global economic change. Here, innovation is to do with repositioning in the value chain, being able to create value (design, services, branding, etc.) for the final customer. KIS (Knowledge Intensive Services) has proved to be a good catalyser. A third challenge is innovation in management. According to a bestseller recently published,[1] the future of management is an unexplored area from the innovation point of view, and here in Spain, companies such as Zara[2] or Irizar[3] are very good examples of what can be achieved. Finally, a fourth challenge is that services are linked to leisure activities, such as hospitality, tourism, travelling or cooking, and thus so is innovation in services. The advantage here is the peculiarity of leisure's added value potential in relation to health, growth or environment.

However, the main lessons we can learn from the actual economic situation are that we are now confronting a new era, where we must think creatively of new innovation paradigms, scenarios, products, sustainability, etc. Many sectors, in spite of their innovative drive, are still anchored in old thinking models which date back to the beginning of the 20th century and the automobile

1   Bill Breen and Gary Hamel (2007) *The Future of Management* (Harvard Business School Press).

2   See Pankaj Chemawat and Jose Luis Nueno (2003), *ZARA: Fast Fashion (Multimedia Case)* (Harvard Business Publishing, 23 June 2003).

3   See Ramon Casadesus-Masanell and Jordan Mitchell (2006), *Irizar in 2005* (Harvard Business Publishing, available as pdf, 15 March 2006).

industry is a good example of this. Others face dramatic strategic changes where new competitors may appear in the industry and the aerospace industry may serve as a good illustration of this.

Ann Ledwith is here to help you with the opportunities available to the services industry; read on to find out what she has to say.

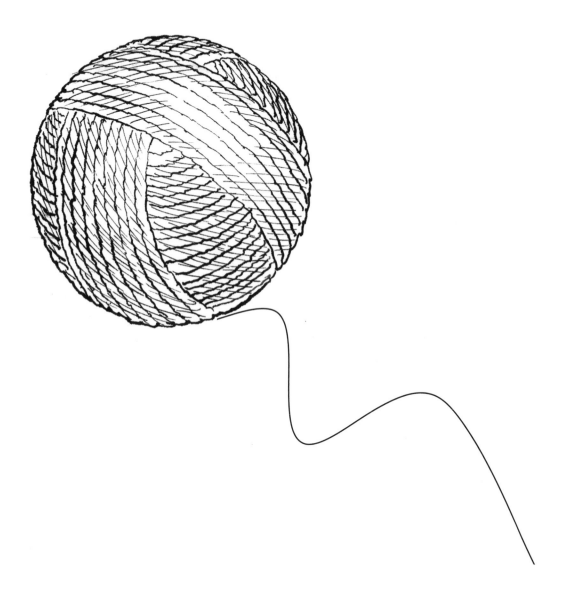

The Future of Innovation is SMEs in Global Niches

Name	**Ann Ledwith**
Affiliation	Enterprise Research Centre, University of Limerick
Position	Lecturer
Country	Ireland
Area	Innovation in SMEs
Email	ann.ledwith@ul.ie

SMEs   small firms   niche markets   global markets   innovation

The future of innovation in small and medium-sized enterprises (SMEs) will depend on their ability to identify opportunities and build key relationships within global supply chains. There are two main forces driving innovation in SMEs. The first is the opportunity offered by the internet and related technologies. SMEs are renowned for working closely with customers, for their flexibility, for adapting their products to satisfy specific customer needs and for their 'can do' approach. Traditionally many small firms have relied on local customers. While larger firms have had the resources to set up international sales and distribution networks the cost of expanding into international markets has been prohibitive for SMEs. But technology, and specifically the internet, has changed this situation. Compared to other forms of promotion, advertising on the internet is cheap – communication with customers and suppliers is easy. SMEs can identify potential customers in any location, multimedia communication can be used to determine customer needs, customer support can be offered online. We have been aware of the power of the internet for several years, but SMEs are not yet fully exploiting this opportunity. A recent survey revealed that fewer than 10 per cent of SMEs are using the internet as a tool for innovation. Small firms who think about innovation in a global context will be the future success stories.

The second force driving the future of innovation in SMEs is the complexity of the technology embedded in most of today's new products. There was a time when an individual could 'invent' a new product: think of Alexander Graham Bell and the telephone, and then think of the number of people involved in developing the latest mobile technology at Nokia. Because of increasing complexity, technical breakthroughs are achieved mainly by teams not individuals. Most SMEs no longer have the resources to develop new products, particularly technology-based products, and to successfully deliver them to the marketplace. To innovate successfully SMEs need to develop relationships and partnerships with larger organisations. They need the skills to identify opportunities and to build the relationships required to exploit these opportunities.

SMEs have always operated within niches; they have developed products that satisfy specific customer needs. Where large firms develop new products to exploit new markets, small firms develop new products to satisfy customer needs. However to survive into the future SMEs will need to innovate within global markets. They must learn to think more strategically about the products that they release and to understand their unique position within the supply chain. But in doing this they must not lose their traditional strengths. Buying from a smaller firm involves a higher risk; customers choose SMEs to supply those products that they cannot buy from larger firms or because of the high levels of customisation and customer care provided by SMEs. SMEs need to continue to offer these benefits.

In summary, the future of innovation in SMEs depends on their ability to retain their traditional strengths but within global internet-enabled markets and supply chains.

We are aware that neither internet nor global markets are new to you; but we wonder how seriously you have thought about them as a driving force. Have you realised that 'fewer than 10 per cent of SMEs are using the internet as a tool for innovation'? Have you ever considered the global market as one whole big playing field? You may well be local oriented, but you can still use lateral thinking to contemplate the opportunities that arise from the internet and the global community it creates. If you have not done it yet, now is the time!

Michele O'Dwyer explores the competitive landscape for SMEs and proposes three types of strategies that should help SMEs to survive in the big wide world.

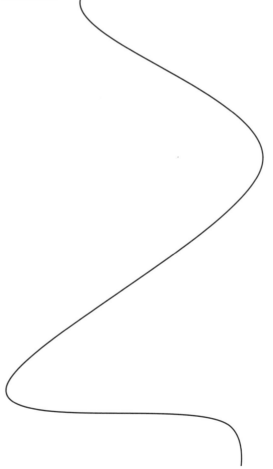

The Future of Innovation is David and Goliath: Integrating Innovation to Build for the Future

Name	**Michele O'Dwyer**
Affiliation	University of Limerick
Position	Lecturer in Entrepreneurship
Country	Ireland
Area	Innovation management
Email	michele.odwyer@ul.ie

**SMEs   competitive advantage   strategic alliances   organisational performance
innovation integration**

Small and medium enterprises (SMEs) face a dynamic environment which challenges their survival. Although large and multinational companies (MNCs) face the same challenges, their resource base cocoons them against the harshest of realities. However, looking to the future, it is this very lack of resources that will force SMEs to be more innovative than larger firms in products services, processes and business models.

These innovations will stem from SMEs having to overcome resource limitations to manage a contradictory relationship with larger firms, firms who in some instances are their customers and in other instances are their competitors. In order to compete with and/or sell to, larger firms, SMEs need to address three key issues: keeping up with the Joneses, Trojan horses and daisy chains.

1. **Keeping up with the Joneses:** Many SMEs attempt to emulate larger firms thereby 'keeping up with the Joneses', however, the systems and approaches used by larger firms were developed to suit larger firms, and literature has established that SMEs are not small large firms. Instead of accepting and adopting these systems and approaches, SMEs need to focus on identifying those aspects of their business which have a direct and proven impact on their performance – keeping them lean and agile. Once these key success factors have been identified SMEs need to innovate to maximise competitive advantage. This integration of innovation across all aspects of the SME will result in more successful new products and services being developed, more efficient processes being implemented and more effective business models being adopted.

2. **The Trojan horses:** Larger firms take a risk when they buy from an SME without a recognised international brand name. In order to reduce the purchase risk to their large-firm customers, SMEs need to mimic a 'Trojan horse'; instead of presenting themselves as a sales-orientated firm interested in an asymmetrical relationship with the larger firm, the SME needs to engage in bilateral relationships, integrating itself into its large firm customers. In adopting this 'corporate lego' approach the SME embeds itself in the larger firms' innovation processes, helping it to cultivate new products and services, while suggesting process and business model modifications which would make both the SME and its large-firm customer more competitive.

3. **Daisy chains:** To help SMEs compete with larger firms, SMEs need to explore more innovative company structures to make themselves appear to a bigger company then they are. One such structural

option would be to form a 'daisy chain', that is, a series of strategic alliances linking SMEs with similar size companies (e.g., key suppliers/distributors/customers/competitors). Such alliances would provide economies of scale, helping to combat the inequities posed by an SME competing with larger organisations for supplies and sales. In addition, the new perceived organisational size would reduce the perceived purchase risk for larger firms buying from SMEs.

Addressing these three issues around the large/small firm relationship will result in unusual and unique solutions and propositions, which in future will generate dynamic performance-oriented SMEs embedded in symbiotic relationships with larger firms.

Don't you just love the language Michele is using? Have you got a shared language around innovation in your organisation? And is it as descriptive and engaging as the language Michele has just been using? Or is it rather formal and technical? And what kind of language do you think is more engaging and inspiring and will help to create stories that will keep the spirit of innovation alive?

Dennis Farrell will close this part by giving us his view on the SMEs subject from the South African and other developing nations' perspective. As one of the solutions for creating a fertile ground for SMEs Dennis suggests to focus on the Work Life Renewal model.

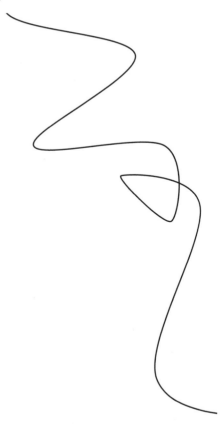

The Future of Innovation is Transforming Communities

Name	**Dennis Farrell**
Affiliation	Alfa and Omega Networked Business Solutions
Position	Managing Director
Country	South Africa
Area	Strategic HR management/small business development
Email	dennis@alfaandomega.co.za

transformation communities human resources SMEs

Transformational reform in the South African and other developing nations is an important business and social imperative to ensure those communities and ultimately the country is stable and sustainable.

Rapid changes in world economies have created new challenges for organisations. Privatisation processes are an attempt by governments to open markets to competition, create globally competitive industries and in this process hopefully attract foreign direct investment and a transfer of skills and knowledge from developed countries. However, these processes are not without consequences – both good and bad. The business enterprise if well managed can become more efficient and competitive. For the individual – this could mean retrenchment, a period of uncertainty and possibly job loss. These change processes are often very sensitive and outcomes are highly dependent on the management of the process, particularly human resources. Part of this process will mean that organisations will also have to communicate and manage a paradigm shift in the way people perform their work and their expectations in terms of alternative career paths. This implies a formal, structured, integrated 'post-employment' process of building support and consensus through effective communications, training, management of stakeholders and motivation.

Such a 'post-employment process' or human resource exit strategy is not a 'financial handout' but rather an investment in the promotion of an entrepreneurial economy founded in economically sustainable small and medium size enterprises (SMEs). Due to the high unemployment rate in the South African scenario, SMEs are of critical importance in the alleviation of poverty, socioeconomic 'upliftment', job creation and the promotion of political stability. In order to narrow the gap between expectations (often emotionally and ideologically orientated) and socioeconomic realities, little doubt remains that SME development founded in sustainable entrepreneurship ventures (business, environmental and social entrepreneurship) is of critical importance in the prevention of a 'revolution within a revolution' in South Africa.

The Work Life Renewal Model is proposed as one of the solutions for creating sustainable SMEs through the integration of skilled and qualified people who either through retrenchments, transformational reforms, political flight and other factors become economically sidelined and retreat into their own worlds to become partners with developing societies and/or individuals by utilising their skills and knowledge in the establishment of sustainable SMEs.

The Work Life Renewal model therefore suggests that organisations should consider supporting the development of SMEs through utilising 'redundant staff' with their skills base to become entrepreneurial Ad-mentors for SMEs. This would support and lead to:

- Higher levels of efficiency in organisations and SME development.

- A better integrated use of resources and capital, including human capital.

- A core strategic focus emphasis that is the top level 'drive' with the organisation for areas such as HR.

- True business partnering models, which will address operational excellence.

- Leverage outsourcing excellence to minimise operational cost growth for the organisation.

- The creation of affordable funding opportunities for the creation of SMEs.

The foreseen deliverables or outputs of the Work Life Renewal Model are illustrated in Figure 4.

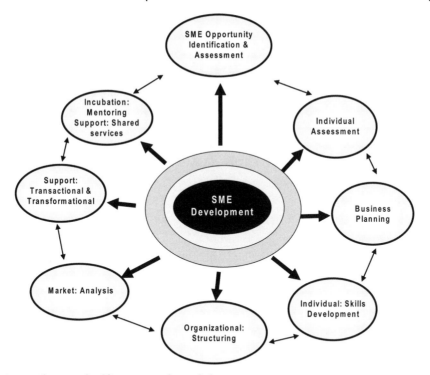

Figure 4   The Work Life Renewal model

What lessons can you draw from the Work Life Renewal Model? How could it help in your economy, today, and what could you do to help facilitate it?

So far we have taking a glimpse at the future of innovation in the fields of energy, chemistry, telecom, services, insurance, health care, TV, FMCG, charity and SMEs. A wish list and provocations for business, consultancy, academics, policy makers, endless and diverse. Yet there is still more to come! We felt that our picture was not complete without offering some national perspectives. At many levels nations are coming together as a global village, yet at others nations retain their specific outlook and personality. What are the implications for the future of innovation? How does the perspective on the future of innovation vary, depending on national context? Read on! The next session offers plenty examples of the many different perspectives and views we received.

Geographic Perspectives

Our geography section of the book is the most colourful with its different flags, nations, countries. We are gaining insights into perspectives on the future of innovation in Romania, Nigeria, Barbados, Mauritius, Japan, Egypt, South Africa, Denmark, China, Taiwan, Malaysia, Brazil, Mexico, Ireland, Spain and the USA. The international journey commences with the outline of agenda for today, tomorrow and the day after tomorrow in the global village.

Jaideep Prabhu starts our journey from the Cambridge of 2009 to the BRIC countries, Brazil, Russia, China and India, of the year 2030. We encourage you to take the window seat from where it will be best to see the potential of the large number of people who are considered 'economic unworthy' by so many. Let us start the engine. We are sure you will enjoy the stopovers where it will be explained to us what kind of innovation is likely to pay off handsomely, and how, finally, we might have one world, united by one set of economic values and benefits. Fasten your seat belts and off we go.

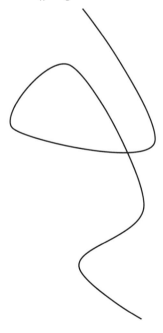

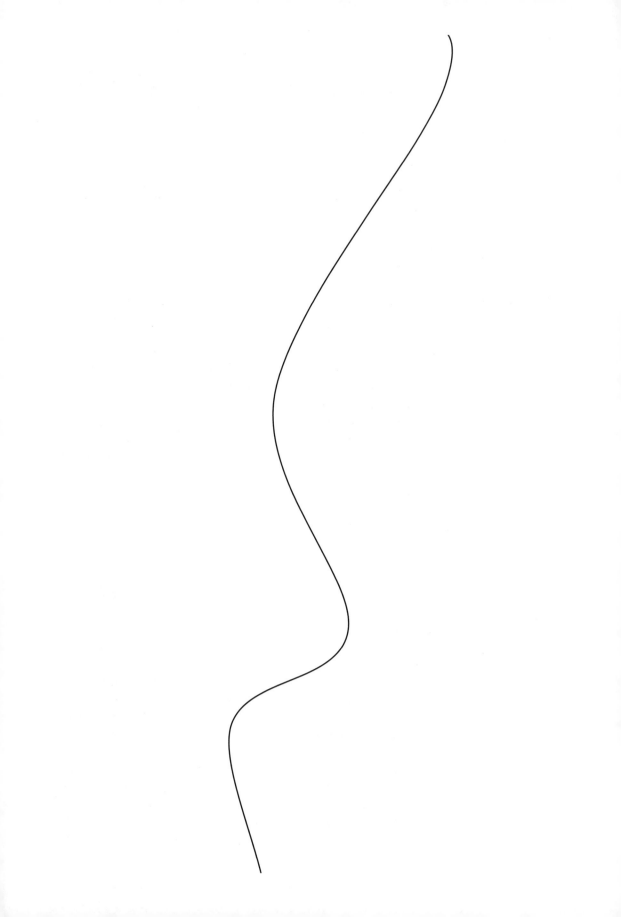

The Future of Innovation is at the Bottom of the Pyramid

Name	**Jaideep Prabhu**
Affiliation	Judge Business School, University of Cambridge
Position	Jawaharlal Nehru Professor of Indian Business and Enterprise
Country	UK
Area	Product/service/business model innovation
Email	j.prabhu@jbs.cam.ac.uk

innovation   future   emerging markets   bottom of the pyramid   global

The future of innovation lies in emerging markets and in the so-called bottom of the socioeconomic pyramid. Emerging markets such as Brazil, Russia, China and India increasingly account for a large part of global economic activity; by some estimates these markets will dominate the world economy by 2030. The so-called bottom of the socioeconomic pyramid – roughly speaking, those who live on less than US$2 a day – accounts for a little over half the global population today: that is about 3.3 billion people in all. A majority of these people live in emerging markets.

So far, technological progress and the consumer revolution have largely passed these people by. Even domestic firms in emerging markets have ignored this large segment in their home countries, preferring to focus on the urban rich and the growing middle class. But this trend will soon change. There is an increasing realisation that these masses of people are not a lost economic cause, but a huge source of opportunity for the future. Embracing them and bringing them within the ambit of the contemporary market system offers huge opportunities for firms, governments and the people themselves.

However, reaching these people and bringing them within the ambit of the global system will not be simple. In fact, it will require considerable innovation, and this innovation will often though not always require the use of new technology. What this innovation will certainly require, however, is designing new products and services around the special needs and lifestyles of the poor. Most importantly, such innovation will have to find ways to radically reduce costs. Consequently, the big challenge for firms will more often than not involve rethinking existing business models entirely; specifically, it will require radically overhauling the existing cost structures around which businesses operate.

This will not be easy. It will require the investment of significant amounts of time, money and labour. But this innovation will pay off handsomely. Not only will it bring the fruits of progress to a large part of the world that is currently denied this, but it will also potentially offer new products and services, at knock-down prices, for consumers in the rich world. If this form of innovation is truly successful, we might, for the first time in human history have one world, united by one set of economic values and benefits. The old ideal of justice for all, at least in an economic sense, may finally be within reach. The future of innovation promises to be exciting indeed. We cannot afford to have it fail.

A fortune at the bottom of the pyramid. Had you come across that before? We guess that many of you will have come across C.K. Prahalad's book of the same title!

Most interestingly, Daniel Arias-Aranda too devotes his contribution on the future of innovation to those living on less than €2 per day. He goes deeper, recognising that corruption is a – if not the – major impediment to reducing poverty via innovation. To diminish inertia in developing countries, concerted international governmental actions will be necessary.

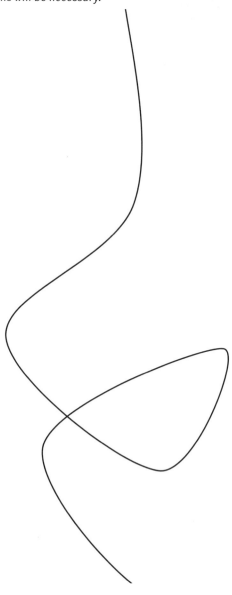

The Future of Innovation is Low-income Targets

Name	**Daniel Arias-Aranda**
Affiliation	Universidad de Granada
Position	Associate Professor
Country	Spain
Area	Innovation management
Email	darias@ugr.es

**low income targets   Third world countries   radical and incremental innovations
information and communications technologies**

The future of innovation is tightly linked to the development of products, services and processes focused on low-income population targets. Nowadays, only a small percentage of the world's inhabitants experience any kind of influence on their lives derived from innovation efforts developed within private or public institutions. However, there is a huge market potential regarding people living with less than €2 per day (in fact they represent more than half of the whole population of this planet). Innovations such are microcredits are already improving living conditions for many of these people. Once they reach an economic level higher than just surviving, they will turn into potential consumers.

Only one obstacle lies in from of the innovation path to decrease poverty: corruption. Corruption kills incentives for people to start initiatives to improve their quality of life. The simple rule of 'present sacrifices lead to future enhancements' is destroyed when corruption takes place. Similar innovation policies work in low-corruption regions or countries while they completely fail in highly corrupted zones. The innovation process itself works under the previous rule. If the individual perceives that the benefits of his/her present sacrifices will go to corrupted pockets, he/she just will not make that effort. International governmental actions will be required to diminish corruption in developing countries.

The generalisation of new information and communication technologies (ICTs) for lower-income populations will accelerate the innovation evolution in third world countries. The innovation process requires high degrees of interrelationship. Most of the poorest communities around the world are located in either isolated or excommunicated zones. Some of them may live near big cities; however, the access of these people to information is very limited. When this barrier lowers, creativity will start to flow as people will be able to apply the acquired knowledge to solve local problems. After that, the innovation effect will grow exponentially improving people's life conditions. Education and health care as the basics to establish a minimum life standard will be achieved in a short time as ICTs will spread the needed knowledge all over the different communities.

Hence, microfinance and ICTs are the two crucial factors for future innovation policy. And yes, it is possible. And it is profitable not only in social but also in economic terms. It is good for the people and good for the firms. Innovation opportunities are hidden behind market niches represented by low-income people which have not still been discovered.

We quite like the idea of microcredits as a way of 'the man on the street' – woman more likely – circumventing corrupt government and banks by creating their own, direct banking system! Have you not heard the story where mobile phones are used to transfer money from island to island, even from country to country? And yet again the importance of ICT as equaliser in the information flow, as well as driver and enabler of innovation.

If corruption and an unequal distribution of information are Daniel's key concerns Paulo Benetti brings us back to yet another highly critical topic and potential obstacles to a bright future of innovation in developing countries: education. Echoing Daniel he too doubts the future of innovation, due to the same reasons, namely corruption, poor education, and a lack of an innovation-friendly environment. Paulo is our tour guide for Brazil, Mexico and Guatemala.

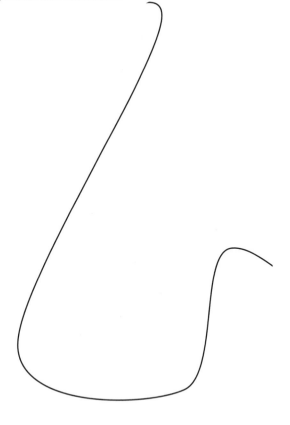

The Future of Innovation is Paying More Attention to Poor Countries!

Name	**Paulo Benetti**
Affiliation	Inteligência Natural Consultoria
Position	Director
Country	Brazil
Area	Creativity, innovation, strategies and project management
Email	benetti@benetti.com.br

poor countries   sadness   low education   educational revolution   brighter future

It would be much more fascinating to write about the future of innovation in technology or the opportunities for innovation in the development of new markets or corporate partnerships. But I live in Brazil, a country where innovation is as yet an unexplored and underdeveloped concept. Even though I have worked in highly developed countries where innovation is on the agenda, I intend to express my opinion and concern for the future taking Brazil, Mexico and Guatemala as examples, for these are countries I know well.

As the world develops and sets new knowledge development as the most important differentiation strategy for companies and nations, it is with sadness that I see how Latin American countries fail to keep pace with the most advanced ones.

We know of the importance of the environment in fostering creativity and innovation. Latin American countries fail to create, in the short term, an innovation-friendly environment. Unfortunately, corruption has become big business in these countries.

Education is not stimulated or valued. And corruption thrives under such conditions. Families are more concerned that their children get a degree. It does not really matter whether they learn or not. Teaching is so poor that it is difficult to acquire new knowledge and to use existing knowledge in different ways.

These countries are lagging behind in comparison with countries where innovation is acknowledged and stimulated. They can do very little and in few niches. Brazil, for example, is renowned for its innovative advances in agriculture and has specialised in it. But this field is no longer labour intensive. One wonders how it is possible to insert 60 million miserables and many more poor people in the consumer market.

What is the future of innovation in these countries? If an educational revolution is not started there, their future will be lost. We can quote Darwin here and say: only the fittest will survive. How can these countries reverse this scenario and adapt to the new world order?

All that is left for small and limited countries like Guatemala is to advance in the creative industry field.

México will have to overcome its dependence on oil and the dollars that are sent home by those of its citizens who have migrated to the US.

Brazil will need to overcome the belief that commodities are good business. Its multicultural society may prove to be its best asset in fostering growth.

So I repeat the question: what is the future of innovation? Developed countries may discuss their options, but the discussion elsewhere will have to dig deeper. I may not know how to describe the required scenario, but I may describe the desired one. I wish we can innovate in the political field and manage to build real nations that can show us a brighter future.

If Paulo Benetti only mentions differences in innovation agenda of highly developed countries and Latin America, Will Pugh focuses on country-of-origin effects. Again, most wonderfully, we will be able to follow Will's mention of Unilever's investment in India with an Indian case study from Mehmood Khan, who is from Unilever.

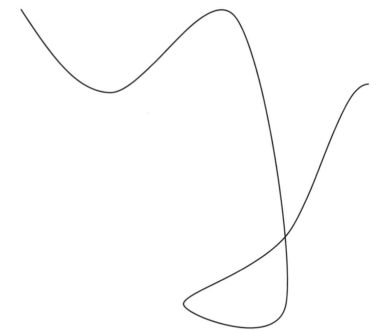

The Future of Innovation is 1709 and all that

Name	**Will Pugh**
Affiliation	Willpower Brands Ltd
Position	Innovation Coach
Country	UK
Area	Innovation management
Email	Will@WillpowerBrands.com

brands   marketing   growth   culture   value

Innovation is often linked to optimism and for some it is very hard to be optimistic at a time of slumping economic output and daily news of job losses. However, the current economic downturn actually offers huge opportunities for those prepared to take a long view. Innovation in adversity can often result in considerable improvements when good times return – look at the civilian application of military technology after the Second World War which led to the huge prosperity growth of the 1950s and 1960s.

Taking a step back to look at the big picture of economic development, we see that the economies of India and China were the largest economies in the world in 1709. 300 years later, they are returning to their pre-eminence. Alongside Brazil and Russia, these countries will have a growing impact on the way that innovation is managed. Innovation processes have come from the West, particularly the US. These processes are imbued with the characteristics of Western, particularly Anglo-Saxon, culture. Now that both India and China have embraced much of Western capitalism, what can the rest of the world learn from them?

It is no coincidence that Unilever, one of the most globally orientated multinational innovators, has recently invested considerable amounts in R&D facilities in both India and China. China and India are both collectivist societies. This is a big contrast to the individualist tendencies in Anglo Saxon economies. Hierarchy is a notable characteristic of both. Both have diaspora that command significant investing power and commercial know-how. Indians have made many investments both in high-technology areas like Silicon Valley and the automotive industry (Land Rover and Jaguar)[1] and steel (Mittal), as well as consumer goods (Typhoo, Lornamead). For China, much of the recent investment and subsequent innovation has come from wealthy Chinese living in Taiwan, Singapore and the West, while much of Africa has felt the strong pull of Chinese need for raw materials. To take one example of how Chinese cultural attitudes affect innovation differs can be seen in the way that there is more focus on corporate values (Haier or Lenovo) rather than the specific brand characteristics. The individualist culture of the West emphasises single brands but the collectivist nature of China means that consumers think about the company. In India and Bangladesh, IT and

---

1   Editors' note: please see Part III, 'Innovation – but not as we know it', for insights on the future of innovation from Al Saje from Jaguar and Land Rover, UK.

microfinance innovation has allowed women to make a much greater contribution to their local economies in spite of cultural norms.

What this means for innovation, whether specific innovation or innovation management, is that the future winners will be those who are able to build an understanding of the very different cultural norms in India and China to achieve success.

Finally, a sense of how these cultures might need different perspective in innovation comes in two quotes:

'You should be the change that you want to see in the world.'

Mahatma Gandhi

'Give a man a fish and you feed him for a day. Teach him how to fish and you feed him for a lifetime'.

Chinese proverb

Do you remember us quoting Gandhi earlier? We have said it before and will say it again: you have to be the change you want to see in the world.

Mehmood Khan takes us to northern India, reporting on the changes a single company can achieve, having set itself some aspirational innovation goals. If you take notes, here is another one for your collection: 'If you educate one girl, you educate a family.' Has that ever occurred to you?

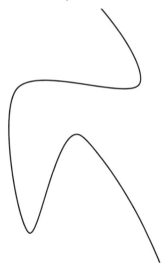

The Future of Innovation is Collaboration and Co-creation

Name	**Mehmood Khan**
Affiliation	Unilever
Position	Global Leader of Innovation PD
Country	UK
Area	Innovation
Email	Mehmood.khan@unilever.com

collaboration   co-occurring   imagination   experimentation
sustainable value creation   India

Collaboration, co-creation, villages as sources of growth, nurturing female power and leveraging global networks are key for global growth.

There are circa 6.7 billion people on planet earth and about 70 millions are added every year.

Various projections show that we will have about 9–10 billion people in total in next 30–40 years after which the population will stabilise or will start decreasing.

Taking India as an example 70 per cent of the population lives in villages and majority of the population growth is happening in villages.

Mewat is a region in north India in which the Meo community has lived for ages. 50 per cent of people live below poverty line. The literacy rate in 2003 was 23 per cent, compared with 65 per cent for the country as whole. The literacy rate among girls was only 2 per cent.

With the help of organisations from voluntary, corporate and government bodies, I initiated an experiment in Mewat. A stakeholder meeting confirmed the following priorities of the people:

- education;

- unemployment;

- health and hygiene;

- water.

We developed an action plan in which more than 80 per cent of the actions were taken by villagers themselves. The state system also responded by appointing 5,000 teachers, to provide one teacher for every 40 students who joined the schools. Now 85 per cent of children of the aged 6–14 are going to school. Quality is still an issue but this will be addressed as we continue on our journey.

The corporate sector responded positively as well: Unilever's company on the ground (HUL) started the Shakti Project through which Unilever has facilitated the training and appointment of 45 women entrepreneurs, Aviva has appointed 15 insurance agents, L&T has taken on a dozen youths for construction work, GENPACT has contributed computers to start computer literacy, Mother Dairy has opened milk collection plants and ICICI Bank has opened a branch and recruited a full batch of graduates who had just passed the six-month computer and English module.

This experiment is young but what it shows is that the enormous issues our world faces can be addressed by bringing stakeholders together.

The corporate world is recognising the power of collaboration and co-creation but has not got on top of it yet. This experiment is providing space for the corporate world to come and participate in their own way without being put in a straitjacket. They experiment in their own ways. Collectively these companies are benefiting each other and people while helping themselves.

By nature this requires spirit of experimentation to co-create and develop these in to fully fledged viable businesses.

Governments have to learn that future job creation will be with the help of large companies who act as nuclei and then smaller enterprises can be developed as suppliers and customers of these large companies. As the majority of population growth is happening in villages it is in everybody's interest to see these as source of growth and help in building their capability.

As the saying goes, 'If you educate one girl, you educate a family.' In this experiment we have seen the girls in the age range of 14–19 as rapid learners and they have become catalysts of change in the family.

Global Networks have contributed for the success of this experiment and the bottom line is that all stakeholders have benefited in this experiment to grow the pie: villagers' income has increased in some cases as much as 50 per cent within one year; the corporate world has benefited from increased sales or cost-effective procurement opportunities or finding cost-effective talent; unemployment has been reduced as youths are finding work commensurate to their skills.

Not only does Mehmood share a very encouraging and successful story, he also gives other organisations who might want to embark on a similar journey some tips and starting points. Staying on the Indian subcontinent let's hear A.S. Rao who is helping us to understand why China is now the hub for manufacturing and India for software outsourcing and development. As if A.S. had conferred with Paulo and Mehmood, he too ponders on the issue of basic education in India and China. The rather thrilling question he asks is, 'Are Indians and Chinese creative?'

The Future of Innovation is From the Perspective of a Risk-Averse Culture

Name	**A.S. Rao**
Affiliation	Government of India
Position	Adviser
Country	India
Area	Open innovation network
Email	asrao@nic.in

culture value system risk Indian innovation fear of failure China

The future of innovation is inextricably linked to the value system of a society, and Eastern economies might find transferring the routines that underlie the philosophy of Western ethos that drives innovation a daunting task. India and China are large economies, and forecasts of their economic prowess vary from analyst to analyst. These potential competitors to Western innovation systems face a major challenge: how to give their citizens 'freedom to fail'? Risk in innovation has been documented and analysed again and again, the success rate may be one in eight or one in ten, but the fact remains, there are more failures than successes. Economic risk can be underwritten by state but social stigma of failure lingers on, which becomes the major inhibiting factor for innovation-promotion programmes to take off; it cannot be brushed aside as of no consequence.

I see the need for a major shift in the innovation programs of India and China which should focus on transforming the education system to allow children to 'experiment and learn' as opposed to 'teach to learn'. Arresting the fall of the 'creative quotient' due to a premium on logical minds would become a national priority.

When could this happen? India and China have traversed the traditional road map, moving from 'learn to produce' to 'learn to design new products/processes' and have reached a stage where China is considered a major player in mass manufacture, with India being strong in services. Can they cope with the recession without transformation? Unlikely, as both cater to the US market and Fortune 500 companies.

These large developing economies need to introspect and re-engineer their innovation systems – as France is doing, converting high-end research into innovations in a seamless manner, focusing on strategic sectors like aerospace and defence. There is no light at the end of the tunnel for most research work in existing government structures for the simple reason that winners cannot be picked that way – only the market can – and that probability improves with quantity.

To stabilise the innovation system, like a production system or a software program, the nation needs numbers, huge numbers of 'creative minds'. China became the 'global factory' because of a massive infrastructure build-up manned by millions of disciplined workers; the software boom in

India is the result of cumulative investment made by millions of middle-class parents in providing their wards with engineering education.

Are Indians and Chinese creative? Fortunately the percentage of creative minds does not vary from nation to nation, and countries with billions of people have a natural advantage here. India and China do not have to produce creative people by genetic manipulations – all they have to do is ensure the creativity minds are not shut down at a formative age.

This brings us to the basic issue of education, primarily science education, of making science teachers great facilitators of learning. With information and communication technologies, multimedia content, the time is ripe to do away with textbooks. Give them reference books and provide them with platforms to experiment (real or virtual) to keep their curiosity alive. Give them an 'opportunity to fail' and they will pay us back in later life by not failing.

Having listen to A.S.'s argument on creativity and education we start wondering, how does the Western education nurture a tolerance of failure. Well, actually, does it? We don't think so!

Sabri Saidam, having his say from the Occupied Palestinian Territories, looks at the future of innovation through the particular lenses of a conflict. If you ever asked yourself whether conflict could be a mother of innovation, Sabri is here to share his perception.

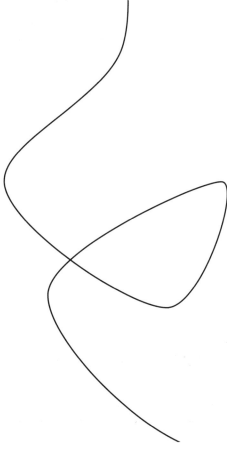

The Future of Innovation is Utilising Hardship

Name	**Sabri Saidam**
Affiliation	Palestinian National Authority
Position	Presidential Advisor
Country	Occupied Palestinian Territories
Area	Social and scientific innovation and ICT for development
Email	s.saidam@gmail.com

ICT   conflict   innovation   creativity   development

In a fast-moving world of constant developments in internet connectivity, science and technology, the global movement towards innovation-blended knowledge building is emerging as a turning point of the intellectual evolution of humankind. Being positively different is the rule that governs humans' innovation race.

Innovation success on the other hand means one should be a leader in introducing different ideas, pioneering constructive change. Yet for a society to succeed in its innovation quest it has to be capable of utilising human knowledge for the engineering of a more prosperous and dignified human life. The society should also collectively utilise human suffering to deploy societal determination in producing better environmental, social, economic and intellectual advancement.

It is certainly true that communities' success in establishing knowledge-based and innovative societies is affected by educational, political, economic and social challenges. It is equally true that aspects of instability exerted by political unrests, wars and conflicts often play a major role in delaying all aspects of development, including e-transformation. Moreover, the emergence and dominance of conflict and poverty often affect local priorities and impose a compulsory move from development to relief with attention given to more pressing issues of concern. Little or no attention and funding are then available for the adoption and introduction of new technologies and innovation, there being the usual scarcity of funds for basic services and infrastructural support. Such decline and lack of governmental control induces a rapid decline in service provision and an evident retardation of societal intellectual capital, giving way to the prevalence of ignorance and extremism which directly feed into the superiority and dominance of conflict.

Conflict is thus the source of pain, loss and severe anxiety. Its existence and prevalence act as major deterrent to individual as well as societal achievements, creativity and most importantly survival.

Conflict to many is, however, a means of inducing survival attempts, plans and policies. It surprisingly can be combined with adaptation mechanisms and possible innovation, and these serve to convert the pressure of conflict into a catalyst for human achievement in defiance of such pressure and consequent devastation.

Innovation should therefore be a tool for survival and life continuity under conflict, poverty and human hardship. Human determination is an asset that should be best invested to facilitate the emergence of more connected societies whose fabric becomes consolidated with communication and access to information as well as the wider dissemination of ICT into citizens' lives, even on the governance level!

Yes, 'need' could well be the mother of innovation! There are living examples from countries around the world of communities that rose out of the ashes. Even communities which were deeply affected by years of wars and disputes made a serious come-back. Therefore, the future of innovation should involve an investment in determination, persistence and the will to live!

Sabri outlines very well the disastrously negative consequences of conflict. Remember in Part VI, where we talked about the role of government and Mario Coccia argued the case that democracy provides the most fertile ground for innovation? And it links to the educational argument; if education fails, if children 'play' war instead of learning to be creative and how to deal with failure, all we do is create a generation of those whose view of the world is black and white, who believe that if I am right you are wrong, and who will not be able to embrace the diversity that is necessary for the kind of innovation we need to secure humankind's future.

Marko Torkkeli continues Sabri's argument and declares that 'in the case of emerging markets, one cannot succeed by offering just updated or cheaper versions of current products or services'. To add to Unilever's efforts, Marko brings another wonderful example of how Nokia is engaging with the needs of the new markets. The story of Nokia implementing the strategy of localisation in Uganda has to become a classic for identifying the needs at the bottom of pyramid, so often spoken about by this book's contributors.

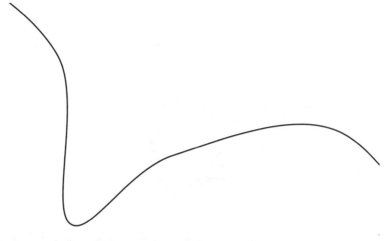

The Future of Innovation is in Emerging Markets

Name	**Marko Torkkeli**
Affiliation	Lappeenranta University of Technology
Position	Professor of Technology and Business Innovations
Country	Finland
Area	Emerging markets
Email	marko.torkkeli@lut.fi

emerging markets   innovation   the bottom of the pyramid   mobile phone

The nature of innovation activities aimed at developing products for future emerging markets (such as Mexico, Indonesia, Pakistan and Turkey) differs markedly from the nature of innovation activities which focus on the needs of developed markets. In particular, in the case of emerging markets, one cannot succeed by offering just 'updated' or cheaper versions of current products or services, since there is a need to create genuinely new products, services and business models based on local customer needs, as well as to develop new kinds of value networks.

In emerging markets, disruptive innovations will be especially important. This is because the focus of innovation activities must be on discovering unmet needs or 'opportunity gaps' where existing products or services do not fulfil the needs of their customers. The needs at the bottom of the pyramid (social and economic) around the developing world are the great unknown and therefore provide numerous opportunities for product and service innovation. Innovations related to energy, infrastructure and the environment, as well as to social networks and information infrastructure/transfer, in these countries are therefore among the key issues to consider in innovation strategies. Consequently, innovations in emerging markets are also often so-called 'social innovations', which means that a company not only tries to increase its profitability and create growth, but also tries to find solutions for social needs or problems in cooperation with local actors. All this requires new approaches to innovation processes and new capabilities from a company.

A good example of this kind participatory approach to innovation and creating new markets comes from Nokia. That is, field observations in Uganda had demonstrated that people only rarely could afford their own personal mobile phones, so that often an entire family would share one cellphone. Therefore, in response, Nokia developed a sharedphone device which permitted up to five separate profiles, contact directories and other personalisation features for the single phone (i.e., with this device each family member could have his/her 'own' phone). And later, as these family members become accustomed to using Nokia's phone, this invention greatly increased the likelihood that they would later purchase the same brand – thus increasing Nokia's sales.

The bottom line here is that anticipating future needs and trends in emerging markets requires considerable efforts from a company. The company must carefully observe how people live and behave at the bottom of the pyramid in order to identify the 'weak signals'. Only through shifting the focus from efficiency issues and streamlining costs can a company better understand users and their needs that lead to the effective design of new products and services. Companies thus need to address the business challenges and opportunities of emerging markets by developing more user-centred design processes and integrating them to their business models.

We find the two examples of two large companies, Unilever and Nokia, experimenting and engaging with the needs of those commonly not considered 'commercially worthwhile' absolutely encouraging and fantastic. And, here we have it again, context is everything. What is the context you are innovating in, what is the context you are innovating for. Where and how can value be created. In understanding that lies a secret of the future of innovation.

Aleksander Buczacki summarises all the above statement on the country-of-origin effects via the phenomenon of 'regional innovation' and the notion of so-called 'islands of innovation'.

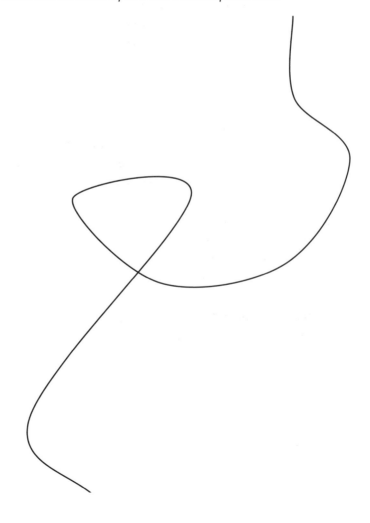

The Future of Innovation is in Regional Development

Name	**Aleksander Buczacki**
Affiliation	Technology Partners Foundation
Position	Secretary General
Country	Poland
Area	R&D management, business processes in research and technology organisations
Email	aleksander.buczacki@technologypartners.pl

regional innovation   inter-regional cooperation   constant factors of regional innovation   variable factors of regional innovation

The subject of the innovation level of individual organisations is extensively studied and being described, while another interesting and so far insufficiently researched phenomenon is that of regional innovation, which captures overall innovation at a regional level. Regional innovation is more complex than innovation considered at the level of an individual unit (enterprise or other organisation) because of the multi-factor nature of the processes occurring at the regional level. Significant factors impacting on the regional innovation level include the innovativeness of the individual organisations operating in the region, although other issues – such as their cooperation possibilities and potential to create a synergy effect in joint undertakings – should also be taken into account. Experience shows that the synergy effect is very difficult, although not impossible, to achieve.

Today in the world there are so-called islands of innovation – regions characterised by high levels of innovation – as well as other regions where the innovation level is low. This situation is interesting in that such differences also occur within individual countries. Innovation development is usually coupled with economic growth and has a fundamental impact on improving the quality of life in a region, and hence in order to ensure sustainable development, regions must pay particular attention to this area.

The regional innovation level depends on the effects of the actions of all the groups of organisations in the region that are involved in innovation processes. The groups most frequently mentioned are:

- The business sector – enterprises.

- The science sector – research units.

- The support organisations sector – organisations that provide support to both entrepreneurs and researchers – consulting organisations and financial institutions.

- Public administration (local and national level).

Only close cooperation and a full mutual understanding of all the groups' objectives can ensure increased regional innovation. A significant element is understanding the role that each group should play. It must be noted that each of the groups presented above possesses a discrete set of instruments which it can and should use to promote innovation development in its region.

In general, it can be stated that the regional innovation level is determined by two types of factors:

- constant factors that exist in every region;

- variable factors that are peculiar to individual regions.

In view of the above, the challenge is to identify and precisely describe the mechanisms that influence regional innovation and analyse the potential to adapt solutions tested in other regions. This will allow for a precise description of the 'constant' factors that influence a region's innovation and assigning to them proper weights. It will also make it possible to determine the areas of 'variable' factors and an analysis of the conditions under which these factors appear. Intensified research in this area will make it possible to develop more effective mechanisms of inter-regional cooperation in the area of increasing innovation output, which in turn will increase innovation in a higher number of regions, thereby evening out the differences between them.

We could not have said it better ourselves! Now, in the innovation ocean, we try to find those 'islands of innovation' with no particular structural approach to the order of appearance.

Geography – Romania

Have you ever been to Romania? Have you heard anything about Romanian technical culture? Are you familiar with the 'not enough money' problem? Luminita Hurbean will now enable us to realise how most organisations in transitional economies, like Romania, are putting serious efforts into creating a climate in which innovation can thrive.

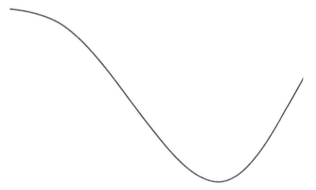

The Future of Innovation is Dependent on Education and People, Not Technology

Name	**Luminita Hurbean**
Affiliation	West University of Timisoara
Position	Associate Professor
Country	Romania
Area	Process innovation, human capital
Email	luminita.hurbean@feaa.uvt.ro

process inovation   ERP   human capital   Romania

In a world in which each enterprise can compete in a global market, growth depends on the ability of businesses to innovate. In Romanian technical culture, innovation is regarded mainly as the preserve of the research and development department, which technically improves a product. Nowadays, global competition calls for the *process innovation*. I will discuss here the integrated information systems (my number one research field) as source of innovation, adding comments related to my country's situation.

The end of the 20th century brought enterprise resource planning (ERP) – a new generation of innovation management software to support leaders, cultures and processes in an organisation. During the 1990s costly ERP software was adopted mostly to improve business processes. In the 2000s ERP systems extended and enhanced their role, becoming a source of innovation. The developed countries took the lead, transforming the functional footprint in the foundation for the next level of ERP development, replacing the operational excellence with competitive differentiation and market responsiveness.

In my opinion, Western nations will maintain their competitive advantage in technology, innovation, productivity and education for the foreseeable future. In transition economies, like Romania, most organisations are carrying on a struggle for survival. ERP has gained popularity among large organisations that seek to increase the efficiency and productivity as well as to streamline their operations. The immature economic environment, weak state support and the low managerial culture have had a critical impact on the state of affairs, especially in small and medium firms. All the global studies point to small and medium-sized enterprises (SMEs) as the key players of the ERP market. In Romania, SMEs play the Cinderella role in the economy – they don't get enough support and encouragement, but everyone expects them to develop and transform into the queens of the economy.

In most of the Romanian enterprises employees operate in a *silo mentality* and don't want to move beyond their boundaries. I believe that changing the state of mind is the most challenging duty in creating a collaborative environment, a cradle of innovation. It is true that many firms are confronting themselves with the 'not enough money' problem when talking about IT investments, but this obstacle is often defeated. Indifference, hostility and isolation are the obstacles that are inhibiting the growth in innovation.

I strongly believe that innovation begins and ends with people, individuals who have the courage to push the boundaries. However, spirited people are reduced to silence in badly managed firms. Innovation is based on a culture that cultivates and rewards creative thinking, where people feel comfortable enough to voice new ideas, no matter how small. A strong leadership should stress the importance of human capital and human talent, teamwork and collaboration, openness and transparency. Leadership should innovate itself.

Facing the decline of value in the university education, the brain exodus to more competitive and appealing economies and the attenuation of research in the academia, Romania should regain its pride and revive the human capital, the main asset of any organisation. Innovation will follow.

What Luminita says about indifference, hostility and isolation – and mindset – as main barriers to innovation resonates deeply with us too. As do the consequences she foresees for a decline in education. However, don't you like the analogy of small businesses as 'queens of the economy'? What or who will be the doves that help Cinderella deal with her challenges? It is not Romania alone; many, if not all nations, even developed ones, encounter similar challenges. Like Luminita, we strongly believe that innovation begins and ends with people, individuals who have the courage to push the boundaries. Usually, if not always, it is impossible to fight with bare hands, we still need some tools.

From a transitional economy we go to a developing nation, Nigeria, to better understand the evolution of the innovation future in this street of the global village.

Geography – Nigeria

We can't help asking you again whether you have ever been to Nigeria? Have you ever thought of your tomorrow in 'the shoes' of a developing economy? To better understand the common future of innovation for developed, transitional, emerging and developing economies, Abiodun Adeyemi Egbetokun is here to help us.

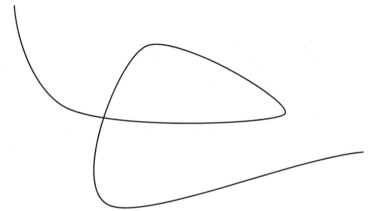

The Future of Innovation is One that has Implications for Developing Countries

Name **Abiodun Adeyemi Egbetokun**
Affiliation National Centre for Technology Management
(Federal Ministry of Science and Technology)
Position Research Officer
Country Nigeria
Area Firm-level innovation, innovation policy and
management
Email abiodun.egbetokun@nacetem.org

diffusion-based innovation   intra-innovation   catch-up   technology transfer developing economies

The future of innovation will hold important implications for developing countries. We are aware, for instance, that the definitions applied in the developed world do not always apply in the developing world. Hence, customised definitions and approaches have evolved through research. We also know that the implementation of innovation based on research and development (R&D) is quite low in developing economies – and especially in my country, Nigeria – but is getting higher in developed economies like the US and UK as well as in emerging ones like China. From that standpoint, I make bold to say that the entire world is approaching an era where innovation will not only explain national competitiveness but will also drive social systems. Today we talk only of product, process, marketing and organisational innovations. There is a new type of innovation that we are adding in Nigeria here, and which I believe will become more popular in the future – that is, diffusion-based innovation or innovation that arises from technology transfer and acquisition of embodied technology. I see many more of such new ideas arising such that we would begin to talk, in the nearest future, of social innovation, intra-innovation and international innovation in the same way that we talk about social, intra- and international entrepreneurship. For developing countries with currently low capability levels, the distance to cover so as to catch up will then be greater.

The future of innovation is also not fuzzy. We can conveniently predict how it is going to go in the coming years, with relatively high accuracy. For instance, given the current national levels of investments in human capital, infrastructure and R&D, as well as the status of these, I can say that not much is likely to be seen as far as radical, high-impact innovation is concerned. Organisation-level and national innovativeness will mostly continue to be predominated by minor incremental changes. At the same time, the rules of competition will become more dynamic because, as organisations better understand the role of innovation, they are likely to proceed on their own to make the necessary investments, thereby stimulating more dynamism in their respective sectors. These necessary investments will mostly centre around the acquisition of embodied technologies, the assimilation and adaptation of these technologies as well as capability acquisition.

It is thus quite imperative for developing nations to continually look inwards and redirect their energies towards the areas where they may have comparative advantage which could be deployed for building competitive advantage in the nearest future. One of such areas is diffusion-based innovation, as mentioned earlier. When we focus more on our perceived strength, it becomes easier to strategically position ourselves for the daunting but surmountable challenges that may come with innovation. It is not a gainsaying that developing countries, especially Nigeria, are richly endowed with a lot of potential. However, conscious and decisive efforts must be deployed towards taking technology transfer or acquisition of embodied technologies to a level where diffusion-based innovation will become prevalent. And as knowledge increase, developing economies should know better to attach developmental conditions to the transfer of technologies to them.

I gratefully acknowledge the contributions of my colleague, Mr Isaac Oluyi, who read and offered useful suggestions on my first draft.

From diffusion-based innovation we go to the other 'islands of innovation' which truly are islands: Barbados and Mauritius. For the time being, Betty Jane Punnett labels the Caribbean 'takers of innovation rather than makers of innovation'. Should this hold true in the future as well?

Geography – Barbados

Do you have in your innovation vocabulary something like 'a blessing' and 'a curse' from an innovation perspective? Betty is here to enrich your glossary and more. We have discussed the future of innovation from SMEs with no particular reference to the size of the country. Now the task is more complicated and even unmanageable – 'small' refers to the country, not the enterprise. What can you add to a solution from Betty: 'Capitalise on smallness!'?

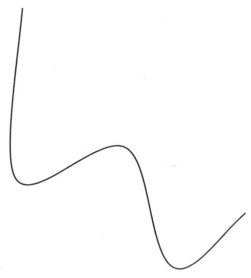

The Future of Innovation is in Small Island States

Name	**Betty Jane Punnett**
Affiliation	University of the West Indies, Cave Hill
Position	Professor
Country	Barbados
Area	Cross-cultural management
Email	eureka@caribsurf.com

small countries   niche markets   island states

From a small island state in the Caribbean, I wonder what to say about innovation in the future. Small island states are takers of innovation rather than makers of innovation. Our heritage is one of accepting the ideas of the colonial masters, and simply carrying out their wishes. To the extent that we have been innovators, it has been in our ability to get around the wishes of the 'masters' through subterfuge. Maybe this is the way forward? Small Caribbean states should be innovative through accepting and using their smallness and their unique 'Caribbean' heritage.

Smallness is a blessing and a curse from an innovation perspective. It's a blessing because being small means you can move quickly and nimbly, and the world of the future is going to demand quick, nimble responses to its challenges. It's a curse because it is hard for a small country to make an impact; limited resources limit its abilities.

The innovation solution for small Caribbean countries? Capitalise on smallness! Seek niche opportunities where customers/users want individual, unique products and services. Do not try to be 'all things to all people' or even 'many things to many people' – rather be 'a few things to a few people'. Innovate on a small scale for a small market. Small countries that succeed in doing this can dominate in small areas and reap the attendant rewards.

Emtek's website illustrates the type of product that can be described as a 'high-value-added, specialty niche product' which is positioned to address a specialty niche market (www.trendworthy. com; www.entrepreneur.com). The product is unusual and high priced, with a special appeal to a small number of consumers. The company started small, with a specific objective and a limited range. Its specialised focus has made it an international success. The Emtek story is one which Caribbean companies can emulate. The key facet of specialised niche markets is that the products are sold on the basis of differentiation, not price. Typically, niche products are perceived as high value and differentiated, and are priced accordingly.

A major advantage for small producers is the flexibility inherent in smallness. Large producers find it much more difficult to shift production than do small producers. This means that small Caribbean companies can capitalize on their size and flexibility to meet the potentially cyclical nature of high-value niche markets. Niche markets are often contrasted with mass markets. Niche products have a special, differentiated appeal to a limited number of purchasers. Mass products have a broad appeal to the undifferentiated mass of consumers. Mass products for mass markets rely on economies of scale and cost efficiencies, and compete largely on the basis of price. Niche products rely on differentiated features, and compete on the basis of these special features, meeting special and even unique consumers' needs. Niche markets, by definition, are relatively small, but they are also associated with relatively high margins; therefore, niche markets can be as profitable as mass markets.

Niche markets are the innovation future for Caribbean countries.

We almost said it after the previous contribution, we definitely have to say it now: it is not only at the organisational level, perhaps even more so at the national level: where lies your innovation strength? What is special about your national (company, individual!) culture that you can contribute to the innovation game? What is your special gift which you can bring to the creation of the future of innovation (and don't tell us it is the same as everyone else's, we are rather certain it is not …).

Paul Pounder is from Barbados, too. After reviewing the governmental efforts taken in the Caribbean, apart from the senior management of the country, Paul focuses on the front rather than back end of the innovation process: the education system. 'Creativity' and 'innovation culture', though intangible, but most vital for innovation to happen and make innovation tangible. Creativity and innovation culture like 'the sun' and 'the blue sky' that make the grass grow green over and over again. Whatever you belong to – SMEs or a small country – wherever you live in – developed, transitional, emerging or developing economies – whatever your age is – get ashamed of being not creative rather than vice versa – this is the new insight.

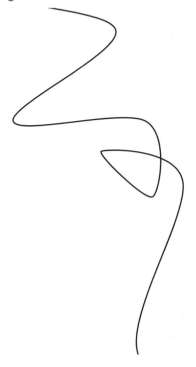

The Future of Innovation is Creating a Culture for Innovation in Barbados

Name	**Dr Paul Pounder**
Affiliation	University of the West Indies
Position	Lecturer
Country	Barbados
Area	Innovation management, SME innovation
Email	paul.pounder@cavehill.uwi.edu

creativity   culture   innovation model   funding   entrepreneur   Barbados

In our time, innovation plays a fundamental role in the creation of wealth, economic growth and the improvement of the quality of life for all. This is certainly the case for Barbados, a small island situated in the Caribbean. Barbados has made efforts to support innovation, but more is needed to embed an innovative mindset in the country. It is understood that though countries can try to create processes to stimulate inventions, it is not the processes that create the innovation: it is the people and their mindset. In Barbados much of the focus has been placed on an organisational perspective and this article aims to highlight some of the steps that the government has taken to stimulate the innovation process, as well as to identify some of the gaps which exists.

In 2001, the Barbados Investment and Development Corporation (BIDC) developed an Innovation Support Programme (ISP). The BIDC recognised that innovative ideas often languish or remain unexploited because the owners lack the financial, technical or other means of pursuing their development and protection. To overcome this challenge, the programme offers technical advice to inventors about the development of novel ideas, intellectual property protection and commercialisation.

In addition to the ISP, the government of Barbados also set aside US$2.5 million in 2003 in a fund called the Innovation Fund. The Innovation Fund is managed by the Enterprise Growth Fund Limited and provides seed capital in the range of US$12,500 to US$125,000 to assist entrepreneurs with the implementation of commercially viable project ideas. The fund is also used to coordinate the National Innovation Competition which encourages management and other personnel to think outside the box in enhancing the competitiveness of their businesses.

In summary, though I believe all these efforts play an important part in the innovation process, I do not believe that a country can try to formalise innovation, as creativity and innovation are very much art forms. As such, it makes good sense to say that the results of any such innovation could only stem from stimulation of the art form and therefore creating a culture of innovation should be people focused, therefore stimulating such creative juices from an individual perspective is definitely one good way forward.

Therefore any future plans should develop around introducing creativity workshops at all levels in the educational system. This is, however, just the beginning as it is also necessary to create an innovation model as part of the transformation strategy to create an innovative culture which is integrated and stimulates linkage and simultaneous interaction between stakeholders throughout the entire innovation cycle on the island. In the case of businesses, an optimal mix between technology advancements, retooling, investments and organisational changes is needed to remain competitive. Therefore it makes justifiable sense to concur that the more people are exposed to developing the correct mindset from an early age, the more a country like Barbados can foster creativity.

'No comment' seems to be the best comment if after Paul Pounder we listen to Hemant Kassean. Incredibly, Hemant Kassean uses the same words as Paul: island, innovation culture, creativity, education ... the slight addition is a 'success story'. Though we cannot resist picking up (again) on his emphasis on people.

Geography – Mauritius

Some countries that possess natural recourses like oil or gas might not feel an urgency to make renewable energy supplies their top priority (at least for now). However, the new mindset realises the earth's resources are finite. One day, better today than tomorrow, a small country like Mauritius will be a good, sustainable example worth following from most big countries' perspective. This is where the quintessence of 'innovate or die' is clearly perceived, becoming strikingly realistic.

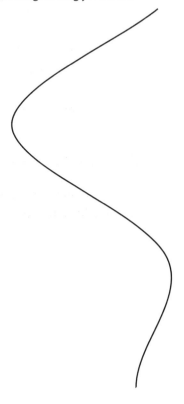

The Future of Innovation is Innovate or Die

Name	**Hemant Kassean**
Affiliation	University of Mauritius
Position	Head, Department of Management
Country	Mauritius
Area	Mauritius
Email	h.kassean@uom.ac.mu

Mauritius   small island state   ethnic populations   entrepreneurial spirit

Mauritius is disadvantaged by being a small island state and more distant from major world markets than the average African state. The adverse climatic conditions we are often confronted with – like strong cyclones, droughts, floods and the recent tsunami – have highlighted how vulnerable we are as a small island economy. Against this background, it came as no surprise when, in the early 1960s, the economist and Nobel Prize winner James Meade prophesied that the development prospects of Mauritius were poor and that Mauritius was a strong candidate for failure, because of being a very typical African economy with a heavy economic dependence on sugar cane only; it was vulnerable due to trade shocks, rapid population growth and the potential for ethnic tensions. But instead of lying down and accepting its fate, Mauritius rose to the challenge and has proved all this to be wrong. Mauritius today is considered a success story and a model for many African states.

Mauritius has been able to transform its weaknesses and threats into strengths and opportunities. The ethnic communities have important links with the rest of the world which have encouraged investments from entrepreneurs in Hong Kong, China, India and France in particular. The diversity of the population has played an important role in the development of participatory institutions. An article in the British newspaper, *The Times*, in 1983, claimed that many ethnic populations in one country would give rise to tensions and the state was not likely to progress economically. In reply to this article, another British newspaper, the *Independent*, referred to the example of Mauritius, an island with many ethnic diversities yet thriving and prospering, with no major tensions.

It is time now for Mauritius to sustain its spirit of innovation in order to meet the challenges of the 21st century. Because we do not have natural resources like oil, gas or precious metals, we need to harness the solar, wind and wave energy which are in abundant supply in our tropical country. We can also use our sugar to produce ethanol for hybrid cars, following the model of Brazil. This will also reduce our dependency on imported oil which is used as a major source of fuel. The government of Mauritius has recently embarked on an innovative project: 'Maurice Ile durable' – 'Mauritius, Sustainable Island' – which has attracted attention from France, the World Health Organisation and other Commonwealth countries, which are following the progress of many of our pilot projects towards a sustainable island state with keen interest.

Our human capital and entrepreneurial spirit are going to play a key role in enhancing our creativity as a nation along with the way we utilise technology to improve our productivity and quality of products and services. Mauritius has been innovative in the field of education and is probably unique as a model where schooling is free at all levels, with free transport. We also have a state university providing free education at tertiary level. The country is also tackling poverty which affects about 10 per cent of the population. Unfortunately, with rapid progress, the country is also suffering from problems resulting from non-transmissible diseases, with Mauritius having one of the highest incidence of diabetes in the world. Mauritius however, is a good example where there is a culture of innovation because as a small island economy, we believe that we cannot not innovate – otherwise we will die.

Listen to the Mauritius experience. How can you transform your weakness into a strength? Do you know what your weakness is? Do you know what your strengths are? May we challenge you: from whose perspective?

Let's move from Mauritius to another island economy, a rather larger one: Japan which is on its latest stage of implementation of 'innovate or die' national strategy.

Geography – Japan

Takeshi Shimada puts us in the middle of the national 'innovation tornado', commencing with 'modular and integral architecture' then going deeper to 'invisible and visible competitiveness'. Extrapolating to Japanese manufacturing companies, he postulates that innovation is much more than technology, and many other complementary resources and services are essential for market success. Takeshi assures that 'a new value can be created by combining various technology elements, such as technologies of one's own company with those of other companies' and we add 'of other countries, too' – collaborate or die.

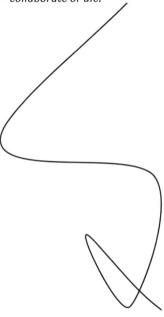

The Future of Innovation is the Future of Corporate Strength

Name	**Takeshi Shimada**
Affiliation	SHIMA Knowledge Laboratory
Position	The Head of Laboratory
Country	Japan
Area	Tokyo
Email	takeshi-shimada@nifty.com

architecture   innovation process   market-led vision   technological fusion combination   Japan

Innovation strategies of Japanese manufacturing companies and future issues: what determines corporate strengths?

From the standpoint of architecture, products can be classified into two categories: those with modular architecture and those with integral architecture. The majority of successful Japanese manufacturing companies have been nurturing organisational capabilities for integrated production that match products with integral architecture because these companies have been growing through a process of capabilities-building competition in the post-war period with poor resources. A product with integral architecture requires the delicate mutual adjustment of respective components dedicated for the product to demonstrate its real performance as a total system. Therefore, strong organisational capabilities nurtured through the development and production processes of this type of product have served as the competitiveness of Japanese manufacturing companies.

The competitiveness of companies consists of 'invisible competitiveness' and 'visible competitiveness.' 'Invisible competitiveness' is assessed by indicators such as productivity, production lead time, development lead time, product quality/yield and in-process defect rate, which is hardly to be seen from the outside, while 'visible competitiveness' is assessed by market factors such as prices, designs, brand images, delivery policies and services. The strong organisational capabilities for production are directly reflected in the 'invisible competitiveness' of the company, but 'visible competitiveness' can be cancelled out by extrinsic factors such as exchange rate fluctuations.

Japanese manufacturing companies are weak in 'visible competitiveness' in spite of their strong 'invisible competitiveness'. As a result, their profits generally remain low. Therefore, to turn technologies to profits by utilising the strong organisational capabilities and 'invisible competitiveness' of Japanese companies, innovations in 'visible competitiveness', the weak point, which includes marketing, branding and strategy making, is necessary.

Pursuit of new technologies is not enough to create competitive products. It is the market that utilises technologies. High-level technologies do not necessarily lead to competitive products; it is necessary to design the manner of approaching the market as well as to predict what added values can finally be created for the product as commercial goods, from the planning and development phases. Furthermore, innovations should not be limited to those in 'goods'; total innovation processes involving products, manufacturing processes, business models, supply chains and others, should be promoted based on the market-led vision.

The future source of innovation lies in the field of technological fusion or combination. A new value can be created by combining various technology elements, such as the technologies of one's own company with those of other companies. Combining various elements may lead to a breakthrough that brings total changes to society, far beyond scientific or technological innovations. No innovation occurs without varied technologies. As technologies vary more, we can apply our ingenuity to solving wider-ranging issues.

What can you fuse, combine, recombine to create valuable innovation? Kayano Fukuda goes up a level from the company perspective Takeshi has shared with us. He explains to us the future of innovation, bringing into focus the innovation ecosystem. In his reflections he touches on industry–government relationships that, despite all fears, made it viable for Japan to succeed in the world's highest industrial R&D intensity. If you are interested in ecosystem principles Kayano explains them for you.

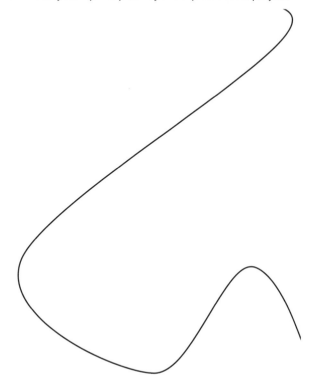

The Future of Innovation is Co-evolving in the Innovation Ecosystem

Name	**Kayano Fukuda**
Affiliation	Centre for Research and Development Strategy, Japan Science and Technology Agency
Position	Fellow
Country	Japan
Area	Innovation management
Email	kfukuda@jst.go.jp

co-evolution   innovation ecosystem   hybrid management   government R&D
Japan

The future of innovation co-evolves with institutions in an innovation ecosystem. Innovation has become a crucial source of a nation's sustainable growth and competitiveness amidst globalisation. The innovation cycle, from its emergence to its utilisation, is critically dependent on the co-evolutionary dynamism with the institutions. Institutions are similar to the soil in that they are necessary for the cultivation of emerging innovation, and can be expressed as the three-dimensional system:

1.   national strategy and socioeconomic system;

2.   entrepreneurial organisation and culture; and

3.   historical perspectives.

In a manner similar to that of the US and EU, Japan's government has taken the initiative in promoting enhanced innovation. The initiative was undertaken by three five-year science and technology basic plan programmes with government R&D investment of 17 trillion yen for 1996–2000, 24 trillion yen for 2001–2005, and 25 trillion yen for 2006–2010.

This initiative has contributed to terminating the stagnating trend in industry R&D investment, reactivating firms' technopreneurial endeavours. In turn it has resulted in increased popularity of quantitative rather than qualitative increases in government R&D investment as well as the bipolarisation of technopreneurial trajectories between those firms that are successful and those that are failing.

Historically, Japan has incorporated a sophisticated resilient structure supported by vigorous industry R&D with intensive efforts in learning and improvement for the assimilation of business models, and an explicit government catalyst function for inducing such industry efforts effectively.

This structure is notable due to the unique industry–government relationship that has made it possible to achieve the world's highest industrial R&D intensity despite the world's lowest level of government support for industrial R&D.

While it was feared that such an invaluable asset disappeared during the course of Japan's lost decade in the 1990s, it has recently been postulated that Japan has changed its structure to be more resilient by fusing indigenous strength and the effect of learning. This structural change can largely be attributed to a government catalysis role that is unique to Japan.

Japan has achieved the hybrid management of technology by fusing indigenous strength and the effect of learning with sophisticated government R&D as a catalysis. This optimal system for a sophisticated combination of industry efforts and government stimulation in maximising the effective utilisation of potential resources in innovation is demonstrated by ecosystem as a masterpiece of the system.

The cycle of co-evolutionary development as it is adapted to ecosystem homeostasis is attributed to the systems function, which is similar to the four ecosystem principles encompassing (i) sustainable development through substitution, (ii) self-propagation through co-evolution, (iii) organisational inertia and inspired learning from competitors, and (iv) heterogeneous synergy.

New insight into the further development of optimal innovation management in a systematic way will make the future of innovation brighter. Ecosystem principles centring around 'substitution', 'co-evolution', 'learning', and 'heterogeneous synergy' will be decisive for sustainable productivity and growth. Efforts should be made to effectively utilise potential resources in innovation thereby maximising the effect of the co-evolution between indigenous strength and the effect of learning.

Isn't amazing how we come back to the same topics again and again? Like to many others Kayano closes with an emphasis on sustainability and co-evolution. Brilliant. Now, would you like a perspective of an innovation ecosystem through a particular set of geographical lenses, say... Egypt? Yasser Tawfik can grant you that wish.

Geography – Egypt

Yasser focuses on the missing part of the current innovation ecosystem in Egypt and reveals elaborating plans for the Arab region. Based on his experience, Yasser proposes rather a sophisticated definition for ever-developing notion of 'innovation'.

The Future of Innovation is as an Ecosystem

Name	**Yasser Tawfik**
Affiliation	The Arab Science and Technology Foundation
Position	Programmes Manager
Country	Egypt
Area	Innovation ecosystem, social side of innovation
Email	yasser.tawfik@astf.net

ecosystem   entrepreneur   education   Egypt

The future of innovation could be seen as an ecosystem. An innovation ecosystem should consist of units functioning together. Innovation ecosystems have been studied before but mostly there is a missing link within the ecosystem described. This missing link that could complete the cycle of a closed ecosystem is payback to the ecosystem, which would close the cycle (that would otherwise remain open). For example, entrepreneurial innovators struggle with their innovations at the early stages of development; once they passed this difficult phase, they go through a period of growth to maturity; but this process is an open loop. To close the loop the company, which has grown as a result of the innovation, should pay something back to the system to balance it – by supporting angel funds and supporting new innovators who enter the ecosystem. Failing to include this final link and close the loop could cause a disruptive effect similar to what sometimes happens when a natural ecosystem is disrupted – the death of a species.

New innovators should learn about the innovation ecosystem in their education, training and business plan workshops. They should understand that one day they must repay the ecosystem by supporting new entrepreneurial innovators who will struggle in the early stages just as they struggled in the beginning.

The future of innovation should include the social responsibility of repaying the bigger ecosystem which is society. A disturbance of the whole society's ecosystem will indeed affect the sub-ecosystem.

In Egypt, the current innovation ecosystem is not a closed loop yet and missing some essential units. However, the future of innovation in Egypt could build upon the fact that any ecosystem should have the ability to recover from a disruptive agent (or missing link) by adapting itself through existing units to reach a balanced state. Existing big companies and investors that understand the ecosystem's nature and repay the current innovation ecosystem will grow the ecosystem and rebalance it. I suggest that all entrepreneurship and innovation training and educational facilities in the world include repaying the innovation ecosystem by supporting new innovators and entrepreneurs, and that this is included in the concept of the social responsibility of a company, not as a charitable action but as a necessary balancing of the ecosystem in which they work.

I am currently managing part of the training and business plan template in an Arab region business plan competition and in both of these I include information about how to rebalance the ecosystem and how to design a social responsibility department from day one of a company's existence.

Thus my definition of innovation would be: innovation is a process by which value is created for customers through public and private organisations that transform new knowledge and technologies into profitable products and services for national and global markets. A high rate of innovation in turn contributes to more intellectual capital, market creation, economic growth, job creation, wealth and a higher standard of living and pay-back to the innovation cycle.

In the sense of innovation's meaning as operationalised by Yasser Tawfik, Jacobus Slabbert raises the issues of 'socioeconomical, political and ecological problems ... in an increasingly demanding and changing global village'.

Geography – South Africa

Through the lens of South Africa, Jacobus ponders upon the dilemma of how to ensure success for non-profit social entrepreneurial ventures, which today are all too often 'inefficient, ineffective and unresponsive'.

The Future of Innovation is a Social Entrepreneurial Spear Point

Name	**Jacobus Slabbert**
Affiliation	African Centre for Social Entrepreneurship
Position	Executive Director
Country	South Africa/USA
Area	Social entrepreneurship
E-mail	cobusslabbert@worldfootprints.us

social entrepreneurship   sustainable development   community development
social problems   Africa

The future of innovation is not limited to technology. With the power to transform peoples' lives, the promotion of entrepreneurial sustainability in small businesses can be one of the most powerful socioeconomic innovation tools for the future. As an integral part of a country's formal economy, a dynamic and innovative small business sector is worldwide recognised as the 'vehicle' to equalise and mobilise economic, social and environmental opportunities. It also tends to be the 'engine' of job creation as well as the 'seedbed' for innovation. Apart from giving people a sense of self-worth and independence and creating value for customers that will ultimately yield a profit for shareholders, entrepreneurial sustainability also implies a responsibility towards the eco-environment, the broader community and future generations.

This broader emphasis on the importance of balancing organisational wealth with community wellness, struck a responsive chord of social entrepreneurship. This dynamic phenomenon, which combines the passion of a social mission with business realities, holds the promise of more effectively addressing the most intractable social problems on the African continent where many of the socioeconomical, political and ecological problems derive from inequalities between rich and poor. However, to reach a point of sustainability, innovative and ongoing change interventions regarding the business modelling of social entrepreneurial ventures are a given reality and pre-condition for success on the African continent. Not only have many global initiatives, governmental and philanthropic efforts fallen short of expectations, but major social sector institutions are often viewed as inefficient, ineffective and unresponsive to societal needs and expectations. Some building blocks to be considered in the structuring of best practice social entrepreneurial business modelling can be summarised as follows.

Firstly, it will be necessary to combine operational models in order to capture opportunities in commercial markets, societal sectors and government systems. More specifically the challenge will be to establish a point of optimum balance between the rule of law (government), stabilising factors and wellness requirements (community), competitiveness, growth and wealth (business organisations) and sustainable development and deliverables (social entrepreneurial ventures) – see Figure 5. Secondly, it is important for social entrepreneurial ventures to move from a purely dependency model to one where the necessity of dependency is lessened by earned income and even profitable business initiatives. Successful social entrepreneurs will have to be driven by a double bottom-line blend of social and financial returns in order to ensure entrepreneurial sustainability and self-sufficiency. This does not mean that the social mission becomes secondary to the financial incentives of earned income and profit making. Thirdly, the management and leadership efficiency profile of social entrepreneurial ventures will have to match that of their profit-only counterparts. Entrepreneurial efforts in non-profits and double bottom-line social entrepreneurial ventures are often doomed because of a misunderstanding of the differences between leadership, management, innovators and entrepreneurs.

Without underestimating the role of government and community leadership, big business corporations in the private sector has a pivotal role to play in this regard. As part of its human resources exit strategy big business corporations can for example add value in terms of opportunity identification, capacity building and aftercare support for social entrepreneurs to a point where earned income, sustainability and self-efficiency will replace charitable contributions, government subsidies and eternal dependency.

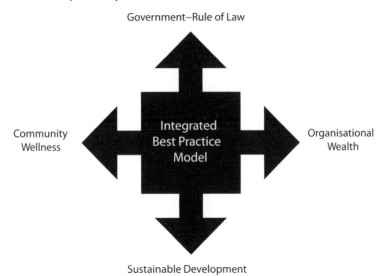

Figure 5   Integrated best practice social entrepreneurship model

What Jacobus Slabbert suggests might seem to be unachievable, unmanageable or even unrealistic – but only if you have not yet read Henning Sejer Jakobsen and the Danish experience!

Geography – Denmark

Henning reconsiders definition, essence, source and leaders of innovation. Through the Danish innovation achievements in the adaptation of alternative energy rather than through the adoption of nuclear power, Henning argues that 'movement activities' are the dominant source for strategic innovations. 'Actions speak louder than words' – this is another proverb for the hoped future of innovation to happen.

The Future of Innovation is Through Movements

Name	**Henning Sejer Jakobsen**
Affiliation	Danish Technological Institute
Position	Open Innovation
Country	Denmark
Area	Open innovation
Email	sejer@teknologisk.dk

definition   art   bottomup movement   mindset   Denmark

It seems that innovation shares characteristics with the future, both being something unexpected and unpredictable. And still we often try to predict the future to find solutions to problems. But if innovation is to lead to changes – not only differences – an approach with 'and *more*' of the same won't bring any new discoveries. As the Danish writer, inventor and mathematician Piet Hein once said about art: 'Art is what you can't do – otherwise it would not be an art' – in that construction, art and innovation have the same definition!

It's often stated that innovation and change happen faster and faster. In areas like IT, electronics, packaging etc. this is an indisputable fact, but in more law-regulated sectors like medicine, the food industry and biotechnology new discoveries enter the market slower and slower, even interminably slowly. Many new innovations in the 'slow' branches are therefore first done in the 'fast' areas, for example new packaging for the food industry, new devices for diagnosis in medicine, financing models for goods,and innovation successes are not any longer limited to technological superiority.

The military industry has in many years been a major source of new radical inventions such as the internet or GPS, but new salient areas such as climate change (in particular CO_2 emissions), new diseases, hunger, health etc. will define new and more complex innovation tasks not *only* to be solved technological and probably with new leading conductors. Based in established underground activities, political statements and movements will arise and be created around beliefs in a *mission* or a cause to fight for, which doubtless will lead to quite new business opportunities. As an example from Denmark, the strong resistance to nuclear power station in the 1970s created an underground movement for alternative energy such as sun energy, wind power and bio-fuel. As the global focus increased, business models were created, and Denmark is today the leading producer of windmills, supported both politically and in the education system – an evolution nobody could predict.

Movements like these, whether in organisations, at the national level or even in political systems, will become a major source of long-term innovation activities instead of forecasting or predictions. Event-based innovation and short-term project-activities will be undertaken by ongoing movements with dedicated personnel, focusing on long-term innovation as an open and continuous process. When focusing on long-term innovation, many smaller innovations appear unpredictable and often a consequence nobody could have reached by small-step innovation. An example of this is the mobile-phone industry which worked on the idea to create internet access, and in the process created inventions like SMS, WAP and MMS. The challenge for societies, organisations and companies, especially SMEs and small countries, will be to find, create, stage or stimulate such new movement activities and have the mind and courage to follow the potential instead of searching for a rationale in a predicted mainstream.

We again feel that Henning is challenging us to identify our particular innovation strength and build on it. What do you believe is the innovation strength of your company, of your organisation, of yourself? And do not forget, innovation requires a rather diverse set of skills, which can be rather opposing but only in combination will they create innovation success.

The challenge of short- and long-term benefits is a destabilising factor for the future of innovation. Stephen Ko is full of caution about the Hong Kong high-tech myth.

Geography – China

Have you ever heard of a 'high-tech harms and low-tech pays!' myth? Is it catching? Or it is already spread all around but we have never yet identified it? And as Stephen asks: 'In the long run, is it true that high-tech harms and low-tech pays?'.

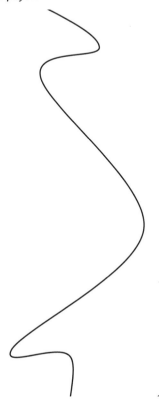

The Future of Innovation is Attitudes Count

Name	**Dr Stephen Ko**
Affiliation	The Hong Kong Polytechnic University
Position	Lecturer
Country	China
Area	Innovation policy
Email	Stephen.ko@polyu.edu.hk

high-tech   low-tech   technology   Hong Kong   entrepreneurship

Hong Kong business people believe in a myth: 'high-tech harms and low-tech pays!' If you are doing something on high-tech innovations here, people will say, 'you are digging yourself into a hole'.

How come? Cyberport, science and technology parks, InnoCentre, renowned universities, a financial hub, the rule of law, the free flow of information, world-class infrastructure, the world's freest economy, low tax, a skilled workforce, an unrivalled location, innovation and technology fund – all these facilities are in place to create an enabling environment for innovations. Why do you Hongkongers still have this belief?

What we are still lacking is something more crucial than hard facts. Attitudes towards high-tech innovations top the list. Hong Kong business people, and the government, are short-sighted. They are looking at returns on investment in a very short period of time. If you are burning money, we don't buy into that. We prefer a quick-fix panacea! The government is *encouraging* innovation but its support is far below our Four Pillar Industries – financial services, trading and logistics, tourism, and producer and professional services – which are believed to be the driving force of economic growth, providing impetus to growth of other sectors and creating employment. High-tech is too *high*. Thus, there are never any innovation-related tax incentives and significant technological spillovers.

The second element is human capital. In the education system, it is generally agreed that our students are under-educated in terms of creativity, innovation and entrepreneurship. They are used to living in a comfort zone due to the steady economy, low unemployment rate and generally acceptable salary levels, which translate into less motivation, persistence and assertiveness. In a utilitarian economy like Hong Kong, the best students would rather go to business or medical school. To them, being a scientist or an inventor is a long way to go. Rewards are too remote and uncertain, though scientists and inventors are accorded a high social status. Why not doing something that can get more immediate benefits, including monetary rewards, a good career and making their parents happy? Life is short, seize the day!

In a recent Global Urban Competitiveness Report (2007–2008), which measures a city's ability to create more wealth in a faster and better manner than other cities in the world in terms of GDP, per capita GDP, per unit area GDP, labour productivity, number of multinational enterprises settled in the city, number of patent applications, price advantage, economic growth rate and employment rate, Hong Kong was ranked only 26th, falling far behind its perennial rival, Singapore. This in fact raised the alarm – Hong Kong is declining in its competitiveness! In the long run, is it true that high-tech harms and low-tech pays?

For the latter question, Yichen Lin is here with her success story on high-tech industries in today and tomorrow of Taiwan.

Geography – Taiwan

In contrast to Stephen, Yichen is determined that the Taiwanese future is tied with the high-tech industries. She provides an overall overview of core areas where Taiwan should, and most probably will, concentrate its efforts of developing through technological innovations, despite all myths that seem to indicate the contrary.

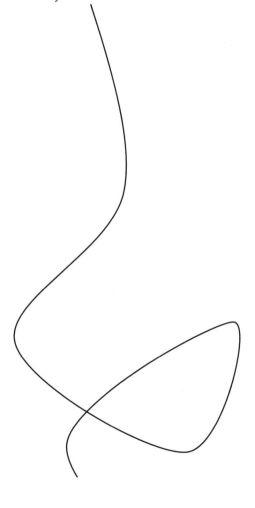

The Future of Innovation is in High-Tech Industries in Taiwan

Name	**Yichen Lin**
Affiliation	Graduate Institute of Technology Management, National University of Tainan
Position	Associate Professor and Director
Country	Taiwan
Area	Product innovations, technology commercialisation
Email	yichen@mail.nutn.edu.tw

high-tech   service innovation   design service   brand   Taiwan

In the past 20 years, the most successful high-tech industries in Taiwan have been one based on the personal computer and the wafer foundry in the semiconductor industry. These are the two foundations of Taiwan high-tech industry. However, we have entered a period of uncertainty where threats are indeterminate even as changes in technology accelerate and innovation. In response to the growing need for innovation, several countries have already developed national policy regarding innovation. Also, in order to foster further growth and sustain our competitiveness, Taiwan must maintain a high rate of technological innovation. It is, therefore, incumbent upon business leaders and policy makers to understand the many forces driving innovation. Building on insights from Taiwanese industry, the Science and Technology Advisory Group (STAG) developed an industry innovation guideline, which points out the five emerging industries that are the most worth investment and development: the electronic industry (semiconductor and display technology), communication (optical communication and wireless communication), information services, biological technology and nanotechnology.

Service innovation is another vitally important issue in Taiwan. The focuses on service innovation are:

- Packing the innovation business model by means of the product.

- OEM and ODM (original equipment manufacture and original design manufacture) firms extend the value creation activity for customer.

- Enhance the middle customer's value by cooperating with the upstream, downstream and the competition.

- Innovation in the traditional service industry.

The semiconductor industry is no longer technology driven. Innovations on the application level are more important than technology alone. Thumb drive and iPod are great examples, simple technology with great success. Nowadays, the technology barrier is low; therefore, marketing and platform establishment become a major focus. In addition, consolidation and synergising among companies will be next step. Companies need to share resources to push innovation forward, and accelerate time to market of the solution.

During the 1990s the US outsourced their production skills overseas, which gave a growing opportunity for the Taiwanese high-technology industry. Nowadays, the US has started outsourcing researching skills. Corporate headquarters in the US focus on their marketing and brands. This also offered an opportunity of transforms and improvements for the Taiwanese high-technology industry. We will start combining US and Japanese design and research to innovate in Taiwan. We will extend the high-technology industry from a production type to a research type, and begin developing added-value production. We ought to even have the ambition to set up our own brands. Thus the Taiwanese high-technology industry could reach to another highlight under the pressure of industry transferring to China.

For further consideration of Stephen Ko's question 'In the long run, is it true that high-tech harms and low-tech pays?', and to add to Yichen's inspiration, there is Farha Abdol Ghapar's wisdom from Malaysia.

Geography – Malaysia

In the words of Farha, 'Malaysian must realise it's time to wake up and be a quick learner'. Don't you agree that it refers to many more nations, not merely Malaysia?

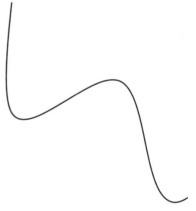

The Future of Innovation is Inspired by the Intellectual Property System

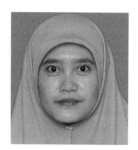

Name	**Farha Abdol Ghapar**
Affiliation	MARA University of Technology
Position	Lecturer
Country	Malaysia
Area	Intellectual property
Email	farha.agf@gmail.com

intellectual property   patent   innovation   technological capability
indigenous technology   Malaysia

Innovation in Malaysia still has a long way to go. Nevertheless, as one of the emerging economies, Malaysia is catching up pretty fast in terms of economic growth in the era of technology and innovation. Moving from post-colonial status to primary product exporter into an industrially oriented economy, Malaysia has a large amount of foreign direct investment (FDI) into the country with large amounts of partial diversification of manufactured foreign products to be exported to other parts of the world. This situation has helped spur Malaysia's economic performance.

Despite of its tremendous economic performance, Malaysia is still seen as being dependent on foreign countries' technological capability. In its (latest) 9th Malaysia Plan, it is reported that even though there is an increasing trend in the science and technology (S&T) indicator output in terms of patents filed and granted by its own residents, the number is still very low when compared with those of non-residents. One of many reasons this might occur is the high rate of manufacturing of foreign products in Malaysia for which the foreigners might want to secure the intellectual property (IP). Another S&T indicator is that royalty payments are also much higher than its receipts, MYR5851 million payments compared to MYR98 million receipts in 2005. This shows that Malaysia is still very much dependent on foreign technological capability.

Even though some might argue that some innovation has never been patented, the patent has been traditionally seen as one of the technological outputs that can earn monetary returns. Back in 1878, Thomas Edison, who holds 1,093 patents (more than any other inventor in history) and who founded the Edison Electric Light Company (General Electric's predecessor), said that, 'Anything that won't sell, I don't want to invent. Its sale is proof of utility, and utility is success.' Some still argue that patenting activities would not bring much benefits to the inventor especially in emerging economies, so why the mountains of patent applications in each and every patent office in every region around the world?

I believe that Malaysia as an emerging economy shouldn't have to be too dependent on foreign technological capability as it matures. Malaysia must realise it's time to wake up and be a quick learner. Malaysians must take the advantage of the FDI that is pouring into the country and learn from their technological capabilities. It is timely for Malaysia to shift its course from becoming the leading manufacturers of foreign products, to innovating its own indigenous technology and grabbing the golden opportunity of the patenting system. The IP is a powerful tool which not only protects the new innovation but also creates more business opportunities in its own country and other countries as well. Malaysians must catch up with the IP system so that there is a bright future of innovation in Malaysia.

Perhaps it is about confidence, confidence in one's own abilities? Let us hear how Luis Cláudio Silva Frade sees the future of innovation in Brazil, considering patents and technical knowledge, as well as innovation culture and national innovation agenda.

Geography – Brazil

Luis starts with the legacy of the past in terms of innovations in Brazil – they are the absence of technical knowledge and bureaucracy. He then discusses a Brazilian national innovation agenda. By the way, do you have a national innovation agenda in your country? And is it time to set a global innovation agenda, too?

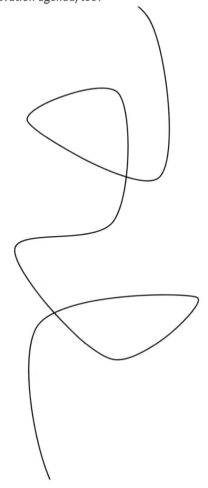

The Future of Innovation is in Brazil, a Craft Nation

Name	**Luis Cláudio Silva Frade**
Affiliation	Eletrobrás S/A
Position	Head of Technological Management Department
Country	Brazil
Area	Research, technological development and innovation
Email	luis.frade@eletrobras.com

innovation   nation   Brazil   improvements   IP

Evaluating how innovations happened in Brazil, over the last couple of millennia, it can said that all efforts to put innovation's instruments into place, such as public policies, laws, decrees, programmes, financial mechanisms, economic subventions, and so on, do not seem to have been able to translate innovation into wealth for people. All these instruments are ineffective in the absence of technical knowledge about innovation and presence of bureaucracy. A consequence of this misalignment is a smaller number of patents deposited compared with other emerging countries: only 384 in 2007.

Much less – almost nothing – was done to create 'in fact', a national innovation culture that could help Brazilian innovators transform their ideas into innovation, delivering value to them and to their country. It is possible to count a lot of factors that have contributed to this situation: teachers who only worry about publishing their papers instead of protecting or licensing their innovations; the National Institute of Industrial Propriety being very slow in processing patents; the process of financing innovation projects being slowed down by the Projects and Studies Agency, and so on.

But, all these things are part of the past. Now the question is: what will be the *future* of innovation in Brazil?

First, innovation needs be understood by all Brazilian people as a simple thing that is accessible to for all – from the initial idea to its development, its protection, and through to its commercialisation. It is necessary to change the minds of people who are heads of funding organisations, intellectual property agencies, teachers and the Brazilian government with regards to the meaning of innovation for society. Mechanics, electricians, carpenters and others have developed new small improvements to their tools, in their processes or in their way of work, but never knew that these incremental improvements could be protected or maybe commercialised in order to provide royalties for them.

Another action could be the creation of a national innovation agenda. It would be necessary to define very well the roles for those involved in such an agenda in both the public sphere and the private sector.

A systematic and coordinated effort around learning of mathematics and sciences for young people as a way to open their minds could provide new innovation ideas that create aggregated value to the society where they live. We should focus on strategic areas where Brazil has natural advantages such as food, pharmaceuticals, software, oil, aviation, manufactured metals and even products created from biodiversity. It is necessary to create networks pursuing R&D in the same strategic area, including institutes, universities and companies. These networks should have access to everything necessary to support innovation, including financing, IP protection and support during commercialisation. Moreover, they need to be integrated through high-speed broadband connections.

Finally, it's necessary to learn from past mistakes but mainly to take a look to the future and remove all barriers in order to put Brazil in the direction it ought to go: an innovation nation.

Luis Cláudio Silva Frade has emphasised the role of young people in the future of innovation, Blanca Garcia looks at that of young students. It is incredible, how similarly and differently we dream, how similarly and differently we make our dreams come true.

Geography – Mexico

Blanca is extremely optimistic about innovation in Mexico, calling it 'brilliant, creative, and full of opportunities' for younger generations.

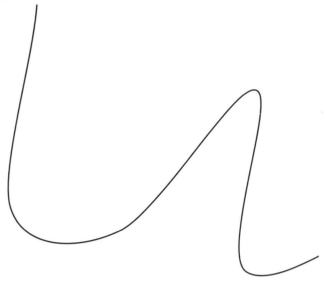

The Future of Innovation Lies in Mexico, and Seems Bright

Name	**Blanca Garcia, PhD**
Affiliation	Universidad Autónoma de Baja California, Faculty of Business and Social Sciences
Position	Coordinator of the PhD in business
Country	Mexico
Area	Human resources and competitiveness
Email	blanca_garcia@uabc.mx

innovation Mexico technology future inventions creativity

The economy of Mexico will evolve into innovation-based processes and products that drive progress into blue ocean strategies that create new needs for the future of humanity.

New value-added products and better processes will be the only way of survival for many businesses and depend upon their ability to innovate.

The creation of new industries will bring new employment opportunities and local inventions.

This highlights the need of investing in research and development and increasing support for universities to develop a higher level of innovation. Only when universities provide the scientific workforce of the future will the country be able to start an innovation cycle; building human capabilities has to be a major objective to achieve technological change.

Creativity is the basis of all innovation. Creativity should be nurtured in those who have it. Innovation depends on a scientifically and technologically creative workforce. Thus, in addition to strong research universities, there should be elementary, secondary and high schools of excellence that bring together the best young minds to introduce them early to science and give them opportunities for creative work. Corporations and government research agencies should support special educational projects, such as science fairs for young students.

In Mexico, there are urgent challenges that in the near future will need a creative solution through innovation such as improving the general health of an ageing population, understanding ecological and environmental issues, providing sufficient food and meeting their basic needs, developing alternative sources of energy and substitutes for increasingly scarce natural resources, providing new technologies to enhance the quality of life while extending those benefits to regions and groups that have not yet shared in them, as well as competing in a global economy through government and political reform that promote enterprise development.

It means that we need to change our beliefs about the future. The future will not be easy for developing countries like Mexico unless we think out of the box and give our young minds freedom to create and support for their inventions to develop and to become into new products and services; the future is here and now and change needs to be done immediately.

Educators have a huge responsibility in planting the seed of change and eliminating the fear of centuries of colonial submission that made our minds narrow and our innovation process latent. Mexicans are creative and happy people that need to feel that their ideas grow and flourish like a big garden full of opportunities, where every new invention is awarded and recognised and where encouragement is given for more.

May the future of innovation in my country be brilliant, creative and full of opportunities for our children and youngsters to create change and bring new devices and processes that meet our needs and make our lives easier and fuller.

Indeed, we think differently and at the same time similarly. Blanca, like many of us, thinks that the future of innovation in Mexico will prosper through creativity, education and changes in national beliefs. Paul Coughlan also thinks about the future of innovation from a country-of-origin perspective, Ireland this time. But he sees the future coming more from top-down rather than a bottom-up approach.

Geography – Ireland

Paul introduces to us the Irish system of innovation. He thinks that many firms in Ireland 'lack the necessary depth of management and international experience to engage successfully in advanced technical cooperation'. Don't we all lack it? We all need a good, a great book on global innovation management, professor!

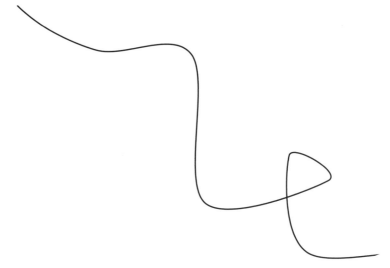

The Future of Innovation is What will You do Tomorrow, Professor?

Name	**Paul Coughlan**
Affiliation	School of Business, Trinity College Dublin
Position	Associate Professor
Country	Ireland
Area	Product development, commercialisation of university research
Email	coughlnp@tcd.ie

commercialising university research   networking   Ireland

In a small open economy, such as that of Ireland, one focus of government attention is on the development, acquisition and application of industrially relevant technologies that can help firms both to develop new products and services for which there is a market and also to improve the competitiveness and quality of existing product-service offerings. Developing such a focus is challenging in the current economic climate, but can be assisted through the transfer of knowledge from university to industry. In particular, formal and informal networking between university researchers, business, government, social and personal counterparts can influence the ability to innovate in individual firms and national economies.

Within the Irish system of innovation, many firms lack the necessary depth of management and international experience to engage successfully in advanced technical cooperation. They are reactive and, because of a low innovative capability, are poorly positioned at the low end of their markets and lose out on adding value from niche strategies in global markets. Many have a shortage of the complementary assets and capabilities to undertake sophisticated sub-supply activities.

Yet, the Irish system is characterised also by:

- a strong European influence on strategy and direction of the national science, technology and innovation effort;

- an increasingly well-funded national effort to increase industrial involvement in R&D and innovation, to raise business expenditure on R&D and to build appreciation of the role of research;

- a conscious national effort to link university research and industry through the development of a public research infrastructure;

- the emergence of universities, not just as generators of new basic and applied scientific knowledge, but also as sources of new firms and of technical expertise for existing technology-based firms.

As a source of new spin-off firms, technology licences and graduates, universities concentrate a large critical mass of scientifically sophisticated individuals who can generate new technologies with potential. The success of policies to channel and diffuse such technologies from the universities to industry depends on active networking among all of the institutional, educational and industrial actors. Here, strategic networking must be regarded as long-term and purposeful to allow the actors/partners to gain, sustain and to demonstrate competitive advantage vis-à-vis their competitors outside the network. Within this strategic network, at least three related types of network are required to overcome the problem of small scale:

- an innovation/research network to access complementary technologies, cost-sharing ideas, potential sources of finance and risk spreading;

- a supply network to improve speed of materials supply and dependability of delivery promises to customers;

- and a learning network to capture experience and to increase the capability to manage survival and growth.

This range of networks underscores the complexity of managing such purposeful interaction and requires capabilities to recognise the requirements – human and financial – for commercial exploitation of university-developed technology, and to reward achievement. These complex cooperation arrangements suggest a continuing need for further research and education on how such arrangements should be structured and the inevitable conflicts resolved.

Have we not heard about the importance of networks many a time? How networked are you, and what do you do to establish the trust and respect that is necessary to let networks thrive?

Staying in Europe we now visit its 'ultra-periphery' – The Canaries – which is what Petra De Saá-Pérez calls the islands she comes from.

Geography – Spain – Canary Islands

Petra brings our attention to the development of innovation in peripheral regions of Europe. She summarises the weak country-of-origin attributes that impact upon the innovation capability of the Canary Islands. We may argue here that being small could be a weak and a strong point at the same time. Yes, it is a weak point from recourse angle, but it is a strong side from the perspective of collaboration, trust, openness. Do you remember Bengt-Åke Lundvall's comment that small Nordic countries have been able to establish 'generalised trust'? You might want to go back to Part II, 'The winds of change', if you have forgotten it. Big is not always good either. Big means distant, separated, scattered.

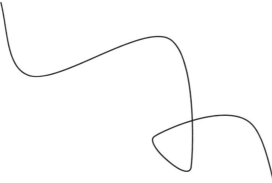

The Future of Innovation is in the Role of Human Resources in Peripheral Regions

Name	**Petra De Saá-Pérez**
Affiliation	Las Palmas De Gran Canaria University
Position	Associated Professor
Country	Canary Islands, Spain
Area	Human resources and innovation
Email	pdesaa@dede.ulpgc.es

innovation   human resources   peripheral regions   Canary Islands

A firm's level of technological development is considered to be one of the principal competitive advantages. Therefore, a firm's decision to invest in innovation-oriented activities becomes an important strategic issue closely linked to the firm's knowledge management process. However, the success of that process is affected by a series of internal and external factors that can differ according to the geographical location of the firm. This is the case of firms that operate in regions like the Canary Islands, in the ultra-periphery of the EU.

Although much effort has been devoted to the analysis of innovation in the more knowledge-intensive regions, there is a lack of studies of innovation in peripheral regions. That lack may be explained by the fact that those regions are zones that face difficulties in transforming their R&D investment efforts into economic activity. Nevertheless, it is necessary to clarify how firms overcome the barriers inherent to that difficult context to implement innovative practices based on their own internal strengths.

The Canaries share with other peripheral regions specific characteristics that influence their innovation capability. First, their innovation system is weak due to the low development of the institutions related to innovation. Second, there is little interaction between the local technological and scientific infrastructures and the higher education institutions. Third, the local market is small. Fourth, there is a lack of confidence in the local suppliers of innovative products, which, in turn, limits the demand for technological products. Finally, the productive structure is dominated by small firms, only a few of which are interested in boosting innovation. Moreover, there has been a lack of dynamism among the actors and support institutions that have promoted innovative and technological change. In general, the region is little developed in terms of networks, training, transfer of technology and other systems to support knowledge management. There is also a clear imbalance in science and technology in favour of the public sector in general and the academic sector in particular. In addition, there has been little development of cooperation and technological transfer between research centres, universities and the private sector.

To overcome those barriers or weaknesses, firms must change their culture to adapt to a more long-term strategic approach that recognises the role of employees as a source of innovative ideas and commits to a style of human resource management (HRM) that supports that cultural change. This new management style must be more consultative than authoritarian and involve employees in the decision-taking process in a way that they feel committed to the firm in promoting innovation. The traditional control-based HRM is not suitable to promote the creativity and autonomy necessary to create knowledge and innovate; it is essential to seek an alternative approach to motivate individuals to share knowledge and actively participate in the innovation process. This new HRM style requires the firm to be more committed to its employees and adopt management systems based on greater employee participation and involvement, which will result in improved innovative outcomes. In sum, firms must use high-commitment or high-performance HRM.

We quite agree with Petra that overcoming the barriers, firms must change their culture; however, we all most probably should change our culture, mindset and outlook from being at individual peripheries to considering ourselves to be part of the global community.

After reading this very book, hopefully, Petra will not think any longer of those features as particularly typical for small territories only. Those traits are as natural for the many small corners as they are for the big streets in our 'global village'.

The final two sets of insights from our journey around the global village come from Tugrul Daim and Ramon Barquin, both hailing from the USA.

Geography – USA

Tugrul and Ramon see the future of innovation through the particular lenses of a highly developed country, the farther and the mother of many financial, organisation, technological, product and process innovation. Are they certain about the future of innovation in the US? Not entirely. Why? Because, even one of world's most powerful economic engines is unlikely to do all, to think for all and to manage all that it takes to create the future of innovation.

Up to now we have been trying to achieve things through competition, which had its time but perhaps it is now the time to move on towards cooperation, collaboration, co-production, co-creation, co-thinking? Don't you think? Well, we somehow believe that the answer is in this book.

The Future of Innovation is Open to Question

Name	**Tugrul Daim**
Affiliation	Portland State University
Position	Associate Professor
Country	USA
Area	Technological innovation
Email	tugrul@etm.pdx.edu

technological innovation   research and development   basic research   USA

I have been an advocate of the strength of US research institutes for many years and have not seen any close competitor. Recent events in the US economy have sewn some doubts on my opinion of the US. I am sure many contributors are defining innovation in several different ways, so I will not attempt to do that; however, I will ask that we think for a moment about technological innovations. Those types of innovations will require years of technical research unlike product innovations which may result from market research. My colleagues in the field of technology forecasting would remember the papers coming from several developed and developing countries participating in national foresight studies. Countries such as Korea do it periodically. However US has not done one for more than three decades. So what happened as a result? We ran out of technological innovations. A good example of this is our automotive industry. Roughly the last two decades we have been riding the wave that was fed with technological innovations resulting from the research done more than two decades ago. Companies have reduced their R&D investments and turned to universities, government has reduced funding for research and universities as a result of that started focusing more on applied, rather than basic, research.

So as a result I am not too hopeful of the future of innovation in the US. I believe we will see more process innovations bringing efficiency to industries that have been behind in adopting innovations when compared to information technology industry. Health care and energy are likely to be leading this type of innovation which will keep many of us busy in terms of analysing how they do it versus how they should be doing it. At this point I would like to challenge many of my colleagues to look for transformational research ideas in assessing, delivering and accelerating technological innovations rather than keeping focusing on incremental product innovations and aiming at incremental theory development for the purpose of getting published in so called management journals. Lately I have been disappointed in the type of research presented, submitted and published in such journals and related conferences. Product development is presented as technology management. In fact it is a mirror image of what happened out in the industry – market-driven R&D replacing R&D centres focusing on much more radical, disruptive or discontinuous technology development.

So what is the picture today? Companies with minimal research capabilities, a nation with a minimal portfolio of technologies and universities with engineering schools totally focused in what industry needs and business schools who are driven by market needs. So what is wrong with this? This put us into the loophole we are in today and has resulted in the worst economic crisis in a long time. We need every player in this loop to get out and start exploring other areas and then get together and compare notes. We have been spending too much time in our comfort zones – it is time to take risks – otherwise there will be no future for innovation.

Now, what has your organisation's reaction to the financial crisis been? Have entire innovation teams been sacked, or are budgets preserved and are long-term opportunities pursued that will come to fruition when the economy has recovered?

Whereas Tugrul paints a rather gloomy picture of the future of innovation in the USA, Ramon has a rather different perspective. Let's see what he's got to say.

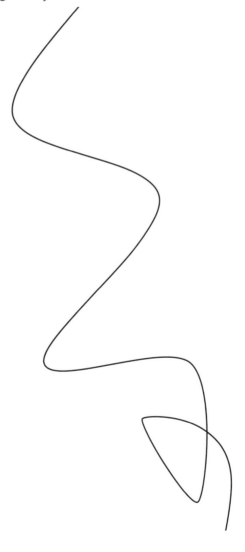

The Future of Innovation is Excellent Because of the World's Huge Problems

Name	**Dr Ramon C. Barquin**
Affiliation	Barquin International
Position	President
Country	USA
Area	Knowledge management, knowledge creation
Email	rbarquin@barquin.com

knowledge-management challenges problem-solving singularity networks USA

The world in general and the United States in particular are on the verge of a massive explosion of innovation. Innovation is about ideas and ideas are tied to problems. Innovation is about finding new ways to do things differently. Given the multitude and magnitude of problems that we face – global warming, depletion of non-renewable resources, economic downturns, meltdown of financial markets, demographic explosion, threats from terrorism – ideas will soon start to emerge addressing each and every one of these issues. Problem solving through innovation will restock our intellectual shelves with a fresh supply of solutions to these challenges.

And this will be very positive for humanity. From these innovations we will derive enhanced economic activity providing employment opportunities where they did not exist before. Value will be created through the application of new processes, new materials, new inventions, and new technologies to the current infrastructure that produces the goods and services essential to civilisation.

Furthermore, much of this innovation will be nurtured, aided and supported by the global networks giving access to the enormous repositories of virtual knowledge we have already launched. As ideas emerge bringing innovation to the fore and applying it to solve existing problems, it will be the internet, cloud computing, the Wikipedia, the blogosphere and the many other components of the emerging knowledge and distribution fabric – the global knowledge environment – that will become the principal mechanism for the refinement, application and dissemination of these innovations.

And if we are to believe the advocates of the coming 'singularity' – the point in the future when machines surpass human intellect and bring an intelligence explosion – there should well be a quantum change in both the quantity and quality of innovation.

The United States will have a central role in this coming outburst of innovation since it still is the world's most powerful economic engine and is currently faced with daunting challenges. Furthermore, much of the world will continue to innovate in attempts to cash in on the market opportunities involved in solving problems the United States faces.

But the rest of the world clearly faces enough challenges of its own. We are starting to see the effect of innovation in low-tech solutions, cultural adaptations to new realities, microfinance approaches to investment needs in many countries. When we see, for example, the emerging impact of cell phones in many African countries where legacy communications infrastructure was non-existent.

So will the coming innovation boom solve all the world's problems? Of course not, and new ones will emerge most surely to replace the current ones. Furthermore we will have to face the challenge of unexpected undesirable consequences of the new ways of doing things. In the same way in which the invention of the internal combustion engine in some way has given us massive pollution and traffic accidents, many of our innovations will lead to problems now unimagined.

As always, we will be able to deal with *what we know.*

Through knowledge management we are getting better at addressing what we don't know we know.

Risk management will allow us to prudently approach what we know we don't know.

But it's *what we don't know we don't know* that will trigger civilisation's next round of innovation.

What richness and what variety of thoughts and perspectives we have seen in this section. We would like to challenge you to look at each contribution and ask yourself: what is in here that can help me in creating the future of innovation; how can I apply and transfer the insights that are offered to me and thereby accelerate my learning? Don't let 'but my situation is different' get in the way of the nuggets of wisdom that are offered: savour what is offered, and make good use of it.

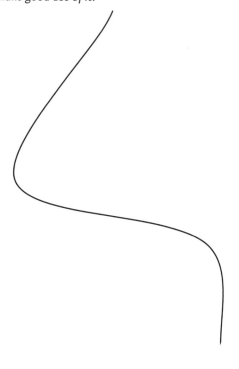

PART XIV
Famous Last Words

Right then, it is time to start summing up – if such a feat could ever possibly be achieved! We will certainly try our best – with the help of some more of our contributors.

So, what then are the main themes that we have found in the richness of the contributions? Some keywords and themes that stuck out were certainly the need for diversity, of collaboration and for a new perspective on innovation that is centred around consideration for sustainability. To bring such a future into the present a change in mindset is definitely required: we need a mindset that values and embraces differences and experimentation and such a mindset needs to be nurtured and encouraged from the outset, meaning that it needs to be the cornerstone of education. In addition, education needs to instil a sense of responsibility in each and every one of us, as well as a new kind of morality that ensures that we weigh the benefits and downsides of innovation carefully, and at a systemic level, before pursuing an innovation opportunity. Such a new code of conduct needs to be shared across the globe as instant communication and access to knowledge makes it increasingly likely that the same kind of new insights or conclusions will be drawn simultaneously in different places around the world.

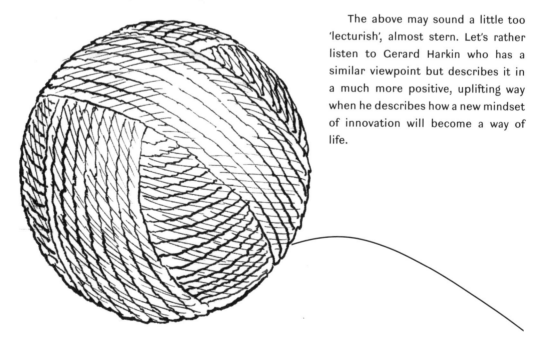

The above may sound a little too 'lecturish', almost stern. Let's rather listen to Gerard Harkin who has a similar viewpoint but describes it in a much more positive, uplifting way when he describes how a new mindset of innovation will become a way of life.

The Future of Innovation is Holistic and Vibrant

Name	**Gerard Harkin**
Affiliation	Edengene
Position	Innovation Consultant
Country	UK
Area	Innovation management, sustainability
Email	gerard.harkin@edengene.com

holistic   purposeful   fragmented   mental model   perspective

I believe 'living' and 'innovating' are one and the same thing and that people and innovation are deeply connected. The ability to innovate is woven into the fabric of our being. It moves and vibrates like a living current within us, wanting to be expressed; I think we are starting to appreciate this quality.

In the future, we'll start thinking about innovation in a more active and personal way and we'll feel a vibrancy when we speak about it. Today, this vibrancy isn't always there when people talk about innovation. Perhaps it's because of the way we've fragmented innovation – for example, books and articles have broken it down into types of innovation, levers, enablers and metrics etc. While the books and articles are helpful, I think we've gone too far in 'breaking apart' innovation and it's time to rekindle its sparkle. Another factor is that organisations occasionally need to overemphasise the intellect and rational facts, but the downside can be a sterile approach to innovation where ignition and passion are lacking. Ironically, in spite of innovation being easier to understand, it's getting harder to do successfully!

I think the future of innovation will be enabled by a simple shift in our perspective – a shift away from fragmented thinking towards a more holistic outlook. We'll let go of what isn't working with our existing models. As this happens we'll start innovating from a place of 'contributing to' rather than 'taking from'. This holistic outlook will lead to a significant change in what and how we innovate. Not only will we ask, 'What should I innovate?' but we'll also ask, 'What needs to be innovated?' Innovating from this place has ignition, vibrancy and unbounded potential.

Harmonious win–win situations will arise, we'll resolve many of the challenges facing us today and sustainability will be an obvious choice. We'll know what to do, when to do it and will be comfortable with ambiguity. Our innovation stories will become richer and heart warming. On the internet, at conferences and within companies, people will be asked to share their personal innovation journeys as well as the facts about what they were innovating – for example, how did the person and team change as a result of developing a new product; audiences will want to hear both aspects. In the future we'll focus more of our energy on meaningful innovations rooted in powerful visions.

We just love Gerard's contribution, it is so full of optimism, positive energy and courageous conviction. Bring on the future of innovation as Gerard sees it: with emotions, with sparkle and with a holistic approach, focused on sustainable outcomes and based on what he refers to as 'inner guidance'. This is clearly a far cry from how innovation is widely understood today. Yet there are others who perceive the great opportunity that lies in the current 'crisis of identity' of innovation and suggest new ways of looking at it – let's read what Alexander Manu has contributed.

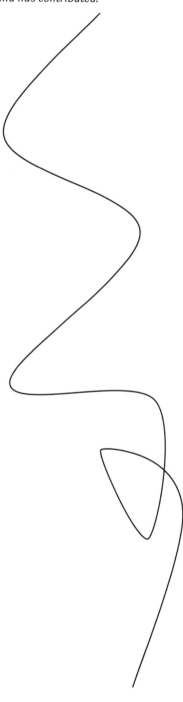

The Future of Innovation is About a Precept Not a Concept

Name	**Alexander Manu**
Affiliation	Rotman School of Management, University of Toronto
Position	Adjunct Professor
Country	Canada
Area	Methods, product and service innovation, business design
Email	alexander.manu@rotman.utoronto.ca

**strategic innovation   strategic foresight   business design   massive innovation
disruptive business**

Innovation is in a crisis of identity. Crowdsourced massive innovation is a reality that calls for the redefinition of what 'innovation' is, in the new context of an empowered and participatory user. At the level of the corporation, we need focus, incentives, tools, scope and precision in the language surrounding innovation, so all stakeholders are on the same page. For focus, I propose the model of Pre-Competitive Innovation as a strategic tool. Pre-Competitive Innovation starts with Innovation Questions rather than Innovation Problems. Pre-Competitive Innovation is a mindset necessary for the creation of beneficial services, products and experiences at the intersection of technology and latent behaviour. Here are a few starting points:

1. The innovation challenge: Innovation is an outcome, not a process

Organisations fancy the latter because processes can be managed, and this is what organisations are good at. This hides the lack of expertise – and mindset – in creating and managing a culture of innovativeness, and an organisational ecology populated by innovation 'connoisseurs'. The management of the outcome is much different than the management of the process, and this is where definitions are important: innovation is an outcome achieved by a multiplicity of processes.

2. Ethos: Innovation has always been pre-competitive

While our first innovations were competitive – we needed to survive and compete with the other animals – humanity moved quickly to pre-competitive innovation. The concept of comfort is one of these innovations. Pillows have nothing to do with need or competitive drive. Innovation for competitive advantage encourages an Innovation Problem Framework – the starting point of a process where the limits for what can be achieved are already defined. This model is no longer sufficient or desirable. This type of innovation does not create a strategic advantage but mitigates a weak position.

3. Labels: There is no 'disruptive innovation'

This label has misstated the nature of innovation. What is disruptive is technologies and emergent behaviours. When behaviour engages technology in an innovation outcome, we have a disruptive business model. Think of Apple's App Store. It is this model applied in business, that is disruptive to the incumbent, and not its component parts.

4. Purpose: Innovation creates culture, not products

Take Apple again: they are not innovating technology, they are innovating ways of engagement with technology for new desired and beneficial outcomes; ways to make us happy.

5. Roots: Innovation is rooted in desire, not need

Organisations need to reconnect with the core of makes us human: desire. Desire not in the hedonistic sense, but in the higher motivational sense of the desire to become better through education, literacy, tools, systems and services, all provisions for the achievement of our higher goals. A company's ability to meet this desire directly contributes to the success of their products and services in the marketplace. As desire is constant, innovation needs to be constant. The variable in this equation is business.

6. Ecology: A new mindset for innovativeness

Where can we find the competence and ability to innovate at 2.0 speed and for 2.0 behaviour? In the corporate ecosystem most likely to encourage the free flow of ideas capable to generate new revenue models. The challenge is that of creating a culture in which platforms for the exploration of possibility are encouraged, funded and free of the day-to-day metrics of the organisation, balancing risk, ambiguity, courage and imagination with a pragmatic business ambition in a timely manner.

How should the future envisaged by Gerard and Alexander come about, and why now, you may ask. Well, let's see what Sandra Castaneda has to say!

The Future of Innovation is Sustainable

Name   **Sandra Castaneda**
Affiliation   Organic Exchange
Position   Business Development Manager (Europe)
Country   Spain
Area   Sustainable innovation
Email   sandra.castaneda@gmail.com

sustainability   social entrepreneurship   environment   conscience   values

We could not be at a better time to focus on innovation, meaning consciously rethinking the way we look at things and coming out with great solutions for the challenges we face. And more specifically, for the challenges at the heart of the system, those which touch upon the foundations.

The Background: Seizing Momentum and Diagnosing

The word 'crisis' comes from the Greek *krinen*, meaning 'to separate' or 'to decide'. Separating and deciding involve previous thinking, analysing a given situation, reflecting on pros and cons, a step one cannot ignore. So times of crises, when something is not working well, are perfect times for intelligent creative thinking and innovative processes.

And we live in times of crises: the crash of the global financial system; scarce resources for a growing population leading conspicuous consumption lives; greater and more glaring inequalities. Therefore, our main challenges relate to rebuilding trust, expanding the scope of awareness in terms of time and space and cultivating fraternity.

The Object: Addressing Global Risks in a Holistic Way

Like people, money and societies nowadays, contemporary challenges are not kept within national borders – taking Ulrich Beck's approach – but have linkages between them, forming a network in which one aspect affects the others – think about the butterfly effect. This means an innovation process in the 21st century has to be wholesome. It needs to take into account several risk areas and stop developing one-at-a-time-challenge solutions. The outcomes will not be perfect, but we need, at least, to think more globally – not only in terms of geography, but also in terms of interdisciplinary, and clarify the purpose of our work.

The Purpose: Making People's Lives Better

Innovation is not an end; it is a means for people to have a better life. The question is: what does 'better' mean? There are certainly as many answers as people in this planet. However, it is now more than ever needed that innovators define the goals if each innovation process and foresee its consequences at the various levels: for technology, science, the environment and societies; north and south, east and west.

The Start: Consciously Redefining Our Common Vision on Well-being

Future innovation starts by designing a new common vision on well-being. Professor Ezio Manzini, from Istituto Politecnico di Milano, has been studying the issue for many years and proposing, more specifically, how designers can contribute to the purpose. But we cannot define our common understanding of well-being unless each of us, individually, is conscious enough. Conscious of his or her freedom and co-responsibility. Aware of his or her surroundings, the long term, others. And we cannot become conscious unless we tear mechanics and fear of change away from our lives. So innovation starts at the individual level, more precisely, at the values and awareness of each and every human being.

Let's take the risk: it will be worth it.

Does wisdom not tell us that we are most likely to be willing to take a risk when our back is against the wall and we have nothing to lose – the current financial, economic and environmental crisis – or if we have just so much to gain – a true chance to revisit some fundamental assumptions and create a better life for people on this planet. Don't you agree with Sandra that this is a risk worth taking?

We would like to call upon Francisco Pinheiro who was – is! – a relentless supporter of the quest to explore the future of innovation. But that support is not the reason for reading his thoughts here. He connects us back to the metaphor of the body – with innovation being in his blood – but also connects the responsibility of innovation to a triple bottom line (people, planet, profit) which was a close second to the chosen structure of the book.

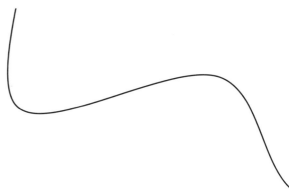

The Future of Innovation is About People, Diversity, Collaboration and Passion

Name	**Francisco Pinheiro**
Affiliation	Atos Origin International
Position	Director, Global Innovation
Country	Spain
Area	International IT services provider
Email	francisco.pinheiro@atosorigin.com

collective creativity   people   diversity   collaboration   passion

The future of innovation relies significantly upon our ability to tap into the collective creativity and experience of all stakeholders in our ecosystem. Imagine the many new ideas, connections, thoughts, insights, synergies, collaborations, intersections and cases of hybridisation, cross-fertilisation and co-creation that will arise out of this inspirational shared journey that Bettina and Anna are taking us on, and the valuable innovation initiatives that will be generated. Explore the diversity of the contributors and their talents, experiences, skills, cultures, perspectives, thinking styles and ideas ... etc. Be open to it. This journey is a good example of *collaboration*; it is full of *diversity*; diversity drives innovation and innovation is about *people*. People have their passions. Have you ever noticed that every great achievement in this world was accomplished by people who are passionate about something? *Passion* also drives innovation. I would be willing to bet that passion is something shared by all contributors to this initiative.

People, *diversity*, *collaboration* and *passion* were definitely the bold innovation drivers that came into my mind and my heart when I eventually decided what to write about for this book. The future of innovation will depend on the holistic approach that you, your team, your business unit, your organisation and your community take in order to leverage these drivers to explore and capitalise on new growth opportunities at a local and global level, making innovation both repeatable and sustainable. The future of innovation will also depend on the way we all practise what are known as the 3Ps of sustainability – people, planet, profit – in our business and in our lives. I would add another P for passion.

However, before an organisation can become the next innovation leader it must fully understand its own innovation architecture, ecosystems and innovation archetypes, as well as its own *people* and their thinking styles, social and professional behaviours, interests and passions. Understanding what your innovation DNA looks like enables management innovators to gain a holistic perspective of which actions will best foster and develop a culture of innovation in all of its forms.

The innovation chain must be considered in its entirety: ideation, project selection, development and commercialisation. It is important to monitor and identify any weak links in this chain in order to take the appropriate action. In order to build a true and successful corporate innovation engine, we need to have, either formal or informal, multidisciplinary and cross-functional teams which understand and appreciate the importance of the various roles which are key to transforming ideas into real innovation within an organisation: an *ideator/inventor*, a *transformer* to shape the idea into something more tangible, a *financial backer* (sponsor) and an externally facing *entrepreneur* (broker) to help sell the innovative asset.

My passion for innovation has not gone unnoticed. When I was putting Ivan, my nine-year-old son, to bed the other day, he stated his desire to be a sports journalist when he grows up, and then he asked me: 'Do you enjoy your work?' I told him that I do, and he responded by saying: 'Innovation runs through your veins'. We laughed and it occurred to me that besides passion, blood is as vital for us as innovation is vital for our business, our society and our future. As far as I am aware, nothing has yet been invented to replace the blood in our bodies, and the same applies to innovation within organisations; it is fundamental. It is essential to keep it flowing, for if it stops or its path is blocked, you may experience serious problems, particularly in the context of the current economic climate.

Does innovation run in your blood? Maybe it is a passion for and understanding of innovation that creates a new morality and not the other way around? And again we hear about diversity and its important role. Sepehr Ghazinoory too talks about diversity yet of a slightly different kind; yet the kind of diversity he talks about is as important to realise the potential of the future of innovation as the kind of diversity Francisco or Sandra talk about.

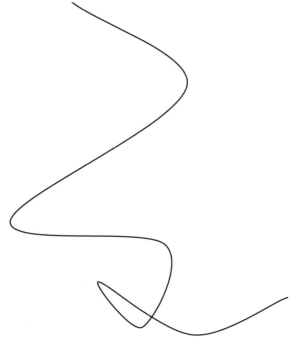

The Future of Innovation is Non-normal Ways

Name	**Sepehr Ghazinoory**
Affiliation	Department of Information Technology Management, Tarbiat Modares University, Tehran
Position	Associate Professor
Country	Iran
Area	National innovation systems
Email	Ghazinoory@yahoo.com

**metaphysical innovations   cultural technologies   extraordinary innovation
different kinds for innovation   converging technologies**

The future of innovation may be concentrated on those missing links that humankind has ignored in its evolution path over recent centuries. If we take a look at the oldest human written works, we realise that metaphysical issues, like the nature of death, sleep, ghost and mind, engrossed our antecedents. Sciences like physics and chemistry emerged much later and had extraordinary advancements but primary human questions are still unanswered.

Maybe the cause of this lag is that scientists artificially limited themselves to sensory and natural fields. This artificial limitation fails to recognise the fact that opinion polls are based on consensus of opinions and according to them the majority of people believe in some kind of metaphysics (religion, ghosts, elves ...) and so metaphysics is an acceptable belief or at least it's logical to conduct researches about that.

It may be necessary that we revise our one-sided research methods in knowledge. Today, when we use the word 'medicine', Western medicine comes into mind as the only way of healing and treatment, but historically and currently different kinds of medicine like Chinese (acupuncture), Hindi (yoga), Iranian (herbal), Islamic (edibles and potables) and tribal (sorcery) have existed and certainly have been effectual to some extent, because if not the people in charge would have been ostracised.

If we liken knowledge to a mountain, then you can climb it from different sides, not only the Western. If you climb different sides, you'll undoubtedly reach new achievements. Using these old but not fully recognised schools for development of science and technologies may help us to satisfy needs that have been unsatisfied till now: the need to feel the happiness and calmness, the need to understand about the past and future, all the things that humans need for the sedation of pain. If not, we should still wait for the development of accessible technologies: cognitive and genetic technologies which are more promising to satisfy mentioned needs.

Today, if humans' cultural and technological achievements are integrating and are creating cultural technologies, if we accepted that four independent technologies (information, nano, bio and cognitive) are converging, if there are some endeavours to prove the convergence of physics (and maybe other natural sciences), then we can imagine that, finally, the convergence of natural scientists' efforts and human metaphysical beliefs will lead to new technologies and inventions which are embedded in innovations will be welcomed by all human societies and consumers. We should not forget that if the objective of previous technologies development was creation of happiness in human mind, Western civilisation has not been successful in accomplishing this objective until now and we must try new ways.

Sepehr's proposition, too, means letting go of the notion that there is one truth, that there is only one right approach which automatically implies that all others are wrong. Different approaches can lead to the goal, different approaches can be equally valid, useful, helpful and successful.

The notion of different paths and different solutions being equally valid is a challenging one for today's education system where multiple-choice questions allow only one right answer. If this notion is embraced, how then can we compare and rank performance of individuals? Well, what is the assumption behind the belief that such comparison is critical? Is it another of those we need to challenge and question?

What also hits home with us from his contribution is a tendency of us to throw out and negate the old when something new comes along, regardless of the value and the qualities of the old. It somehow seems to us that the innovation wave that is currently sweeping management thinking might drown an appreciation of operational excellence. Yet, as we have emphasised before, we no longer live in times of 'either or', we live in times of 'and'. And that means that we have to learn to balance – and Lucio Pieroni provides a list of some of the many things that will need balancing in future.

The Future of Innovation is in Achieving a Balanced Performance

Name	**Lucio Pieroni**
Affiliation	Mars Inc
Position	Global Vice President, R&D Pet Care
Country	Belgium
Area	Innovation management
Email	lucio.pieroni@eu.effem.com

balance   creativity   discipline   ambidextrous organisations   diversity

The future of innovation lies in the achievement of a *balanced performance* across seemingly opposing competencies. Balancing, for example:

- innovation (new products meeting new product needs) with renovation (upgrading current products, i.e., caring for the core business);

- the portfolio between continuous improvement (usually smaller but safer opportunities) with disruptive innovation (bigger but riskier opportunities);

- creativity and divergence at the front end with rigour, discipline and convergence during delivery;

- performance with cost of goods to deliver superior value;

- depth of consumer insights with technical brilliance to go beyond what consumers can actually articulate;

- the professionalism of a market leader with the entrepreneurship of a start-up;

- the strengthening core competencies while developing new skills;

- the 'redundancy' needed for prototyping with a lean approach in development and execution;

- the need for maximising global reach of activities with the understanding that projects are born locally.

Achieving such balance is not simple, as it requires in depth analysis of what drives the field in which you innovate. In addition, and more importantly, it requires that the institution that innovates is made of people of very diverse skills and beliefs, yet working seamlessly together. The latter is possibly the most difficult balance to achieve. Companies usually stick to what has worked best for them in the past. And, even more importantly, 'like hires like'. Yet, an institution is likely to attract realists, pragmatists and project managers and frustrate dreamers and visionaries, or vice versa. By the way, the same is true for consultants, so it is important to use a blend of consultants to step change innovation. Finally, achieving this balance requires, as Loren Gary said in his 2003 *Harvard Business Review* article, 'ambidextrous organisation', that 'senior teams must be able to act consistently with the inconsistencies among the innovation streams'. It is the lack of these key talents with broad perspective, that in 'foresight' terminology are called integrators, that generates the 'one size fits all' approach. Instead, innovation requires a blend of diverse competencies, diverse skills, diverse reward systems and a differentiated and balanced portfolio to thrive.

How good is your organisation – are you – at managing these balancing acts?

Back to diversity – the essential ingredient in the difficult challenge to find balance between many different demands. How are we going to achieve all this: the balancing, the dealing with diversity and uncertainty, the collaboration with strangers? Perhaps Barbara Perry has an idea ...

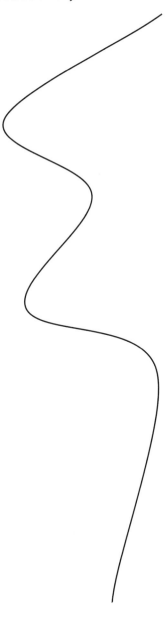

The Future of Innovation is the Case for Hope

Name	**Barbara Perry**
Affiliation	Barbara Perry Associates
Position	Cultural Anthropologist
Country	USA
Area	Ethnographic research
Email	barbara@barbaraperryassociates.com

strategic   proactive   collaborative   hope   front-end

The future of innovation will be:

- **Strategic.** Innovation efforts will be integrated into and directly impact the organisation's long-term vision and strategy. Gone are the days when resources (time, money, and the human spirit) can be squandered in random, superficial, 'busy-ness.'

- **Proactive.** As innovation becomes more strategic, more emphasis will be placed on doing the front-end right in terms of people, process, and leadership. The leader's role will be to 'hold the container,' protecting the micro-culture of complexity and ambiguity necessary for true insights and learning to emerge. The leader's own willingness to challenge assumptions and champion open-ended, exploratory customer research will demonstrate the commitment within which innovation thrives.

- **Collaborative.** As innovation becomes more proactive and strategic, it will necessitate earlier and deeper cross-functional (perhaps cross-company) partnerships and collaboration. The world is moving too fast, the innovation challenges too holistic and complex for linear processes and silo mentality, particularly at the front end. Dialogue will be the core competence of this inclusive world, grounding stakeholders in shared reality and interpretation.

The Case for Hope

In his election campaign, President Obama said:

> For many months we have been teased, even derided, for talking about hope. But we always knew that hope was not blind optimism. It's not ignoring the enormity of the tasks ahead or the roadblocks that stand in that path. Hope is that thing inside us that insists, despite all the evidence to the contrary, that something better awaits us if we have the courage to reach for it and to work for it and to fight for it.

Obama has it right. In our 20 years of researching hopeful organisations and leadership, we have learned that under the 'safe' words we use – morale, engagement and, especially, innovation – hope is the animating force. Innovative organisations have to be hopeful organisations. Hope is forward focused, inspires action, is rooted in reality and engages our heads, hearts and hands.

It results in positive energy, enhanced performance, personal commitment and faster learning. Hope impacts us every day in large and small ways.

In In our book, *Putting Hope to Work*, Harry Hutson and I have identified five principles that, woven together, create the fabric of a hopeful organisation:

1. Hope is born in possibility – our shared dreams, visions and goals.

2. Hope is energised by agency – my personal ability to make a difference.

3. Hope is inspired by worth – the meaning of my work.

4. Hope is informed by openness – a culture of risk-taking, truth and learning.

5. Hope is completed in connection – to co-workers, customers and reality.

While not 'spiritual,' these principles speak to the human spirit at work. Actionable in big and small ways, they are the foundation for building a healthy front end of innovation, which is, after all, the birthplace of hope for the future.

It is in the human spirit to overcome obstacles, to defy defeat and to rise from the ashes. It is the belief that it is possible to create a better future. What we perhaps need to do to create a better future is to challenge what is currently classified as 'desirable'. It cannot be consumption for everyone everywhere to the levels we have become accustomed to in most of the Western world over the past century. As Sepehr pointed out, following the Western belief system we may have 'achieved' a lot yet we have become, overall, unhappier in the process.

We would like to close on a humorous note – humour is something fundamentally human, and can be a highly lubricating element in the innovation process: it releases tension, it opens the mind, it even establishes new connections between the different parts of the brain. So, let's have it from Marko Seppänen!

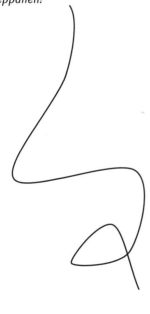

The Future of Innovation is For Your eyes Only

Name	**Marko Seppänen**
Affiliation	Tampere University of Technology
Position	Senior Researcher
Country	Finland
Area	Business model innovation, creativity
Email	marko.seppanen@tut.fi

movie   quote (or quotation)   timing   creativity   insight

The future of innovation appears in the profound insights expressed in quotations from famous movies. Innovativeness is a renewable, scarce natural resource, which becomes manifest when *we have a problem*.[1] Human evolution shows that while *nobody is perfect*,[2] people are usually at their best when *the going gets tough*.[3] Life's problems are commonly solved using tried and tested solutions. However, many problems test our ingenuity and creativity to the full, and after *rounding up the usual suspects*,[4] we find it necessary to adopt novel thinking and fresh approaches.

However, the best innovations usually just appear out of the blue: *like a box of chocolates; you never know what you are going to get*.[5] Problem solving is rarely straightforward; *using the force*[6] rarely helps. Indeed quite the reverse; perseverance is of the essence. Edison, for instance, performed over 1,200 experiments before finding a durable filament for the light bulb. Humans are inherently inventive and being innovative is *elementary, my dear Watson*.[7] We must release our creativity through curiosity and think broadmindedly, outside the box, without fear of failure. Stumbling and fumbling in the dark in search of novel solutions may sometimes induce a strange sense that *we are not in Kansas any more*.[8] It is this serendipitous journey, which induces the right creative mindset. Achieving that final breakthrough promotes that heady sense of triumph when at last you feel that *you are the king of the world*.[9]

But never forget that your innovative ideas might turn to *your precious*.[10] More often than not, those nice basic ideas will need a good deal more tweaking before they can conquer the market.

1   *Apollo 13* (1995).

2   *Some Like It Hot* (1959).

3   *All That* (1994).

4   *Casablanca* (1942).

5   *Forrest Gump* (1994).

6   *Star Wars* (1977).

7   *The Hound of Baskervilles* (1959).

8   *The Wizard of Oz* (1939).

9   *Titanic* (1997).

10 *The Lord of the Rings: The Two Towers* (2002).

Even the hardened innovator can be faced with a confrontational statement: *Show me the money!*[11] The temptation to shoot back, *Go ahead, make my day*,[12] should be resisted by *making an offer he cannot refuse.*[13] Then you can tempt him with offers of early performance trials with potential customers to tailor the original idea to the needs of markets. Also, beware the advice of experts and theorists because *there is a difference between knowing the path and walking the path.*[14] Persistent and determined commitment is what it usually takes; innovation rarely results from epiphanies.

Timing is crucial for innovations to succeed. Much of excellent ideas do not take off because of timing. However, what might be tragic for the individual may be merely a statistical footnote when millions are concerned. Most of humanity's major challenges are overcome sooner or later; even inventions mouldering in the vaults of obscurity might eventually see the light of day. Innovators' success is the outcome of hard work and common sense, and the success of new ideas is largely based on a desire to share and collaborate with other people. The resourcefulness and ingenuity of humankind should teach us we have no need to be running scared of life's challenges. Problems exist only to be solved. So, *fasten your seatbelts, it is going to be*[15] brilliant times ahead.

That's all, folks.[16]

Thanks Marko – and thanks to all of you who have taken the time to share their thoughts. What an amazing journey it has been, and how rewarding, humbling, joyful, exciting – and exhausting too.

Indeed there are brilliant times ahead – but we also need to realise that there is not much time left to start the journey! In fact, we probably do not have any time left, it is the 11th hour and we are the ones we have been waiting for. We have no time to waste, that is why we need more time to identify the things that really matter, that's why we need to continue asking the question 'why' until we are certain that we are addressing the causes and no longer the symptoms. Carbon trading is pushing the 'bad penny' from one person to another. Hedging and hedging the hedges is pushing the 'bad penny' from one person to another. We can no longer afford to do that. We need to start casting away our most basic assumptions and start seeing the unexpected, the unimaginable as possibility and potential new reality. Only with courage and care and wisdom can we hope to preserve the planet that is the only home there is, for us and for future generations.

The future of innovation, our future. We have heard a lot about it, is it not time we started creating it?

---

11 *Jerry Maguire* (1996).

12 *Sudden Impact* (1983).

13 *The Godfather* (1972).

14 *Matrix* (1999).

15 *All About Eve* (1950).

16 *Porky and Daffy* (1938).

Postscript:
Sixth Stage: And in Every Ending There is a New Beginning

We started this book with sharing the stages we went through; now, this is the final stage. And it is the stage where we had over to you, the reader, to take the story forward, to become part of it.

We can imagine, dear reader, that you might still think about the future of innovation in terms of a riddle! You most probably ask yourself is the discovery in human capital? Consumers? Co-creation? Global networks? Clusters? Open innovation? National innovation systems? Ecosystems? Smart or green technology? Renewables? Solar energy? Eco-innovations? Radical innovation? Service innovation? Process innovation? Product design? Industrial design? Technology management? Innovation management? Knowledge management? Diversity management? Brand management? Cross-cultural management? Change management? Project management? R&D management? NPD management? Creativity? Idea generation? Fuzzy front- or back-end? Innovation drivers? Process drivers? Technology transfer? Knowledge transfer? Knowledge economy? Shareholder economy? Emerging markets? Cross-cultural diffusion? Ethnographic research? University research? Innovation training? Organisational learning? Organisational development? Absorptive capacity? Dynamic capability? Discontinuity? Sustainability? Roadmapping? Foresighting? Communication? Exploitation? Intrapreneurship? Entrepreneurship? Catalysts? Innovacians?

Well, of course it is all of the above! We believe that this book has provided a lot of insight into innovation and its future! Though is there perhaps something that is its nucleus, quintessence, vigour, soul, lifeblood; the heart of innovation? Yes, still you may wonder; this quest reminds us of a tale about the Human Body.

Once upon a time there was a talk between the parts of the human body.

'We', said the Eyes, 'are very useful to Man. We not only see things, but we also make Man's face pretty'.

'Don't forget us,' exclaimed the Hair, the Forehead, the Cheeks and the Chin in chorus. 'We make Man's face pretty, too'.

'I beg your pardon,' exclaimed the Mouth, 'I am very useful to Man, for with my teeth he bites his food'.

'Don't forget me!' cried the Tongue. 'Without me he cannot speak'.

'Oh, oh', said the Ears, 'please remember that Man has two ears to hear much and one tongue to talk little'.

Then a thin small voice was heard: 'You all think yourselves very useful. But you must understand that I, the Nose, give Man real pleasure. He can smell the pretty flowers of the garden with my help'.

'You all talk too much and do too little', exclaimed the Hands. 'We, with our fingers and thumbs, do Man's work, therefore we are necessary for his happiness'. 'And without our help Man cannot walk', said the Legs and the Feet.

Then there was a short silence after which the Heart said: 'There are blind men who cannot see, dumb men who cannot speak, deaf men who cannot hear and even men who have no hands to hold things with, but there is not a man without a heart. I warm Man's blood, at the same time I put colour into his face, life into his arms and legs and in fact into his whole body. Without me, he cannot live!'

Indeed, which part of innovation can innovation not live without? Innovation process? Innovation structure? Innovation vision? Innovation leadership? Innovation environment? Innovation policy? Or innovation culture?

For a difficult question there should be a simple answer. If looking at the Innovation Future straight from the heart, we say ... *the heart is the future of innovation!* As simple as that!

'I love it!' is the highest feeling! Highest devotion! Highest admiration! And highest praise! Innovation has to be done with love, with passion, from the heart! Remember this in the making of the future of innovation, for yourself, for our and for *all* of your future! Whatever it is – new product development, technology transfer or innovative thinking – do it with passion, from your heart! Love for people, for your country, for our planet, and for yourself! Love makes us go on, and will be the energy that nurtures the future of innovation!

The final insight we have to offer you here, dear reader, from our experience of venturing into the future of innovation, is: trust in global collaboration. You may say that globalisation and innovation are the two terms that seem to be on top of most firms' agendas today. Yes, but we would like to give a slightly different slant. What we mean is that there is always a helping hand. Never say 'I can't do this'! Nor say 'Never' to those who are asking you for assistance ... especially if this request comes from outside your country. Our innovation community is transported to the future by a global force, and friendly support. Only together can we create a future that is worth living (and innovating) for.